Customary Law in the Modern World

Customary Law in the Modern World is the study of a coherent and well-established legal system, which is now operating in the context of a modern nation-state and therefore poised between remaining relevant and the threat of marginalization.

Focusing on Sudan, the author places customary law in its historical and cultural context, analyzing the fundamental traditional values that underlie customary law and the impact of the war between the North and the South that lasted intermittently for half a century. He deals with the substance of customary law, covering a wide variety of areas: family law, property law, torts, and criminal liability. Drawing on interviews conducted with judges, legislators, and practicing lawyers on customary law and its future in the modern context, the book challenges the development of customary law to build on the positives of tradition and the reform of its shortcomings, particularly in the areas of human rights, gender equality, and the protection of children. This book fills a gap in the literature on customary law, and will be of great interest to anyone interested in law, anthropology, and politics.

Francis M. Deng is the UN secretary-general's special advisor on the prevention of genocide. He served as Sudan's minister of state for foreign affairs and ambassador to the United States, Nordic countries, and Canada. He holds a doctorate from Yale Law School and is the author or editor of more than thirty books.

Customary Law in the Modern World

The Crossfire of Sudan's War of Identities

Francis M. Deng

Routledge
Taylor & Francis Group
LONDON AND NEW YORK

First published 2010
by Routledge
2 Park Square, Milton Park, Abingdon, Oxon OX14 4RN

Simultaneously published in the USA and Canada
by Routledge
711 Third Ave, New York, NY 10017

Routledge is an imprint of the Taylor & Francis Group, an informa business

Typeset in Times New Roman by
Taylor & Francis Books

First issued in paperback 2013

British Library Cataloguing in Publication Data
A catalogue record for this book is available from the British Library

Library of Congress Cataloging in Publication Data
Deng, Francis Mading, 1938–
Customary law in the modern world: the crossfire of Sudan's war of identities / Francis M. Deng.
p. cm.
Includes bibliographical references and index
ISBN 978-0-7103-1338-6 (hardback : alk. paper) – ISBN 978-0-203-87357-1 (ebook) 1. Customary law–Sudan. 3. Sudan–Ethnic relations. I. Title.
KTQ449.3.D46 2009
340.5'2624–dc22
2009003724

ISBN13: 978-0-415-84690-5 (pbk)
ISBN13: 978-0-7103-1338-6 (hbk)
ISBN13: 978-0-203-87357-1 (ebk)

Contents

Part One

Customary Law in Context

1 Introduction to Part One

A paradox surrounds the way customary law is viewed in Southern Sudan. The educated, modernized elite largely see customary law as backward and incapable of addressing the needs of a rapidly changing and modernizing society. Yet in the context of the civil war that has raged intermittently for half a century between the dominant Arab-Muslim North and the subordinated South – where the overwhelming majority adhere to traditional beliefs or are converts to Christianity – customary law is seen as an integral component of the identity the South has been defending against Arabization and Islamization from the North. Moreover, the reality is that most of the people in both the North and the South – estimated at more than 80 percent – are governed by customary law. Simultaneously, then, customary law is seen as something to be discouraged and eventually done away with, yet also something to be preserved, promoted and developed.

In the context of the Comprehensive Peace Agreement (CPA) that was concluded between the government of Sudan and the Southern-based Sudan People's Liberation Movement and Army (SPLM/A) on January 9, 2005, the revivalist perspective on customary law appears to be heightened. Customary law is being projected not only as a central element of the Southern identity for which the people fought, but as an important source of legislation, constitutionalism and the rule of law for the government of Southern Sudan. Although the shortcomings of customary law are recognized, the general tendency is to idealize the cultural values behind it even as a basis for promoting and realizing the principles of the universal human rights regime. There is, however, a gap between the positive rhetoric and practical measures for making effective use of customary law as postulated. Rather than being an unbridgeable gap, this dilemma is presenting the leadership and those responsible for the legal system with the challenge of turning the aspirations into practical programs and strategies.

Following this introduction, Section 2 of Part One relates the political history of Sudan leading up to the CPA, looking at how a well-functioning legal system bequeathed by the British has fallen into disarray and explaining how customary law has become a central part of the clash of identities between the Islamic North and African South that fueled the war.

It is not possible to understand customary law without appreciating the cultural values that underpin it. The third section therefore lays the necessary foundation for this understanding by outlining the key cultural concepts that underpin traditional society, and tracing their implications for conflict resolution methods, court procedures, and the selection of judges and leaders.

At present, the situation remains open-ended, which – despite the uncertainties involved – offers potential for legal reconstruction and reform? What direction law reform will take will depend very much on whether the country will remain united or divided. If the country remains united, the question of how to manage constructively the diversity of three sources of law – the received Western law, Islamic law, and African customary law – will require a great deal of creativity. This is the subject of the fourth section, which traces the complex historical interplay of the three divisions of law – civil, Islamic and customary.

If the country gets divided, the challenge then becomes contextualized within the North and the South. The North will presumably continue to consider how to develop along the lines of an Islamic legal system, while the South will have to struggle with how to integrate customary law into a unified administration of justice. Section 5 examines how the Sudanese People's Liberation Movement/Army (SPLM/A) – which fought for the South during the last two decades of the civil war and now forms the Government of the Southern Sudan – approached customary law during the war, and what role it sees for traditional authority in the Southern Sudan's new legal system. It also traces the ambiguous effects of the war and broader social change on the role of traditional authority and the place of customary law.

With or without the North, the South faces great challenges in developing a viable legal and administrative system that builds on its cultural values and makes effective use of the common law system bequeathed by the British. A strong sense of customary law revivalism is matched by an acceptance of the need to reform customary law to bring it in line with the structures and values of the modern state. The final section explores the areas in need of reform, and the emerging thinking of Southern Sudanese leaders in developing practical programs and strategies for achieving this

2. Historical Background: Law, War and Identity

Sudan is geographically the largest country in Africa – about one million square miles – and comprises several hundred ethnic groups. These have generally been clustered into the Arab-Muslim North and the African South, whose people generally adhere to traditional religions but have been converting to Christianity since the advent of British colonialism. To complicate the picture, there are groups in the North who, though Muslims, have retained their indigenous cultures and even practice an indigenized version of Islam. The political and legal history of Sudan plays out against this complex demographic background, turning conflict into a war of identities.

This section traces the political and legal history of Sudan since colonization, looks at the role of law in shaping the identities that lie behind Sudan's civil war, and explains what the Comprehensive Peace Agreement envisages for the political and legal future of the country.

2.1 Pre-independence: formation of state and legal system

The history of Sudan is one in which the formal and informal legal systems have coexisted and interacted for a long time. Foreign rule in the country began with the Ottoman invasion in 1821 and the establishment of the Turko-Egyptian administration that lasted until it was overthrown in 1885 by a fundamentalist Islamic movement led by Mohamed Ahmed, who became known as the Mahdi, the Islamic Messiah. The Mahdist state was in turn overthrown by the joint British-Egyptian forces in 1898, followed by the establishment of the British dominated Anglo-Egyptian administration that ruled the country until independence on January 1, 1956.

Although both the Turko-Egyptian administration and the Mahdist state claimed to apply Sharia, much of the rural North was administered by customary laws that claimed to reflect Islamic principles, but were for the most part indigenous. The South remained outside the control of these regimes and what prevailed there were customary practices guided by the moral and ethical values associated with traditional religious beliefs.

From the start, the British introduced a formal system based on English common law, which was adapted to the conditions of the country. As the

British were very careful not to offend the religious sensitivities of the Muslims in the North, they recognized Sharia to apply in personal matters. However, they also realized that most of the North observed customary practices that were different from Orthodox Sharia, so they established a system of informal justice to administer customary law. In the South, where the societies were largely unaffected by Islam, a purer version of African customary law applied.

A penal code and a code of criminal procedure were adopted to be applied by the state courts. But local courts, which primarily applied customary law, were also guided by the statutory law in criminal matters. The code of civil justice also empowered state courts to apply customary law as appropriate to the parties concerned. Since all these systems were recognized components of the law of the land, it could be argued that they became part of the formal system. This unique tripartite system is described in more detail in Section 4.

In due course, Sudan established a legal system that was as formal and effective as any in sub-Saharan Africa. Legal education started early under the British in what was then known as the Gordon Memorial College and eventually became the University of Khartoum. The Faculty of Law of the University of Khartoum was considered one of the best in Africa. It admitted about thirty students a year and graduated around twenty-five. Most of them joined the Judiciary, some joined the Attorney General's Chambers, increasingly some opted to join the bar and practice privately, and the top in the graduating class were appointed to the Faculty. Over the years, graduates went first to the United Kingdom and later to the United States, including Chicago, Harvard, and Yale Law Schools, for postgraduate studies.

By the time Sudan became independent, it had a well-established, efficient, and effective system of justice. The independence of the judiciary was highly prized, observed, and effectively invoked, even against the Government. The Bar Association was a vibrant, active body that "played a significant role in the profession and in public life in the defense of human rights and fundamental freedoms."[1] Sudan even provided other African countries with legal professionals – judges, lawyers, and teachers. Today, however, the legal system has fallen into disarray, described by well-informed legal professionals as "really chaotic and confused."[2] In many ways, this deterioration reflects the conflict of identities that has characterized post-independent Sudan, and has been responsible for both the undermining of, and recent revivalist sentiments concerning, the role of customary law.

2.2 Post-independence: instability, Islamization and civil war

Since independence on January 1, 1956, three related factors have served to plunge Sudan into a state of fragmentation and identity crisis. The first is the periodic military usurpation of power, usually followed by a purging of the professionals to favor the policies of the military rulers. Coups took place in 1958, 1969, 1985, and 1989. The intervening civilian governments either tried to introduce changes favorable to their party's objectives or lacked the capacity for effective reform to undo the damage done by the military.

The second factor has been the Government's persistent efforts to reverse the policies of British colonial rule, which administered the country as two separate entities in a framework of loose unity, to replace them with the policies of Arabization and Islamization. These policies began to gain practical ground with the introduction by then-President Jaafar Nimeiri of the so-called September Laws of 1983, which imposed Islamic law. Prominent Muslim leaders did not recognize them as a reflection of true Sharia, but rather saw them as a part of an opportunistic political ploy by a man who had been anything but a good Muslim. Nevertheless, the laws were not abrogated when Nimeiri was overthrown. Instead, the National Islamic Front (NIF), which seized power by a military coup in 1989, began to expand and entrench the wholesale application of Sharia. The Islamization of the legal system made many professionals who had been trained in the common law become defiant in that they continued to apply the old law, formal changes notwithstanding. Even in the Faculty of Law, pressures for the teaching of Sharia as the dominant framework only introduced confusion, as members of the faculty continued to teach the law they knew. Unfortunately, the academic staff began to leave the country en masse and spread all over the world, most of them to the Gulf States.

Perhaps the factor that has had the most pervasive and debilitating impact has been the civil war. The first phase of the war, from 1955 to 1972, was primarily a struggle for the independence of the South. That war ended in 1972 with a compromise that granted the South regional autonomy and recognition of their belief systems, both Christianity and traditional religions. While there was relative peace for eleven years, the war resumed in 1983 as a direct result of Nimeiri's imposition of Islamic law, which, along with the division of the South into three weak regions, constituted a unilateral abrogation of the peace agreement. That triggered a return to armed struggle under the Sudan Peoples Liberation Movement and Army – SPLM/A. The conflict initially pitted the Arabized Muslim North – whose identity is seen as welding race, ethnicity, culture, and religion into an integrated whole – and the South, which is more indigenously African in race, culture, and religious beliefs, with Christianity as a religion of modern conversion. Although the North is in fact a hybrid – not only in its racial composition, but also in culture, Islamic beliefs and practice of its overwhelming majority, particularly in the rural areas – the dominant group at the center sees itself as monolithically Arab and Islamic and wants to project those as elements of the national identity that determine the distribution of power, wealth, services, and development opportunities.

The declared objective of the SPLM/A, contrary to the first war, was not the secession of the South from the North, but the liberation of the whole country from the Arab-Islamic domination and the creation of a New Sudan in which there would be no discrimination due to race, ethnicity, culture, religion, or gender. This recasting of the objectives of the struggle began to appeal to the marginalized regions of the North, especially those who had been subsumed under the Arab-Islamic label, but had in effect remained African in race, ethnicity, and culture, and with an Africanized version of Islam. In the mid-1980s, the Nuba of Southern Kordofan and the Ingessana or Funj of Southern Blue Nile who border the South joined the SPLM/A in the struggle. The Ngok Dinka of Abyei, who, though racially, ethnically, and culturally part of the South, but administered in the North, had fought with the South since the first war.

The war has indeed cost the country dearly since 1983. In addition to the ruthless use of its own forces against the rebels and their sources of support, the Government recruited, trained, armed, and deployed Arab and other tribal militias who inflicted on the civilian population of the South unmitigated atrocities – burning villages, killing indiscriminately, looting, and otherwise terrorizing the people. With the war came massive movements of millions of Southerners to the North as internally displaced persons seeking safety, with half a million fleeing as refugees to neighboring countries and scores of thousands resettled abroad, particularly in the United States, Canada, the UK, and Australia. Thousands of children and women have been abducted and taken to the North into slavery. Over two million people have been killed or have died from war-related causes.

2.3 Impact on the legal system – formal and customary

Because of this turbulent series of events, the history of constitutional development and the rule of law in Sudan is a tortured one. As one constitutional authority has observed: "The political experience of the Sudan, in half a century of independence, has been so unsettled that the adoption of a nationally accepted constitutional document has not yet been realized."[3] As noted above, the series of military regimes suspended or abolished previous constitutions, or instituted self-serving provisions. The 1983 promulgation of the September Laws went beyond imposition of Sharia, to include also the amendment of several laws, the imposition of a state of emergency, the granting of extensive powers to security organs, the establishment of special courts, and generally the creation of a reign of terror that ultimately led to the overthrow of the regime. The new military regime of the National Islamic Front,[4] which came into power in 1989, suspended the Constitution, imposed a state of emergency, dissolved all political parties and trade unions, suspended the newspapers, and detained most political leaders, trade unionists, lawyers, and human rights activists. The once-vibrant Bar Association was one of the new regime's first victims:

> The first direct intervention in the Association occurred on the first day of the coup d'etat of June 1989. Together with political parties, trade unions and professional associations, the Bar Association was dissolved and its

> properties taken over. A Steering Committee was appointed by Presidential Decree to run the Affairs of the Association. Subsequently, the whole Chapter of the Bar Association Law relating to its general assembly independence and election of its executive committee was deleted. Although lawyers are self-employed, the Association was made part of the trade union law which empowers the Registrar of Trade Unions to determine the dates and organize and supervise the general meetings and election of the executive officers of the Association.[5]

Hundreds of judges, police and army officers, and civil servants were dismissed "in the public interest."[6] Military and special security courts were set up for trial and punishment of political opponents. Security organs exercised arbitrary powers of arrest, search, detention, torture, and prevention of travel.

Sudan was subjected to severe criticism and condemnation internally and by the international community, not least because of alleged involvement in international terrorism. The war in the South was intensified into a "jihad" holy war against the "infidels" and enemies of Islam, and also added to the breakdown of the rule of law. Repression, persecution, and egregious violations of human rights became the pattern. Reliable sources reported that Khartoum prisons were overcrowded with Southerners who were detained for years without trial, while Southern women were lashed and imprisoned for such minor offenses as brewing local alcoholic beverages to support their families.[7]

The imposition of Sharia had clear and direct consequences, such as the replacement of hundreds of common law-trained judges with those schooled only in Sharia, and the creation of "public order courts," which, as the name implies, dealt with the breaches of public order, such as drunkenness and noncompliance with the Islamic dress code.[8] Yet, while the system is supposedly fully Islamized, political Islamists themselves – with pragmatic opportunism – explain in appropriate circles that the Islamic laws they have so religiously enshrined are not all that Islamic after all, and that the English common law that provided the country with its main modern source of law is still intact.

In an interview with the Minister of Justice following the CPA, he explained the way the present regime had reformed the September Laws of Nimeiri and argued that the Sudanese legal system, though now described as Islamic, is in fact overwhelmingly still based on the common law system. As he put it, "for me, as a student of common law, who has also done some reading in Islamic law, I can say with confidence that the common law system is not touched … We have never deformed the common law system in the Sudan. It is still intact; it is touched, but not destroyed." He acknowledged, however, that "for the Muslims, they can say that it is Islamic because there is no contravention between what they believe and what they can see applied in the courts."[9]

What the Minister was arguing is not that the legal system has not been Islamized, but rather that the process of Islamization has not substantially changed the substance of the common law. He concedes, however, that they included in the criminal law the Islamic *hudud* penalties which entail amputation of hands for theft, stoning to death for adultery, and flogging for distribution or consumption of alcohol. He reports, "We made some explanatory notes to make things easier in the application," and proudly announced that "since 1989, amputation of hands is minimal."[10]

Omar El-Farouk Shoumena and Amin Mekki Medani, two prominent legal scholars and practicing attorneys, affirmed the position of the Minister regarding continuing application of English common law – but with major qualifications. According to Omar Shoumena, in the area of commercial law, such laws as the Companies Act, the Bankruptcy Act, and the Business Exchange Act are still based on the common law system. In the Law of Contract, the Law of Torts and the Law of Agency, the relevant legislation, including the Contract Act, Sale of Goods Act, and the Agency Act, were based on the English Law, and are supposedly still applicable. To that extent, Shoumena argues that "the bulk of the laws which are applicable today are really common law."

On the other hand, the situation is complicated by the laws that were introduced under the Islamic system, such as the Civil Code promulgated by Nimeiri and the Social Justice Act, which makes it mandatory for the court to apply Sharia when any applicable law is in doubt. Shoumena sees this as a source of confusion. "Most of the judges are Sharia judges and they tend not to recognize legislative law ... They are creating havoc." Shoumena illustrated his point by discussing a murder case in which the 1929 Penal Code – which is still applicable – provides grave provocation and sudden fight as mitigating circumstances. "They say murder is murder. In Sharia, we don't know sudden fight and we don't know provocation." Fortunately, Shoumena says, these decisions are usually reversed by the Appeals Court. Asked what the legal practice was under those circumstances, Shoumena responded: "Chaotic. One of the duties of the lawyer is to predict what the court will say about the law, and in a system that is intact, you can be pretty sure that the court will say so and so, but now you cannot be sure at all."

Amin Mekki Medani agreed and elaborated with reference to the Judicial Act of 1983, which provides that the judge will have to apply the principles of Sharia according to a certain hierarchy of legal principles. But, in the end, if no clear principles are applicable, the judge is empowered to resort to his own opinion. According to Medani, this was the reasoning used by the Sharia judge who sentenced to death Mahmoud Mohamed Taha, the revered elderly leader of the Republican Brotherhood, who was executed on January 18, 1985, for the crime of apostasy:

> Apostasy at that time was not an offence in the penal code, but the judge applied his own creativity under the principle of *ijtihad* and came out

> with the judgment "This is *ridda-apostasy.*" And they executed the man without there being a specific offense for that. Now, this principle of individual interpretation has been eliminated from the criminal law, but it is still part of the civil law. This disguises what the civil law is or is not, because it is left to the discretion of the judge. And there is no direction. You don't stipulate that the discretion of the judge is to be exercised according to the legal principles of a particular school of jurisprudence, Maliki, Shafie, or Hanbali, or Hanafi, or Shia, or whatever. So whatever he finds, he will use it and give you a judgment. That is how the system works in an atmosphere of total uncertainty and unpredictability.

Amin Mekki Medani also emphasized the current state of uncertainty and confusion in the legal system: "You read judgments – some people will quote Egyptian scholars, some will quote Abu Hanifa and others Savigny and now Deng. So the law is really in a state of flux. You don't know what the applicable law is. That is my opinion. And because of the recruitment of these [Sharia] judges, courts will recite the Koran instead of other legal sources. It is a matter of religion rather than law. This is what has happened to the law; it is a total confusion."

What needs to be emphasized is that the issue of Islamic law has become an acutely divisive identity factor. Even if the legal system were 99.9 percent Islamic but is described as secular, it would be objectionable to the Islamists, and, likewise, even if it were 99.9 percent secular and is described as Islamic, it would be objectionable to non-Muslim secularists. The issue is symbolism, not the substance of the law.

Indeed, the perspective of the aggrieved regions of the country, in particular the South, highlights the extent to which Islam, together with Arabism, connoting a combination of race, ethnicity, and culture, have been used as bases for discrimination and for fashioning a national framework that is intrinsically discriminatory. It is in this context that the imposition of Sharia law has been pivotal. This has made Southerners not only embrace secularism, but see their own identity as Africans closely connected with their customary law as a counterforce to Sharia. Religion and related legal systems became emotionally charged beyond the actual substance and merit of the law and related cultural or moral values.

2.4 The comprehensive peace agreement and implications for the legal system

After more than twenty years of brutal war, the Inter-Governmental Authority for Development (IGAD), a subregional organization, with the support of the US government and the international community, helped the Government of Sudan and the SPLM/A to negotiate the Comprehensive Peace Agreement (CPA) that was concluded and signed on January 9, 2005. The agreement accommodates the differences between the North and the South, but lays down a foundation for the promotion of the vision of the New Sudan, a country reconstructed to uphold the ideals of freedom, justice, democracy, and equity for all. The CPA gives the people of the South the right to decide by a referendum after a six-year interim period whether to remain within a united Sudan or secede and become an independent state. According to the interim arrangements premised on the principles of "one country, two systems," Islamic law will apply in the North, while the South will have a secular, democratic system in which the source of legislation will be "the values and customs of the people."

The power-sharing arrangements give the South a large measure of autonomy, with its own legislative and judicial branches, and provides for participation on an equitable basis in the Government of National Unity, with the President of the South becoming First Vice President of the Republic in a collegiate Presidency. Security arrangements give the South the right to keep its own army (SPLA) on par with the Sudan Armed Forces of the central government, and provides for Joint Integrated Units that will constitute a nucleus for the future national army, should the South vote for unity. Wealth-sharing arrangements give the North 50 percent of revenues from oil produced in the South and 50 percent of national non-oil revenues generated in the South. A third source of revenue will be taxation by the Government of Southern Sudan. There will be a National Central Bank, but the South will have its own branch, which will follow a conventional banking system, while the Northern branch of the Bank will continue to follow the Islamic banking system. The CPA also makes special arrangements for Abyei, Nuba Mountains, and Southern Blue Nile areas, which were allied with the South in the SPLM/A.

As the late Dr. John Garang de Mabior, former leader of the SPLM/A, put it: "The CPA is a unique Sudanese achievement that I believe shall forever change Sudan as well as have a fundamental and positive impact on our region and Africa."[11]

The CPA and the Interim National Constitution introduced values that provide promising bases for the rule of law, despite the anomalies of the Sharia legal system in the North and its built-in discrimination against non-Muslims and women. In an interview with the author, the then minister of justice, Ali Osman, expressed optimism about the future in light of the peace agreement: "We are doing our best to comply with the provisions of the agreement. We cannot afford any conflict between the constitution and the enabling law or the current law in the country."[12]

Nevertheless, the lack of certainty about the legal situation in general, and particularly in the context of the CPA, will continue to pose pressing issues for consideration. While the CPA provides for Sharia in the North and a secular legal system in the South, the situation of non-Muslims in the North and Muslims in the South is left uncertain. In an interview with the author, Omar Shoumena recalled discussing the situation with Garang shortly after he was sworn in as First Vice President: "I said to him, 'If you want to make peace attractive, you have to sort out the legal situation. Let there be no more confusion.' At present, there is a lot of confusion." Garang showed great interest and later told Shoumena that he had taken note of that point. Shoumena re-emphasized, "There is real confusion now. You cannot speak about the judiciary when the chief justice is Sharia judge and you want a fusion between the systems in the South and in the North. You tell me that the chief justice is a Sharia judge and at the same time you have a Supreme Court for both the North and the South. How can that be?"

The challenge for the post-conflict legal system will settle on how to reconcile these conflicting perspectives – the Islamist orientation of the center, the secularist orientation of the South, and the liberal Islamic orientation of the marginalized non-Arab areas of the North. There is also a strong secularist trend in the Arab-Islamic North that is increasingly aligning itself with the South and the marginalized regions of the North. Whether the Sudan will succeed in creating a constitutive and legal framework that will accommodate all the diverse trends and transcend the divisions based on race, ethnicity, religion, culture, and gender is the question for which the transitional period is expected to provide an answer. Whether or not the North will make unity attractive to the South will only be judged by the Southern vote in favor or against the unity option in the referendum after six years.

Prospects of a positive outcome will, to a significant degree, depend on the North understanding and appreciating the cultural values behind customary law, which, for the South, are central to the identity they have been fighting to defend and promote. Indeed, the CPA has led to an upsurge in interest in customary law, and there is a general assumption that it must underpin the legal future of the South. Southern Sudanese see customary law as an integral part of the identity they have fought so hard and so long to preserve against the threat of Arab-Islamic assimilation and domination. As the Southern Chief Justice, Ambrose Riiny Thiik, said, "Customary law is a manifestation of our customs, social norms, beliefs and practices. It embodies much of what we have fought for these past twenty years. It is self-evident that customary law will underpin our society, its legal institutions and laws for the future."[13] In the interviews the author conducted with judges and attorneys in the Southern Sudan in February 2005, following the January 9, 2005, Comprehensive Peace Agreement (CPA), this was a recurrent theme. Deng Biong Mijak, who chairs the Customary Law Steering Committee, charged with the development of customary law in the Southern Sudan, had this to say: "The war we have just ended was a cultural war … The North thought the South was suffering from a cultural vacuum, in Arabic, *el faragh el thagafy* … The system in Sudan was trying, of course, to build itself on … Arab and Islamic culture and our argument in the South is definitely that we are a people with cultures." Attorney General Michael Makuei noted: "It was the policy … to see to it that customary law did not find any home, and should not be developed. Our customary law is rich … Time has come now for us to develop it." The challenges involved in realizing this ideal will be explored in Section 6 of Part One.

3. Customary Law in its Cultural Context

Law is not an abstract concept neutrally poised above political, social, and cultural realities of a given community but is, to the contrary, a normative framework that regulates the society's constitutive processes. These processes themselves are guided by overriding postulates that determine the distribution of power, wealth, and other values, both substantively and procedurally. Law is thus an instrument of power for regulating relations between people, promoting values, and managing resources. This is why the study of customary law must go beyond legalistic principles to probe into the complexities of the social order and its determinants.

This section seeks to identify and elucidate the cultural concepts that are most necessary to forming an understanding of customary law in the South: procreational immortality, the ideals of unity and harmony, the interrelated dignity of the individual and the group, and the attributes required of leadership. It further discusses how these concepts are translated into a system of conflict resolution, involving law, decision-makers, and the process of decision-making. Understanding these overriding goals of the society's culture is necessary to understand their law, and also what reforms will be required to adapt the law to today's changing conditions – the subject of the final Section 6 in Part One: "The Challenges of Reform."

A methodological note is necessary here: there are many ethnic groups in the South with varying degrees of diversity in their cultures and customary laws, and it will be impossible to do justice to them all. The author's particular expertise is on the Ngok Dinka of Abyei – the Dinka, in their various groupings, are the majority in the Sudan – among whom he conducted extensive field research in the 1950s and 1960s. What should be emphasized, however, is that despite significant differences among the various ethnic groups, there is much in common in the customary laws of the South. Furthermore, this being a study not of, but about, customary law, the conceptual issues it raises are much more generic than would be the case with a discussion of the laws of a specific group.[1]

3.1 Procreational immortality – women, children and clan identity

Virtually all traditional African cultures are deeply entrenched in a lineage system in which the ancestors, seen as close to other deities and ultimately God, play a pivotal role. This is a concept of immortalization that aims at ensuring the continuity of every person after death, with a permanent identity and influence that is reflected in the dual world of the dead and the living, which remain interconnected and interactive. This is what the Dinka call *koc e nhom*, "standing the head (of the dead man) upright," and which is responsible for what anthropologists call "ghost marriage," marrying for a dead man so that children can be born to his name, and the *levirate*, an inheritance by which a widow of childbearing age lives with a relative of the deceased to produce children in the name of the dead husband.

Although this concept favors the male line, the role of women is pivotal – not only through the physical dimension of procreation, but also because it is the mother who inculcates in the child at the earliest stages the ancestral value system. Despite the acceptance of male dominance in the public forum, the influence of the mother is considered so great that it must be contained by encouraging loyalty to the agnatic group. The place and influence of women in many African societies is therefore extremely complex. The challenge of reconciling this position with international human rights standards is discussed in the final Section of Part One: "The Challenges of Reform."

Children are most prized, for they provide the pillars on which the ancestral line is built and maintained. Boys add their names to the line, while girls, through the bride's wealth, provide the means for their brothers to marry and beget children, particularly sons, to perpetuate the ancestral line. The son is more directly identified with the father, while the daughter, though also identified with the father, is permitted to be closer to the mother. To be called a son of a woman, which implies being close to the mother and under her influence, is a serious insult no child wants to risk. In polygynous societies, children are encouraged to show affection to their stepmothers and should be seen to be even closer to them than to their own mother. They must also demonstrate solidarity with their half-brothers and half-sisters.

The nuclear family then expands into the extended family and on to the lineage and its largest expansion, the clan, comprised of all those who can trace their descent to an original ancestor, from whom the clan gets its name. Beyond the clan, identity becomes primarily territorial: family ties become interfused into the territorial structures, and the principles that govern family relations in turn become interfused into those of the territorially based relations through the sections, the subtribes, or the entire tribe, each of which becomes viewed as a fictional family.

3.2 Unity and harmony – the concept of *cieng*

The lineage system has an overriding goal of continued combined individual and group identity and influence. This requires an emphasis on unity, solidarity, and harmony with the members of the group. The characteristics of this set of values can best be described by examining the Dinka concept called *cieng*, which occupies a pivotal position in their community processes. The Nuer have an identical concept known as *ciang*. Dr. Lienhardt wrote: "The Dinka … have notions … of what their society ought, ideally, to be like. They have a word, *cieng* or *cieng baai* (*baai* means home, family, village, community, tribe, or country), which used as a verb has the sense of 'to look after' or 'to order,' and in its noun form means 'the custom' or 'the rule.'"[2] Father Nebel translates morals as good *cieng* and benefactor as a man who knows and acts in accordance with *cieng*. He also translates *cieng* to mean behavior, habit, or nature of, or custom.[3]

But *cieng* is far more complex: as a transitive verb, it also means to inhabit, to live together, to treat (a person), to dominate, or to wear (clothes or ornaments), and as an intransitive verb it also means to last long. As a noun, it means conduct, human relations, way of life, or culture. Wherever the word "law" will apply, the Dinka use *cieng,* usually with an emphasis on "our *cieng*." These usages represent a multiplicity and a unity, which may be either descriptive or prescriptive, combining what "is" with what "ought to be." Every individual relies on other fellow members of the family, the lineage or the clan for his own prospects for being immortalized into a permanent identity and influence. So, his group is indispensable to his destiny. And, since it is the sum total of individuals that form the ancestral line, the individual is vital to the group's interest as a family, a lineage, a clan, and the wider community.

What, then, is the hierarchy of authority among individuals and groups involved in the shaping and sharing of values within the traditional system? At the top of the hierarchy are, of course, God and the other deities conceived of as being above, in the sky. The ancestors, though buried in the ground, are also believed to be spiritually close to God, the deities and spirits in the sky. In various ways and forms, these spiritual entities are in continuous contact with the living. They can be approached through prayer and sacrifices, and requested to provide protection and, if necessary, to intercede with other spirits and God. The deities, too, make their demands in a variety of ways, sometimes through dreams, or by afflicting a person with a credibly identifiable condition that brings illness or a positive manifestation of spiritual power in that person. Divination by credible spiritual functionaries is also a way of revealing the wishes of the supernatural actors in the worldly political, social, and economic processes. Among the living, the oldest members of the clan are viewed as the closest to the world of the ancestors, the spirits, and God. They manage family affairs in an autonomous decision-making process that aims at observing the ancestral values and reinforcing the unity, solidarity, and harmony of the family and the extended groups. Only major conflicts on which consensus within the family or extended groups is not possible are taken to territorial leaders – the different hierarchy of chiefs and the elders in council.

3.3 Individual and collective dignity – the concept of *dheeng*

Another value predicated on the overriding postulate of continuity is respect for every individual as a revitalization of the ancestral line. Dignity, on which respect is premised, ensures that the name, the image, and the overall reputation of every individual are valued assets to the group, just as the group is an asset to the individual. *Dheeng* is a word of multiple meanings, all positive. As a noun, it means nobility, beauty, handsomeness, elegance, charm, grace, gentleness, hospitality, generosity, good manners, discretion, and kindness. Except in prayer or on certain religious occasions, singing and dancing are *dheeng*. Personal decoration, initiation ceremonies, celebration of marriages, the display of "personality oxen" – indeed, any demonstrations of aesthetic value – are considered *dheeng*. The social background of a man, his physical appearance, the way he walks, talks, eats, or dresses, and the way he behaves toward his fellow human beings are all factors in determining his *dheeng*.

The youth, both men and women, are organized into an age-set system in which young men at a mature age are initiated into adulthood as *adheeng* (sing. *adheng*), "gentlemen" warriors. The corresponding age set of women are partners who follow men in war, provide them with food, reinforce them with the traditional weapons of war – spears – and provide support and humanitarian cover for the wounded and the fallen who, according to traditional war ethics, must no longer be harmed. The age-set system provides a life-long camaraderie that transcends narrow family loyalties and provides corporate identity and partnership in many aspects of life, social, economic, and, of course, cultural.

Every individual strives to represent his or her group with dignity and to protect and serve the interest of the community, just as the community protects the welfare and security of its individual members. This intragroup value-system is projected to the relations between and among component groups in the wider community, without which the integrity and security of the society cannot be safeguarded.

3.4 The moral attributes of leadership

A final set of concepts – crucial to the values of leadership – comprises: *dom*, establishing control over a group (a related notion of which is *mac* symbolized by tying a rope on the necks of cattle and tethering them to a pig), *muk*, maintaining and sustaining the group; and *guier*, improving the lot of the group. Each of these concepts connotes the observance of the principles of *cieng* and *dheeng* through *dom* (and *mac*); a chief establishes control and "holds" the land or group, not only by the mere fact of wielding power and authority, but also by using his position wisely to ensure peace, security, and prosperity. The continuity or stability of that state of affairs is maintained through *muk*, which literally means "keeping," a word also applied to child-rearing, including handling, feeding, looking after, protecting, and raising. *Guier* goes a step further to imply improvement of the existing situation, through reconstruction and/or reform. These values are mutually reinforcing and cyclic in nature. When a chief has taken over the reins of power (*dom/mac*), has stabilized his benevolent control over the situation (*muk*), and has introduced reforms to ensure a constructive and stable leadership (*guier*), he is described as having held (*dom/mac*) the land.

These elements of the normative worldview, which are widely shared in the Southern Sudan, mean that the temporal and spiritual worlds are closely interconnected. The chief is indeed believed to be a man endowed with spiritual powers to see right and wrong, a man with "a cool heart, *raan lir piou*," inspired by God to seek and find divine wisdom, and guided by God and the ancestral spirits to lead his people in the path of righteousness and societal ideals. His virtue is, however, unique only in degree and not in kind, for every person shares something of the divine, spiritual, and moral order. This is what makes the Dinka and indeed the indigenous Africans, both as individuals and as a people, profoundly religious, but without formalized or institutionalized religion. To the Southern Sudanese societies, legal norms are intrinsic components of culture, and so is religion, and all are part and parcel of their way of life.

3.5 Implications of the value-system for customary law

The Dinka, of course, never claim to live up to the ideals of their cultural values. This is not simply a gap between idealism and reality; it is the offshoot of the family orientation of society. Unity of purpose conflicts with divisive personal interests, inevitably generating tensions and conflicts that threaten to undermine the ideals of unity and harmony. It is by reference to both the successes and the failures, an appraisal often expressed in songs, that these values are reaffirmed. There are several noteworthy implications of the value-system for customary law and the management of conflict.

First, customary law itself is an integral aspect of the traditional way of life, with a well-established normative code closely associated with the social and cultural processes subsumed in the principles of *cieng* that are central to the ideals and ethos of unity and harmony in human relations. In order to facilitate human interaction in ways that meet the desired standards, the society, over time immemorial, has developed normative principles that are widely recognized, respected, and generally observed by members of the society. While specialized decision-makers, such as chiefs and elders, are more knowledgeable on the law than ordinary people, almost every adult member of the community is conversant with the principles of the normative code.

And while these principles are flexible enough to adapt to the needs of the changing times, either through interpretation or innovation to meet new situations or remedy obvious shortcomings, there is a degree of stability and predictability to the law.

The law may be regulatory in the sense that it provides guidance on how to behave in order to facilitate harmonious human relations – how to do what one is permitted to do, such as marriage. The law may also be prohibitive in the sense that it forbids certain acts or behaviors perceived as wrong and injurious to others in society – what should not be done, such as homicide, adultery, or defamatory insults.[4] In traditional society, this is not only a social or temporal prohibition, but also a spiritual one whose violation carries punitive sanctions from God and the ancestors. What Douglas Johnson observed of the Nuer also applies to the Dinka:

> As offences such as homicide, adultery and incest also involved a spiritual contamination (*nueer*) which had to be removed before a case could be completely settled, the land priest's other duty was to perform the necessary rituals of spiritual cleansing. The settlement of many cases thus involved both political negotiation and spiritual atonement. The spiritual and judicial were interwoven to such an extent that Nuer did not readily differentiate between the two.[5]

Breaches of both regulatory and prohibitive rules may result in wrongs that could be considered "criminal or civil," depending on the gravity of the injury to others involved. In reality, because of the segmentary structure of traditional society and the emphasis laid on intimate groups, public and private interests were largely undifferentiated and the punitive aspect of sanctions was intertwined with the restitutive aspect.

Second, while the community at the broadest level of organization is governed by an inclusive code of conduct in the shaping and sharing of power, wealth, and other values, every level down to the family and even to the individual is autonomous. The role of the authoritative decision-makers, who could be senior members of the group or higher authorities, depending on the gravity of the conflict, is merely to regulate relations between and among the diverse groups, to resolve conflicts between them, without interfering in the management of their internal affairs. The objective of such intervention is not punishment in the Western sense, but the achievement of an outcome both sides will accept as a fair basis for settlement and the restoration of unity and harmony. Reconciliation is a cardinal principle of the traditional method of dispute settlement. Payment of compensation or restitution by the culprit is nearly always the desired outcome. As Douglas Johnson observed with respect to the Nuer, whose cultural values are almost identical to those of the Dinka: "Their procedure was not designed to pronounce on guilt and innocence, or to enforce deterrent punishments. It was instead a system of arbitration."[6] Severe punishment is resorted to only when the individual disregards the sense of the community after a lengthy attempt at persuasion, thus alienating group regard for him or her. Such a punishment entails ostracism and isolation that may force the individual into self-exile – which was traditionally viewed as the worst that could happen to a person, short of death.

Third, the importance of the group means that kinship loyalties behind individual disputants are crucial to dispute resolution. To impose a judgment without mobilizing the public sentiment, including that of the wrongdoer's group, provokes not only the individual concerned, but also all those who owe him or her loyalty. Instead of settling the case, it may intensify the conflict between the parties. Indeed, cases usually take the form of groups versus groups – an insult aimed at an individual quickly assumes a slander against his or her group and can provoke intergroup hostilities – although this does not mean that individuals do not litigate or suffer the consequences of their wrongdoing personally. Furthermore, problems for litigation usually concern personal matters, particularly those resulting from a complex network of marriage affinities. These issues, being of a domestic nature, involve people who must often return to the same "doorway," *ghot thok*, or "fireplace," *mac thok*, words which are patently definitive of family bonds. Emphasis has therefore been placed upon reconciliation to bring about the harmony necessary for the maintenance of minimum tranquillity and order within the immediate and expanded communities.

This emphasis on reconciliation does not fit well with more formal legal systems. Douglas Johnson reports the Dinka of the Bahr el Ghazal in the 1940s expressing dissatisfaction with "the haste at which courts reached decisions, before persons were reconciled."[7] Ironically, speedy resolutions may actually prolong conflict, as kinship obligations keep relationships alive, and insisting on full and immediate payment of debts is a sign that relationships are broken. This is presumably why there is no time limitation to claims in customary law and obligations can be passed on from generation to generation. As Johnson explained with reference to the Nuer: "The courts' insistence on a precise and punctual repayment of obligations seems to have emphasised, in practice, what was owed the individual rather than the community … In this way the legal system imposed strains on Nuer society in the very process of trying to strengthen it."[8]

Fourth, the system was geared toward a conservative preservation of the value-system. Since the core elements of the worldview and ancestral values were cyclical, interrelating life with death and continuity in the hereafter, the notion of a linear approach to change viewed as a process of development or progress was unknown to traditional society. The principal objectives of life were achievable and for the most part actually achieved. One could have few or many children to continue one's name. The unity and harmony of the family and the community could always be better. And so with the status of the family, whether derived from its wealth or its ancestral image. One could be more or less endowed with material wealth or other resources, could accumulate large herds of cattle, cultivate bigger plots of land, or build better and larger homes, but those were all within the capacity of members of society. While ancestral values and kinship solidarity were deemed to be inherently respectful of the rights and duties of every individual, as a member of the group, and of the rights and duties of the group over its members, obviously, the basis of the value-system, specifically the continuation of the ancestral line, to the extent that they aimed first and foremost at the perpetuation of the male line, were inherently discriminatory to women and children. By the same token, these otherwise disadvantaged groups were accorded special compensatory privileges which had the effect of sometimes disguising the inequities against them. Among the Nilotics, members of youth warrior age sets, for instance, preoccupy themselves with aesthetics of cattle camping, singing, and dancing, and are prone to excessive use of force as attributes of their distinctive identity and avenue to dignity. Women, on the other hand, find their principal source of dignity by identifying themselves with the status of their husbands and formally recognized male friends – so much so that in their songs of self-exaltation, a woman alternately refers to her husband or boyfriend as "I" and takes a special pride in his wealth or social prestige, which she sees as hers.

Since there were hardly any alternatives outside the system, the forces favoring conformity were almost insurmountable. A close probing will lead to the conclusion that even though there appears to be a consensus behind fundamental values and the normative framework they shape, there is an awareness of the inequities of the system, which were accepted, or perhaps tolerated, presumably because alternatives did not seem feasible in a close and relatively isolated society. The only alternative that was traditionally available was self-exile into the unknown world of a potentially more hostile environment, a risk only the foolhardy or the most daring would choose. The overwhelming majority not only succumbed to their position in society, but, as is true of women, became a backbone in support of the system to enhance the relative benefits and minimize the threat of punitive measures. Because of the subtleties of the traditional stratification and discrimination, the more assertive modern promotion of universal human rights and humanitarian standards is viewed with unease as founded on a misunderstanding of the cultural values and the benefits they accord women and children. The challenges this poses to current efforts to reform customary law will be explored in Section 6.

3.6 The process of selecting decision-makers

Although the People's Local Courts Act of 1977, as its predecessors, the Chiefs' Courts Ordinance of 1931 and the Native Courts Ordinance of 1932, provides for the appointment and dismissal of the members of the traditional courts, these are for the most part traditional leaders selected in accordance with the traditional rules of succession, with authority embedded in their own legitimacy among their people, in conformity with indigenous values for leadership. While the principles involved have been significantly affected by change and the modern state requirements, they persist, making the situation a blend of tradition and modernity, with ambivalences, dilemmas, and paradoxes. In particular, it is important to note that despite the modern tendency toward democratic elections of leaders, the ideals of ancestral supremacy and continuity through the male line not only still favor the leadership of certain clans or lineages, but also men over women and children. This means that the leaders, whether administrators or judges, are, for the most part, men, although efforts are now being made to promote the representation of women in the political and judicial organs.

A significant aspect of the traditional system was that the decision-making functions were integrated. There has been a trend toward separating the roles of traditional leaders as political authorities, administrators, and judges, but traditional societies still perceive these functions as intrinsically interconnected. Sometimes, the functions may be separated but are still exercised by the same personalities. And even when the personalities are separated in accordance with their special functions, there is still a tendency to see administrators and judges as "chiefs."

In traditional society, the authority of the clans that produced leaders was derived from the divine powers inherited from their ancestors and ultimately from God. Colonial rule undermined traditional leaders by turning them into agents of the state, but it also reinforced them through indirect rule and the coercive force of the state. In many cases, traditional leaders were replaced with salaried government chiefs whose sole source of authority became the secular force of the state. However, even in the case of government appointed chiefs, because of the importance of the religious dimension, myths of divine origin to their authority will develop to support their otherwise secular authority.

Traditionally, leadership was hereditary and held for life. Under colonial rule, some form of election was introduced by which the will of the community was ascertained through consultations with representatives of the different segments of the tribal structures. In most cases, elections were used when the person entitled to succeed was viewed as incapable of leadership, or in the event of ambiguity about who should be the rightful heir. Increasingly, there is a tendency to open up the position of the chief for election, albeit within the family of the deceased leader. Even where succession is hereditary, the facts surrounding the case permit at least two people to compete and elections through representative group voting are held. Admittedly, these elections are very much influenced by the government authorities, but the fact is that the people have come to regard some form of election as normal. The method of election is usually collective; that is, by families, clans, sections, or subtribes according to the importance of the position in question. And a consensus is usually arrived at through broad consultation. More and more people who are not the eldest sons of the most senior wives or whose line once held the disputed chieftainship but lost it for one reason or another are now entitled to compete. Yet, the importance of descent in the eyes of the people remains intact. Authority based solely on personal attributes is still unknown.[9]

In the interviews conducted with judges and lawyers in Southern Sudan, skepticism about the emerging tendency toward the Western electoral system was strongly voiced. There was a general tendency to prefer the traditional method of consultation aimed at selecting the person best qualified for leadership. According to Deng Biong, Western-style democracy creates tensions because "the chief who is elected will not be at peace with some of the people who did not support him. The traditional notion of democracy is that people sit, they nominate the candidates, and people debate, through dialogue, until they come to a consensus, and select one of them." Michael Makuei, the attorney general, described how the traditional way of selecting leaders led to a consensus: "The elders will be observing what the young people are doing. At the end of the day, when they come to the selection of a leader, they will not ask you, the young people; they will just say that so-and-so is the chief. And that's that. Nobody will question their wisdom, because if I am selected from amongst my age-mates, they already have known the role I play among them." It is obvious from these reactions to the Western-style electoral system that a tension is developing in the way chiefs are chosen. The traditional method is still prevalent, but there is a strong emerging demand for a more democratic system of election that will be constrained by descent. The choice, then, is between leaders groomed and prepared to lead by their hereditary legacy and those self-made persons who have demonstrated their qualifications for elected leadership. It is a legitimate tension that may, in the end, be transitory, since the global trend is toward free and fair elections, through one person, one vote.

3.7 The process of dispute resolution

Because the aim of Dinka law is reconciliation, a guiding principle is that disputes should be settled out of court whenever possible. Family disputes are ideally resolved within the family or at lower levels of the leadership hierarchy outside formal court. The initiative to mediate such disputes may be taken by one of the parties, probably the aggrieved or the wrongdoer, eager to resolve the matter and be reconciled with the wronged. Any other member of the family or the local community who is aware of the conflict may also initiate the process.

The mediation process will then require convening a council or a meeting of a limited number of elders in a manner not dissimilar to a Chiefs' court, though limited in size. The initiator of the mediation will then introduce the case. If the initiator is the wrongdoer, he or she will state the case with an admission of the wrong, a willingness to address the wrong in an amicable manner, and a plea to the elders for arbitration and reconciliation. The wronged party will then state his or her case, initially without directly responding to the offer of redress or reconciliation. A lengthy process follows, in which those present contribute their own statements, all aimed at facilitating a settlement on an appropriate basis, including the value of compensation or restitution required. In this type of mediation, an *agamlong* – whose role is to repeat, clarify, and summarize statements in a raised voice for the benefit of the court – is not involved.

However, mediation out of court may also be much more expanded and formal, depending on the seriousness of the issues involved or the status of the individuals in conflict. These mediation processes are not significantly different from formal court procedures and an *agamlong* is engaged, although no records are made, as are required by the regulations of the formal courts. Furthermore, the customary law principles applied in the resolution of such conflicts are essentially the same as those applied by formal courts, although the nature of the relationship and the added importance of restoring unity, harmony, and amicable family relations will naturally influence the outcome and the value of the settlement.

Even when the case goes to court, the possibility that a settlement can be negotiated outside the court is always an option. Those elders who take part in an attempt to reach a settlement outside the court may still insist on that option, and they may endeavor to persuade the court to refer the matter back to the elders for settlement outside the court, or they may urge the court to persuade the parties to compromise. The desire for conciliation is so strong that courts may decide to revise their own judicial decisions on that basis.[10]

In formal court proceedings, customary law does not see the judge as an umpire in an adversarial process in which the parties are represented by partisan attorneys. The whole notion of adversarial procedure is alien to the Dinka. A case is popularly known in which one of the Dinka witnesses, frustrated by the bizarre behavior of the hired attorney in speaking solely in favor of the accused, burst out, "The way you are talking, you must have been bribed." Justice to the Dinka means that anyone involved in the settlement of a dispute must balance the opposing positions and try to reconcile them. The objective is a genuine search for the truth in the interest of justice. The procedure under customary law makes the judge or the court the investigator of facts during a trial, eliciting the best evidence from the litigants in order to pass a fair and mutually acceptable judgment.

Court procedure begins with the statement of the invocation to the adjudicating authority in formal court or in a council of elders, with a wider public audience. No person can state his case if he is not authorized by the court through the *agamlong*. A case is introduced if the *agamlong* responds or is ordered by the court to respond to the plaintiff's statement of his claim by repeating it in whole or in essential part. This practice of repetition, apart from encouraging the court to keep track of the statements, also helps to ensure order. This is equally true where a statement by a witness or an opinion by a court member is involved. According to John Makec:

> no trial or hearing takes place unless [the *agamlong*] is present to play his ... role ... Every person who speaks in court, including the president and court members, speaks through him ... He is an orator who has a command of the language of the court. He is capable of reducing the long and clumsy statement of a speaker into a precise and comprehensive sentence. Apart from repeating the words aloud and precisely, it is a part of his duty to direct the parties, witnesses and the court as to what steps to take at the next stage of the proceedings. He is well versed in court procedure.[11]

The statements of the parties, their witnesses, and the court members are often lengthy. Speakers often digress into stories, proverbs, and even jokes, but they always connect them to the point at issue. The whole situation is thus brought together and objective truth is sought to restore unity and harmony. Godfrey Lienhardt described the process in the following words: "The Dinka and the Nuer are a warlike people; and have never been slow to assert their rights as they see them by physical force. Yet, if one sees Dinka trying to resolve a dispute, according to their own customary law, there is often a reasonableness and a gentleness in their demeanor, a courtesy and a quietness in the speech of those elder men superior in status and wisdom, an attempt to get at the whole truth of the situation before them."[12]

While the range of admissible evidence is wide, there is a general bias against any evidence which tends to aggravate the indignation of litigants and thus impede settlement. Direct evidence is preferred to circumstantial evidence, because the possibility of error is higher. Likewise, interested evidence – but not evidence of an interested party – can only widen the gap between the interest groups involved. An interested person may speak, although he may decide not to. Should he speak, he is usually expected to emphasize the wrong of the side in which he is interested. This attitude is especially important among the judges, and since the process of litigation involves the gathering and the evaluation of evidence simultaneously, it must be demonstrated throughout the proceedings.

Of course, a person to whom the judges are known to be related, or in whom they are at least interested, has a higher expectation of winning the case. A tactful judge or elder can best favor his relative by condemning him; unless the wrong is too apparent, such an attitude often encourages the court to find in favor of the relative. Even when the wrong is apparent, the indignation of both the wronged person and the court is mitigated by the alignment of the chief with them against his own relative. If a chief or any court member is an immediate party to the case, he may not act as a court member, for among the Dinka, as in the Western justice system, no one can be a judge in his own case.

As the case concludes, court members pass their judgment in ascending order, beginning with the junior judges and ending with the president of the court, usually the most senior chief. Having listened to the views of the other court members, the president pronounces what he views to be the closest to a consensus of the court, one whose wisdom the litigants will accept. Where the case involves a president less than the paramount chief, a dissatisfied litigant can always appeal to him. Nowadays, there is also the possibility of an appeal to the formal judicial authorities, although the judgment of the paramount chief is likely to be upheld by those authorities. Also today, the court proceedings are recorded by the court clerk, and can then be forwarded to the appellate authority.

4. Customary Law and Legal Pluralism

As described briefly in Section 2, the customary and formal legal systems in Sudan have coexisted and interacted for a long time. The British introduced a system of legal pluralism, in which customary law, Islamic law, and English common law each had a statutorily prescribed role. This system preserved the application of customary law among those living in traditional settings, while undermining it by limiting its jurisdiction and subjecting it to principles of "justice, morals and order," inevitably defined by the values of outsiders. That system was kept more or less intact until the Islamization movement in the 1980s. During the 1983–2005 war, in areas controlled by the Government of Sudan, Islamization had the effect of further relegating customary law to an inferior status, while rendering the role of native courts ambiguous. In areas controlled by the SPLA, the British system remained in place, yet customary law was deeply affected by the war and social change, as will be explored in the next section.

4.1 Three systems of justice: Islamic, customary, and civil

During the colonial and the postcolonial period until the imposition of Islamic law in the 1980s, the legal system in Sudan was a complex mixture of dualism and tripartism. It had two hierarchies – Islamic and civil law. But the term civil law was also used in contrast to local or customary law within the civil system, so in fact there have been three divisions of law – Islamic, local, and civil.

The Islamic division consisted of Islamic or Sharia courts, which were established under the Sudan Mohammedan Law Courts Ordinance of 1902, and which formed an independent hierarchy headed by the Grand Gadi. They were empowered to apply the authoritative doctrines of the Hanafi jurisprudential school, unless the Grand Gadi otherwise directed by judicial circular or memorandum that such other doctrines of the Hanafia or other Mohammedan jurists be applied.[1] The courts covered such personal matters as succession, wills, legacies, gifts, marriage, divorce, family relations, or the constitution of *wakfs*.[2] This applied where both parties were Muslims or in the case of mixed or non-Muslim parties where both parties consented to the jurisdiction.[3]

Although the majority of the Sudanese are Muslims, Sharia courts functioned within a relatively small community. The greater portion of the Muslims fell under the jurisdiction of tribal or native courts. Virtually all the Sharia judges were trained only in Islamic law in Egyptian universities or in the branch of the Khartoum Law Faculty that specialized in Sharia. Consequently, these judges administered Islamic law in isolation from the other branches of the law that formed the legal pluralism in the country, while the other branches were required to be sensitive to the tenets of the Islamic orientation of Northern Sudanese society.

The local division, dealing with customary law, was composed of Native and Chiefs' courts. Native courts were applicable to the six provinces of the North, excepting the Ngok Dinka of Abyei in the Northern Province of Kordofan. Chiefs' courts were applicable to the southern provinces and later to the Ngok Dinka of Abyei in accordance with a special order of the governor-general in council of 1944.[4] Native courts were originally instituted by the Sheikhs Courts Ordinance of 1922, amended in 1928, and re-enacted in the Native Courts Ordinance of 1932; Chiefs' courts were instituted by the Chiefs' Courts Ordinance of 1931 and served the same function. The ordinances empowered them to try criminal and civil cases involving the natives of the territory according to the customary law prevailing in that territory, provided it was not repugnant to justice, morality, and order. In both the North and the South, the Chiefs' and Native courts were manned by judges, chiefs, and elders, most of whom were illiterate. The chiefs were largely hereditary, with changes favoring some form of elections as discussed in the previous section. Chiefs received salaries from the state, although their financial burdens as tribal leaders exceeded their official means and they had to depend on the traditional support system.

The idea behind the Chiefs' and Native courts was pragmatic: to make use of existing local structures of authority, while – through the repugnancy clauses – giving the more enlightened local administrators freedom to reform the substance of customary law. Douglas Johnson explains the thinking:

> There were two aspects to "indirect rule" as it applied to the Sudan: (1) it was intended to keep costs down and administrative organization simple by allowing the Sudanese to get on with "non-essentials;" (2) it had an evolutionary aim to develop native institutions through "the inevitability of gradualness," shedding what was "evil and barbarous," but nurturing those aspects which administrators deemed locally valuable. In this system courts were to provide both cathartic entertainment and justice in order to improve public security.[5]

The civil division consisted of common law courts and were the least limited in terms of people and the territory they governed, as well as the laws they applied. In criminal jurisdiction, they applied the Sudan Penal Code (1925) and the Code of Criminal Procedure (1925) together with other criminal statutes and regulations. In civil jurisdiction, they generally applied English common law, but deferred to Islamic and customary law on certain matters, mostly affecting personal status. Section 5 of the Civil Justice Ordinance of 1900, re-enacted in 1929, provided:

> Where in any suit or other proceeding in a civil court any question arises regarding succession, wills, legacies, gifts, marriage, divorce, family relations, or the constitution of Wakfs, the rule of decision shall be:
>
> 1. Any custom applicable to the parties concerned which is not contrary to justice, equity or good conscience, and has not been by this or any other enactment altered or abolished and has not been declared void by the decision of any competent court.
> 2. The Mohammedan law in cases where the parties are Mohammedan, except insofar as that law has been modified by such custom as is above referred to.

Subsection (b) was a device to cover tribal communities in the North who, though Muslims, applied an eclectic amalgamation of indigenous customs and Islamic principles.[6] Under the provision, pure Islamic law does not apply to those people to whom customary law is applicable; rather, Islamic law as modified by their customs will apply to them.

The People's Local Courts Act of 1977, revised up to 1981, repealed the Chiefs' Courts Ordinance of 1931 and the Native Courts Ordinance of 1932, although it was essentially a continuation of the British system. Section 2(1)(a) of the Act provides that "any Court established under any of the aforesaid [Ordinances] shall continue to decide cases until the warrants of establishment of the new Courts are issued in accordance with the provisions of this act." The warrants now issued by the chief justice are essentially the same as those that were issued by the governor-general under the Anglo-Egyptian administration. As was the case under the Ordinances, the Act makes separate provisions for the North and the South, with respect to the establishment of the local courts, their jurisdiction and powers, and the hierarchy of appeals, although the differences are relatively minor.

The Act stipulates in article 11(1) the composition of a people's local court to consist of a president, vice president, and "sufficient number of members to be selected by the Chief Justice." According to article 11(2), the members are selected pursuant to recommendation of the resident magistrate, in consultation with various local officials before it is submitted to the chief justice. Nonetheless, most of the judges, particularly at the higher levels, such as president and vice president, are hereditary leaders whose legitimacy in the eyes of their people is vested on that background, with government authority behind them being more a reinforcement rather than the foundation of their moral authority. In reality, while the court officially consists of the appointed members, it is open to the public, and anyone of appropriate age and social standing can give his opinion.

In the North, appeals from the judgments of a people's local court or a bench of magistrates exercising the powers of a People's Local Court under the Act went to the intermediate local court (if any), then to the magistrate of the first grade, then to the province judge, then to the court of appeal. Appeals against the judgments of a Special People's Court went to the authority designated by the chief justice from time to time. In the South, appeals from the decisions of People's Local Courts or Benches of Magistrates exercising the powers of a People's Local Court under the Act went to the Regional People's Courts, from which appeals went to the Main People's Courts, from which appeals in turn went to the magistrate of the first grade, then to the province judge and finally to the Court of Appeal, as in the North.

Section 17(1) provides that People's Local Courts shall be subject to supervision by the most senior magistrate of the first grade within the local limits of whose jurisdiction the court is situated. In accordance with subsection (2), the chief justice shall appoint a sufficient number of inspectors to carry out periodic inspection of People's Courts for the control of their good performance in the administrative and financial matters.

Perhaps the most contentious issue with respect to the People's Local Courts relates to the so-called repugnancy clause. Section 13 of the People's Local Courts Act provides that: "A People's Local Court shall administer the custom prevailing within the local limits of its jurisdiction provided that it is not contrary to justice, morals or public order. It shall administer the provisions of any other law, the administration of which is authorised by its warrant of establishment or the regulations accompanying the same." This is basically a restatement of the law as it had been under the Ordinances. As John Wuol Makec noted, despite the repeal of those Ordinances, the status of custom as one of the sources of law in the Sudan has not been diminished. In addition to the People's Local Courts Act, customary law has been emphasized by Section 5 of the Civil Justice Act 1983, which regulates the overall formal justice system in the country. Further, local courts' warrants issued from time to time by the chief justice authorize those courts to apply the local custom applicable to the contesting parties.[7] In addition, "judicial decisions have, from time to time, given recognition to custom as one of the sources of law in the Sudan."[8]

Nevertheless, the qualification which requires conformity to "justice, equity and good conscience" or to "justice, morality and order" implies not only control over local custom, but also the relegation of customary law to a lower status than statutory law or Islamic law.[9] The standard of reasonableness and its equivalents in the Sudanese administration of justice pose serious cross-cultural problems, since, as Makec has noted, a custom by its very nature must be reasonable to the people who observe it, and it must be presumed to be in conformity with "justice, equity and good conscience" or "justice, morality and order." The question arises only if those making the judgment are alien to the value-system represented by the custom concerned. In the Sudanese context, the judges were for the most part English during the colonial period and after independence mostly Northern Sudanese Muslims. "[T]here is usually a tendency on the part of the judges to be subjective in their determination of what is or is not reasonable, or what does or does not conform to justice, equity and good conscience," Makec observed. Another Southern Sudanese legal scholar, Natale Olwak Akolawin, noted: "There is in each one of us an underlying philosophy of life which gives coherence and discretion to our thought and action. This philosophy of life is an outcome of inherited instincts. Traditional beliefs and acquired conviction and what one may consider just and equitable or in accordance with good conscience is necessarily limited by the above factors."[10] Ignorance of customary law is also a major factor that can cut both ways. I had a personal encounter with this problem during my research into the customary law of the Ngok Dinka of Abyei. While I was interning with a district judge, he told me that I could attend his court of appeal but should not expect to learn from it since he, though the appellate authority, knew nothing about Dinka law. He explained further that in any case, since they did not want to embarrass or undermine the chiefs – whose influence depended largely on the extent to which his judgments were respected by higher authorities – they will usually allow their judgments to prevail. It is true that the influence of the chief depended largely on the extent to which his judgments were respected by higher authorities, but the concept of appeal will be meaningless if this concession were carried to an extreme. A happy medium cannot be reached in ignorance of the law.

Since the imposition of Sharia, Muslim judges have generally contended that such repugnancy clauses as were applicable to customary law could not be applied to Islamic law, since it is God's prescription. This problem, from the Southern Sudanese perspective, has been very much aggravated by the attempt to impose Islamic law on the whole country, including the non-Muslim South. As much as Sharia law is favored, customary law is disfavoured. A number of factors account for this. First and foremost is the fact that customary law is seen in opposition to Islamic law and is, accordingly, resented. Besides, as noted earlier, since customary law in the North has assimilated Islamic principles, customary law as commonly understood is identified with the South and to encourage it will be to impede national integration.[11] There is also the point already made that customary law is considered inferior and therefore something to be ashamed of, or at least not to be encouraged by any means, including the mere knowledge of it. Yet, an estimated 80 percent of the population were governed by customary law, and through original jurisdiction, revision, and appeals, civil courts were and still are continuously confronted with customary law.[12]

Despite their objection to colonial rule, Southerners now look back on British administration with favor when compared to the Arab-Islamic domination of the independence era. As a senior Southern judge put it, "The first colonialists – the British – were to some extent lenient, merciful and sympathetic to our traditions than our second colonialists – the Arab, Muslim minority clique based in the capital Khartoum. I, for one, thank the British for protecting our culture, identity, and customs through, among other measures, imposing the Closed Districts Act 1922 and enacting the Chiefs Courts Ordinance, 1931, by which traditional chiefs in the South were allowed to apply their customary laws."[13]

Although the place of customary law in the pluralistic context of modern Sudan, as presented in this section, may appear to be part of a cohesive national legal system, the situation today has been much affected not only by the Islamization the system has incrementally experienced since independence, and accelerated over the last two decades, but also by the civil war in the South that has devastated the country since independence and has witnessed an erosion of the principles of the rule of law, which, though limited under colonial administration, was soundly grounded in the administration of justice.

5. Customary Law, War, and Social Transformation

It was noted earlier that customary law, as described in this section, represents both continuity and change – what *was* (to a degree still *is*) and the changes the society has undergone and is still undergoing. There are several ways of looking at the impact of change on customary law, among them the general process of modernization, which implies transition out of the traditional social context, and reactions to the inequities of the traditional system. The most radical transformation is associated with the impact of the war that has raged in the country for decades. The need to cope with these changes, together with a strong sentiment of cultural revivalism and a desire to restore the positive values of tradition while recognizing the widely accepted need to reform customary law are the contradictory forces at work, reflecting both conservativism and radicalism.

5.1 Overview of social change

Although the overriding cultural values are still acknowledged and revered, the specific principles emanating from them – especially insofar as they relate to the stratifications based on descent, gender, and age – are being questioned and even openly challenged and violated in practice. Social change is, of course, a natural phenomenon associated with historical evolution. In today's Africa, this is closely connected with modernization, a process that has largely been a function of education, conversion to Christianity or Islam, occupational opportunities, and emigration out of the traditional context. Education challenged the traditional value systems insofar as it opened minds to radically different worldviews. The self-contained, largely homogeneous and cohesive social order of tradition became exposed to diversities in perspectives. Conversion to Christianity and Islam undermined the fundamentals of the indigenous cultural value-system, especially as they relate to ancestral continuity and its religious implications. Opportunities for employment, ranging from urban labor to professional careers, opened doors to new sources of income, which inevitably had an impact on traditional obligations and dependencies on which conformity was grounded. All these changes have challenged the traditional structures and hierarchies for shaping and sharing of values. Power structures based on descent are increasingly contested. Gender roles are being seriously scrutinized, especially as women under the destabilizing circumstances of war have proven to be more resilient and productive than men and have assumed greater responsibilities than they had been assigned under the traditional system. The same is true of the role of youth, many of whom acquire modern skills, more earning capacity than their elders, and greater independence.

The civil war has profoundly affected traditional values in a variety of ways. People have been massively displaced, both internally and to outside the country. In some cases, people have been exposed to modern values that undermine their belief in or adherence to indigenous norms. Within Southern Sudan, this has entailed a great deal of intercommunal interaction, with unavoidable conflict of local cultures. The normative standards of ancestral continuity, unity, and harmony through *cieng*, personal and collective dignity through *dheeng*, and the combined temporal and spiritual authority of traditional leaders, are evidently losing ground.

Biong Bol Bulabek, an elder of Ngok Dinka community that has been largely displaced to Northern Sudan, described the impact of the war on the Ngok society:

> When your cow is robbed and you are not allowed to cultivate otherwise you are killed, then your home has completely been destroyed to the extent that you cannot live in it any longer. Our people fled their homes for those very reasons. Some ran away pinning their hope on their daughters thinking that they could bring for them cattle in the future. But after they have grown up in Northern Sudan most of the girls do not even listen to their mothers. If a mother tells her daughter to behave herself in order not to spoil her chances of marriage, the daughter will dismiss her mother as being out of date and that the days have changed. And even if the girl was lucky to be married then only little cash is given to the father with an agreement that cattle will be sorted out if people return home … Even at home now people have no cattle any more. Only very few people escaped the raids of the government militia. Therefore if somebody approached you with five heads of cattle then you have to give away your daughter in marriage. The question is no more about the number of cattle but of a person who can look after your daughter during this difficult time.[1]

These developments have been immensely complicated and aggravated by the militarization of society. The introduction of guns has impacted on the spiritual values that were associated with the rituals and methods of resolving homicide cases. According to John Luk, "Nowadays, someone accused of having killed in a fight may argue, 'I was fighting on this side of the battle; I could not have shot and killed someone on the other front.' But previously, with spears and sticks, you knew your victim immediately; you were immediately identified. These days how do you get the evidence? Who did this? It is a problem."[2]

Although the SPLM/A in some ways sought to engage local communities constructively by recognizing their customary laws and traditional social structures, constant interference with traditional social institutions by some officials has contributed to the weakening of those institutions. While traditional authorities have rendered a highly valued service to the rebel movement, commanding officers and soldiers have not always been deferential to them or to the civilian population that offered them grassroots support. The standards of human dignity traditionally observed and in many respects supportive of universal human rights standards are losing ground and violations of international human rights and humanitarian law are reported, although they are perceived as the result of individual misconduct rather than of SPLM/A policies.[3] This is, of course, quite apart from the egregious violations of human rights by the national authorities that have been well documented by the relevant agencies, intergovernmental, governmental, and nongovernmental.

During the 1994 SPLA/SPLM national convention, the traditional leadership was able to forge a united front and ask the political and military leaders to reassert a positive role among local communities. Measures to establish civilian, as distinct from military, administration were adopted, but the need for the movement to use the limited resources available to achieve certain military and political objectives restricted its flexibility. In some instances, the differences between civil and military leaders led to further conflicts and struggle for authority. According to Monyluak Alor, the demand of traditional leaders for respect toward cultural values transcended concerns about their individual powers. Their concerns were over the breakdown of the social order and the declining morality, especially among the young. Traditional societies were suddenly experiencing an unfamiliar rise in crime rates, destruction of property during intertribal fighting, and the killing of women and children, previously unknown. They saw those developments as endangering the integrity of their society and attributed them to the failure of the movement to cooperate with the local leadership on matters of public concern.

It is too soon to have any coherent view of the impact change has made on the traditional legal system. Changes are taking place even within the traditional legal system, as the old rules get reinterpreted, amended, or even replaced by new rules to adapt to the imperatives of social transition. But more reform is dictated by the radically transformed conditions outside the traditional context, both inside and outside the country.

5.2 Customary law and traditional authority in the new order

Despite these negative trends, the role of customary law appears to have remained of crucial importance, even as it is threatened by all the negative consequences of the war. In fact, customary laws were always in force in the liberated areas. Section (2) of the SPLM laws of 1984 recognized the application of the local custom of each community within the SPLM/A liberated areas. While the military established three military courts, namely the summary court martial, the district court martial, and the general court martial as the final appeal court, the ordinary courts that were in force before the establishment of SPLM/A authority were recognized. Sudanese Government laws were rendered irrelevant in SPLM/A areas, and only the customary laws of the Southern communities were upheld. The customary laws of Bahr el Ghazal, which had been codified under the leadership of the then-speaker of Bahr el Ghazal regional assembly, John Wuol Makec, before the commencement of the war, remained in force under the name "The Re-Statement of Bahr el Ghazal Region Customary Law (Amendment) Act of 1984."

In line with the growing sentiments of cultural revival, customary law was given a further unequivocal recognition in the SPLM's statutory reforms of 2003. Section 3(2) of the New Sudan Penal Code, 2003, provides: "In the application of this Code, courts may consider the existing customary laws and practices prevailing in each area."[4] The civilian court system established by the SPLM in 1999–2000 incorporated customary courts as the two lowest levels of the six-tier judicial hierarchy. With the establishment of the Government of Southern Sudan in 2005, court jurisdictions will be modified to reflect new geographic boundaries, with a single Supreme Court, three regional Courts of Appeal, High Courts for each of the ten states, and County courts. Below the County courts are the Payam courts, each composed of three members. Below them will remain the two levels of traditional courts. The regional courts, now called Boma courts, on which sit five members drawn from two or more chieftaincies, have regional as well as appellate jurisdiction over the Chiefs' courts. The latter, the lowest in the hierarchy, comprise the chief of each tribal jurisdiction as president of the court, assisted by four members.

Chiefs' courts are empowered to deal with both criminal and civil cases as dictated in the warrant of establishment issued by the chief justice in much the same way as the old system, with wide powers to deal with both criminal and civil cases. In the criminal cases they may use customary law to deal with crimes ranging from theft through criminal breach of trust to murder (particularly where the killing(s) result from tribal or sectional fighting). Their powers in civil cases may range from marriage through custody of children, incest, and divorce. Appeals from the Chiefs' courts should in principle go to the regional court, but in practice appeals from both go directly to the Payam court, which is empowered to deal with customary and statutory law cases, both criminal and civil.[5] Given severe personnel and infrastructure shortages in the formal courts, as well as the lack of a formal legislative framework, nearly all disputes are resolved in customary courts. The challenges of integrating the two systems will be explored below.

There is also a genuine cause to believe that the Government of Southern Sudan will reverse the trend in the war that has led to the weakening of traditional authority. Despite the encroachment on traditional authority and the occasional abuse of military power by some field commanders and the military rank and file, there is, generally speaking, appreciation of the role played by the traditional leaders. This was symbolized and indeed demonstrated by the conference of chiefs and traditional leaders that was held in New Site in June 2004. As John Luk observed:

> The Movement in fact recognizes the very important role they have played since the inception of this war. They have preserved the integrity of the society. They have fed our army. They have contributed selflessly to the struggle. During this the hour of peace, are we going to discard these leaders, and you forget them? And are your structures, which start with the Boma [the lowest administrative level], going up to the Payam and the county, going to establish a system of local administration that will tend to push the traditional authorities away? Will they be replaced by other bodies or will these others coexist with them in exercising the authority of governance at that level? These traditional authorities, who have persevered our institutions of indigenous governance during all these years, what are we going to do with them, to make them part and parcel of our governance structures, and part and parcel of the peace that we have achieved, their share in the victory of peace?[6]

A number of the leading thinkers and policy-makers made similar comments on the role of traditional leaders. Commenting on the anticipated reform of the system, with particular reference to the role of leadership, Paul Mayom noted: "Many reasons can be given for advocating an important role for them, such as their support of the movement to come to where we are now. It is one of the areas for which we should find time and resources, and sit down to develop a well-considered opinion on what constitutes traditional authority and what role it should play in our system of governance. And traditional authority really has behind it our very history. We cannot easily begin to abandon it." Paul Mayom went beyond that to envisage a system where the traditional leaders absorb the modern system of local administration instead of the other way around: "Instead of bringing the local authority to absorb traditional authority, let the traditional authority absorb the elements of the local administration, which should strengthen, and create systems that can be efficient in service delivery as well as keeping the traditional values that we will want to preserve."[7]

It is quite obvious from the forgoing that the impact of the war has had mixed results. On the one hand, the pervasive dominance of the military, which was dictated by the war, has undermined and weakened traditional authority. On the other hand, the support these leaders gave the cause of the liberation struggle generally and the SPLM/A specifically, in addition to their contribution to the administration of justice under challenging circumstances, has been, and is still much appreciated. Traditional authorities have also benefited from the sentiments and aspiration for cultural revivalism associated with the struggle. The post-conflict challenge now is to develop a practical program for the reform of the legal system, both formal and informal, and to address the role the traditional authority is expected to play in the administration of justice.

6. The Challenges of Reform

On the whole, the tone for the need to preserve traditional values and the customary law in which they are manifested is generally not sufficiently critical, considering the demand for change under the contemporary circumstances. This is an understandable defensive response to the culturally based denigration, humiliation, and domination that the South has suffered since independence, indeed since the advent of foreign domination, which dates back even further. Theirs is a revivalist sense of attachment to the culture as a component of a highly valued identity for which the South fought a prolonged war and in which millions died. There is also ambivalence about the human rights pressures for reform related to the status of women and children, for which the traditional system has been strongly and rightly criticized, but on which customary law is, as a reaction, becoming romanticized and idealized. And yet, despite the consensus in support of customary law, there is a realization that changes to customs, beliefs, and practices throughout Southern Sudan are inevitable.

What this means is that there has to be a delicate balance between the stability of conforming to traditional norms and adjusting to changing conditions, perspectives, and expectations. Some of these changes are already dictating themselves and the law needs to catch up with the realities on the ground. In other areas, the law needs to play an educational role by prescribing normative standards that transcend the traditional code. The precise details of what is needed to bridge the traditional code with the imperatives and the ideals of a new framework corresponding to modern imperatives and principles of nondiscrimination based on gender or age still need to be worked out. Because of the delicacy of the issues, change must be a self-propelled process of improvement from within rather than an imposition from outside.

Reflecting on reform in both programmatic and substantive areas of both the informal and the formal systems, a realistic approach will envisage three interactive processes: resolution of the formal national legal system, presumably of common law origins that will meet the needs of the emerging modern society; classification of the principles of the informal system needed to address the needs of the indigenous community at the transitional phases;

and the development of an integrated national legal system that will build on the principles of both informal and formal systems, ultimately producing a national code that will synthesize the most desirable principles of both systems.

6.1 Challenges of integrating the formal and informal justice systems

The challenges of reform in the Southern Sudan legal system, both formal and informal, are formidable. What adds to the magnitude of the challenge is that there are still prospects of a new, united Sudan in which the elements of the old legal system, English common law, Islamic law, and customary law, will continue to coexist. Even without the North, these three sources of the law will continue to be considered in the South. And what is more, the dichotomy between the formal and the informal systems has never been that clear-cut in Sudan. The fact that the Comprehensive Peace Agreement and the Interim Constitutions of Sudan and Southern Sudan recognize custom and popular consensus as the principal sources of legislation in Southern Sudan raises questions of whether formal and informal law will remain separate and be coordinated as mutually reinforcing branches of the law, or will be integrated into one national legal system.

Adding to the challenge is the fact that the formal system of administration of justice needs to be built literally from the ground up. Although the SLPM now has the rudiments of a judicial system, a ministry of justice, attorney general chambers, and capacity in all sectors is lacking, or is severely limited. According to a recent study, "The judiciary at every level lacks trained judges, support staff, or resources. Courts are rudimentary and lack even the basic essentials, like recorders and clerks. Records of proceedings are written in longhand often by the judge. Many judges admit to having limited knowledge of the customary law of the area in which they are serving. Cases outside the remit of the customary law courts or on appeal from those courts are not dealt with promptly."[1] As the backlog grows, so does discontent with and distrust of the system.

The police forces that must maintain and enforce the law are in an even worse state – due to "an acute shortage of personnel" in the Ministry for Legal Affairs and Constitutional Development. As the Chief Justice explained, the function of prosecuting cases rests with the police, but many young, able-bodied men from the civil police joined the liberation struggle, and were replaced by men too old or too injured for combat: training in policing skills remains minimal. The result of all this is that there are few police who know how to investigate crime or to prepare evidence for hearing. The Chief Justice went on:

> The police force also has its own challenges. It is not well organized, not well trained and it has a shortage of personnel as well. And so are the prison services. They too have serious problems. These are some of

> the challenges that face the justice system in the SPLA held areas, the New Sudan or the Southern Sudan ... And their implications for the delivery of justice service are considerable. You have now judges that find themselves trying cases that are never well investigated. Sometimes, it is not easy to apprehend the criminals, or people accused of crimes. Even if they are arrested, sometimes keeping them in custody has its own problems. When they come before the courts, the courts tend to impose fines rather than custodial sentences because of problems pertaining to the prison system. These are some of the challenges facing us. They gravely affect the kind of justice system that we are delivering.[2]

There are serious logistical difficulties in enforcing sentences. But for those who end up in prison, there are limited or no resources to support the prisons, which makes them very unforgiving places. Women prisoners are particularly affected as their incarceration usually means rejection by their families, leaving them without even the basic means of survival. Most of them depend for their lives upon charity, predominantly foreign. Not surprisingly, there is public complaint about the lack of justice.

Against these realities, policy-makers must consider how the formal and informal systems might be integrated and what law they will apply. The general view is that custom, or more precisely customary law, should not only be recognized and applied by the traditional institutions, but should be the main source of legislation and governance in all areas, except for those where modern exigencies require adopting from outside sources. This is a radical departure from the usual approaches that relegated customary law to a subordinate status. A major challenge in the expected tension between the two systems will be the extent to which the adversarial nature of the formal system will accommodate the conciliatory orientation of the informal system. It is contended that "a system based upon reconciliation must routinely clash with one based upon punishment and deterrence. This is even more likely if the judges who interpret statutory law have a manifestly different cultural viewpoint from those who interpret and execute customary law."[3]

Key to resolving areas of tension between the two systems will be the education of the judiciary in the various customary laws systems of Southern Sudan. Also vital will be a system that records and distributes case reports, to enable the use of precedents in both the formal and informal systems. Deng Biong strongly endorsed the need for training of judges: "And apart from training in substantive customary law as a sitting judge, there is the question of how you allow a custom to govern a case. In case of conflict of customs, what custom should apply to a suit that is a suit of personal matter. These are issues that you have to train judges about."[4] The role of paralegal professionals could also be of crucial value: "If the future legal system of Southern Sudan, including the application of customary law, is to survive and grow to meet the needs of a new society, it will require major investment of resources to produce the trained manpower and resources at every level."[5] There also appears to be strong support, particularly among the senior judges, "for the creation of paralegal staff within the judiciary system and paralegal training for key members of the current legal structure. This important first step in capacity building will require training in customary as well as statutory law."[6]

6.2 Areas of needed reform of customary law

When it comes to the reform of customary law, the primary focus of outside observers tends to be on the area of human rights, particularly as they relate to women and children, two aspects that have become widely recognized as calling for radical reform. As noted in Section 3, the role of women is seen as one of wealth-generation and distribution as well as cementing family ties through "bride wealth" and producing children. Although these cultural practices have evolved over countless generations and survived half a century of war, to those whose culture is based on protecting the rights of the individual, the status of women in this system is viewed as approximating that of property. There is a demand for reform, which is being championed by women themselves.

Several areas of the law clearly discriminate against women, or at least reflect significant inequality. As noted above, the institution of marriage – including "ghost marriages" and "the levirate" – are primarily for the perpetuation of the male line and sometimes without much regard to the position of the woman concerned. And even though the consent of the girl is often sought for practical purposes, it is not a legal requirement and pressure is often exerted for her to conform to the will of the family. The area of property ownership among the Dinka also subordinates the position of women.

Justice Chan Reec Madut of the Federal Court of Appeal, in an article, "Customary Law from the Perspective of Human Rights," sees the disadvantages associated with the status of women as outweighing the positives: "There are myriad of stereotypes about women which tend to belittle them in the society and the men, whether husbands or male relatives, tend to be domineering in their attitude vis-à-vis women. What is more, customs do not seem to provide sufficient protection of their rights."[7] Justice Madut then outlines areas of the law in which women were discriminated against, among them ownership of property, mostly cattle and land; the husband's power of chastisement or beating of wives; inheritance rights; widow inheritance, marriage, and divorce.[8]

Justice Madut notes that "it is not uncommon to find families marrying off their daughters against their will."[9] The rules relating to divorce are also gender biased. "Women find it increasingly difficult to divorce even cruel husbands unless the wife's life is really threatened … Generally families are less inclined to approve divorce because they will lose bride wealth, and also because they prefer to maintain the social relations created by marriage."[10] Similar ambivalences apply to the status of children in traditional society. On the one hand, children are at the core of procreational continuity and are considered as a blessing and as the social insurance for their parents when they reach old age. However, certain practices in traditional society tend to violate children's rights. Among these, Justice Madut lists corporal punishment; unequal educational opportunities that favor boys over girls; early marriage for daughters; school drop-out due to pregnancy; favoring the father over the mother in the custody of children in the event of divorce; and scarification and other harmful practices.[11]

Justice Madut concludes his review of the status of women and children in traditional society with a plea for reform: "Some customary laws and practices are clearly against human rights. This calls for appropriate legislation and the adoption of policy to eradicate such practices. In addition it is important that traditional societies be sensitized on the evils of some of the harmful practices."[12]

In the past, these inequities were widely accepted, including by the women, as an integral part of a culture that was esteemed and from which there was in any case no escape. With changes dictated not only by the normal process of development and women's education, but also by the demands of international human rights standards, the pressure on the informal justice system is mounting. Deputy Chief Justice Bullen Paancol adds his voice to the need for gender equality: "Women are known to have suffered in the past, even in Europe and America. Now, women are claiming their rights … We Sudanese must recognize that women must be brought up to equality with men. This should be the position of the law in my view. We should abrogate, modernize, or otherwise reform those areas of the law that seem to discriminate against women." Deng Biong gives the example of gender discrimination in the law of property, reporting that "generally speaking, ownership of property by a woman in Dinka society is difficult if not impossible."

Peter Nyot raises the issue of adultery as another area of discrimination. In the past, adultery in customary law was an offense committed by men, who were made to pay compensation to the husband. Nowadays, it seems that women are also punished for the crime with imprisonment, but for some reason they appear to be carrying the brunt of the punishment. This is an issue that is being highlighted by women in many legal forums. According to Peter Nyot, the traditional way of obtaining evidence of adultery, when women are pressured to confess, is now being contested by women. "And they put the case on the basis of equality. They want that rule also applied to men. Let the men be asked to confess, 'Have you slept with other women?' Of course, it was not applied on the men. Women took that as a case of discrimination, 'Look what is required of us, while the same thing is not required of men.' In Rumbek, it was actually abolished. So people no longer require women to confess."[13]

The issue of gender inequality figured prominently in the contribution of Kuyang Anade, the only woman participant in the group discussion with judges and attorneys in Rumbek in February 2005. She noted that although there are arguments in favor of the custom of widow inheritance – it provides for continuity in the family and for the maintenance of the widow – it was implicated in spreading HIV/AIDS. She also raised the issue of inheritance in the event of the death of a male spouse in the family, when "Women in the family become beggars." Kuyang commented: "We are looking at a culture that looks at the men as a superior group of persons."[14]

There is, of course, no doubt that traditional society stratified the gender positions in favor of men – although there is also no doubt that the position of women was a lot more complex and ambivalent than might be easily detectable by a casual observer. There is now no question about the need for reform in favor of gender equality. The challenge is to change traditional attitudes, a process that will have to come from within. This can only be done in the short run by public debate, and in the mid- to long run through policy-oriented education, formal and informal.

Allegations of miscarriage of justice, favoritism, coercion, arbitrary imprisonment, or extended detention without trial have been levied against the Chiefs' courts. Some of these may be the result of the breakdown of the system and the creation of courts whose presidents or members are of dubious qualification by traditional standards or values. Traditionally, of course, the chiefs did not have the power or the capacity to commit such abuses, which in any case were repugnant under the indigenous moral code. Under the modern system, when imprisonment and other means of state coercion have been made available to the Chiefs' courts, they are subject to the supervision of superior judges in the judicial hierarchy. Abuses of power or favoritism of course existed, but were checked through the appeal system and state oversight. These allegations must therefore be viewed as part of the overall breakdown of the justice system associated with the war and the disintegration of the traditional order. To the extent that they now exist, whether because of structural deficiencies or personal inadequacies of the court members, they need to be remedied through better discipline or training of the traditional authorities managing the courts.

The issue of land ownership and use is considered to be an area where Western concepts of individual ownership come into conflict with the traditional African concept of communal ownership. This is an issue in which the government, claiming that all unregistered land belongs to the state, and the SPLM/A claiming communal ownership, could not agree in the peace negotiations that resulted in the Comprehensive Peace Agreement. In particular, there is the issue of potential foreign investment in the South, which will require creating a conducive climate. Peter Nyot argued that "the government will have to deal with the question of collective ownership in a more understandable way than is being done at present. On the one hand, important investors will be interested, definitely. They will want security of tenure from the government to hold the land long enough to make economic sense. On the other hand, there are culturally prescribed principles of land tenure, which are very sensitive and to which people adhere religiously. How are these conflicting considerations going to be managed?"[15] The approach to the problem must be phased. In the short run, it is important to protect the communal rights and grant limited rights of usage to outside investors. In the longer term, opening up land ownership to investors must continue to prioritize the interest of the community above exploitation of the land. The community members must continue to be seen as the owners and the primary beneficiaries of any returns from investment in their land, and the rise in their standard of living must be visibly commensurate to the profits made.

6.3 The process of reform: bridging the gap between enthusiasm and knowledge

What is remarkable about the discussion of customary law and the need for its development in the context of a reform of the national legal system is that there is a wide gap between aspirations and performance. Customary law is currently viewed with enthusiasm as part of the identity for which the South has fought for so long. And yet, it is only sentimentally felt and not known. Compounding the knowledge gap is the fact that there are thought to be over fifty separate tribal groups in Southern Sudan, each with its own discrete body of customary laws.

There is therefore a degree of ambiguity in the advocacy between reinvention or rediscovery of customary law as opposed to recognizing and upholding a system that has been in use and might now be adapted and reformed to meet emergent circumstances. In a way, it is both. There is ample evidence indicating that society has been both formally and informally governed largely by customary law. What is required is an elevated recognition of what is in fact already functioning. But to the extent that knowledge of customary law is rudimentary at best, advocacy also implies a search for something known to be there, but not fully known, understood, or appreciated. In this ambiguity lies the foundation for the reform and modernization of customary law.

Such a reform should be the outcome of an in-depth understanding of the political, social, cultural, and economic processes that underpin the traditional legal system. This should include the fundamental norms of society, how to determine patterns of distribution, who benefits the most from the system, who is disadvantaged, to what extent, and who suffers gross injustice in the system.

Michael Makuei acknowledged this up front:

> In fact, if you go to our own documents, we talk about customary law being the source of legislation. But we have not even gone down to know it. What is that customary law which we are making our source of legislation? We need to study it thoroughly. Then we can develop it, so that we make it a source of legislation based on a particular understanding. We have a great deal to learn. The field of customary law in the South is vast. And there is a lot to learn. In some areas, there is even a conflict of

> customary laws. These need to be recorded. We need to identify their origins, record them, and then harmonize between them. After harmonization, we need to go down to enacting them ... There is need for us to adopt these customs, so that they become our source of legislation.[16]

Recording, analyzing, comparing, and synthesizing customary law of the various tribes is therefore widely recognized as perhaps the most compelling and urgent first step on the reform agenda. Some useful work has already been done. In the 1970s and 1980s, chiefs in the then-province of Bahr el Ghazal succeeded through conferences in overcoming differences in application of their customary rules and restating them in a code embodying law related to personal status, property, personal injury, defamation, and other areas. These rules are of common application in the courts to this day. The most notable and productive efforts have been those of John Wuol Makec, who, as speaker of the Bahr el Ghazal People's Regional Assembly, helped to draft and enact the Bahr el Ghazal Customary Law Act 1984, comprising the customary law of three groups: Dinka, Luo, and Fertit.[17] In 1998, a conference was held in Aweil, Bahr el Ghazal, at which it was agreed by the Dinka and the Luo that their respective codes should be harmonized into one body of law. In 1984, the three principal tribes of Upper Nile, the Dinka, Nuer and Shilluk, recorded their respective customary laws in written form, although revision and elaboration are required.

There also exists in written form a body of customary law that serves a number of ethnic groups of the central Sudanic people, the Kakwa, Kuku, Pajulu, Kaliko, and Luguara tribes in Yei and Kajo-Keji Counties of Equatoria Region. The document is said to have an approximate but not verifiable date of 1996 and, in the expert opinion of one of the authors of the World Vision study, is probably outdated, although it remains a key tool for county court judges in the region.[18]

Nevertheless, the idea of codifying customary law is still a controversial issue. A distinction must be drawn between the recording and the codification of customary law. Recording is merely making the law available. Codification through a legislative act makes the law formally binding. There is a broad consensus on the need for recording customary law, but there is resistance to codification. Some people believe that codification is antithetic to the essence of customary law as a living, dynamic system. To codify it will be to freeze it and impede its capacity to adapt to changing conditions. According to Monyluak Alor, "The experience in some parts of Bahr el Ghazal Region proves the indifference of leaders of such local communities to the idea of codification and indeed their insistence to interpret the application of the rules of social control in a way that will serve the timely interest of the community."[19]

Recognizing the need to take a systematic and comprehensive approach to customary law, the SPLM created the Customary Law Steering Committee in 2004 to formulate and guide the process. Currently under the Ministry of Legal Affairs and Constitutional Development, the committee, chaired by

Justice Deng Biong, is charged with determining how to incorporate customary law into the modern state. As a first step, the committee is planning a comprehensive coverage in recording the customary law of about fifteen ethnic group clusters, with a view to ascertaining the law, harmonizing it between the ethnic groups, determining where there are gaps or inconsistencies with modern life and human rights, and ultimately incorporating what is acceptable into legislation. Deng Biong outlined his main reasons for recording and developing customary law in the Southern Sudan. First, as customary rules are the main source of law under the new legal system, there is a duty to ascertain, establish, and write down the customary rules – otherwise anybody can claim anything to be a customary rule. Second, the civil war has claimed the lives of many of the elders who carried the content of the law in their minds; if what the remaining elders know is not written down, their knowledge may be lost forever. Third, many people have been displaced by the war and are living on other communities' land, so when disputes arise, diverse customary rules come together in conflict. There is a need to establish which customs should have precedence. This is especially difficult when deciding on compensation for the life of a person killed by someone from a different community. Fourth, unlike in the past, the New Sudan laws do not confine the application of customary law to matters of personal status, but allow them to cover crimes and torts, thus necessitating a thorough understanding of the rules in those areas. Fifth, unification of customary rules is essential if they are to form a basis of legislation. And finally, in order to reform practices that are contrary to human rights, such as discriminatory practices, it is necessary to know first what such practices are.[20]

The process of recording, analyzing, synthesizing, restating, unifying, and codifying the customary laws of the various ethnic groups is bound to be a protracted one and by no means easy. If the law is an expression of societal values, then each system must be approached in depth and its logic and integrity understood and built upon in order to introduce well-considered reforms that address the shortcomings of the traditional system. The process must be well planned and can be expected to be intensive, extensive, and time consuming. Perhaps what is needed is a phased process that will allow what is learned to be applied, even as more information continues to be collected and processed. Whether the ultimate goal should be the full integration of the customary laws of the country or a separate development of each of the major regimes, is a question that can only be addressed after a thorough appreciation of the situation.

6.4 The role of international partnership

A central theme from my studies and interviews is that Southern Sudanese leaders appear to be torn between wanting to control their own reform process, and welcome cooperation with international partners. There is ambivalence about the way in which international humanitarian organizations have supported pioneering indigenous NGOs that campaign for women's rights. But the Southern Sudanese authorities are very open to, and even solicitous of, international cooperation in the development and reform of the legal system. Michael Makuei, the attorney general, in the tape-recorded interview cited above, notes the need for "technical assistance" in drawing up new laws for Southern Sudan.

But he says that external assistance with research into customary law must be coordinated: "You find that most of the NGOs will rush in with their money and they come and say, 'we are conducting research in this field' … After finishing the research, they don't know where to present it." He saw the setting up of the Customary Law Steering Committee as a remedy. The policy now is that whatever organization has interest in the study of customary law should liaise with the committee: "There is no way we will allow people to conduct research here and there, which is not controlled. People come up with very wild conclusions. This has been putting us into crisis with some of our constituencies. So, this customary law research should be organized, systematized."

The Customary Law Steering Committee involves representatives from the judiciary, legal affairs, women and child welfare, local government, and the law society. Deng Biong, the chairman of the committee, in the tape-recorded interview already cited, explains how cooperation with NGOs can work well if it is coordinated: PACT funded a conference in Nairobi, at which "there were agencies that were interested in specific issues. UNICEF was interested in women's rights, and in child rights, and FAO was interested in issues to do with land, because of food security." Sooner or later, this body is expected to be developed into an institution that will be more established than a committee.

As was the case with the previous sections, there is much more clarity on the need for reform, and even on the principles on which the reform agenda should be based, than on the practical means of getting to that end. This is perhaps where collaborators could help to chart the way forward and, within available means, provide material support and expertise. The final section offers some thoughts in that direction.

6.5 Program of action

The required program of action could be divided into several areas: field work, desk work, discussion groups, and documentation of outcomes for the consideration of policy formulators and decision-makers, whether legislators, administrators, or judges.

Field work will involve engaging a team of researchers to record the customary law of the fifteen groups that have been already identified by the Customary Law Steering Committee. According to Deng Biong, the chairman of the steering committee,

> "these 15 groups, we have proposed, will be covered by 15 or so teams of researchers. Each research team will have one international expert, plus

> some 4 or 5, depending on the area occupied by that cultural group. So, they will be supported by the data collectors, about 4 or 5 depending on the size of the area … We want to target every group in Southern Sudan, and then we will ascertain and record all the customs related to many aspects of life, issues to do with marriage, or with family law in general, torts, and all that."

Desk work, wherever it will be carried out, will entail collecting the results of the field work and other already available materials on customary law, analyzing the data comparatively, identifying areas of agreement and conflict among the various customary law regimes, and exploring a framework of uniformity, while allowing some room for local diversity in the administration of justice.

Discussion groups are a step removed from desk work, for what is envisaged is a round-table discussion of the results of field work and desk work, with the view to formulate ideas that might help policy-makers, administrators, and judicial authorities to make informed decisions.

Documenting outcomes means preparing reports from field work, desk work, and discussion groups to produce documents that are authoritative and capable of being used by legal professionals

Connected with this will be organizing legal training sessions to familiarize the legal profession with the available knowledge and the challenges facing their profession.

On the broader issue of the relevancy of customary law to legislation in general, governance, and constitutionalism, more thought and dialogue need to be invested. At present, there is a considerable gap in the thinking. On the one hand, there is the conventional view of customary law as "an informal system" that contrasts with the "formal system," with the connotation that it is marginal and subordinate. And yet, Southerners at all levels seem to take pride in their customary law as part of their identity and self-determination that should influence all levels of their life, informal and formal, private and public. It is seen almost as a mirror image of the Muslim view of Sharia as the correct path, which view the South has been violently resisting.

Whether customary law or, more broadly, traditional culture, will be able to provide a practical and viable normative framework for legislation, good governance, and effective administration must be a debatable issue.

All this goes to show that there is clearly room for international partnership, but one that must be delicately forged, with due sensitivity to cross-cultural perspectives on the issues involved. Apart from support in funding some of the activities outlined above, international support is said to be needed on the training of judges, attorneys, and the police, the preparation and evaluation of the constitutions of Sudan and South Sudan, and the drafting of the laws of the Southern Sudan Government, as well as support for conferences and workshops to discuss the various products and ideas generated by the reform process.

The recommendations made by various studies and interviewees, and which this study endorses, may be divided into two: generic ones for the government of Southern Sudan and those related to partnership with the international community.

For the government of Southern Sudan the challenge of reform is to:

- Clarify the policy on the place of customary law as it relates to the administration of justice, legislation, governance, and constitutionalism;
- Determine what making custom or customary law a basis for legislation means and whether it means integration into the entire system or keeping it separate and using it as a source and inspiration for legislation;
- Record the customary laws of the various ethnic groups in the Southern Sudan, analyze them comparatively, synthesize them, and restate them with the view to reform;
- Analyze existing laws with the view to harmonizing them with the terms of the Comprehensive Peace Agreement, the interim constitutions of Sudan and Southern Sudan, including the place of customary law;
- Prepare from existing studies and documents materials for the training of judges, lawyers, and the police on customary law and its place in the national and Southern legal system;
- Conduct special training programs for traditional authorities to understand their role in the overall administration of justice;
- Determine whether the rules of customary law and the traditional authority will remain a separate branch of the system or be integrated into the national system, and how; and
- Prepare materials on the extent to which the rules of customary law support or contradict international human rights standards and make them available to both the traditional authorities (in the language they understand) and to national authorities in the relevant branches of the government.

International partners are called on to:

- Support with funding in areas of mutual interest with the organization concerned;
- Assist with the training of judges, lawyers, and administrators on the generic function of the informal system (customary law) in partnership with formal system (statutory law), building on the experiences of other countries;
- Provide expertise in the drafting of the laws of the Government of Southern Sudan to deal with generic problems that confront a modern state, to manage the diversities within the South, to forge a culturally sensitive democratic system, and to promote a human rights agenda that builds on the values of the indigenous society; and
- Support brainstorming conferences, workshops, and discussion groups to discuss the results of research, policy analysis, and recommendations with scholars, policy-makers, and practitioners, and to generate more

recommendations for the government of Southern Sudan and the international community.

While these recommendations point at areas of obvious need, the challenge of developing and reforming customary law is a complex and daunting one that cannot be reduced to a few sets of disparate recommendations. As noted earlier, a comprehensive, well-planned, and integrated approach is needed. These recommendations and others from various sources should be viewed as merely providing material and a framework for discussion with experts and practitioners in Sudan and other countries that have faced similar challenges in the development and reform of customary law. It is from such discussions that a conceptual framework and plan of action can be developed.

Part Two

Substantive Examples of Customary Law

individual and family or group autonomy in religious practice as contrasted with the policies of the Sudanese state in favor of Islam and the restriction of the Christian missionary work in the South. The law relating to wealth included bride wealth, inheritance, barter and sale, custody of livestock, gifts, theft, acquisition and rights of ownership, labor and produce. Well-being concerns physical health and the relevant areas of law were presented under homicide, bodily injuries, liability for animals, employment of curers, and "health insurance." Skills and the law discussed such things as payment for experts in the settlement of feuds connected with homicide, divination, and song composition, some of which are more symbolic than of significant material value. Under enlightenment and the law, matters relating to responsibility for the guardianship and education of children were discussed in broad terms.

Above the value-processes and their legal expression, Lasswell and McDougall postulated the overriding goal of human dignity, defined as the broadest shaping and sharing of all values. Put in other words, this is essentially a principle of equity and inclusivity, in a free and democratic society.[1] This also implies a holistic observance of all human rights and fundamental freedoms and liberties. In this context, human dignity as defined provides a normative basis for evaluating the roles of the various participants in the traditional system, the changes the society has undergone or is undergoing, and the consequential need for reform.

The areas from which the following selections are made cover four value categories and their legal expression, two from the deference values – affection and respect – and two from the welfare values – wealth and well-being. In more conventional legal categories these include: family law, law of defamation, law of property, and homicide and bodily injuries.[2]

It should be noted that while the law is described in the present tense, society has already undergone substantial change in practice. The normative perspectives underlying the traditional legal system and the substantive content of the law have either changed commensurably or are lagging behind. Since the situation implies both continuity and change, the legal system is described in terms that alternate between the present and past tense, depending on the context.

Finally, as noted in Part One, there are many ethnic groups in the South with varying degrees of diversity in their cultures and customary laws, and it will be impossible to do justice to them all. The author's particular expertise is on the Ngok Dinka of Abyei – among whom he conducted extensive field research in the 1950s and 1960s. What should be emphasized, however, is that despite significant differences among the various ethnic groups, there is much in common in the customary laws of the South. Furthermore, this being a study not of, but about, customary law, the conceptual issues it raises are much more generic than will be the case with a discussion of the laws of a specific group. Even with respect to the studies of the Dinka, while some people may tend to see the differences and perhaps even instinctively resent highlighting the laws of other groups, rather than their own, many Southerners from other groups have generally found the substance of those studies of significant relevance to their own societies. They indeed provide a framework for a more detailed discussion of specific situations in the other groups.

2. Family Law

In view of the interconnectedness of values and their merger in the institution of family, the legal issues involved permeate the social process. This section delineates the discussion of family law to a few categories: marriage, divorce, legitimacy of children, and offenses affecting family integrity. This is one of the areas in which the stratifications of gender and age are most pronounced.

2.1 Marriage

From what has been said about procreational continuity as a fundamental goal of Dinka society, the importance of marriage will be self-evident. "In Dinka society, continuity of the lineage of the person is not only of primary importance, it is also sacred … in the sense that it is fulfillment of the Will of God that the lineage of a person, whether male or female, is not allowed to become extinct."[1] To marry not only fulfills an individual objective, but also discharges a social duty to the agnatic kin group. Since continuity through procreation involves the whole lineage, marriage is not simply a union of a man and a woman, but an alliance between their respective bodies of kin. This transforms the personal desire for marriage into a social obligation. Central to this system is the principle of perpetual identity and influence as expressed in procreation.

2.1.1 Forms of marriage

Conspicuous expressions of the role perpetuity plays in Dinka social and legal processes are found in the forms of marital unions. The various forms of marriage are simple marriage, the levirate, and ghost marriage. Simple marriage is the normal union between a man and a woman. Levirate marriage is the practice of transferring the union of a widowed woman to her dead husband's nearest agnate. Ghost marriage is performed between a dead man (one who died too young to be married) and a living woman. Each form of marriage is discussed separately, bearing in mind that the fundamental purpose of marriage in Dinka society is procreational continuity.

abide by his original consent. However, the marriage did not take place because the girl rejected Ayii and could not be persuaded otherwise.

Normally, the consent of the bride herself to a suggested union is given little, if any, consideration. Some fathers do not consider it necessary to consult with their daughters before accepting a proposal. Most fathers feel that it is at least desirable to consult their daughters, but this consultation, to be more accurate, is merely providing information with the view to persuasion should she refuse her consent. Without her acceptance, marriage can hardly work. In practice, most girls accept the decision of their fathers, although perhaps with complaints. The desire to have a large bride wealth paid as their value also plays a part in their decision to accept men otherwise objectionable to them. Dinka girls are largely accepting of the fact that their male agnates will be the ones to choose their husband and so, as the case of *Ayii v. Allor* illustrates, only those who detest their proposed husbands or are in love with other men refuse.

Flirtation and courtship usually attract proposals that are not objectionable to the brides. This leads people to think that Dinka "men and girls choose their own mates," but that "in practice the girl does not accept a man who will bring disgrace on her by not being able to pay a proper marriage price in cattle to her family."[12] Should a girl refuse consent, then various pressures, including ostracism, beating, and scolding are used by the relatives to gain her consent. Even the court may authorize such measures. In the past, such situations were sometimes settled using "lawful rape," by which a man was authorized to consummate a marriage forcefully, although this is no longer practiced. In his UNDP study Deng Biong Mijak wrote: "the practice of forcible consummation of marriage, by which a bridegroom is helped by his age-mates to have sex with the unwilling bride, is not remembered by most sources, but considered as part of the past by those who had witnessed some instances of it."[13] Such pressures are dangerous, because a determined girl has many ways by which she can deprive her kin of bride wealth. These include elopement, impregnation by a man of her choice, or, rarely, suicide.[14]

The types of difficulties which may result from imposing marriage on a girl who refuses it are illustrated by *Akot Ral v. Lal Ayoum.*[15] Akot had paid a bride wealth of nearly 100 cows for a girl who loved Lal Ayoum, with whom she eloped to the North. After some time, they were discovered and she was taken back to Akot's house, while Lal Ayoum was imprisoned and made to pay compensation to Akot. After Lal's prison sentence was over, the lovers escaped and were discovered again. The process of escape and discovery was repeated several times. During their escapes, she gave birth to two children. Their biological father was Lal but, being "children of the cows," they were legally those of Akot. In the final action, Akot claimed and was awarded the children, as well as compensation for adultery. Such cases occur quite frequently.

Interpreting the evidence and the cases collected from the Ngok Dinka, Dr. Farran argues that a case like the one outlined above "points to a crude realization that the bride's consent is a prerequisite to a lawful marriage. Why, otherwise, will there be need for the beatings and scolding? The tribal marriage laws in effect require consent, but – at least in the past – some of them have not been scrupulous as to how such 'consent' was obtained."[16] O'Sullivan also observed this and concluded, erroneously, that "no girl is obliged to marry anyone unless she is herself willing ... Fear of beating is used to influence a girl to consent, but such coercion is against tribal law."[17]

The objective of this interpretation seems more prescriptive than descriptive. Even so, it is somewhat paradoxical that a system of law that requires consent will not only permit but enforce undue influence and coercive measures to obtain it. Dr. Farran himself admits that such torture is sometimes carried out "under the authority of a Chiefs' court."[18] To call "submission" under such severe threats "consent" is a contradiction in terms. The more attractive interpretation is that Dinka customary law does not regard the girl's consent as necessary, but her acceptance facilitates marriage – for without it, consummation of the marriage will be difficult and the objective of the marriage might not be fulfilled. This is why a girl who refuses to marry the man chosen for her must be persuaded or coerced into accepting him, not because her consent is legally required, but because the fundamental procreational goal of marriage will be threatened.

In his study of Ngok Dinka law, Deng Biong Mijak notes that "unlike the past, when the only important consent to marriage was the one of the spouses' parents, most informants say, today, while the consent of the parents should be holding, it should be combined together with the one of the girl and the boy."[19] In any case, the changes the society has undergone, including urbanization and massive displacement due to war, have significantly weakened family bonds and parental control over young members of the family, both men and women.

2.1.4 Bars to marriage

Bars to marriage are based on affinity and alienage. Affinity includes relationship by blood, nursing, marriage, adoption, age-mate relationship, and friendship. Alienage covers relationships with feuding groups.

(a) Bars based on affinity

Any traceable blood relationship between the agnatic and cognatic sides is an impediment to marriage. Even members of a clan separated long enough to fall within two tribes cannot intermarry. There is one exception to the rule: intermarriage of relatives falling beyond a certain degree of agnatic or cognatic relationship, who are descended from a common male ancestor with intervening female ancestors on both sides is permitted. The degrees of female intervention need not be the same. Among the Ngok Dinka of Abyei, this is known as *kwot yeth,* literally "the neck of a gourd," symbolizing that the relationship becomes "too small," that is, remote. The question of how many generations are necessary in order to reach *kwot yeth* is not certain. The Dinka merely say that "it must be far." The general opinion was that five or six generations will not suffice. The counting begins with the generation of the first intervening female.

The marriage of relatives is an issue about which the Dinka hold and voice very strong feelings and, while there are changes threatening the tradition, it remains a subject of heated debate, with some even conceding that marriage between relatives now takes place openly and often. Deng Biong Mijak's study of Ngok Dinka law reveals some of the views involved in the debate. "Incest or sexual intercourse or marriage with a blood related woman was difficult in the past," an elder named Akuei Bol told Deng Biong Mijak in a tape recorded interview:

> But your generation … is showing indifference or might be supporting it. Now we cannot determine at what degree of affinity a related couple should marry. We shall leave it for you to decide. In the past it was suggested by late uncle Mijangdit … [grand father of Deng Biong Mijak], that people had multiplied enough to warrant fears of incestuous marriages in the future. He went on to suggest that "*alaraan amou*" (blood relationship be drowned) in the river. A cow was supposed to be slaughtered and cut into two parts. It was said those who were to carry out those rites were going to die soon after that. Mijangdit volunteered, but nobody else joined him among the elders named. That was in late sixties. In late 1980s, uncle Acuil (Acuil Bulabek Biong, father of Chief Biong Acuil) brought it up again, but nobody stood up with him until he passed away. Now people are regretting.
>
> In the past and according to our customs, the degree of affinity that could be allowed to marry was *kwot yeth* (gourd's neck), meaning blood relationship that is so thin and tiny that it could be undermined. But from the clan's center it was and still should not be allowed.
>
> There are clans which may be in different sub/tribes, but not supposed to marry each other. It used to be but nowadays it has been broken e.g. Pajook of Abiyor should not marry from Pajook of Kondit in Diil. But that has been violated several times. A striking example was furnished by (late) Chief Kwol Kon Tinglooth himself when he married a daughter of Wieu Nyandeeng Biong of Pajook clan of Abiyor sub-tribe despite the fact that he was Thon e Pan e Kon (literally meaning a bull of Kon's family) of Pajook clan of Diil sub-tribe who are related by blood to the former. Chief Acuil and even P/Chief Deng Majok protested, but in vain. There are so many examples to cite of violations.[20]

Elder Arob Minyang Chan added:

> Marriage among people related by blood was highly forbidden by our ancestors. But your generation is making terrible violations these days. Ayuel Kiir Choi married the daughter of Deng Bek Deng. She is his wife now. We shall watch and see what will happen in his case. This is the first time I am witnessing a marriage between relatives in our society. I do not know whether it will be good or bad. In the past it was forbidden, because it could lead to death or *e Koc waany guop* (like albino?) or makes the couple give birth to an albino (*menth ce bek*).

As for the purification rituals performed to correct an incestuous affair, Chief Biong Acuil and Akuei Bol jointly said to Deng Biong Mijak:

> First the man pays 3 H/C *as* Aruok, if the girl is pregnant or 1 heifer, if he merely eloped with her but no pregnancy. Then people sit down to examine the issue of *alaraan* (blood relationship). Elders will normally decide the following measures for purification. First the man pays *Awec* (appeasement). A head of tobacco is brought. *Nyieth* (a palm tree reed) is brought. *Dau* (rope) is brought.
>
> Both *nyieth* and *dau* are wrapped around the tobacco head. The boy's father is asked to hold that tobacco's head and the girl's father the lower end. An elder comes with a very sharp spear and cut that tobacco in the middle into two pieces to signify that *alaraan* is split. Nobody will die as a result of it again since the girl's father goes away with his half and the boy's with the other half. No marriage is allowed. But if the couple insist on marriage, the marriage wealth brought to the girl's family will be grabbed and divided at random such that they are not traced later on to remind people of that shunned relationship.[21]

Even when no punitive action is taken, or rituals of severance are performed, and no apparent consequences (such as death or illness) are attributed to the violation of rules of exogamy, a violation creates cleavages and conflicts within the wider kin group that are difficult to resolve and sometimes result in violence against the offending couple. A case in point is that of Kiir Deng Baar Kiir and Nyangeer Deng Majok. Kiir's paternal grandfather was the brother of Nyangeer's father's maternal grandfather, which made their parents cousins and themselves second cousins. This was as close a relationship as the rules of exogamy could unquestionably allow. Nyangeer became pregnant and eventually revealed the identity of the father, with whom she was apparently in love. The family could not entertain the idea of marriage between them. Nevertheless, Nyangeer and Kiir eloped and lived together as husband and wife, even though no marital ceremonies were performed. The couple became ostracized and were even subject to violent attacks by overzealous young men from Nyangeer's family. While the couple remained together, it soon became obvious that the hostility against them exacted a heavy toll on their relationship, and the long-term prospects of their union remained in doubt.

The exception in marriages of affinity, *kwot yeth,* is significant. While males perpetuate the clan or the lineage directly, females play an important role by providing bride wealth to be used in the marriages of agnates and extend affection circles. Although marriage takes them out of the group, they remain part of it and continue to share in the bride wealth of their descendants. At the excepted degree, the descendants of a common ancestor no longer have claims to the bride wealth of their kinswomen. It thus becomes opportune to reaffiliate through marriages in order to revive mutual assistance in lineage perpetuation.

A nursing relationship occurs when a baby is suckled by a woman other than its mother, and the baby is then considered a relative of the wet nurse. If the baby should be female, then the suckling woman is entitled to share in her bride wealth. A marriage bar is created which prohibits marriage between the children of the wet nurse, the suckled child, and any other children whom she has suckled. The Dinka conceive of a fusion of blood in this relationship and therefore, though limited to the second degree and descendants thereof, it becomes akin to blood relationship.

Another requirement of exogamy is "illegal conjunction," which introduces prohibitions into in-law relationships. Traditionally, the rule was that a man, his brothers, or his children could not marry into his wife's lineage. An apparent exception to this rule is the custom of substitution of a dead wife with her close relative, who may be a sister.[22] Since the substituting party steps into the shoes of her dead relative, the union is not a new marriage, but a perpetuation of the old marriage comparable to levirate, except that whereas the children of a levirate union identify themselves with the dead pater, the dead wife is not considered by the issue of her relative as their mater. This is not deemed significant, since the fundamental objective is the perpetuation of the male line.

The next bar to marriage is adoption, a common practice among the Dinka. The ties between a man and his adopted child are socially and legally recognized as constituting full kinship. Likewise where a woman who has a child is married to a man other than the biological father and the biological father has not legitimated the child, who is then adopted by the stepfather, such a child acquires his name and is affiliated with his kin. An illegal conjunction will therefore result from his marriage with a member of his stepfather's kin.

A form of adoption, which is now mostly obsolete, relates to relationships originating with slavery. The Dinka enslaved Arabs during the wars of slavery – although the Dinka were mainly the victims of Arab slavery, rather than perpetrators. Their leaders rescued enslaved Southerners who, after being freed, often decided to live with their liberators either because they could not trace their origin or because they simply wished to stay. Both the captured Arabs and the rescued Southerners were assimilated into the capturing or the rescuing lineages. Technically, they were known, but generally not referred to, as "slaves," *aloony.* They assumed the identity of the lineage into which they were affiliated. In the case of females, their bride wealth went to the lineage of the adopter, and the rules of exogamy were applied to those thus affiliated. The degree of application of the rules is uncertain, however, for opinion is divided on the point. Some Dinka elders argue that it is identical with kinship, while others argue that it is not carried so far.

There is no doubt that both opinions are influenced by the case of the marriage of Deng Majok and Nyananyuat, discussed earlier. The authority of this decision is still disputed by many Dinkas, and one cannot deny the effect of Deng's position on the outcome. In any case, it has established a widely publicized precedent. Although the Dinka are not easily led to disbelieve the likelihood of danger merely because of the passage of time, the fact that Nyananyuat has borne children and that she and her children are not afflicted with the evils of ancestral curse may work in favor of the precedent.

The Dinka make an exception in case of a male slave. He cannot marry within the lineage of his adoption. Since the lineage is traced through the male, the role of a male slave in the pursuit of permanent identity and influence is direct and only depends on his marriage. The female slave, on the other hand, contributes indirectly by attracting bride wealth, which may then be used by the males of the lineage for marriage. If she is taken as a wife by her adopters, there is more gain than is the case with male slaves, for she will have had to go out of the lineage, while he will not. The Dinka thus choose between two alternative ways of obtaining her contribution; either she does so through bride wealth from outside the lineage, or through marriage into the lineage. The facts indicate that different people choose according to the particular situation. This reasoning is similar to the exception made for female agnates or cognates whose descendants, *anyaal*, after a certain degree become *kwot yeth*. They are choosing intermarriage because their distant kinsmen will be unlikely to share in the bride wealth of their females. Marriage thus helps bring them closer to the lineage. *Kwot yeth* requires more degrees of descent than adoption by slavery because of its stronger blood and marriage ties.

Another ground for exogamous bar, according to the Ngok Dinka, is age-mate relationship. A man may not marry the daughter of an age-mate, for common initiation of males creates a solidarity comparable to kinship. We have seen that age-mates are closely involved in marriage and have certain entitlement by virtue of their association. If a man were to marry the daughter of an age-mate he will be his age-mate's father-in-law, creating a discrepancy in status directly opposed to relationship of age-mates. Chiefs have married daughters of men of the same age, though not initiated together as age-mates, normally regarded as violations by the Dinka. Although, a violation by analogy, violations by leaders, if endorsed, become innovations.

Akin to the barrier of age-mate relationship is friendship, particularly a special "friendship agreement," which, when confirmed with the rite of blood fusion, symbolizes kinship. The rules of exogamy, whether based on blood, marriage, adoption, age-mate relationship, or friendship, are based on the notion of extending affinity by compelling marriage outside the present circles.

(b) Bars based on alienage

Converse to bars based on affinity are the prohibitions against marrying those considered too distant from the kinship to be affiliated. The most rigid are those with whom the kin group is in a feud. When a person commits homicide, culpable or accidental, a feud arises that requires vengeance unless ended by ritual reconciliation, *peek*. This is more easily done where the killing is not culpable. Unless it is done, the two groups should not drink or eat in each other's homes, nor should they associate. This continues even after payment of blood wealth, although it no longer requires vengeance. Without *peek*, intermarriage is not permitted. If the feud has lasted for more than two generations and *peek* has not been performed, a special rite is performed to authorize intermarriage. First, more cows are paid to appease the deceased. They are paid to the person charged with the duty of marrying a ghost wife for the deceased and are known as *ghok kooj e nom*, "the cows of standing the head." They do not count as part of the bride wealth. A ram is sacrificed in ritual atonement.

Great care is taken by the Dinka to avoid a breach of marriage prohibitions. When a boy and a girl meet, their introduction includes their paternal lineage, and clan identifications. During the social processes of marriage, intense investigation is carried out by both sides to the proposed marriage. If the parents of the parties to a proposed incestuous union agree to it despite the opposition of less important relatives, those relatives are authorized to seize the bride wealth to prevent the marriage. Should the bridegroom demand the return of his cattle, the court may direct that the cattle taken be considered compensation to the relatives for the insult to their feelings caused by the undesirable union. Presently, seizure of cattle is dying out and the whole issue is fought in court.

2.1.5 Formalities of marriage

In a system where the social and the legal processes intermingle, it is both difficult and undesirable to differentiate them too rigidly. This is particularly the case in marriage formalities, many of which, though important, are not necessarily addressed by the law. Marriage among the Dinka is not a momentary ceremony, but a long social transaction, stretching over at least two years. The important components of this transaction are *ting nya*, "seeing the girl"; *leer atooc*, "conveyance of marriage proposal"; *leer amec*, "delivery of the betrothal cattle"; *kuen thiek*, "discussing the marriage"; and, finally, *geem nya*, "handing over the bride." There are also different procedures connected with such practices as competition in marriage, and wrongful but customary processes of affecting an impeded marriage.

*(a) Seeing the girl (*ting nya*)*

Ting nya, "seeing the girl," may be performed by a prospective groom or by any of his relatives and friends. It is more than the simple fact of seeing, for it is associated with investigating the girl and her background, courting by the man and his age-mate relatives in order to know her well, and agreeing within the family that she should be pursued. *Ting* thus begins with seeing and admiring, but covers a wide range of preliminary considerations leading to an affirmative family decision. The most prominent role in initial *ting* is played by the prospective groom himself because the man is expected to familiarize himself with the girl through courtship. Dinka girls are brought up to be courteous to men, but also to be prudent. Since the status of a Dinka girl in her kin group and in the society depends largely on her marriage, a girl's response to suitors often depends more on the prospects of marriage resulting from the friendship than on the mutuality of affection.

On the assumption that a mutual affection exists and the two wish to marry (it is more important that he wishes to wed her), the young man will declare his wish to his real or marriage "father." This is, of course, necessary where the young man or someone else had done the "seeing" or where the father had made a suggestion conditional to his son's confirmation. When the matter has been settled between the young man and his father, many other significant kinsmen are informed. The bride wealth will be gathered by this circle, and the broader the circle, the more facts about the girl and her kin group will be examined. Once informed, relatives explore various areas to determine whether any legal impediments to the marriage exist or whether it is desirable for the two to marry. The man's female relatives become especially active at this stage. They may informally engage someone who is related to the girl to observe her in her home when she is most natural and unlikely to put on such an impressive show as she is bound to display to them. The man himself may engage a male friend to observe her in this way. This intensive process of investigation and consultation among the relatives goes on for quite a long time until a consensus is reached or until at least the pivotal decision-makers agree.

*(b) Conveyance of marriage proposal (*leer atooc*)*

Once an agreement is reached, the second step, *leer atooc,* the conveyance of marriage proposal, follows. *Leer atooc* begins with the man's kin sending word to the girl's kin announcing their intention to visit them. The girl's relatives will then fix a date for the visit, allowing ample time to arrange for festivities. At the appointed time, the important relatives of the man, including his "father" or the representative of his father, visit the girl's relatives.[23] This may be for two or three days. The relatives of the prospective bridegroom must observe rigid restrictions on their movements in the bride's home, as they must always continue to do – an aspect of respect for in-laws which the Dinka value very highly. They are not to enter the houses of the bride's people and when the Dinka used to go naked, they must have been clothed when moving in front of the female relatives of the girl. When the time for negotiation comes, each side plans who should say what and when at the meeting.

The assembly is then convened in the presence of *abathook*, the public, who will act as the court of arbitration. From then and throughout the marriage ceremonies, the prospective bridegroom's family is referred to as *koc moc*, "the people of the groom," while that of the bride is *koc nya*, "the people of the bride" – descriptions which have acquired a technical usage and are consonant with the communal characteristic of Dinka marriage.

At the beginning of the negotiations, the people of the girl formally request the people of the man to state the purpose of their visit.[24] The man's kin then state their offer in modest terms. The theme is often something like this: "In our hearts is a lie [perhaps an exaggerated wish] we would like to attempt." By this, they mean that they are asking for a girl who might prove too expensive. It represents a kind of modesty, which may be good manners or may be calculated to moderate the claims of the girl's relatives. A lengthy dialogue follows their proposal which is typical of Dinka meetings, and which in the case of marriage is always carried out, however much in agreement the parties may secretly know themselves to be. One weakens one's bargaining position if one easily endorses the views of the other side, and yet one must treat relations-in-law with the greatest deference. In most cases, therefore, the girl's relatives first refuse their consent or make it exaggeratedly conditional, even though they have planned to accept the offer. It may be that while the majority accept, at least one important relative objects. Though expected, such pretenses give marriage additional dignity in Dinka eyes, for they tend to augment the bride's value in the eyes of the man's kin.

The girl's relatives then explain their refusal or reluctance. When their reasons are minor grievances (as in the case of the marriage of Wor, when one relative opposed the marriage because the knock on the gate of Wor's house was not responded to) they are more speedily given. However, if serious grounds exist, such as infectious, supposedly inherited, diseases, then consent may never be given. Between these two extremes are many grounds, which are easily or reluctantly given. When they are resolvable, such as when some important kinsman is indignant, the *abathook* (the public) will impose appeasement compensation and an agreement is reached. The *abathook* may not be able to resolve serious objections, but this may not end the proceedings. If the girl's relatives agree or it is apparent that their refusal is not seriously intended, the man's relatives then express their desire to return and send "a little something" (another gesture of modesty) as a betrothal consideration. The girl's relatives, in a combined acceptance-and-refusal manner reply, "do the thing of your hearts; guests should not be rebuffed," so that they permit them to bring the cattle while allegedly not committing themselves.

It is such circumstances that make it difficult to decide what constitutes offer and acceptance in contract terms. The Dinka call this "the seating of the offer." It is a form of acceptance of the offer for the purposes of further negotiations, a kind of acceptance of the invitation to discuss further rather than of the offer in the usual sense. The Dinka say that refusal does not really end the matter, for the man's relatives will go ahead on the presumption that no genuine refusal is meant, or that the girl's relatives can be persuaded to agree.

*(c) Delivery of the betrothal cattle (*leer amec*)*

What approximates offer and acceptance follows with the next stage, *leer amec*, when the man's relatives return with the betrothal cattle. The number of the cattle will depend on the age of the girl. If she is below the age of puberty and it is expected that several years will pass before the marriage is concluded, a token payment of a few cows is made; if she is of age, the number is greater, depending on the estimated total bride wealth. It is desirable that among these cattle be special cows particularly selected for the most important mythical participants of the girl's lineage. The cows are driven by the bridegroom and his age-mates, but the elders are the people who negotiate. The oxen in the herd are decorated with tassels, collars, and bells, and the young men and the women who meet them in the girl's home display their singing and dancing skills around the cattle and the oxen.

Great festivities follow, with slaughtering of beasts, brewing of beer, and much cooking. The prospective bridegroom and his closest elders – such as his father and uncles – do not partake of the food; they are to continue abstaining until "their mouths have been washed," according to the custom of *wak thok*, which means that an abstaining relative must be paid a cow or two by the bride's relatives before eating or drinking anything from the bride's home. The bridegroom does not eat or drink in the home of the bride until some time after the marriage has been completed.

Negotiations are then resumed in which the girl's relatives are formally asked to accept the cattle. They then decide whether to accept the *amec* or reject them. The Dinka say that even if they should not be accepted, the man's relatives, if decisively interested in the girl, should not be provoked into taking them back but should leave them, and the girl's relatives, or at least some moderates among them, will look after them, pending final decision. This also indicates the anomalies of a Dinka marriage and the difficulty of deciding just when betrothal and even marriage may be considered concluded. The Dinka word *amec* is used for cattle possessed by one person but owned by another. We are thus led into thinking that the betrothal cattle, even when accepted, are still owned by the man's relatives. Generally, however, they count as the property of the man's relatives for detrimental purposes and as those of the bride's relatives for beneficial purposes. Should they die before the final settlement of bride wealth, they are considered the property of the man's relatives and are not counted as part of bride wealth. But should they increase naturally before the settlement, their offspring count as the property of the girl's relatives and will not be counted as part of the bride wealth.

After betrothal, an important custom known as *mioc*, "offering," may follow. In normal usage, *mioc* is the act of serving food to men by women. As a feature of marriage celebrations, the bride and several members of her age-set visit the man's family carrying food. Although the idea is to bring food to the groom, these gifts are often distributed among relatives, since the groom cannot eat anything from the bride's home before "washing the mouth." *Mioc* is not an essential part of the marriage proceedings, and it is not always performed, but it is an important custom. In the past, it conferred certain rights of "husband" and "wife" upon the betrothed couple, which now depend on the mere fact of betrothal.

*(d) Counting the bride wealth (*kuen thiek*)*

The next important ceremony is *kuen thiek*, "counting the bride wealth," which is primarily concerned with negotiating the bride wealth. *Kuen thiek* is done soon or long after *leer amec*, depending on the total length of the marriage celebrations. It is both a festive and "businesslike" occasion. Several bulls and rams may be slaughtered and plenty of beer and food is prepared; dancing is at its highest.

Traditionally, *kuen thiek* is associated with the cattle byre, and is sometimes referred to as "entering the cattle byre," a concept that associates the ceremony with the place of cattle. The parties sit opposite each other while representatives of *abathook*, the public, sit in the center. All those connected with the bride who claim a share in the bride wealth attend to voice their claims. Many of the groom's relatives who will be asked to contribute also attend. Each side utters invocations calling upon its ancestors and divinities to witness the negotiations and facilitate agreement. The bridegroom and the bride, together with their respective age-mates, continue with celebrations and are thus excluded from the ordeal. The girl's people are then requested to state the number of cattle they claim. Their objective being to get the maximum possible, they are sure to aim high. The people of the bridegroom politely reject and counteroffer. Amid much pipe smoking and courtesy, which ideally marks the relations of in-laws, a clamor grows. Clamorous bargaining is not done by the fathers of both parties, but by other relatives. By this time, the relatives of the girl will already have investigated the cattle of the groom's relatives and will make demands specifying by color pattern what cattle they would like included in the marriage. One ox or cow may be pivotal in the negotiations. Usually, the best cattle are demanded for the ancestral spirits, *yieth*, but the father of the girl, and other relatives such as the girl's brother, also have specific claims for high-quality cattle. The people of the bridegroom are normally not reminded of the quality of the girl's mother's share which, though limited to a cow with a cow calf, is always among the best, a consideration for the attachment between the mother and the daughter. Negotiations usually end with a compromise. The amount of bride wealth ranges considerably from an average of about 50 head of cattle to as high as 200 cows for the daughters of wealthy or prominent families. Once the amount of cattle is determined, the precise time of payment is then debated. Negotiations having ended, usually with a considerable compromise, all return to the festivities in a profoundly amicable fashion, for now the betrothal, and therefore the marriage has attained a high degree of validity and stability.

*(e) The giving away of the girl (*geem nya*)*

The final stage is *geem nya*, literally "the giving away of the girl." On this occasion, the people of the man visit the people of the girl and formally request that she be given to them. Normally, unless an important condition in *kuen thiek* has not been fulfilled, there will be no further impediment. A promise being given that "their wife" will follow, the people of the man return to prepare themselves to receive her.[25] Meanwhile, her kin perform a ritual ceremony in which a bull is sacrificed for the ancestral spirits who are invoked once again to bless the union. The bride then goes to the home of the bridegroom's father accompanied by a group of her age-mates. As a safeguard against *tiel* and as an expression of solidarity, she stays in the house of the groom's stepmother or other step-kin, rather than in the house of his own mother. Another large celebration follows and the age-mates of both parties have several days of badinage, eating, drinking, and singing, with the festivities sometimes lasting all night. The bride and the groom share their first exclusive night and the marriage is consummated.[26]

*(f) Competition for brides (*teer nya*)*

A significant feature of Dinka marriage is the custom of *teer nya*, competition over the bride. Once it is realized that a Dinka girl is primarily a source of wealth, competition is easily understood. For the same reason, and also because of the enmities it creates, it is avoided by the relatives of a man and is only resorted to when really necessary. It is more frequent among the rich. In case the competitors are related, one party is usually propitiated or appeased with compensation and persuaded to surrender. When competition ensues, the cattle received as betrothal consideration are kept apart by the girl's kin, who are expected to inform the competing groups if one side increases its betrothal cattle. In response, the other group adds more cattle. The process goes on until one party is forced to surrender. In competition, there is no *kuen thiek* – that is, settlement of bride wealth. When one party is defeated, special cows from among the bride wealth are allotted to the ancestral spirits, the sacrifice to them is made, and *geem nya*, the handing over of the bride, concludes the ceremonies as in normal situations.

The process of competition is a very tense one in which the parties will use any means to defeat each other. In songs, anything that can destroy the reputation of the adversary is used. Open physical clashes may result. To minimize this, the right of courtship is regulated; the rule is that the first to betroth the girl is the lawful bridegroom and the rights of betrothal accrue to him. He is thus the one entitled to courtship. One of the ways of determining the stage of validity of marriage is when sexual intercourse with other people counts as adultery, or when sexual intercourse of the girl and groom ceases to be wrong. While sexual relationships are discouraged prior to the conclusion of the marriage, should it occur it is not an offense. Should the girl conceive, the issue is the lawful child of the marriage. In the case of competition, if the girl should conceive by the first suitor, he is not held liable and the child is his even though he is eventually defeated. The second groom, on the other hand, is not even permitted to court the girl. Should he do so, he commits an offense, as will be seen later under violation of rights in women. If he has sexual intercourse with her, he commits "adultery," and should he be defeated, he is supposed to compensate the winning suitor.

While most relatives of a girl welcome competition, the practice is not universal. Some fathers consider it disgraceful to put a daughter on the market. Indeed, the custom is waning, and, as is true of many other cases, the paramount chief has led the way. In one case, Acai, the daughter of Chief Deng Majok, was betrothed to a Ngok Dinka, and a betrothal wealth of about 100 cows was paid. Chief Bol Col, one of the prominent chiefs of the Tuic Dinka, sought her for one of his sons. He offered 150 cows for betrothal and undertook to pay a total bride wealth of 200. As in most marriages to the chief's daughters, the objective of Chief Bol was diplomatic. Deng Majok's kin group was predominantly in favor of marrying the girl to Bol Col's son on the grounds that, according to tradition, a girl is an item of trade and higher payment should prevail. They were supported in this by the tribe, who claimed that a daughter of the chief, especially in intertribal marriages, was a daughter of the tribe and so their opinion should count. The matter went to Abyei court for arbitration. Deng Majok argued that the bridegroom's father had died after the betrothal, and that as the chief he had a general obligation to his needy people and to the bridegroom, whose father had died believing his son to be the chief's son-in-law. Secondly, he argued that his tribe will be inviting an insult to him and therefore to themselves if they made him accept a marriage on grounds of a more profitable offer. The court, convinced by the reasonableness of his grounds, persuaded the kin group and the tribe to endorse it.

The difficulties of traditional marriage, seen from both the man's and the girl's standpoints, prompt certain actions which the Dinka judge wrong but that, because of their frequency, become recognized as part of the marriage process in certain circumstances. These are elopement with an unbetrothed or a betrothed girl, and abduction and/or authorized rape of a married but unconsenting girl. Here, we are not concerned with these acts as offenses, but as measures which Dinka youth take in order to influence marriage proceedings where they disapprove of the normal course.

Jon nya, elopement with an unbetrothed girl with a view to marriage where that is otherwise difficult or impossible, is considered the most serious, particularly if the elopement has been consummated. Depending on his assessment of his kinsmen's reaction, the man may take the girl to the home of the one in charge of his marriage, or even to the chief's home. This is naturally preferred to elopement to far-off areas, a practice which is on the increase as interaction with non-Ngok Sudanese increases. Whichever form it takes, elopement is a serious act. In the past, the girl's kin, if they desired the proposed union, would go armed into the cattle camp of the man's kin and seize all the cattle they could find. This is the custom known as *thel*, and serious, often fatal, fights would ensue.

More prudent kinsmen of such a wrongdoer would not attempt obstruction. Instead, if they wanted their son to marry the girl, which would be preferable, they appealed to the chief to summon the girl's kin so that marriage could be discussed. On the appointed day, both sides came to the Chiefs' court and a reasonable amount was fixed by the court as the bride wealth. A set-off was then made. If the cattle seized were less than the amount fixed, the difference was paid; if more, the excess was returned. If the girl's people insisted on her return they could do so but would not get compensation unless there had been consummation, in which case they were given a cow called "the cow of the leather skirt." She then had to put on a bridal skirt and continue to dress as a married woman whether married to this particular person or not. If she conceived, then additional compensation was paid. The relatives of the man might also refuse marriage and in theory, similar measures as above are taken to restore the status quo, but in practice, settlement was rendered more difficult.

Elopement with a girl already betrothed to the man taking her is a less serious offense. This is implicit in the term the Dinka use for it, *jon tik*, literally "elopement with a wife," for once betrothed, she is thought of as a wife. Such elopement may occur for several reasons, including the inability to meet the bride wealth demands of the bride's kin or to secure the consent of some pivotal figure. Usually, the bridegroom takes the bride to the home of his father. However, the couple may want to ensure their marriage by going beyond the reach of their relatives until their union will have been confirmed with children. *Jon tik* generally facilitates marriage in favor of the eloping parties. As in *jon nya*, negotiations are concluded in the Chiefs' court and, except in a few cases, the return of the bride to her kin is not necessary. Should she be returned, marriage ceremonies are accelerated and previous impediments are greatly modified.

Where *jon nya* or *jon tik* takes place without the consent of the girl, it is called *guem*, "abduction." *Guem* is a most serious offense, and a bloody conflict is inevitable, whether there has been consummation or not. *Guem* may be authorized by the girl's relatives if after the conclusion of marriage ceremonies the girl still refuses her consent. Incredible brutalities can result from *guem*. The age-mates of a bridegroom may seize the girl and physically force her into submission.[27] Once consummation is effected, the girl is forced into dressing like a married woman and, it is hoped, will be too shamefaced to leave him. Many surrender, but some determined girls continue to reject their supposed husbands until they eventually secure a divorce.

2.1.6 Validity of marriage

Although we later examine the validity of Dinka marriage in the context of legal pluralism, we are here concerned primarily with the stage at which customary marriage is recognized as valid and giving rise to rights and obligations. Since marriage ceremonies are so lengthy, this stage is not easily determined.

As betrothal is considered a degree of marriage among the Ngok Dinka, a betrothed man is said to have an action of "adultery" against third parties. A failure to appreciate the fact that betrothal is part of marriage in the customary laws of traditional African societies has led some writers to conclude that "'adultery' here is used in a loose sense, for it covers sexual intercourse by the wife before marriage."[28] Since the protection of betrothal lies mostly in its anticipation of marriage rather than in the institution of betrothal itself, many societies require any compensation paid for adultery with a betrothed girl to be transferred to her relatives if the betrothal is subsequently broken. Among the Ngok, whoever weds her is entitled to it. Because of their misunderstanding of the true nature of such betrothal, some people are surprised to learn that "any child born to a betrothed woman 'belongs' to the intended husband."[29] For this reason, the man and his kin receive compensation for her injury. The same is true of any other rights over her that are violated. With these rights, the betrothed man and his kin also assume certain obligations for the girl. For instance, if she wrongs other people, the man and his kinsmen will pay compensation.

Identifying betrothal as a degree of marriage is only a starting point for delineating the stages of validity in the extensive proceedings of the Dinka betrothal period. In this, Ngok law has undergone some changes. In the past, the validity of marriage giving rise to rights and duties was determined by one of two tests. The first was whether the cattle paid as a preliminary part of the marriage consideration included cattle dedicated to the bride's ancestral spirits and clan divinities. The second was whether the bride fulfilled the custom known as *mioc*, by which a betrothed girl visits her groom's home with gifts of food. Today, the decisive factor is whether any cattle have been paid and accepted as *amec*.

In *Deng Ajith v. Magwith*,[30] Deng Ajith was betrothed to a girl and paid *amec*. Magwith eloped with the girl and went to a distant area. After begetting two children, they were caught and returned to the tribe. Deng brought an action of adultery against Magwith and claimed the children as "the children of the cows." Magwith pleaded that the girl had been his girlfriend long before she was betrothed to Deng. In fact, the first pregnancy occurred prior to the girl's engagement to Deng, a reason for their elopement. The court of first instance sentenced Magwith to six months' imprisonment for eloping with and impregnating "a married woman." The court also ordered the payment of six cows to Deng as compensation for the elopement and the adultery. The children were held to be his.

Magwith appealed to the Chiefs' court of appeal on the ground that their first relationship had occurred prior to Deng's payment of the cattle of *amec* and therefore should not count as adultery to entitle Deng to compensation, nor should it entitle Deng to the offspring of that relationship. On proof of the facts, the court allowed his appeal. With respect to the first pregnancy, he was made to pay three cows compensation to the girl's relatives for the impregnation of an unmarried woman, and was entitled to the child on further payment of legitimization wealth.[31]

As we saw in *Ayii v. Allor*, once the cows of *amec* have been paid not even the girl's father can interfere with the marriage. In *Koryom Arob v. Bol Duper*,[32] Koryom had paid thirty-nine cows as *amec* for the daughter of Bol. Bol subsequently gave the girl to another man who went outside the tribe with her. Bol was detained in jail while attempts were made to bring the girl back. Koryom, however, decided to "divorce" the girl and the court accepted his grounds. As obiter dictum, the court said that had he wanted his wife back, he would have been entitled to an action of adultery and could have claimed any adulterous children as the offspring of his cattle. As it was, the court ordered immediate return of his betrothal wealth.

2.2 Dissolution of marriage

Dissolution of marriage may be the result of the wife's death (not the husband's) or of divorce. Among the Dinka both are disapproved of and restricted.[33] Even the death of a wife may not justify the husband to dissolve the marriage and withdraw the bride wealth cattle. However, a substantial amount of litigation in Dinka courts is concerned with the consequences of dissolving marriage. Under the current law, reference to court is necessary.

2.2.1 Consequences of a spouse's death

Only the wife's death can justify dissolution of marriage in that it may be used as a ground for a postmortem divorce. Because of levirate, the husband's death does not dissolve the marriage. Even the death of the wife is rarely a ground for divorce. Other considerations have to be made before a divorce decree may be granted; the most important is whether the woman died without issue. If she had two or more children, the marriage subsists and her widower will not be permitted to claim the return of the bride wealth. In such a case, the relatives of the dead wife are requested to pay him cattle of *duot yic*, literally "tying the belly." This expression originates in a mourning custom by which a man, who must not cry with tears but is believed to cry "inside," ties a piece of cloth or leather around his abdomen, a practice associated with controlling the expression of one's grief. Thus, the compensation paid by the wife's kin is in essence a gesture of sympathy and assistance. They may also help the man to marry again. While anybody may pay cattle of *adut*, as *duot yic* is sometimes called, payment by the wife's kin is compulsory. If a wife dies with only one child, the likelihood is that the marriage will not be dissolved, especially if that child is a male. However, should the widower desire its dissolution, he is entitled to it and will be returned his bride wealth with the exception of a number sufficient to retain his paternal rights over the child. Should he receive all the cows, he loses his rights over the child.

If a father who has lost his paternal rights over his orphan child wishes to reclaim him or her, he must "marry" the child. This notion applies whether the child is male or female. It recalls the fundamental base of Dinka marriage, and is a fictional restoration of the status quo ante so that the husband is in effect envisioned as remarrying his deceased wife in order to reclaim his child – hence, "marrying" the child. The number of cows a man needs to pay for his issue differs according to the sex and age of the child, with more paid for girls and older children. In *Bol Malek v. the Maternal Kin of Ajang Bol*,[34] the facts of *Bol Malek v. the Relatives of Awut* came to the Chiefs' court once more. When Ajang reached marriageable age, Bol Malek reclaimed her. At this stage, when a daughter is about to attract wealth, her father's wish to "marry" her is not easily accepted by her maternal kin. Ajang's maternal kin demanded more than Bol was willing to pay. Dispute arose over the matter and Bol brought an action for the recovery of his daughter. The court held that in view of Ajang's age and marriage potential, Bol should "marry" his daughter for twenty cows in order to resume his paternal rights over her. This he did. Soon after he recovered his daughter, Ajang was married with a substantial bride wealth.

Where a deceased wife leaves no children, dissolution is more likely to be granted. This requires further qualification, for although there may be dissolution of the marriage, the wife's kin and the husband with his kin may perpetuate their in-law relationship by sororate, that is, by substituting the deceased with another girl who may be her sister or a relative. This is illustrated by *The Relatives of Salvatore Atem v. the Relatives of Athilueth*.[35] Atem, a Roman Catholic, married Athilueth by customary law. Athilueth died during her first childbirth. It was said that one of the relatives of the girl who had unsuccessfully opposed the marriage had inflicted a curse upon the marriage, saying that Athilueth will never live to bear children to Atem. Her death therefore recalled the curse. Atem's kin group sued for the return of their full bride wealth. During the litigation, one of Atem's kinsmen proposed that a girl be given to them as a substitute wife. Both sides agreed. Athilueth's relatives suggested three girls, one a full sister and the others half-sisters of

Athilueth. Atem's relatives chose the full sister because she was educated, as was Atem. Atem, who was absent on government service, was not informed of these measures. When the choice was made, the court ordered that a nominal number of cattle be paid by Atem's relatives to the girl's relatives as cows of *put*, that is, "cows of spraying with ashes" – a blessing rite to establish the new union independently of the dead wife and thus to avoid the implications of incest. This, it must be noted, is different from the symbolic action of alleviating the evil consequences of experienced or feared incest. It is essentially indicative that the marriage of Atem and Athilueth had been dissolved by death and the relationship of in-laws could only be maintained by a new marriage.[36] This case illustrates the subordination of the individual parties to the marriage. Not only was Salvatore Atem not present at the proceedings, but the girl who was offered as a substitute was not there either and might not have been consulted. Sororate must be distinguished from levirate and ghost marriage. Whereas in the levirate the previous marriage subsists, sororate is a new marriage. Ghost marriage may seem closer, but the union *inter vivos* is entered into in the name of the deceased; in sororate, death gives rise to a new marriage. In sororate, the objective is to perpetuate the name of the living and not the deceased, as in levirate. Indeed, if the deceased wife had children, sororate will not be possible, for they will then be a tangible symbol of the permanence and the success of the previous union.

2.2.2 Grounds for a husband's claim for divorce

A man may request a divorce on any one of many grounds, including the barrenness of his wife, theft, habitual insults, badness of mouth, adultery, witchcraft, mortal disease, *jiliiu* or *dejook*, gross indecency, desertion, and giving the wife to another man. The first and most obvious ground for divorce, when examined in the context of the procreational goal of marriage, is the wife's barrenness, which in Dinka eyes is a failure to fulfill the fundamental obligation of marriage.[37] The bride wealth is returned, with the exception of "a cow of the leather skirt," that is, compensation for having put her into her status as a married woman, which reduces her marriage potential. In *Mithiang Aguek v. Malek Deng*[38] Mithiang married Malek's sister, who proved barren. Mithiang sued for divorce. Malek counterclaimed compensation from Mithiang for having been cohabiting with his sister. The court held that Mithiang was entitled to divorce, but had to pay *weng biong*, "the cow of the leather skirt," to Malek.

If the wife bears a child before her barrenness, sufficient cattle to preserve the legitimacy of the child will be left with her kin. If barrenness comes after the birth of two or more children, it is unlikely that divorce will be granted. When a man's wife does not conceive, the Dinka usually suspect the woman of barrenness rather than the husband of sterility or impotence, and this is often linked with some indignation on the part of the participants. If propitiation and appeasement rites have been carried out, the wife is either suspected of some wrong or simply believed barren.[39] Analogous to barrenness is mortality of the wife's offspring. The woman is often suspected of hiding some evil, particularly a sexual offense, for which the death of children is a supernatural punishment.[40]

The second ground for divorce is theft, which involves punitive measures by the age-set of the alleged thief and is therefore a public scandal.

Habitual insults by the wife constitute a third ground for divorce. Such insults must be grievous and injurious to the reputation of the husband or his lineage, a question decided by the court in the light of all the circumstances. A case cited by John Makec indicates that even one insult can provide a ground for suing for divorce. In that case, *Bona Mou Ngot v. Alek Nyang Dhieu*, the wife insulted the children of her husband (it is not clear whether her own children or those of another wife) by saying, "any child of Bona Ngot will not be satisfied even if the oil pours down his or her anus." This was an allegation of greed that was assumed to be genetic, a serious insult for a Dinka. Although the court denied divorce, it imposed appeasement compensation of two heifers on the relatives of the wife to be paid to the husband.

The fourth ground is "badness of the mouth," *rac thok*. This is similar to the third ground, but *rac thok* does not need to entail actual insults; it concerns a wife who nags and grumbles so much that she wearies the husband to an unbearable extent. This is essentially a matter of character and does not necessarily need to be directed toward the husband; it will suffice that the wife cannot get along with others. This ground requires such notoriety that proof is easy.[41]

Adultery is the fifth ground for divorce, but normally a man will prefer compensation rather than divorce unless the wife is persistently adulterous.

The sixth ground is witchcraft discovered after the marriage. If a man marries a woman knowing that she is reputed as a witch or that witchcraft is practiced within her lineage, he cannot use it as a ground for divorce. Even when subsequently discovered, witchcraft is rarely used as a ground for divorce because of the seriousness of imputing it and the difficulty of proving it. As the court becomes more empirically oriented, witchcraft becomes more difficult to prove and is therefore less utilized as a ground for divorce.

Mortal disease, of which tuberculosis and leprosy are typical examples, constitutes the seventh ground for divorce. However, the court usually persuades the husband against divorce on the ground that the disease is an act of God. Another factor is that imputing such diseases is often considered defamatory and, whatever the justification, the tendency is against such imputation. Only in the most obvious cases do people sue for divorce on this ground.

The eighth ground is *jiliiu* or *dejook*, which are very complex words. A woman who is a *jiliiu* or a *dejook* is untidy, careless, ill-mannered, indecent, bad at cooking, at bringing up children, at keeping the house, and the like. The Dinka themselves say that *jiliiu* and *dejook* cannot be easily defined. They are believed to be so intricate that sometimes the court has to rely entirely on the husband's subjectivities about his wife. These are sometimes better not said, but from the circumstances of each case, the Dinka believe that *jiliiu* or *dejook* may be objectively determined.[42]

While *jiliiu* or *dejook* are essentially matters of general character, a ninth and somewhat similar ground for divorce relates to acts of gross indecency. This ground is wide and may include acts that, in the opinion of the court, violate the obligation of respect that a wife owes her husband, or which in-laws owe each other. Like *jiliiu* or *dejook*, if the husband can substantiate his point without necessarily specifying the cause of grievance, the court may be lenient in its requirements for evidence in order to save him embarrassment. The act need not be by the wife herself: conduct of her close relatives may count against her, though in such a case the court is more likely to rule that instead of divorce, *awec*, conciliatory payment, be made to the offended husband. In *Madut Akoc v. Monytooc Deng*,[43] Madut was married to Monytooc's sister, Kuei. Monytooc, in conflict with Madut, went to see him. Without adequate warning, he walked into the house to find Madut and Kuei in private circumstances. Madut sued for divorce. The court ruled that although Madut was justified in his claim, in view of his wife's innocence he should accept conciliatory payment and be reconciled. Madut accepted and Monytooc was made to pay him two cows.

The tenth ground for divorce is desertion. If a wife runs away with another man, the husband will normally seek to have her returned and accept compensation from the man with whom she had eloped. But if she is not returned or she continually deserts, he will be entitled to a divorce. In *Mithiang Dut v. the Relatives of Adit*,[44] Adit, Mithiang's wife, bore six children, all of whom died. Believing the source of death to be with her husband, she brought a suit for divorce, but her claim was dismissed. She then eloped with another man. They were caught and she was returned to Mithiang. Her lover was made to pay compensation to Mithiang, and was sentenced to imprisonment. Soon after serving his prison sentence, they eloped again. The process was repeated so many times that Mithiang became tired of litigation and asked for a divorce, which the court granted.[45]

The final ground is giving the wife away in marriage to someone else. It is obvious that such a transaction is not marriage, since the girl's relatives cannot contract another marriage while a valid one subsists. This is the case even if there has been only a betrothal. If, instead of enforcing his rights as a husband, a man prefers divorce, it will be granted. This ground is analogous to adultery and desertion; but it is contracting another marriage, though null and void, which constitutes the ground, as we saw in *Koryom Arob v. Bol Duper*.[46] In *Akuek v. Madut*,[47] Akuek was betrothed to a girl who did not like him and was determined not to live with him. When her refusal was dismissed, she indulged in illicit relationships to dissuade Akuek. When this strategy was not fruitful, she eloped with Madut. This time, her relatives felt themselves compelled to endorse her choice and contract a marriage with Madut. Though Akuek could have sued Madut for adultery and her relatives for giving his wife in marriage, he chose to sue Madut for the return of his bride wealth. The court held that, according to custom, in the event of a well-founded divorce and a subsequent marriage, the bride wealth is to be paid by the new husband, or the wife's relatives, or both, whichever is most conducive to prompt payment.

Where a widow marries a woman to beget children for her and her deceased husband, she is entitled to the rights of a husband including the right to divorce her on justified grounds. In the case of Adut-dit cited earlier, Adut-dit was allowed to divorce Achol because Deng, the relative she had invited to beget children with, had joined the SPLM/A and wanted to take her and her baby away. Adut-dit objected to Achol and the baby going with Deng. When they insisted, Adut-dit sued for divorce on the ground of desertion. The court held that Deng had no authority over Achol, save sharing her bed. The court ordered the divorce and Adut-dit was entitled to the return of her bride wealth cattle and the baby son, provided she paid the customary cattle for claiming the child to Achol's relatives.

Although in most cases we have talked of the husband and the wife as parties in divorce actions, in fact the suits often involve kinship groups. Only if the husband can justify his cause to his kinsmen will they back him in his divorce proceedings. In most cases, a combination of grounds is necessary to establish good cause. Divorce among the Dinka can only be effected through the court.

2.2.3 Grounds for the wife's claim for divorce

The wife's grounds for divorce are fewer and often required to be more compelling than those of the husband. Life with her husband has to be terribly hard for her to win the sympathy of her kin and the court. Her family obviously has much more to lose, not only because the cattle of her bride wealth will have multiplied far beyond the number they can possibly hope for in her remarriage, but also because her divorce often works against her chances for a good remarriage. The wife may, however, succeed on a number of grounds, including impotence or sterility, incest by the husband, failure to provide, insults to her relatives, desertion, or cruelty.

The first ground is impotence and sterility. A man is rarely suspected of impotence and sterility, especially if he has only one wife and there is no way of telling whether the defect is his or hers. Generally, women are embarrassed to adduce this as a ground for divorce, but it is sometimes a cause of wives' unfaithfulness. In normal cases, the impotence or sterility of the husband does not entitle the wife to divorce. Since the primary object is that she should procreate, the matter is secretly settled within the family, and a relative of the man may step in to produce children with her while the offspring are considered those of the husband. If the husband objects to such an arrangement, the wife is entitled to divorce.[48] Many husbands will rather have a relative secretly procreate with the wife than risk publicity over their impotence or sterility and so this ground is rarely used.

The second ground for divorce is incest by the husband. The Dinka believe the consequences of incest to fall on the wife and her issue. It is she and her kin, therefore, who are keenest to avoid incest. If a man marries a girl related to the wife, the wife is entitled to divorce him. Even courting such a girl may give the wife good cause, although this is not settled. In *Bashir Deng v. John Ajuong*,[49] Bashir married the ward of Ajuong. Bashir and his wife quarreled frequently, and ultimately separated. Bashir later sued for the restitution of conjugal rights. Ajuong brought a counteraction demanding divorce on the ground that Bashir had courted Ajuong's sister. Ajuong's sister testified to this fact. The majority of the court was of the opinion that courtship, short of marriage or sexual intercourse, was not a ground for divorce by the wife. Accordingly, divorce was denied, and Bashir was made to pay Ajuong a conciliatory fee. As an obiter dictum, the court held that if Ajuong was known to have sufficient cattle to repay the bride wealth, it might have been wiser to grant divorce. Their ground for this dictum was incompatibility resulting from frequent nagging and quarrels rather than from incest.

The wife's third ground for divorce is the husband's failure to provide maintenance. It is his duty to cultivate her fields and provide her with cows, sheep, and goats. The court will first attempt to make the husband provide for his wife according to the wealth in his family. Should he be uncooperative, the wife may then be granted a divorce.

The wife may also be granted a divorce if the husband continually uses insults directed at her relatives. This ground is somewhat similar to the one mentioned for the husband, but whereas insults against the husband personally will give him good cause, in the case under consideration the insult must touch on her lineage rather than her personally. Imputations of leprosy or witchcraft are examples. This ground rarely succeeds because the court will usually persuade the wronged party to accept a conciliatory fee and be reconciled.

The wife may also divorce on grounds of desertion. In most cases, however, she is requested to cohabit with one of the husband's relatives so that children may be begotten to the name of the lineage. A woman may inform the chief of her husband's desertion, who will then call upon her relatives to bring the husband back. If, for one reason or another, her relatives fail to restore cohabitation, then the wife will be entitled to select a man from among his close relatives to live with her. If, instead, she insists on divorce, then it may be granted. If a man deserts his wife for a long period, especially without maintenance, and then returns to restore cohabitation, the wife may justifiably insist on divorce.

Cruelty provides another ground for divorce. Normally, a man has the right to reprimand and even beat his wife, and interference by her relatives is considered reprehensible. However, if he persistently ill-treats her, or beats her without good cause, her relatives may intervene and divorce proceedings may ensue.

The wife, even more than the husband, relies largely on convincing her kin that suing for divorce is necessary and justified. Her chances of convincing them are much poorer than those of the husband with his kin. Although her kin do not benefit from children as much as do her husband and his relatives, their most important consideration is that their daughter should procreate.

As is the case with the husband, the wife and her relatives may insist on a divorce contrary to the court decree. In such an event, they will be compelled to repay the bride wealth promptly and only "the cow of the leather skirt" will be deducted, unless there is a child, in which case further reductions will be made equivalent to those of impregnation. If they have good grounds for divorce, the court will direct the husband to wait for the wife's remarriage and order that he be compensated from among the cattle paid by the new husband. The rules of ownership and custody of the children mentioned above are applicable in such situations.

Makec gives an additional ground for divorce as "a serious deterioration of the relation between close relatives of the spouses" which "may be brought about by disputes over cattle, or if the wife's relatives encourage or support her in causing trouble for him and his relatives, or when the wife is generally mistreated by the husband and his relatives. It may also be caused by grave acts of misconduct committed by one or more relatives on the one side of the marriage against the other side."[50]

Once a divorce decree has been granted to the spouse who claimed it, the ceremony known as *cuet arob*, "the spraying of the sacred ashes," is carried out to emancipate the wife from the status of a married woman.[51] She is brought into the Chiefs' court, and her legs are sprayed with ashes from the burnt dung of the chief's cattle, which is regarded as sacred.

Notwithstanding the grounds of divorce by the husband, the wife, or their respective relatives, it must be emphasized that divorce is extremely rare among the Dinka because of the complex web of kinship ties involved and the serious consequences connected with the cattle exchanged and widely distributed among the relatives. As Howell observed, "It is … in the interest of all those persons to see that marriage is a successful and stable one and the system is one which makes for stability in marriage."[52] Usually, the greater the number of kinsmen who contribute bride wealth or who share in receiving it, the greater the stability of the marriage will be. In the past, these cattle were hardly ever sold, at least during the early years of the marriage, and since they had to be returned if the marriage was dissolved, they represented a pledge that both sides were interested in ensuring its stability. As John Wuol explained, "Divorce cannot be easily allowed since it adversely affects the social and economic interests of both parties. The elders, among the people, make all necessary effort to resist it. They can only persuade the parties concerned to go to court when the reasons for demanding divorce are very strong or when they fail to convince the parties to change their minds. Even when the divorce suit has been raised, the court has the last opportunity to persuade the parties to reconcile, or it may exercise its discretionary power to reject the suit."[53]

According to Howell, the stability of Dinka marriage is largely due to the great care the Dinka place on choosing the right partner.

> The stability of marriage among the Ngork (sic) Dinka … cannot, however, be attributed solely to the deterrent effect of the complications involved in a divorce … The main factor making for stability is to be found in the slow process of flirtation, courtship and marriage, which gives Dinka youths and girls the maximum opportunity to find the right mate. Occasionally, of course, girls are forced by their families to marry old and rich men whom they do not favor and it is sometimes said by the Ngork that it is difficult for a young man to get married at all. This does not, however, appear to be the rule, for although many old and important men have a large number of wives, most men of thirty have at least one wife.[54]

While Howell is correct on the role of courtship and long betrothal, his emphasis on the freedom of choice must be correlated with what was said earlier about the predisposition of most Dinka girls to accept whoever proposes to marry them unless cogent circumstances compel a refusal. It is true that this is often the same man or one of the men who will have been "dating" the girl, and it is also true that she can discourage anyone she particularly disapproves of from proposing; but it is equally true that she is often quite neutral so as not to repel a potential proposal. To understand the stability of Dinka marriage, one must understand the considerations facing a Dinka woman. First, she wants and is wanted, and expects and is expected, to marry and ensure the stability of her marriage. Second, she is better off if she likes the person she marries and continues to like him.

2.3 Legitimacy of children

The concept of illegitimacy is restricted in Dinka law. A child may be illegitimate in relation to a particular person but not in the sense that he or she occupies an independent status of illegitimacy. Children are the greatest treasure, and a child is at all times someone's legitimate offspring with all the rights implicit in that status. We have seen that the factors surrounding the values and institutions of marriage and procreation cause deprivations which in turn prompt violations of the norms. Consequently, universal legitimacy, though a very humane aspect of Dinka law, is marked with correlative deprivations and conflicts over children.

A child is legitimate if born during a valid marriage. The stage of such validity is betrothal upon at least partial payment of bride wealth. Any children born to the bride after that are legitimate children of the intended husband regardless of their actual paternity. Because of the levirate and ghost marriage the "father" may have died when the child was conceived or even when the mother was married. If a man divorces his wife while she is pregnant, he loses the child, unless he leaves sufficient cattle to retain his claim over the child, or unless the child, usually in the case of sons, later demands return to the original father, in which case he transfers his legitimacy by the father's payment of legitimization fee. It then becomes legitimacy by adoption and not by birth in lawful marriage. If a child is born of adultery, he is still the legitimate child of the marriage unless the mother is divorced while still pregnant with that child, in which case the legitimacy of the child is transferred either to the mother's kin or to the man who marries her subsequently.

The principle that the child belongs to the marriage cattle, that is, a marriage that has not been dissolved and cattle returned, can sometimes be so rigid as to impose hardship on those involved. Monyluak Alor Kuol reports a 1987 case involving Arob Lual from Wol Lual's area in Tonj District. Arob Lual married a girl from the Nuer area of Bantiu. He paid the required bride wealth and received his wife. After having two daughters, the couple quarreled and the woman went back to her family with her two young girls. She remained there for years. When the first daughter was married and the bridegroom informed her father, Arob, in accordance with tradition, went to claim the bride wealth. There he discovered that his wife had had two additional daughters with another man. Arob not only received the bride wealth, but also sued for adultery against the other man and claimed to be given back his wife and all the three daughters, the second unmarried daughter and the two young girls of 12 and 9, born of adultery. The court held that since the marriage was never dissolved and bride wealth returned, Arob was entitled to the children and their biological father was found guilty of adultery. However, the court ruled that he did not have to pay compensation for adultery because of the contribution he had already made in bringing up the children. As Kuol noted, "The woman and her daughters were distraught by the order of their transfer from the Nuer community to that of the Dinka, which was completely strange to the three girls. The court's decision nevertheless prevailed."[55]

Legitimization may be by the biological father, or by a stranger. The first case usually occurs in connection with the impregnation of an unmarried woman. Makec has argued that while "it is essentially the bride wealth which legalizes paternity over children … it must not be understood … that the bride wealth legitimizes the children." His reason is that "the term 'legitimation' or 'legitimization' in the context of other legal systems has legal notions which accompany it and these are not part of our law."[56] While Makec is presumably guarding against the implication that these terms imply the existence of the status of illegitimacy until remedied by "legitimation" or "legitimization," what is intended in the Dinka context is the transfer of legitimacy by payment of cattle, which Makec prefers to call legalization. Used in this sense, the biological father may "legitimate" the child by a subsequent marriage or by the payment of a "legitimation" fee in addition to the damages on account of impregnation.[57] Failing adoption by the biological father, a child is adopted by anyone who subsequently marries the mother. A child who is not legitimate by birth or by adoption belongs to the maternal kin.[58] He assumes all the obligations and is entitled to all the rights of a legitimate child.

By whatever means a person acquires his legitimacy, he is fully legitimate and no serious social stigma is attached to the discrepancy in biological and legal parentage. In certain cases, a child may suffer emotional strains and conflicts. Even an otherwise accursed child, once he survives, is entitled to the privileges of legitimacy. It is a serious wrong to remind a relative of the peculiarities of his legitimacy, whatever the provocation. Should any discrimination against him come to court, the judges are most likely to be biased for him and will reprimand his adversaries with unusual emphasis. He, in turn, is also reprimanded strongly if he tends to differentiate himself by attributing ordinary incidents of ill-treatment to the peculiarities of his status. Despite their legal equality, such children may be discriminated against in subtle ways, and in any case are often emotionally insecure.

Frequently a man who has been ill-treated by his father addresses himself to the lineage in songs with such words as "Am I not a son of the clan?" "Did I come with my mother?" "Was I adopted?" and the like.[59] Since such a status is not rare, considerable problems of suspicion about the nature of their legitimacy by persons who feel discriminated against are to be expected. Because of this discrimination, however subtle, sons often return to their biological fathers who will at that stage be only too glad to legitimate them, thus bringing together biological and legal parentage. Since daughters change their residence and domicile, the problem is not so acute for them, and as a rule they do not seek their biological parentage. It is to be noted that once a child has been declared the legal child of someone other than the real father, all links are broken with the real father. The only exception is with regard to exogamy: a child cannot marry into the lineage of either the biological father or the pater.

Implicit in these practices are the hardships to the parents and children who are separated by the strict application of the legitimacy laws. The law approaches the whole matter from the viewpoint of the lineages of the parents involved and whether they can agree so that biological parentage may coincide with legal parentage. Failing such agreement, a parent and child are torn from each other with little or no regard of the consequences to the individuals involved. Such deprivations and the serious conflicts connected with them are frequent. As we saw in Arob Lual's case, there are cases in which children have been taken away from parents who had isolated themselves for years in secret, illegal unions in the hope that if they begot children the people and the law will be sympathetic enough to legalize their marriage. Instead of cementing their love with marriage, they are further deprived of their affection as parents of their children.

2.4 Sexual offences

The Dinka emphasis on maintaining the male line implies that sexual wrongs are defined as those that interfere with the procreative process. Such wrongs can therefore be committed only on women even though the moral responsibility of the female partner may be seen as greater than that of her male paramour. The categories of sexual wrongs are adultery, seduction, and abduction.

2.4.1 Adultery

Adultery is recognized as both a criminal offense and a civil wrong and is abhorred so much that it is believed to result in spiritual contamination likely to cause death to the woman, her children, or a relative unless it is redressed and certain rites are carried out. A woman who has committed adultery feels her guilt in physical pain of a religious significance, which cannot be alleviated unless she confesses. Labor or illness in suspicious circumstances is sufficient to move older women into pressuring the woman to clear her conscience and confess any adulterous acts. It is believed that the presence of an adulterer near a sick person may be a fatal contamination. An adulterer runs the risk of serious injury or even death at the husband's hands. In the old days, the wronged husband's lineage would rise and attack the seducer's lineage and a bloody fight might ensue. Today, criminal sanctions as well as compensation, more effectively enforced by modern administrations, have established a more peaceful solution than the traditional methods.[60]

There is a tendency to take the wife's evidence as almost conclusive. The wife is placed under oath if there is a dispute over the facts. The presumption is that her evidence is correct. Theoretically, should she later be proved guilty of perjury by the curse of false oath manifesting itself in illness or death, or should she confess to having given false evidence, she will be purified ritually and the presumed adulterer may then have his cattle of compensation returned. In practice, however, the court will be reluctant to return the compensation.

Alienation of affection is not an actionable wrong, but it may be evidence of an illicit relationship in an adultery action. Those who induce a wife to have wrongful relations with another man or to desert her husband are subject to criminal punishment. Abduction and rape are aggravating circumstances to liability for adultery. In the past, a fight between the adversary kinfolk was inevitable. Today, severe penalties are inflicted upon the culprit, although civil liability is not affected. If the wife is abducted, adultery is strongly presumed, but the amount of compensation is not increased.[61]

Abetting elopement with a married woman is a severe offense which imposes on the abettor a penal sanction and an obligation to look for the eloped parties if their whereabouts are unknown and bring them before the court. This is so even if the abettor is the guardian of one of the eloping parties and desires the dissolution of the existing marriage. In *Gok Aguek v. Mabok and Others*,[62] Gok was married to the daughter of Mabok. After years of married life, Gok's wife deserted her husband and eloped with another man called Miyan. Several times they were caught, Miyan was punished, and the woman was returned to her husband. One time when they were caught, Gok accompanied a policeman sent to summon Miyan. While they were on their way to the court, Miyan insulted Gok as a son of a leper, and a quarrel ensued. To avoid a fight, the policeman told Gok to go separately while he walked with Miyan. Miyan escaped from him, ran to where the woman was, and they eloped again. The policeman then arrested the woman's guardian, Mabok, and his wife on suspicion of abetting the elopement. The court also summoned the relatives of Miyan on the same suspicion. They were tried and found to have instigated the series of elopements in the hope that Gok would divorce the woman and a marriage between her and Miyan could be contracted. The court decided that they all should be detained until the couple reported. It was believed that news of their elders' detention would move the eloped couple into returning. The question of the ultimate punishment to be inflicted on the abettors was left open pending the return of the couple.[63]

The Dinka conception of the nature of adultery suggests certain principles. For instance, although the adulterer may not use the husband's impotence as a defense, the wife is likely to adduce it as a justification for her unfaithfulness. Furthermore, we have seen that the attitude of the husband's kin and the wife's kin is that the wife's procreative power should not be allowed to be dormant. So, if she cannot bear children regularly, she may use this evidence to justify adultery from her point of view.

The fact that sexual activity must be directed toward marital goals means that the husband cannot profit from his wife's affairs. Consequently, if a married woman's morals are such that she is a "loose woman," her husband cannot recover compensation from an adulterer. As Makec notes, "Where a married woman commits adultery for the second time or more, she will be regarded as a loose woman and therefore no cattle will be paid to her husband as damages. At the same time, the law protects the society by removing the temptation on the part of the husband and his wife to make the act of adultery a continuous source of acquisition of wealth."[64]

Adultery can be committed even when the husband is dead. By the custom of levirate, the widow is not at liberty to cohabit with anyone, relative or not, before the genitor is chosen. Sometimes, more so today, a widow is allowed to choose the lover "to enter the hut with"; however, her choice is usually limited to the relatives of her deceased husband. Once the choice is made, the rest of the husband's kinsmen are excluded. If any of them enter into a sexual relationship with her, it is an offense against the legal heir to the wife as the representative of the dead man. It may be that the deceased husband's legal heir delegates the right of cohabitation to another relative with the consent of the widow. The marital rights of a dead husband survive his death, and if a person commits adultery with the widow he is subject to criminal as well as tortuous liability. In *Deng v. Gwiny de Col*[65] a widow of Deng's father was living with a relative, Achwil, by agreement with Deng. Gwiny committed adultery with her. Deng, as the heir, and not Achwil, brought an adultery action against Gwiny. The court sentenced Gwiny to five months' imprisonment and ordered him to pay the traditional compensation of three head of cattle. Howell, then colonial officer in that area, states that the rank of the parties in this case must have influenced the outcome because "it is doubtful that in ordinary circumstances '*arwok*' (compensation) will be enforced against a woman living in 'widow concubinage.'"[66] Of course, there is an increasing tendency today to give the widow more freedom to decide her own destiny, but once she chooses to live in levirate, she is expected to be exclusive. For all intents and purposes the levirate widow has the ordinary matrimonial rights and duties of a wife.

What has been said about levirate is also generally applicable to ghost marriages. The woman is usually chosen by the genitor, he courts her as he will his normal bride, and he performs all the aspects of an ordinary marriage. His relationship with her is therefore more intense and personal than that of levirate. This fact is relevant only to the psychology of the vicarious relationship rather than the substance of the law. The levirate legal principles are theoretically applicable to ghost marriage, even though a genitor may overlook the adultery of his brother's widow more readily than that of his "ghost wife."

Although a blood relationship between the adulterer and the husband might legally be considered as a mitigating factor in adultery, the gravity of the emotional injury to the husband arising from adultery between his wife and his relative is particularly grave and requires special and more substantial redress. The Dinka saying goes: "A wife belongs to the whole kinfolk except in her bedroom."

Makec discusses the ambivalences involved in such situations with nuanced insight into the complexities of the considerations and emotions involved. First, he concedes that: "Because of the strength of social or kinship ties among the Dinka or among African communities in general, it is possible that tortuous acts committed by kinsmen may be tolerated or the degree of reaction against a wrong committed by a relative may be less vigorous, in spite of the degree of bitterness it must have caused." But then he emphasizes the exclusivity of the husband's sexual rights over his wife:

> A man has an absolute right over the sacred parts of his wife. In the Dinka concept, a married woman may be described as the "wife" of all the relatives of her husband in so far as her services are concerned. She may be required to do anything for any relative of her husband, but her private body is never a subject of joint ownership. There are a few exceptions where a man may be permitted to have sex with the wife of his kinsman, for instance, if the husband is impotent. Even this is not always

> possible if the husband refuses it. But the main reason why a relative may be permitted to have sex with the wife of his kinsman is the procreation of children which, as previously stated, is the prime objective of marriage.

Makec is emphatically affirmative on the issue: "Frankly speaking, sex cannot be shared. Blood relationship is not a license for anyone to have sex with a kinsman's wife and expect a less vigorous reaction."[67]

Nevertheless, Makec, viewing the situation from the perspective of shared ownership in the family wealth, which had been contributed by the kin group in the marriage of the woman involved, states:

> There is an element of truth in [the] emphasis upon the closeness of the relationship between husband and adulterer. This point will hold good if, for example, a man goes with his brother's wife or his father's wife. It is a wrong against the whole family which includes the accused. The aggrieved husband, if he is seriously provoked and does not want to forgive his brother or son, may relieve himself by taking a penal action against him. But if he resorts to an action in customary law, he may not expect much, if any, benefit since the property, out of which he will expect the damages to be paid to him, is their common or family property. But if the wrong-doer is, for example, the son of a paternal uncle (i.e. son of one's father's brother), the law is in favor of the aggrieved party, provided the son or his father never made a contribution towards the bride-wealth. However, it is possible that recourse to the legal processes may be waived if the elders intervene to make an appeasement or if relations between the families are very cordial.[68]

The court will give the injured husband one of three choices: a purely legal remedy where the adulterer is ordered to pay the normal compensation *(rwok)*; a family settlement where the adulterer is required to pay compensation in the form of a conciliatory payment *(awec)*; or a spiritual curse where the adulterer is debased and the husband's compensation is the revenge he attains. The matter is normally settled by an assembly of family elders, but the courts may be asked to mediate. The amount of a conciliatory fee varies from case to case. The wrongdoer will usually prefer reconciliation to a legal settlement in the interest of harmony among kinsmen; the plaintiff will also often prefer mediation because he is likely to receive substantially more compensation.

Since betrothal is part of marriage, it is protected in the same way as marriage, and sexual intercourse with a third party gives rise to an action of adultery. In *Deng Ajith v. Maguith*,[69] Deng Ajith was betrothed to a girl by payment of some cattle toward her marriage consideration. Before she was betrothed, the girl had been Maguith's girlfriend. Soon after her betrothal the girl confessed to impregnation by Maguith, and Maguith eloped with her outside the tribe. Thereafter, the girl gave birth to two children by Maguith.

Believing that Deng Ajith would no longer want her, Maguith returned to the tribe with the girl to regularize their union. Deng Ajith sued him, and the court made Maguith pay compensation for adultery and impregnation of a married woman, including the pregnancy which occurred before betrothal. Maguith appealed on the grounds that he had courted the girl with the intention of marrying her long before she was betrothed to Deng Ajith and that, if liable at all, he should at least not be liable in adultery for acts committed before the girl was betrothed. The court held that it was not sufficient to intend to marry; one must in fact pay at least part of the marriage consideration to manifest intention to marry. On the second issue, the relations between Maguith and the girl before formal betrothal were held not to constitute adultery but merely impregnation of an unmarried girl, for which the compensation was less.

Although flirtatious association with a betrothed girl is a criminal offense, certain circumstances may give rise to a defense. In *Dau v. Kwol Kon*,[70] Dau was betrothed to a girl whom Kwol Kon had wanted to marry but whose family had refused Kwol Kon. Subsequently, Dau eloped with a different girl whom he had wanted to marry. When they returned, the girl was taken from him, and the court ordered that, in the absence of cattle with which to compensate her relatives, Dau should deduct some cattle from his betrothal consideration. Although the relatives of the betrothed girl were offended, they decided to maintain the relationship if Dau would increase the marriage consideration (a demand which was not fulfilled at the time of the case). Meanwhile, Kwol Kon maintained his association with the betrothed girl. One day, Dau saw them in company and became so provoked that he attacked and injured Kwol Kon. The court, while conceding that Kwol was liable criminally for courting a betrothed girl, held, nevertheless, that Dau's conduct could mislead a person to think that he had intended to repudiate the betrothal agreement. Because of the peculiar circumstances, no criminal sentence was inflicted upon Kwol Kon – but he was warned to keep away from the girl.

As with abduction of married women, elopement with betrothed girls calls for penal sanctions and raises a presumption of adultery in tort. Every act of elopement creates a new cause of action, as in *Akot Ral v. Lal Ayom*.[71] If the betrothal relationship is broken, any compensation paid for adultery is returned to the girl's relatives. If the dissolution is because of the adultery, it does not count as adultery but as seduction of an unmarried woman. Since confession by girls not yet fully married follows pregnancy, such compensation will be for the impregnation of an unmarried woman, and the girl's relatives will be the people entitled to it, but the prison sentence will not be affected. Thus, in *Col Ajing v. Patal Abdullai*,[72] Col was betrothed and had completed the payment of most of the bride wealth, but the final ceremonies were not yet performed. The girl committed adultery with Patal and became pregnant. Col then repudiated the betrothal. The court sentenced Patal to six months' imprisonment and ordered him to pay the girl's relatives three head

always end in marriage, for the man may lack the required number of cattle and the girl's family may choose to marry her to a wealthier person. When there is no marriage, the man will be made to pay compensation, particularly if he has consummated the relationship, or criminal sanctions may be inflicted instead of damages.

A culprit is better off if he is economically able to marry. Abduction is not so much a wrong in itself as it is a disruption of the vested interests of the girl's family in her marriage opportunities. The procreative prospects are so dominant in all torts relating to an unmarried girl that her own interests are ruthlessly obstructed unless they are conducive to the family goals.

As in the case of seduction, abduction is also on the increase among the Dinkas who migrate into the urban centers to find work. The restrictive order mentioned under seduction applies to abduction: a guardian who permits his daughter to migrate for labor forfeits his right of action. As was said earlier, this order was calculated to be a deterrent to migration, especially of women, and is probably not strictly applied. With mass displacement by war and migration into Northern towns, the situation has radically changed and traditional controls are no longer applicable.

2.4.4 Parties entitled to sue

In sexual wrongs, Dinka law recognizes only the male as the perpetrator. Women are not liable for sexual offenses except socially and morally. This implies that a woman cannot sue another woman for adultery with her husband. The nonliability of women is sometimes explained in terms of male aggressiveness and female vulnerability. As an elder put it, "It is men who lead women in these matters." The Dinka word for adultery is "seeking (another man's wife)," *akor*. However, the Dinka do not deny the fact that a woman can be the aggressive party.

The myth of female vulnerability to male aggressiveness is correlated with the position of males as the primary beneficiaries in procreation, so that any sex violation is considered damage to males by other males. Adultery, seduction, and abduction are all regarded as wrongs against the husband, father, or guardian, respectively. These roles may, of course coincide, in one person – the head of the family. But since the head of the family is the custodian or the principal manager of the family property, whatever benefits him benefits his family. Again, his position may be affected by broader family connections such as the reciprocal interests of the extended family or the kinship.

In the case of adultery, the husband is normally the person entitled to sue. In the cases of levirate and ghost marriage, the genitor – that is the man living with the woman – is entitled to sue. In one case, a genitor in a levirate marriage sued for adultery. He won his case in the court of first instance, which was a tribal court. The adulterer appealed to a higher court in which the judge was a Northern Sudanese Muslim, who dismissed the case on the ground that the woman's husband – the person rightly entitled to sue for adultery – was dead. As a widow, she could not have committed adultery, since she did not have a husband. The case then went to the province judge, who was a Dinka familiar with customary law. He reversed the decision in favor of the levirate husband. He then wrote a note to the Northern judge, which included the sentence, "For your information, a Dinka husband never dies."[77]

In a polygynous family, if the adultery involves a young wife and the husband has a son, the son may bring the action in his father's name.[78] The brother of the husband may recover for adultery in the name of the husband and may take the compensation for himself. In such a case the husband has no further claim. John Makec disputes the view that a son can sue for the adultery of his father's wife (obviously not his own mother) or that the brother of the husband can recover for adultery. In his view, "It is doubtful whether it has ever been part of the law that a son can raise a suit of adultery while his father is still alive … Furthermore, it is also doubtful whether it has ever been part of the law that a husband's brother can sue for *akor* (adultery) and take the cows for himself."[79]

While Makec may be right about Dinka law in general, certain exceptions exist. One example is a case where a chief asked his son to represent him in a case of adultery with his wife, and he indeed represented his father and the compensation went to his father. Since the man accused of adultery was the chief's half-brother, it may well be that he found it humiliating to confront him in court. Makec is probably correct, because even in the case cited it was clearly embarrassing for the son to confront his uncle over a case of adultery with a stepmother. Although I am not aware of any case concerning a brother suing and recovering for adultery with his brother's wife, it is more plausible.

In cases of adultery with betrothed girls, the plaintiff may be the guardian of the injured boy. Compensation may then go to the bridegroom or it may be used by the guardian. In rare cases, a senior widow may sue for the adultery of a junior co-widow or the wife of her son. Such women will have assumed a status of responsibility quite comparable to that of a family head. In cases of wrongs with respect to unmarried women, the guardian of the girl is the person rightly entitled to bring the action. The guardian may be the father or any relative who is allotted the paternal obligations and rights in respect to her marriage.

Whoever pleads the case is not necessarily entitled to take the proceeds to the exclusion of the other members of the family. As there is only one right of action, the family head is the primary beneficiary, but the family may decide how to distribute the compensation. Any disagreement is usually arbitrated in front of the family or kinship elders, or even in front of the chiefs. Serious conflicts may be officially adjudicated.

The association of indemnity with procreation is further illustrated by the fact that the husband, father, or guardian is supposed to dispose of the cattle in marriage or as a gift to a relative. At least, he himself must not drink their milk, eat their butter, meat, or any food produced by them even indirectly, as when a cow is sold and the money used to buy grain.

In the light of Dinka emphasis on procreation as the basis of liability in sex offenses, we may speculate that the plaintiff views the wrongful act primarily as a violation of his procreative rights in a woman demanding material indemnification, rather than as an alienation of her affections, which is too emotionally injurious to be soothed by compensation. This is particularly so if his wife has already fulfilled the role of procreation. We have seen that mutual "love" in the Western sense is not a prerequisite to Dinka marriage. Consequently, the fact that a wife has been unfaithful does not necessarily imply the insult that her husband has failed to maintain her affection. His marriage success is proved by the mere fact of having children. If he is betrayed during betrothal, he could not yet have been a failure. This notion is supported by the fact that where a man is impotent or sterile and cannot produce children, he will normally avoid litigation so as not to advertise his failure in marriage. Even if he insists on suing, he might be denied remedy. The same may be said of seduction and other sexual torts relating to unmarried women. Such torts are regarded as resulting in the reduction of the girl's marriage value in terms of the amount of bride wealth obtainable. With this economic possibility is linked the chances of maintaining the male line.

2.4.5 Vicarious liability

Among the Dinka, the ultimate ownership of family property is vested in the head of the family. He is responsible for indemnifying for torts committed by any member of his family. Although his wife and children are protected against extremely unreasonable conduct leading to their deprivation, and although he will normally consult them, the powers of the head of the family in respect to property are almost unqualified.

The head of a family is considered the guardian of his unmarried brothers if their father is dead. Similarly, a man may assume guardianship of his dead brother's unmarried children and will be considered responsible for their torts.

The emphasis on the family as an agency for procreation has the effect that capacity is determined by marriage. Once a man is married, the status of matrimony bestows upon him full capacity with rights and obligations. Male children, as long as they are unmarried and attached to the parents' home, are regarded as minors. The parents are supposed to control and protect them, and a child's bad behavior is attributable to the parents. The cause of action itself may be against the child; but once the child is held liable, the father is ordered to pay for the damage and may be compelled to do so. Cases where the father refuses to pay seldom arise. Where a child has become particularly notorious or has hopelessly and deliberately failed to observe his duties to his father, the relationship may be severed – provided the child is old enough to be emancipated or another relative is willing to assume his protection. The severance is done by ritually breaking grasses in front of the chief. After severance, the father will be asked to give the son his due share of property, and for all legal purposes they cease to be father and son. Such extreme measures are detested and will rarely be allowed.

The relations between a married son and his parents are by no means entirely severed. If the parents are old and with insufficient means, he must support them and assume responsibility where they cannot discharge it. The child also inherits his dead parents' liability, as was the case in *Chol v. Ring Aguer*.[80]

The situation is different for girls. Women remain in a position of dependence forever. An unmarried woman, just as her male counterpart, lives under the control and protection of her own kin group until marriage. Marriage conveys her control and protection to her husband and his kin, and it is he and they who benefit from rights and incur liabilities connected with her. The scope of the family varies with the nature of the liability. Only the head of the immediate family will be responsible for minor torts of the members, but cases of homicide will require the contribution of the entire kinfolk.

2.4.6 Intrafamily liability

The solidarities in the Dinka family preclude any tort liability between family members. Children are considered a projection of their father's personality and the wife is a means to that end. All unite to form one legal entity in the person of the father. Generally, therefore, the spouses cannot sue each other, nor children their parents, nor brothers and sisters one another. This is not to say that disputes do not arise within the family, but whatever conflicts arise, they are normally settled as family matters, even if by the courts.

Should there be matrimonial complaints between spouses concerning minor injustices, they are usually referred to elderly kinfolk who act as mediators. In more serious cases, however, a wife's own family will come to her assistance. Thus, in matrimonial cases like divorce on grounds of impotence, cruelty, or neglect, her kin will assist her in the action against her husband. Indeed, the case is normally between the respective kin groups rather than the spouses, although a wife may sue alone. However, it is uncommon for Dinka courts to entertain ordinary suits brought by one spouse against another.

Domestic disputes between parents and children commonly arise when a male child seeks to establish his rights. It is considered admirably courageous for a son to face his father about his rights as he sees them, and the senior relatives of the family will always be quick to appreciate the son's claim and support him. If the family elders fail to settle the dispute and it proceeds to court, they will aid the son if they find him in the right – and the father is likely to be defeated. Should the son be found in the wrong by the council of elders or by the court, he will be reprimanded severely and made to submit to his father's authority.

Disputes between children are very unlikely during their father's lifetime, since any claims they may have are directed against and to the father as the manager of the family. In a polygynous family, however, there are often conflicts that materialize upon the father's death. Here again, senior kin members are consulted and their advice is usually persuasive. If reconciliation cannot be effected, the case is taken to court for further mediation. It is important to keep in mind that intrafamily disputes over reciprocal family rights and obligations are connected with aid in marriage payment and maintenance; they are not in the nature of tort actions. These familial causes are usually settled by arbitration, but the court may legally enforce a settlement.

3. Law of Defamation

Although respect has a pervasive significance in law, I select defamation to illustrate some of the major aspects of the legal expression of respect. The goals of permanent identity and influence, with correlations of unity and harmony, can only be approximated in an atmosphere of mutual respect. Permanent identity and influence is directly linked with the maintenance and the perpetuation of a good name. Respect for a man's name is part of his immortality. Members of society owe each other the duty not to "spoil" another man's name, and defamation is a serious matter. Because of the family orientation of Dinka society, anything that degrades a man threatens to reflect on his family and the gravity of the offense is largely determined by the descent and the generational factors involved, with the result that defamation is graver the higher the stratification of descent and age.[1] In relation to women, its seriousness is greatest in situations of in-law relations. Among the warrior youth, personal imputations are hardly recognized as defamatory, but what is basically personal may still bring shame on a descent group, as when a man is accused of theft or indecent practices. Most insulting to the name of descent groups are those statements that directly touch on ancestors.

In the past, defamatory utterances led to breach of the peace – especially by the youth of the descent groups involved. Today, they are normally brought to court where civil or criminal measures, or both, may be taken against the wrongdoer, but the youth still resort to violence. Defamation is a matter that the Dinka do not ignore and, however trifling the matter, the court will take corrective measures. The name of the complainant does not have to be spoiled; as long as it could have been spoiled by what was said, an action will be taken. Thus, it is not essential that people believe the accusation or alter their attitude toward the defamed.[2]

Generally, the defendant's intention is immaterial, but in certain circumstances relief may be refused on the ground that, considering the status and the relationship of the parties, no defamation exists. It is, for instance, customary that members of an age-set, especially young men, jokingly insult one another. There is often a competition in such insults, and one tries to be creative and amusing in ridiculing the adversary; the audience, by laughter or the like, acts as umpire. Where it has been habitual to insult playfully and nothing unusual happens to change this understanding, the court will dismiss the action. This is presumably because no breach of the peace is expected, nor is the name "spoilable" while a game of creativity, distortion, and hyperbole is being played. Should the particular occasion be unsuitable, such as among strangers, or people with whom the plaintiff, to the knowledge of the defendant, has a special respect relationship (e.g. in-laws), or if the insults are made in such a way that they are likely to be taken seriously by the listeners, the defendant will be held liable.

3.1 Modes of defamation

The mode of defamation is significant in assessing its magnitude. Depending on the circumstances in which the defamatory statements were uttered, the Dinka speak of direct imputations, imputations by way of "gossip," and imputations through songs.[3]

3.1.1 Direct imputations

Direct imputations are those directly addressed to the person defamed, and have been witnessed by a third party. This form of defamation is considered grave because it is likely to cause a breach of the peace. It is immaterial that the imputation is not about the person addressed, as long as it is about a person related to him so as to justify his indignation. Nor is the plaintiff necessarily the person addressed. A relative who is defamed by such a statement may bring an action, but there is only one cause of action. The statement does not have to be specific, as long as it brings or is feared to bring shame or embarrassment to the person addressed or to those about whom it is made. Such statements as "If I insult you, you will cry" have been held to be defamatory. Direct defamation is so serious that, even where the wrong is trifling, the court will at least award nominal damages, inflict a nominal penalty, or reprimand the defendant and warn him against such conduct.

3.1.2 Defamation by gossip

Defamation may arise out of repeating a defamatory statement to someone other than the person to whom it was addressed, or to the defamed person himself, or it may be an original statement to a person other than the one defamed. These may be somewhat arbitrarily called "gossip." For repetition to give rise to a cause of action, it must be *male fides* and unprivileged. When a person hears a defamatory statement, he should not repeat it except in court as a witness or to a person to whom he owes a duty. For instance, in marriage, a father refusing his consent because of things he has heard about the girl's family may repeat that information to his son. A person may report anything to the chief that is a threat to security and order. Where a person, provoked by a statement about another, repeats it to someone else in condemnation of the person who originally made the statement, or in support of the person defamed, he is considered acting in good faith. He might, however, be told that the situation is better served by silence. It is no defense that the statement has been accurately repeated, but if the statement is distorted, the offense is aggravated.

Generally, repetitions to persons other than the defamed are not likely to cause a breach of the peace. However, word may eventually reach the defamed person and a breach of the peace may result. Thus, a repeater both defames a person and instigates breach of the peace. Where the repetition is made to the defamed person, the defendant is deemed directly responsible for any breach of the peace that may ensue. A particularly detested person is one who gossips with both sides. He might be encouraging the defendant to confide in him in order to inform the plaintiff. Apart from being civilly and criminally liable, he will be hated, shunned, or ridiculed. An original statement constitutes a less serious defamation than repetition. While a person who repeats what he hears is also to blame, first utterance is single defamation.

3.1.3 Defamation through song

Defamation through song is aggravated by the fact that it is addressed to the society as a whole. Defamatory songs may be women's songs, ox songs, age-set insult songs, war songs, or other types of songs. In *Macok and Maguith Malual v. Matiok Nyok*,[4] Macok's brother, Maguith, wanted to marry a girl in whom Matiok was also interested. Maguith's relatives betrothed the girl to him. Matiok, who was wealthier than the brothers, decided to compete in marriage and paid more cattle to the girl's relatives than they had given. Provoked by Matiok's attitude, Macok and Maguith composed songs imputing tuberculosis to Matiok's family. Matiok retaliated by composing songs imputing "evil eye" to Macok and Maguith's family. The two brothers then brought a case in defamation against Matiok, who pleaded provocation by defamation. The court held them all guilty of defamation and fined them. No one was compensated. Defamation through songs acquires its widest dimension in age-set insult songs and war songs, which often provoke violence between age-sets and territorial units.

3.2 Objects of defamation

The object of defamation is the person against whom a defamatory statement is made, usually the plaintiff himself or his relative. Groups may be involved through individuals or directly in different degrees according to the nature of the imputation and the status of the person against whom it is made. Whether the imputation is against the plaintiff personally, his relatives, or his group, age and descent are important factors in determining the gravity of the offense.

Although personal insinuations against the plaintiff may lead to a breach of the peace, the fact that they do not touch on descent makes them less serious than imputations against relatives or families that implicate the plaintiff as a member of the group. Thus, if a young man is insulted as a thief or accused of indecent conduct, the defamation is basically against him individually. In *Wol Miyan v. Mareng*,[5] Mareng was enamored of Wol's girlfriend but she did not return his love. Hostility developed between the two men and Mareng accused Wol of seducing the girl in the forest. In the trial that followed, Mareng admitted his statement to be false. He was held liable for defaming both the plaintiff and the girl, and was sentenced to three months' imprisonment.

Imputations relating to inherited diseases such as leprosy and tuberculosis are fundamentally connected with descent. Witchcraft and evil eye are also linked with descent. Imputations of this nature may be alleged against the plaintiff himself, his relative, or the descent group. In the case of a senior member, not only is the family defamed, but, in addition, the rule against abusing anyone who is senior in age or rank is also violated. The person defamed need not be a living member of the family. The logic of maintaining the name of a dead man means that he can be defamed in death. Furthermore, permanent identity and influence means that his defamation implicates his living relatives, and the more senior he is, the graver the offense.

The interdependence of the individual, his relatives, and the underlying principles of lineal continuity are illustrated by *Juac v. Mior Col*.[6] Juac gave Mior a goat to satisfy a debt. Subsequently, Mior married a girl related to Juac. According to custom, if a man owns property that once belonged to his fiancée's relative, that relative may reclaim the property as part of marriage consideration, even though he might not have shared in the distribution of the bride wealth in normal circumstances. Juac reclaimed the goat. Mior insulted Juac by saying that, as he was not marrying Juac's mother but only a distant relative, he was not willing to return it. Juac was provoked and answered that it was the same reckless talk which had made Mior's father a very repulsive and lonely man all his life. Mior retaliated, "If I insult you, you will cry." Juac asked what that insult could be. Mior said Juac will be better off not hearing it. Juac answered, "You cannot compare yourself with me; none of our lineage has ever had an evil eye." Mior said that he could not see how Juac could be better than him when his father had died of starvation. Juac then brought action on defamation. The members of the court, who had known the fathers of both parties, expressed indignation at their assertions. Both were sentenced to eight months' imprisonment, commuted on appeal to fines.

Defamation touching on descent groups, whether directly or through individual members, is a much more serious offense than personal defamation because it affects a wider range of people. If a grandfather is said to have leprosy or tuberculosis, for instance, his grandchildren are affected. This partially explains why it is more serious to defame an elderly man or woman.

There are many imputations against groups that are not taken seriously and rarely give rise to litigation. A man may sing against maltreatment by the police, tax collectors, clan heads, or court members with impunity, depending on the generality of the defamation and the degree of group spirit it is likely to arouse. If the subtribal chiefs are insulted as a group, partly because of their small number, but mainly because of the sensitivity of the society to their integrity, the chances are that the wrongdoer will be convicted.

Because of the violent disposition of warrior age-sets, group defamation is serious among them. Within the subtribe, a senior warrior set composes songs defamatory of a junior age-set, either about individual members or about the group. This is one of the usual causes of inter-age-set fights within the subtribe, but it is so institutionalized that it is hardly ever litigated. Age-set sensitivity to defamation becomes acute in subtribal situations. Subtribal identity rotates around unity behind the territorial chiefs and the age-set system. Competition is most dramatic between the corresponding age-sets of the different subtribes. Defamatory war songs are often a cause of subtribal wars. There have been recent administrative attempts to discourage such songs. When a song is obviously defamatory of another subtribe, it is forbidden in war dances. This has induced an attempt to disguise the insults. A typical example is where the age-set of one subtribe hunts and kills a wild animal, after which the adversary age-set is named. The adversary then composes insulting songs about the animal, exaggerating incidents that had occurred in a prior war with the enemy subtribe. As representative of a territorial group, an age-set is provoked by songs defaming them not only as individuals but also their chief or elder.[7]

Age-set defamation does not always take place through songs, nor is it necessarily by groups. Any conduct may constitute a group insult and as long as the individual responsible for it is seen as a member of a group, indignation may be aroused against his group.

3.3 Publication to a third party

The Dinka say that until recently a statement did not constitute a cause of action in defamation unless it was heard by a third party, *neen*.[8] *Neen* must actually have heard the statement from the defendant. Where there was no *neen*, the court maintained that the plaintiff, by complaining to the court, had defamed himself.

The basis of this requirement is uncertain. The maintenance of a name implies that one's name is known in society, and the name cannot be "spoiled" without the society hearing the defamatory information. On the other hand, it may be argued that, in most cases, the defendant's allegation implies his knowledge or at least his belief that the allegation is founded. This is not substantially different from the third party hearing the statement. Where the defendant makes an original statement knowing that it is false but calculating to shame the plaintiff, the plaintiff's name does not suffer unless the statement is heard by a third party. The requirement of *neen* has recently been made evidentiary rather than necessary. Only if the defendant denies making the statement is *neen* required.

3.4 The defense of justification

The use of justification as a defense requires that the defendant maintain or show sufficient reason for having made the defamatory statement. It is particularly concerned with the truth of the statement.[9] Dinka law has no rigid rules about using justification as a defense, but whether truth is a defense or not depends on the necessity to protect society by revealing the truth. Legal or moral guilt requires verification. But where the imputed evil does not endanger society, justification will not be allowed as a defense. We illustrate the first category with theft and the second with tuberculosis and leprosy.

For example, it is considered important to identify thieves because they are dangerous to society and must be punished. To facilitate this, truth is a defense. In the case of tuberculosis and leprosy, there is no legal or moral guilt attached to them to require punishment. Yet, the knowledge of their existence makes one's reputation suffer seriously. It may be argued that it is in the interest of the society that such diseases be exposed in order to be avoided. However, the Dinka do not believe they are contagious. They are thought to be hereditary. For this reason, there is a defense of privilege where a father or anyone *in loco parentis* imputes such diseases to dissuade his child from marrying into a family afflicted with them. The argument could be pushed further so that, for the relatives to know and avoid marrying into such families, it is expedient that the diseases be exposed. Here, there is a balance of gain and loss. A person interested in marrying is expected to make a thorough study of the family he wants to marry into, but in a small society there is no need for unnecessary exposition to learn about people. The loss for the families accused of such diseases will be much greater than the interest of the society in terms of marriage.

3.5 The defense of privilege

The defense of privilege exempts the defendant from liability on the grounds that he made the statement in the performance of a duty, whether this duty is political, judicial, social, or personal. As in justification, the Dinka have no definite principles about privilege as a defense. A person *in loco parentis* is permitted to inform his ward of any mortal diseases in the lineage of his or her intended spouse. What is said in good faith or in the interest of the plaintiff is also privileged. Furthermore, in court, defamatory statements are repeated in the interest of justice.

Privilege must be exercised sparingly. It is said that a person should avoid making the defamatory statement in the course of duty unless he cannot discharge it otherwise. Good faith and the plaintiff's interest as defenses are interpreted narrowly. When songs, especially group songs, are repeated in court, security measures must be taken to prevent the outbreak of violence.

3.6 Redress against defamation

The form of redress varies with the nature of the defamatory matter and the relationship of the parties. Here, we classify defamatory matter into imputations other than wrongs and those of wrongs. Relationship classifies parties into relatives and nonrelatives. Those who are senior in status compose a special category. When a person is defamed, he complains to the chief, who summons the alleged wrongdoer. In the trial the plaintiff restates his claim. Where the defamatory matter is contained in a song, the court may direct that the song be sung in court.[10]

Since imputations other than wrongs often concern diseases like leprosy and tuberculosis, it is considered undesirable to investigate the truth of the imputation. In the past, however, the plaintiff took an oath and denied the allegation before the defendant was held liable. It is said that the reason for this was merely to exonerate the plaintiff. It did not imply recognition of truth as a defense. In practice, it seems to have made truth a defense; only those who knew that the imputation was false will litigate, since litigation itself caused wider publication.[11] The oath having been taken, the court usually levied conciliatory compensation, *awec*, payable in cattle. *Kueng*, a ceremony of reconciliation, was then carried out by the chief in court. By this ceremony, the chief willed that misfortune should fall upon the party who will initiate further conflict.

The requirement of oath-taking has now been abolished. If it is proven that the statement had been made, then the defendant is held liable. Instead of conciliatory compensation (which is still maintained in special circumstances, such as where the parties are relatives or the plaintiff is a chief) a prison sentence is now imposed. Imputations of wrongs call for a different treatment. Examples of such wrongs are the possession of an "evil eye," *peeth*, and theft. When a person is accused of an evil eye, the accusation is usually associated with his lineage. The liability of the defendant is contingent on the plaintiff's proving that he knows of no evil eye in his lineage. In the past he did this through an ordeal called *lau*, by which he picked up a stone from the bottom of a pot of boiling water or oil. The belief was that only if he was wrong would he be burned. This obviously put the plaintiff at grave risk and it is not known how often it was used to prove the facts or if only to intimidate those seriously suspected. In any case, it is doubtful that the ordeal was widely applied or that people suspected of *peeth* would sue for defamation.

According to Makec, society had an interest in exposing *peeth*, which the Dinka believe poses danger to innocent people: "*Wuuth* or *peeth* is the power and the person alleged to possess it is called *wuth* or *apeth*. The wuth or *apeth* is believed to have the power of killing others with his or her eyes or by staring at them and this, according to the belief, is inherited." Makec argues that a person who complains about being defamed as a *wuth* or *apeth* cannot benefit from the fact that such power is not scientifically provable. "What amounts to defamation should be understood according to the belief of the local population. Hence, although I do not believe that there are people possessing such power, I submit that imputation of *wuuth* or *peeth* to one of the families locally believed to possess such power does not amount to defamation." It is, however, more appropriate that it is the defendant in this case who is supposed to take oath that his accusation is true. He may also call witnesses who will support his case. But a statement constitutes defamation if it is published against a member of a family who is not locally known to have such powers.[12]

Theft among the Dinka is very rare and when it occurs the offender is subjected to severe sanctions. To accuse an individual of theft alerts the society of a grave offense and defames the accused if not true. Traditionally, once theft was alleged, the age-set of the alleged offender would seize his personality ox or, if a woman, her brother's personality ox, a symbol of a man's identity and dignity, as a way of compelling the culprit to clear his or her name and therefore theirs, or as a punishment if he or she actually committed the offense. If the alleged thief desired to clear his or her name, his or her age-set joined in the proceedings against the person accusing him or her. The court would then investigate the truth of the statement. If the plaintiff won the case, he or she was compensated by both the age-set and the defendant, and his or her age-set was entitled to an ox from the defendant. If the plaintiff lost, then, apart from the general ostracism from society, the brutal skewering of his personality ox by his age-set remained uncorrected as a punishment. There was no imprisonment. However small the object alleged to have been stolen, the consequences were the same. Where the age-set had no reason to believe that their member had committed theft, they would refrain from seizing his personality ox and might even initiate proceedings against the person making the allegation on the grounds that a personal defamation of an age-mate amounts to age-set defamation.

The introduction of modern criminal proceedings and the weakening of the age-set system have affected the consequences of alleging theft. Age-set seizure of a personality ox is discouraged and made contingent on proof of theft. During the defamation suit that follows, truth will be a defense and will, when proved, entitle the age-set to seize the plaintiff's personality ox. The defendant is also made to compensate the plaintiff and the age-set for the insult.

The relationship of the parties may affect the nature of damages payable to a successful plaintiff and may also determine whether imprisonment is more appropriate. Where the parties are relatives, conciliatory compensation is the most appropriate. Since the objective is to reconcile the relatives, such compensation is payable even in cases which might otherwise be justifiable. In such cases, no imprisonment is imposed on the wrongdoer. It is said that by the defamation of a relative, the defendant has also defamed himself. This is especially true in cases of imputations essentially associated with descent.

When the parties are not related, imprisonment or fine, or analogous sanction, such as payment of an ox to the plaintiff's age-set, is imposed. The defendant may request that he be allowed to make conciliatory payment and be reconciled with the plaintiff. The court may permit this, but the amount will be much higher than is normal. In practice, the descent orientation of the society does not make conciliation between nonrelatives imperative. Relatives, being in more intense interaction, must be more united and in harmony to lead normal lives.

4. Law of Property

Wealth permeates Dinka law. It is central to livelihood and a means of satisfying claims by way of damages or fines as well as the law of contract. In this section we discuss Dinka concepts of wealth acquisition and rights of ownership, the institution of bride wealth, the law of inheritance, contractual arrangements relating to barter and sale, custody of livestock, and the offense of theft. Although the institution of blood wealth is one of the fundamental aspects of the interaction of wealth and the law and has much in common with bride wealth for purposes of perpetuation, it is better left to the section on well-being since it is primarily retributive rather than a means of wealth distribution.

4.1 Acquisition and rights of ownership

The Dinka recognize the concept of ownership as distinct from limited rights, such as possession. The nature of ownership, conditioned by the cumulative interests inherent in the principle of perpetual identity and influence, is both collective and individual in a hierarchical sense. This fact must not blur the distinction drawn between ownership and limited rights, though it also limits the rights of ownership.

The Dinka do not have a single word for the English word "ownership." Instead, they use such expressions as "It is mine," "It is yours," "It is ours," or "It is theirs." A Dinka can dispose of that which is his at will, subject to any limited claims there might be from others. A cow might, for example, have been pledged as security for a debt, or paid as betrothal wealth, pending the completion of marriage.[1]

Because of the collective-individual nature of agnatic acquisition and rights of ownership, a man may say, "It is mine" when his claim to it is part of a wider common claim. Thus, if a son of a component family unit speaks of cattle allotted to his mother as "his," his claim to ownership is to be seen in the light of his father's overriding claims, which must in turn be seen in the light of ancestral claims. Being the highest worldly owner, the patriarch has greater effective control over wealth than his dead superiors.[2]

That ownership is recognized as distinct from limited rights is obvious in that a Dinka will not say, "It is mine" where he is keeping another person's property either as security for a debt, as betrothal wealth, or in similar situations. A man will rather say that it is a cow of "a debt," or "marriage," or "custody," or merely of a named person. An owner will say, "It is mine" even if the property is in someone else's possession.[3]

The hierarchic structure of ownership means that the Dinka concept of ownership is more limited than the Western concept. This is especially the case with land, which, because of its immovability and its closer association with ancestors, is more in line with lineal continuity than movable property. In discussing acquisition and rights of ownership, therefore, we should treat land, livestock, and other types of property separately.

4.1.1 Land

The land of the Dinka was originally occupied either by peaceful settlement where there were no prior inhabitants or by conquest.[4] In their migrations, the Dinka were led by members of dominant clans whose lineages founded (and still hold) tribal or sectional chieftainships. The conquering leader in a tribe distributed land among his original followers and thereby formed the subtribes. The heads of these subtribes re-divided the land among their internal groups, and so on, according to the segmentation for which the Nilotic society is known. Thus, rights in land, grazing, and fishing and drinking pools are held by the descendants of the original settlers of the area. Those who followed only acquire rights by association with these lineages. This is not of much practical significance today. So complicated and intricate are the problems associated with land tenure that to use words like "ownership" loosely is futile.

Today, every Dinka has the right to settle and cultivate a piece of land, provided that it has not been occupied by any other person. Grazing areas are usually used by the members of the section in common. These areas may be near residential land, or may be in the far-off *toc* or *gok* where only young men and women go with cattle.

As various rights to land are vested in a hierarchy of social and political institutions, the nature of interests in real property is complex. Although the individual member of the community is relatively free to acquire land subject to territorial division, theoretical control, at least, is vested in the chief. It is he who allocates land to newcomers; it is he who protects the land against outsiders; and it is he who by virtue of divine power controls elements conducive or destructive to production (such as rain, birds, or locusts). He should not eat of new crops until he thanks God and ancestral spirits through a ceremony called *mioc piny*, "offering to the land," which, though observed by every family, is most elaborate and festive in the chief's family.

The control of the chief over land is minimal with respect to members of his tribe. There is no need for allocation among them, since land is abundant and there is land for everyone to occupy without friction. Disputes about boundaries do, of course, arise, but they are often solved by local headmen. Only those concerning sectional grazing areas reach the head chief.

In whatever manner the possession of arable or residential land is acquired, a man and his family have the exclusive right to use that land. It is passed from generation to generation. In a compound family, each house, with co-wives, owns and cultivates certain fields collectively. Each of the co-wives usually has her own plot of land. In such polygynous families, the head usually has cattle byres and fields that are commonly owned by the family; in addition, each wife within the family has her own huts and fields with her children and dependent co-wives. The husband cannot interfere with these.

The right of the individual over his land is so strong that even if abandoned the land must be kept unoccupied unless he consents to its use by another occupant. A long-abandoned area is still referred to by the name of the owner who had once occupied it. Even if someone else is allowed to use the unoccupied land in the absence of the owner, on the owner's return it must be surrendered to him. Continuous use is not a prerequisite to maintaining ownership.[5]

In Dinka law no one can sell land. Land has strong religious significance, particularly the link with ancestral spirits and clan divinities. Objects sacrificed to God, ancestors, or divinities are offered to the earth, or to the river for the spirits of the water. Land can therefore not be evaluated in material terms alone. By analogy, cattle dedicated to God or spirits cannot be alienated in any way except in marriage and similar considerations of perpetuation. Furthermore, although a piece of arable land may be known as the land of someone, all of the relatives of that person have potential or actual interests in the land that qualify the person's ownership and right of alienation.

Huts and cattle byres can be sold. In such cases they are either dismantled and their rafters and grass used for building elsewhere, or they are used where they stand on the understanding that when they fall the purchaser must leave. In Dinka law, houses are not real property.

The individual can, however, make a gift of his land to a member of his group. Any change of residence from one section to another must be with the permission of the chiefs of the sections concerned and of the head chief. Since family and lineage members tend to live together for defense purposes, and since intrusion by anyone outside the group may be resented, gifts of land are made either to close relatives or to neighbors who have become affiliated with the group. Such gifts may be for short or indefinite terms, but normally the owner has the right to reclaim the land at any time, subject to the rights of the donee over the fruits of his labor, even if still attached to the land, as in the case of crops before harvest. In Dinka law, crops are not real property.

4.1.2 Livestock

The customs governing cattle differ from those relating to land. Whereas rights in land are more communal in nature, ownership of cattle is more personal. Such ownership is vested in the head of the family, subject to the use of family members. Cattle are allocated by the pater, according to the seniority of the houses. Within a house, cattle are re-divided among the individual wives. Any cattle that are not allocated by the head of the household are the collective property of the family. The sons of each house inherit from their father the cattle under their control. While the father is alive, neither the wives nor the children can dispose of cattle without his consent. The means by which the individual acquires cattle is often connected with his kinship. The cow comes to him through the kinship structure and will be paid to some kinsmen in discharging an obligation or will be passed on in marriage.

The manner in which a person acquires cattle corresponds to his reciprocal obligations to his kinsmen. Cattle are in constant circulation. A man receives cattle from marriage only to dispose of them in marriage; he gets help from a relative or a friend only to return the favor another time. A Dinka will refer to his own cattle as "cattle of my grandfather" or "cattle of my father," another demonstration of the lineal attributes of acquisition. Akin to bride wealth is blood wealth. In both cases, the cattle are contributed and distributed among relatives within the lineage and the family.

In the distribution of what are known as personality oxen – castrated bulls used for aesthetic or artistic display – there is a significant custom by which each son is allocated a color pattern, *kit*, according to the seniority of his mother and a known hierarchy of color patterns. The eldest son of the first wife gets the most senior color pattern.[6] When a bull calf is born from a cow belonging to any member of the family, or when it comes to the family as marriage consideration, the son whose color pattern it bears will claim it. The color patterns are so intricate among the Dinka that frequent litigation centers on their determination. Although the allocation of a color pattern is determined by birth, it is officially effective when a young man is initiated. From his color pattern he derives his ox name, *mior*, by which he is known and addressed. Apart from its proprietary significance, the color pattern becomes a symbol of a man's identity and social position.

The fact that kinship is the normal source of acquisition does not exclude individual ownership; rather, it strengthens the individual's sense of obligation toward his kinsmen. For practical purposes a person can dispose of his cattle without the consent of the dependent members of his family, but in the exercise of his powers he is governed by his obligations toward his kinsmen. There has recently been a general tendency among the Dinka to individualize their self-acquired property, so much so that courts have had to enforce kinship obligations, a necessity which would have been regarded as scandalous in the past.

There has been some recent regulation of the sale of cattle. Registration must be made with the market clerk in any sale. The purpose is to trace the seller in case his title is subsequently questioned and to trace the cow should the buyer lose it and it returns to the seller.

4.1.3 Other personal property

The ownership of personal property other than livestock, unless it is of spiritual or ritual significance – such as a sacred spear – is rarely a matter of claims in Dinka courts. It is in this field that ownership in its ordinary sense is least limited by perpetuity. However, even here kinship claims are strong, depending on the parties' positions in the lineal hierarchy. Dr. Farran cites the present writer on the effect of marriage on a woman's property.

> Evidence suggests that among the Ngok Dinka at least the harsh old English rule applies: a bride's beads or other trinkets or pieces of household equipment (whatever small property she has) are ostentatiously taken from her by her husband after the marriage ceremony and given to her mother-in-law or a senior wife (if such there be).[7]

According to Dr. Farran, this is "to show that she is in subjection to her husband's wishes, in this, as in other matters." One may add that it is not merely a question of subjection to the husband, but also a symbolic action emphasizing the group spirit embodied in the principle of permanent identity and influence. The bride's property is given to another wife, and she is given new property or that of another wife. Ideally, what a man acquires is that of his father, brother, or any other relative. Similarly, the property of a father belongs to a son, though in subordination to his father.

Giving to a kinsman what one acquires is balanced by receiving what a kinsman acquires. While the process of counterclaims by kinsmen is continuous, and common interest in the property is encouraged by the kinship source of acquisition, individual identity in ownership is marked. Although the acquisition and rights of ownership of personal property other than livestock are less complex than those of more valuable kinds of property, they are governed by the identical group–individual combination.

4.2 Bride wealth

The Dinka family is founded on bride wealth, which must be paid in cattle. Its payment before, accompanying, or after the marriage ceremonies is *a sine qua non* to the validity of marriage and the legitimate claim to children. Any marriage in which the bride wealth is not paid in cattle is not treated as valid in the eyes of the law. Where money or anything else is paid by the bridegroom or his relatives to the bride's parents or relatives during the engagement, it is not usually treated as part of the bride wealth; it is treated as a gift only.[8] Misconception of its meaning has led some people to consider bride wealth in purely economic terms. It has been given the misnomer "bride price" to indicate that marriage is the sale and purchase of the bride and her potential offspring.[9]

4.2.1 The nature of bride wealth

Bride wealth is central to the value-system and, in accordance with the stratification involved, has implications that tend to lower the status of women. But this is different from the assertion that every transaction of marriage represents a sale. Rather, it is perceived as an honor, and the greater the amount of the bride wealth, the greater the honor. Many songs by both men and women praise female agnates through whose marriages men acquired their personality oxen. The ox may be referred to as the ox of the girl for whose bride wealth it was paid, and she is praised for possessing the virtues that attracted the man to marry her. Jean Buxton observed that "Girls like to be married for a lot of cattle, and will boast about this. Cattle reflect the girl's value, her beauty and social position, intelligence, popularity and so forth; ugly and inferior girls cannot command many cattle. A girl likes to do better than her age-mates and see their envy."[10] Admittedly, the mere fact that the higher the bride wealth, the higher the status attached to a woman, does not mean that she has not been purchased. However, the implications of bride wealth are different from those of purchase. Marriage binds the two families or bodies of kin among whom the bride wealth is collected and distributed.[11] This link may even survive a divorce and the woman's return to her kin. In any case, a woman cannot be considered "sold" if, as happens, her kin retain the right to protect her if her husband should mistreat her. Furthermore, the family of the bride has to make a counter-payment equal to approximately one-third of the bride wealth.

This suggests that bride wealth is more complex than an economic institution; it has a legal significance, which permeates the kinship system. First, it legalizes the union between man and woman with the primary objective of establishing the legal paternity of the offspring. Second, it brings together formerly unrelated groups and gives emphasis and legality to their reciprocal obligations. Third, it stabilizes the marriage. If the girl or her relatives are responsible for the failure of the marriage, they are expected to return the bride wealth promptly, with certain reductions for children. Since the cattle will have been distributed far and wide, this is a task to be avoided. If the man is at fault, he forfeits his cattle unless the woman is remarried to someone who can afford to compensate him. Since his cattle will have multiplied, it is difficult to compensate a former husband. If he has sufficient wealth for another marriage and does not need the return of his cattle, he might better be a polygynist than divorce. If he can not afford marriage without the return of his cattle, then to divorce is to abandon the only hope for progeny. Divorce is therefore very rare. Fourth, bride wealth is a compensation for the loss of a member. When a woman is married, her lineage loses her and her contribution to their value maximization. Bride wealth compensates them, and introduces them to wider circles and other compensatory values through these circles. It makes it possible for her brother or other agnates to marry. It is in this sense that bride wealth and blood wealth are correlative. But it is important to qualify this identification of the compensatory nature of bride wealth and blood wealth. While the former is primarily a means of wealth distribution, and the loss which necessitates compensation is self-imposed for other supposedly more beneficial purposes, the latter is an externally imposed deprivation of a punitive nature. In a way then, it parallels other compensations for injury. Fifth, by including in the bride wealth cattle dedicated to the man's ancestral spirits, and by giving the woman's ancestral spirits their share in the bride wealth through dedication, the dead are symbolically linked with the living, and their blessing is secured.

4.2.2 Participation in bride wealth collection

The collection of bride wealth is the task of the bridegroom or his father with the help of kinsmen on his father's and mother's sides, as well as of in-laws. The assistance is reciprocal, so that, generally speaking, those who give are the same who will receive in a reverse situation. Between friends of a special contractual category, there is also a reciprocal understanding to assist in each other's marriages. Reciprocity is nowadays enforced by the Chiefs' court.

The standardized contributors in bride wealth collection include: the "father," as the elder in charge of the marriage is called, and he need not be the real father, though the real father often contributes the bulk of the bride wealth; paternal uncle, who may be the "father" appointed to arrange the marriage with the obligations of the normal father also makes a substantial contribution; maternal uncle, who is expected to pay at least a lactating cow with its calf; paternal aunt, in effect her husband, who is expected to pay a lactating cow with its cow calf; maternal aunt, in effect her husband, who is also expected to pay a lactating cow with its cow calf; paternal half-uncle should contribute five cows to the nephew corresponding to him in seniority; and optionally, maternal half-uncle, though not obligated to assist, may choose to do so; sisters, both full and half-sisters (i.e. their husbands), should contribute a cow and a cow calf; other relatives and friends may choose to help, but, in such a case, are also entitled to be helped on the occasion of their own marriage or marriages for which they are responsible.

4.2.3 Value of bride wealth

The amount of bride wealth among the Ngok is unlimited and varies according to the social and political importance of the bride's family. Howell reports that "A man may hand over as many as 40, 50 or even 100 head of cattle for the daughter of an important man but the average appears to be between twenty-five and thirty."[12] There are cases in which daughters of chiefs have been married for 200 cows.

Sometimes, a girl is given in marriage to a poor man after a nominal payment on the grounds that sooner or later his female relatives will be married or somehow he will acquire wealth to enable him to discharge the debt. In such cases, the amount is not discussed. If the husband acquires wealth and there is disagreement on the amount to be paid, the court will fix a reasonable amount. There must always be prompt, even if partial, payment to validate the union. If a girl is given on deferred payment with a nominal validating fee, her relatives will not be permitted to revoke the agreement. If it is proved that the husband can afford to pay but does not want to, he can be forced to pay, but the woman's family will then be given the option of repudiating the marriage agreement.

Generally, bride wealth must be paid in cattle. Even sheep and goats are regarded as too inferior for marriage. Until recently, money was entirely unthinkable, but with its increasing importance, the Dinka are beginning to employ it, but still value it in terms of cattle.[13] The practice is only resorted to in special circumstances and is not common. Payment of money in lieu of cattle is disadvantageous to the bridegroom's kin, for while cattle multiply, no interest is accorded to money, and should there be divorce, the same amount or its equivalent is refundable. If an amount is paid which is too small for a cow, it is considered a gift not forming part of the bride wealth, but should there be divorce, the amount may be reclaimed. Even nowadays as the Dinka have been massively displaced internally and around the world, the practice is still to set a money value for a cow and count the money as cows. In the United States and Europe, US$100 has been adopted as the value per cow. The bride wealth is first discussed in terms of cattle and then paid in cash.

4.2.4 Distribution of bride wealth

Distribution of bride wealth covers relatives of the paternal, maternal, and in-law sides according to a common formula. Just as the paternal kin pay the bulk of the bride wealth, they receive most of the incoming bride wealth. A bridegroom may claim his fiancée's share in her sister's bride wealth soon after a betrothal agreement is reached between him and her relatives. It is immaterial how many cows he has already paid, as long as the total bride wealth to be paid justifies the amount he claims, for his share is dependent upon his completing the payment of the agreed amount. In Maguith's case, Maguith paid six betrothal cows of which two were still in his possession, though the title had passed to his in-laws.[14] Before the completion of the marriage, Maguith eloped with the girl. The girl's relatives brought the matter to court, which decided to consider the marriage completed on the understanding that Maguith's relatives should promptly pay an additional sixteen cows. They agreed to do this when their cattle were back from the dry-season camp. In the meantime, a sister of the bride was betrothed with a betrothal wealth of thirty cows. Maguith claimed a share of three, which was proportional to the twenty cows agreed upon. His in-laws rejected his claim on the ground that his payment of the additional sixteen was a condition precedent to his sharing in his sister-in-law's bride wealth. The court held it immaterial whether a person had actually paid or not, provided the amount was settled and will be paid. In accordance with the amity demanded by the custom of a man's sharing in his sister-in-law's bride wealth, Maguith was authorized to select three cows from among the thirty. The court then turned to Maguith and urged him to pay the sixteen cows as soon as his herds were back from the camp.

Friends receive according to the nature of the friendship. A woman who has suckled a child is entitled to one cow. Anyone who has assisted the girl or her mother in a notable manner may claim a share. Thus, if the girl or her mother was saved by the blessing of a remote relative, or a friend, or by that relative's or friend's sacrificing a beast, that relative or friend may claim a share of a cow, though he will not have been entitled to do so in ordinary circumstances. Furthermore, a friend who has assisted the bridegroom's father or brother in the payment of bride wealth may claim a share, depending on the value of his prior assistance. Even a friend who might not have done any particular favor may claim a share and this will entitle the bride's father or sister to share in a subsequent bride wealth of that friend's sister or daughter.

4.2.5 Enforcement of bride wealth

Bride wealth may be enforced by the action of the bride's kin or by a court decree. The bride's kin may seize cattle from the bridegroom's kin in cases such as elopement. If the girl is already given in marriage, her family may invite her for a visit, hold her, and insist on the payment of bride wealth as a condition for her return. Still, she will be regarded as married, so that no other marriage could be contracted. After the lapse of a reasonable time, her relatives may be entitled to sue for divorce and welcome new bidders. The man himself may use this as a ground for divorce and claim the return of whatever he has already given in part payment of the bride wealth. In either case, the court is more likely to enforce the bride wealth rather than grant a divorce. In *Pajok Monytooc v. Matiok Atem*, Pajok married Matiok's daughter and received her before completing payment.[15] Upon Pajok's failure to pay the remaining portion in reasonable time, Matiok took his daughter and her three children to his home, threatening to retain them until Pajok discharged the bride wealth debt. Instead of paying or demanding their return, Pajok left the tribe for a number of years. On his return, Matiok sued for divorce. The court ordered Pajok to pay Matiok nine cows promptly as a condition for the return of his wife and children.

Instead of withdrawing the woman and her children, the wife's relatives may sue for the rest of the bride wealth and the court may compel the husband to pay. Since the court judgments are now enforceable by police force, this is a more effective alternative.

4.2.6 Reverse payments

There are a number of payments which the bride's kin must make to the bridegroom's relatives and his age-mates. They must pay the bridegroom's kin a certain fraction of the total bride wealth from their own cattle, and not from the cattle given them by the bridegroom's kin. This is called *arueth*. There are no rules for calculating the amount payable. The Dinka themselves do not use any fixed proportion, but they will readily give the corresponding reverse value of any amount of bride wealth given them as an example. It is commonly stated that forty corresponds to one hundred, and six to forty, though it is not explained how these figures are arrived at.[16]

The purpose of this reverse payment is not clear. Originally, it was to help found a herd for the bridegroom, who will then have become more independent. Now, the cattle are distributed among his kinsmen according to their shares in the collection of his bride wealth. A person will assist a friend or a relative to increase the amount of bride wealth for the purpose of enhancing the bridegroom's status on the understanding that he will be refunded from the reverse payment. Reverse payment is compulsory. Indeed, a great deal of litigation concerns failure to discharge the obligation.

The second payment, *wak thok*, literally "the washing of the mouth," is a payment of one cow or more to the husband which formally requests him to eat and drink for the first time in the homes of his in-laws. Such abstention, as described earlier, is a gesture of respect for oneself and for the in-laws. It reinforces the rules of avoidance. Its duration varies according to when the wife's kin pay the cow or cows of "washing the mouth." It may follow soon after the conclusion of the marriage or may last for years after the marriage. Apart from her immediate family, the circles of his wife's kin in which a man wants to abstain are usually a matter of his choice. These circles may be multiple, in which case each of the relatives pays a cow to break the abstention in his own home. Where the in-law relationship is remote, a sheep or a goat will suffice. The husband's relatives may also abstain from eating or drinking in the homes of his wife's relatives and may receive payments of "washing the mouth" differing in value according to the relative importance of those involved and the proximity of their relationship. *Wak thok* is optional, though refusal to pay can strain the marriage and catalyze conflicts.[17]

There are two further payments. The first is *biol*, which is an ox of hospitality paid to the bridegroom's age-set to be slaughtered for meat. The other is *akuath thiek*, literally "the driving of bride wealth," also an ox, supposedly a gesture of appreciation to the age-set for driving the bride wealth cattle to the bride's family. It is immaterial whether they actually did so or whether an ox was slaughtered for those who did, if other than the age-set.

4.3 Inheritance

If, as we have maintained, the principle of permanent identity and influence is at the core of Dinka economic life, inheritance must be conceived of as a perpetuation of the deceased's ownership through his heirs. Thus, the ownership of the chain of ancestors is continued. Inheritance is therefore a "stepping into the shoes" of the deceased, who had also stepped into the shoes of those before him.[18] This determines who should inherit what rights and obligations. The system being patriarchal, the sons are the rightful heirs, and failing them, their sons. Stratification within these circles is based on the seniority of the mother and of the son. Within the broader lineal circles, and in the territorial units, descent determines succession.

Although there are broad principles governing who should inherit what, the will of the deceased, though too limited to affect descent stratification, has some significance. Except for specific objects of ritual significance, which automatically accrue to specific heirs, a man distributes most of his wealth in his lifetime to his family units, that is, his wives and through them, his children. Although basic stratification is governed by the order of seniority in the family, the quantum of what a man allocates to his wives and their children is largely a matter of his prerogative. Sometimes, this results in a junior wife receiving more than a senior wife. This will, however, be a violation of the norms and will probably affect only the lower segments of the pyramid. While he distributes his wealth, he remains the owner and can dispose of the property, though often in consultation with the wives and children to whom it had been allotted.[19]

The Dinka revere the last will of a dying man, and relatives will gather to catch every word he says. This is called *cien*. It governs how the family should be run after his death and what basic reorganizations or changes need to be made. A man may allocate the part of his wealth which has not yet been allocated through gifts similar to *donatio mortis causa*. But if the father has treated any one of his sons unfairly, other brothers may be compelled to make good on the father's injustice. Since the idea is to perpetuate lineage ownership through his progeny, a man cannot make a legacy to outsiders. Generally, his ownership was from the group, for, excepting recent innovations, wealth normally accrues through inheritance or through bride wealth. A man may, of course, make reciprocal donations *inter vivos*, provided they are not extravagantly depriving to his family, but this right is eliminated on his deathbed.

Heirs inherit not only a man's wealth, but also his claims and liabilities. A dying person may distribute these claims and liabilities; otherwise, they normally fall on the eldest son, who may then distribute them among the heirs. The eldest son inherits what is allotted to him in his father's lifetime. But, if he is of age, then he is the representative and the executor of his father, and must ensure that his last instructions are carried out and his affairs settled. It is the eldest son who inherits *panom*, the homestead of his father, where shrines of their clan divinities and ancestors are built and where major sacrifices to them are made. Even if the eldest son has a separate residence, on his father's death he must transfer to his father's *panom*. He also inherits other objects of ritual significance, such as the heirlooms of the family. Furthermore, through primogeniture, the eldest son succeeds to any administrative or ritual position his father might have held.

Where a man dies unmarried, we have seen that he leaves behind an obligation to have a wife married to bear him children. Connected with this obligation is succession of his property. It passes to the person whose duty it is to marry him a wife, and those objects that can be traded are sold or exchanged and ultimately converted into cattle to be used toward the payment of the deceased's bride wealth.

Inheritance among the Dinka is thus an aspect of family continuity implicit in the principle of permanent identity and influence behind procreation. Just as wealth is acquired through the lineage, it is passed on through the lineage, and except within these confines, the will of the deceased has little or no consequence.

4.4 Barter and sale

Prior to the introduction of money, the Dinka traded by exchanging various commodities. This is essentially barter, but the concept of sale also existed. The Dinka distinguish exchange of livestock of one kind, usually based on the sex of the animals, from exchange of different kinds of livestock or of different commodities. The former is *dil*, "barter," and the latter is *ghoc*, "sale." Most cases of *dil* concern exchanging bulls for cow calves and rams or billy goats for ewes or goats. They occur mostly in situations requiring the killing of a male animal (e.g. for hospitality or sacrifice). The reason may also be to acquire a personality ox. If both animals are available, they are exchanged immediately; otherwise, a specific animal not immediately available is designated, or the transfer of the bull is made on a promise to give in exchange any animal of a certain description. The agreement may be to give the first cow calf to be born by a specified cow. Should no cow calf be born, alternatives may then be discussed. A man may promise payment on the marriage of his female relative. There is a great deal of litigation out of such postponed payments, since most people are reluctant to pay when the time comes. Another disadvantage of postponed payment is that there is no profit unless an animal was first designated and left in the possession of the transferor, who subsequently disposes of it for a different purpose. In such a case, the natural increase of the animal is traced and either it reverts to the first person entitled or its equivalent is paid. If the animal cannot be traced, a reasonable increase is assessed by the court.

While *dil* primarily concerns animals of the same kind, there are a few cases when rams and billy-goats may be exchanged for bulls. These are cases where a man desperately needs a ram or a billy-goat and either is obliged to benefit the person providing it or pays more in appreciation of his assistance. In most such cases, there is no immediate payment of the bull. The owner of the ram is also expected to give *ajuek, a* payment, usually of a female sheep or goat, in addition to the ram or billy-goat. Both the payment of the bull and of *ajuek* are often deferred. If a particular bull is designated but is then disposed of before delivery, profit may be dependent on how it was used. Thus, if it were exchanged for a cow calf, the debtor will pay the value including the increase.[20]

Sale, *ghoc*, concerned such exchanges as sheep or goats for a cow or bull, and chickens, hoes and spears, ornaments, and the like for a sheep or a goat. A few people who grew a surplus of grain also traded it for cattle, sheep, or goats. With the introduction of money, most of these objects are now purchased in cash, though a man must often sell a cow, a sheep, or a goat to acquire it. While the Dinka are still reserved about selling their livestock, their animal population is decreasing rapidly because of the very low prices paid by merchants who then sell them in the North at great profit and buy goods they then sell to the Dinka at exorbitant prices. This applies to other commodities and is especially severe in the case of grain, which the merchants buy very cheaply from the Dinka during harvest and then sell at very high prices during the lean seasons. This is behind the restrictions which the chief imposed in the late 1950s against sales of grain.

4.5 Custody of livestock

The Dinka have a common contract by which a person entrusts his animals to the custody of another for a definite or indefinite purpose or period. This custom is known as *mac*, "tethering," which implies that the custodian has only the possession and not the ownership of the animals.

Giving cattle for custody may be done for any one of several reasons. A person may want an expert on animal husbandry to take charge of some of his animals. A friend or a relative may need milk cows for his family. A man may want to disguise his wealth to escape the risk of his cattle being claimed in discharge of kinship or other obligations or the envy of less fortunate people. A young man may want to accumulate independent wealth unknown to his seniors. Finally, custody may simply be prompted by lack of space in the cattle byre for one's herd.

There are two main classes of such agreements: those that confer possession to the custodian for a definite purpose and period, and those that specify no terms except to keep the cattle. In the former case, the agreement comes to an end when the condition has been fulfilled. For example, A gives B a lactating cow to provide milk for B's family. The cow must be returned when dry, unless the agreement anticipated a long-term provision of milk, in which case it will continue into the cow's next lactation period. A might have given a cow to B to assist him during a famine. In such a case, it should be returned when the famine is over, whether dry or not. In unspecified conditions, it is implied that the custodian will keep the animal for a long period during which he takes the milk for his own use. Generally, he must not use it for purposes detrimental to the owner; but in cases of need, the custodian, usually a relative or a friend, may use the property with the view of restitution. For example, if one of his family is dangerously ill and a sacrifice for which he has no animal is needed, he may sacrifice the animal under his custody but he must report the matter to the owner. They then decide whether it was a loan or a gift.[21]

Since the purpose of such long-term custody agreements is to encourage the increase of the animals and to discourage the owner's being tempted to alienate them, the custodian may trade with them. Thus, he can exchange cattle for goats or bulls for cows. If done in good faith, the fact that he ultimately loses does not obligate him to the owner. On the other hand, if he incurs a loss to the owner in his own unjustified interest, he must account for the loss.[22] John Makec discusses *mac*, in terms of *amuk* or *amec*, which both mean "keeping" or "custody." But he sees the concept primarily in terms of security, or pledge for the repayment of debt: "'A' may obtain a loan from 'B'. 'B' may demand an immediate delivery of some property to him as a guarantee for the repayment of the debt, because there may be a doubt as to whether 'A' will ultimately fulfill his obligation. 'A' will then be bound to deposit some property with 'B'." This is, of course, done in cattle, "the most important medium of exchange." Makec, however, recognizes that *amuk* or *amec* may take the form of a situation whereby "The owner of property makes a decision to transfer its possession to a person who accepts to hold it in trust."[23]

4.6 Gifts

The Dinka say, "What is given circulates, and what is consumed is wasted." This explains much about the reciprocal nature of gifts among the Dinka. While the Dinka are very generous, gifts are made on the tacit understanding that the donee will assist the donor in the future. This is derived from the fact that gifts are often in the form of cattle, and that cattle have particular significance to permanent identity and influence, so that ancestral claims intervene to supersede the donor's right to dispose of property without consideration.

A Dinka will not hesitate to "beg" a relative or a friend for help, because the concept of begging in their society, except for certain items, lacks connotations of indignity. There is nearly always a special relationship between the beggar and the person he approaches. Professional begging is unknown. A man whose personality ox dies may take the rope and approach the chief, a prominent elder, or a relative, asking for a substitute ox. A man whose favorite cow is dead will take the meat to the family of a female agnate, who, by accepting it, obligate themselves to pay that relative a cow either immediately or from a daughter's bride wealth to which he will otherwise not be entitled. Asking for help is extended to members of society who in the judgment of the beggar are able to satisfy his need.

There are kinds and degrees of requests for material help, but the major ones that come to court are those relating to assistance in bride wealth payment. Gifts are also exchanged in the special form of "contractual" friendship discussed earlier. Since such gifts are reciprocal, they may be withdrawn if there is later a substantial breach of the friendship obligation on the side of the donee. The friendship is then dissolved and the status quo ante restored. This return of the gifts exchanged is termed *dhiel*. The Dinka defend *dhiel* on the ground that cattle are divine and "to throw them away" without valuable consideration is to invite ancestral curse manifested in illness or poverty. While *dhiel* originated in the social importance of cattle, it was extended to other types of wealth, like sheep and goats, to which the divine attributes of cattle are extended. It must not be assumed that the Dinka are likely to withdraw any gifts where withdrawal is justified. The custom applies only to those types of property endowed with special attributes. Even then, it is not universal to reclaim gifts on the dissolution of friendship.

In *Matet Ayom v. Deng Majok*,[24] this customary law was invalidated. Matet Ayom, a sectional chief and a close friend of Chief Deng Majok, was held vicariously liable for his brother's elopement with Deng Majok's half-sister. Matet, offended by Deng Majok's attitude, began to agitate politically, whereupon he was arrested and convicted. After serving a prison sentence, Matet claimed formal severance of his friendship with Deng Majok and the return of cattle he had contributed to the bride wealth of Deng Majok's marriages. His claim was rejected by the Abyei Chiefs' court on the ground that as Deng Majok will not claim the return of anything, although it was common knowledge that he had helped Matet far more than Matet had helped him, it was not equitable for Matet to have his cattle returned. Matet appealed to the district commissioner, Sayed Mohammed Ibrahim, who said in dismissing the appeal that if the custom were upheld, he, for one, would be reluctant to accept even a cup of tea from a Dinka.

4.7 Theft

The Dinka distinguish between theft of ordinary property, ordinary theft of cattle, and theft of cattle in self-help. The term *cuer* is applied to the first two, which are not only strongly condemned but are very rare. The last is called *kap* (seizing) by the Ngok and is hardly considered theft.

In an earlier discussion of age-set activities, we saw that theft of ordinary objects gives rise to the skewering of one's personality ox or, as in Nyanluak's case, the ox of one's brother. The stolen object, depending on its value, may then be forgotten or restored.

Ordinary theft of cattle, sheep and goats is even rarer than that of ordinary objects. The obvious reason is that it is not easy to conceal the crime. The Dinka are well informed about a neighbor's stock and the source of a new animal will almost certainly be investigated, if only for curiosity. This is why most thefts of cattle, sheep, and goats are accompanied by the slaughtering of the beast for meat. Even in such a case, it may not be easy to utilize the skin, for its origin will be of interest to associates. A more serious reason arises from the attribute of cattle as divine animals closely associated with human life. Stealing them is said to invite spiritual contamination which might cause death to the thief or a relative. Since some ordinary objects are exchangeable for cattle, sheep, or goats, a somewhat similar feeling is applicable to them, though to a much lesser degree.

Theft of cattle in self-help is more frequent, but does not provoke the ordinary moral disapproval of ordinary theft. The origins of this, as of self-help in general, have already been attributed to the ineffectiveness of traditional judicial process. There was the need to compel an uncooperative defendant to appear in court, to speed up litigation, and to execute court judgment. Seizing a cow thus facilitated the process of claims. It was not regarded as an offense, though the likelihood of violence was great if the person was caught in the act. Usually an individual seizing a cow for rightful cause will take it to the chief's home, pending final settlement. Most seizures, however, were instigated by one's own sense of right and wrong, which might be in conflict with the opinion of the court. This has now been greatly modified but not eliminated. Seizure of cattle is now regarded as an ordinary case of theft, and receives the newly introduced prison sentence of six months, partly because its rationale has disappeared and partly because of administrative misunderstanding of its true nature. Nonetheless, society still considers it to be different from ordinary theft. Even the court does not entirely equate them. The ordinary rules governing theft and the sentence normally inflicted on thieves will only apply in cases where the circumstances of seizure are aggravating. Thus, in Manyuol Dongbek's case, Manyuol seized a cow and took it outside the tribe.[25] The court found him guilty of theft but promised to release him if he promised on oath to return the cow. Manyuol refused to do so and was sentenced to six months, imprisonment.

4.8 Labor and produce

4.8.1 Land use and cultivation

A family usually works its own land and builds its own huts and cattle byres. They may hire others to help with the building, to cut grass for thatching or poles for rafters, for example. Such employment may be settled by payment or by inviting friends to a feast of beer and food. An exception is work for the chief, whose huts are built by the age-sets of the various subtribes. Even then, he gives them beer and beasts for meat. But whether a hut is built by a wife herself or by the whole family for her, she is entitled to it.

Each "house" in a polygynous family cultivates its own field. The head of the household often cultivates his fields separately from those of his wives, although he usually assists them. A man or a woman can always get help by giving a feast with beer, meat, and other food to which he or she may invite friends or neighbors. Gratuitous aid of blood relations or relations-in-law may also be obtained. The chief may ask any age-set to work his fields and may also be assisted by litigants awaiting their turn in his court during the cultivation period. The reason behind this custom is that the chief has no time for his own work since his judicial and administrative duties occupy so much of his time. Besides, his status exempts him from menial work.

In cultivation there may be a division of labor. Some young men regularly go to far-off cattle posts with the herds, leaving the older people to work in the fields. This practice is sometimes employed to exempt from work young men whose relatives wish them to *toc* ("to lie down") during the cathartic period. This custom is now discouraged so that all may work to increase agricultural production.

Each family is entitled to the crops reaped from its fields. A now defunct custom had decreed that some of the corn reaped by a family must be presented to the chief, because it was understood that he was also responsible for the poor. Furthermore, his court, as the tribal meeting place, had to provide food for the tribe. Although these responsibilities of the chief have remained, the custom has been abolished. Within the family, each wife owns the crops from her fields. The crops reaped by the head of the household in his fields are common family property, but he must discharge obligations to assist kinsmen. This obligation is extended to neighbors whose crops have failed. Apart from specific obligations toward kinsmen and neighbors, there is a general obligation of hospitality to all in need. This was based on the expectation of reciprocity, for the giver today might expect to be the receiver tomorrow. Refusal to assist hungry kinsmen might lead to fission and the severance of relationship. Nowadays, hospitality may be enforced, and the Ngok Chiefs' court has honored many such claims.

Apart from these rights, a person has the right to deal with his crops in any way he thinks fit. He can exchange grain for cattle, sheep, goats, domestic utensils, etc. A husband cannot sell grain from the field of a wife or dispose of it without her permission. Nor can a wife sell her grain without his consent. Cattle, or other objects bought with a wife's grain belong to her household and can be inherited by her children; but her husband's right in the property amounts to ownership by him.[26] A wife may make gifts of hospitality without her husband's consent, but if a gift is extravagant, he can interfere, though at the risk of gaining the reputation of a miser. Men are generally believed to be more extravagant in hospitality, and a female miser is more tolerated than a parsimonious male (except with respect to cattle, when parsimony is a lesser evil).

4.8.2 Animal husbandry

Herding of cattle is generally collective except for the few cows kept permanently at home for milk. A single family cannot protect its cattle alone, so the cooperation of territorial groups becomes necessary. Cattle are usually herded together, within either the section of the tribe or the subsection. The group may, collectively or by families, use cattle to fertilize the soil. Dinka cattle are tethered together, each to its own peg, so that field after field receives a sufficient deposit of dung and urine. This, with the rapid breakdown ensured by the climate, maintains the fertility of the soil. Thousands of cattle may be tethered in this manner. Within this collective herding, each person has to tether and care for his own cattle except during grazing, when they may be tended by members of the group in turn.

Every wife can produce butter from the cattle of her own house. With this she trades and buys more cows. Among the Dinka, butter produced from cattle dedicated to God or ancestral spirits may not be disposed of to strangers.

When a beast is slaughtered, the meat is divided between kinsmen according to strict rules. An age-set shares cattle which accrue to it as a body, as when a beast is seized from a member who has disgraced the age-set, or when the age-set is awarded a festive beast by the bride's relatives in honor of the marriage of one of its number.

4.8.3 Hunting and fishing

The Dinka are not keen hunters or fishermen, as these are considered a poor man's occupations, but they do hunt and fish to supplement their diet. Hunting and fishing are done collectively. Meat from hunting is distributed among the hunters. Ivory is subject to more definite rules since it is a valuable commodity which is often exchanged for cattle. The Dinka also use ivory for bracelets and bangles, which are highly regarded.[27] In fishing, every person takes his own catch. But there is a custom known as *dom* by which the first man to grasp the fisherman's spear after the fish is speared gets the fish. He need not physically seize the spear as long as he states his claim. The claim is subject to the acceptance of the spearer who has the right to refuse, but who usually will not, as that would be ungentlemanly.

4.8.4 Collection of wild fruits and honey

When collecting wild fruits or honey in a far-off place, people usually go in groups for the sake of protection, but each person is entitled to his own collection. A person may make a beehive, or mark any tree where bees are likely to swarm, thereby ensuring that any honey produced is his private property.

5. Homicide and Bodily Injuries

The objective here is to illustrate the principles underlying the legal expression of well-being, a value which permeates Dinka legal processes. Toward this end, the focus is on homicide, bodily injuries, and liability for animals.

5.1 Homicide

Although the capital aspect of homicide has ceased to be governed by customary law, its tortuous aspect is left to local courts to be governed by appropriate customs where the circumstances permit (e.g. where the accused is not sentenced to death). In homicide, the broadest familial identifications come into perspective. In the past, kinship solidarities were vital for self-defense since the effectiveness of social control was not sufficient to provide security amid widespread hostilities between various units of Dinka society. An act of homicide immediately gave rise to a blood feud and the need for vengeance. The obligation to avenge fell on the dead man's kin but might extend to territorial groups, depending on the circumstances of the homicide. An entire subtribe might remain hostile to another, irrespective of the kinship relations of their members. If the vendetta was settled by payment of blood wealth, collection fell only on those who could trace paternal kinship to the killer, although maternal kinship and marriage affinity sometimes created the obligation to assist. The exception here is where death occurred in a fight between the subtribes, in which case collecting the blood wealth was more broadly shared.[1] Thus, the duty of vengeance was not necessarily correlative to the obligation to assist in the payment of blood wealth, except in intertribal wars.

While vengeance was usually carried out by youth, whether as relatives of the deceased or as warrior groups, the settlement of a vendetta and the compensatory payment were the duties of the senior members of the lineages or the territorial groups involved, with the overall mediation of the chief. Today, retaliation has been replaced by state action, but homicide still gives rise to feuds that must be settled on traditional lines. This customary settlement still takes the form of blood wealth payable in cattle. The amount paid as blood wealth varies from tribe to tribe. Among the Ngok Dinka it is forty cows, while Makec reports that it is thirty cows among the Dinka of Bahr el Ghazal.[2] Underlying blood wealth is the fundamental principle that the deceased should continue to have children begotten in his name. Of course, the dead man's group loses in ways other than those connected with procreation, but the dominant factor is that his procreative potential, both for his own sake and for his contribution to the kin group, has suddenly been terminated. He must therefore be married posthumously with the cattle paid as compensation by the killer's kin. This is clear in the manner of collection and distribution of the compensation. The contribution of cattle on the side of the killer is generally made by the same persons who will assist in marriage, and the distribution among the relatives of the dead is also quite similar to the distribution of bride wealth. The remainder will go to the man whose duty it is to marry a wife to the deceased. As soon as he can afford it, he is expected to carry out the obligation, lest the curse of the dead man befall him.

John Makec questions this linkage and argues that, "If the need to marry a wife for the deceased were the basis of the compensation, there will be no need for the deceased relatives … to share those cattle among themselves." He also argues that even when a man is already married and has many children, blood wealth is still paid. These arguments can, however, be countered with the argument that the people who share the blood wealth are the same people who contribute to the bride wealth and that the procreative potential and value does not end with having already had children, however many they may be. A Dinka man continues to marry, if he can afford it, and have children into old age and perhaps until death, if he is physically able to perform conjugal obligations. At whatever age that is terminated, compensation must at least in part envisage a contribution to a levirate marriage. Makec in fact seemed to consider this when he wrote, "Of the thirty cows paid as compensation, there are … two cows usually selected … one for the 'head' and the other for the 'legs' of the deceased."[3]

Makec is correct that marrying for the dead man is not the sole objective of the compensation but it is a factor. The association between blood wealth and bride wealth has the effect that if blood wealth for a murdered wife is more than her husband had paid in marriage, he will be expected to keep only a number of cattle proportionate to what he paid. The rest of the compensation goes to her family. One of the ominous implications of the system is that a man does not pay compensation if he kills his own wife, for he will have to pay it to himself. He will, however, be expected to pay two or three cows to her kinsmen to reestablish peaceful relations with them. These cows are known as "the cattle of blood," *ghok riem*. According to Makec, among the Bahr el Ghazal Dinka, the marriage is automatically dissolved and the bride wealth is used as compensation to the deceased's family unless it is less than thirty cows, in which case the difference will be paid.[4] If a woman kills someone, her husband, with the assistance of her kinsmen, is responsible for the compensation, with some assistance from her family. As in other torts, payment by a wrongdoing kinsman is generally regarded as a fee of appeasement. It varies in value according to the circumstances of the case and may be more or less than the rate of normal compensation. In cases involving relatives the matter is more localized, and is determined by the nuclear or extended families involved rather than the kinship at large.

5.1.1 Forms of homicide

The Dinka recognize various forms of homicide, determined largely by the manner of commission, which affects the gravity of the offense and the indignation of the dead man's kin. They may be summarized as secret killing, *loc piny*; killing by stealth, *dheng piny*; killing by magic, *awok, wiel, wal*, or *peeth*; ordinary intentional killing, *nak raan*; negligent and accidental killing, *weec*; and death incidental to other wrongs, such as breach of taboo, *jok*.

Loc piny occurs when a person kills secretly and conceals the offense. This is very serious, for apart from its depriving the victim's relatives of their member and their due compensation, it invites spiritual contamination on the kin groups of both parties and might cause death. A blood feud creates a spiritual barrier between the groups concerned and gives rise to observances and taboos, which, if broken even in ignorance of their existence, constitute a serious threat to all concerned. A man must therefore confess any homicide to enable those concerned to follow the necessary observations and taboos. If a man is later compelled by the evil consequences of concealment to confess or he is somehow detected, a higher scale of compensation is demanded. The indignation provoked by such behavior calls for greater punishment and more pecuniary benefit to appease the wronged group.

Dheng piny is a surprise act in which the killer takes unfair advantage of his victim, thereby giving him no opportunity for self-defense. Such a cold-blooded murder outrages the Dinka sense of dignity and honor. Appeasement is difficult in such circumstances, and only a higher scale of compensational punishment can atone for the wrong.

Killing by magical charms, though difficult to prove, is also very serious. The Dinka explain in detail how evil medicine, *wal*, evil eye, *peeth*, and other such antisocial practices affect the victim. The symptoms of each of these are said to be so clearly established that the difficulty is not so much what kind of death is involved as who has caused it. Usually, people suspect those who might have had a motive, such as those who had animosity with the victim or with his close relatives. Should any additional circumstantial evidence lead to a reasonable conclusion as to the identity of the killer, he will be personally attacked and killed. In the past, a fight was bound to occur between his relatives and those of the victim. Compensation for death caused by magic is difficult to settle. Since magic is strongly associated with descent, to admit that a member has caused death by magic is so serious that it is hardly ever done.

Ordinary intentional homicide involves such cases as killing in a fair fight. This is the standard case in the absence of aggravating or mitigating circumstances.

Weec covers cases of both negligent and accidental killings. The former is less serious than intentional killing and graver than the latter. In determining negligence, the Dinka use a concept comparable to that of the "reasonable man." In an interview with the chiefs and elders, an English lecturer with whom I was investigating Dinka customary law asked them whether Dinka law had the concept of the "reasonable man." I interpreted the question into something like "When you judge a person do you consider what a man with a head and a heart (a prudent person) would have done?" Their reaction was tantamount to "What a silly question! Of course we do." One chief went on to give an example based on actual cases. If one saw cornstalks waving in a field immediately behind the huts during a season when corn is ripe and assumed that there was an animal destroying crops and speared it, but it turned out to be a human being, his assumption will not be a good defense because "a man with a head," *raan de nom*, and a heart, *piou*, should have known that a person might be in the field picking corn.

In one of the cases from which the example was derived, a man killed his neighbor's wife in a durra field a few miles away from the homestead. He had been on friendly terms with the deceased and her family, and used to eat with her husband. When the incident occurred, her husband was away and she was cooking for this man since he was unmarried. One afternoon, he went to guard his fields from birds and animals. Before he left, he saw the hut of the woman closed but did not wonder whether she was inside or had gone somewhere. On reaching his fields, he saw the durra stalks moving in the adjacent fields of his neighbors. Thinking that monkeys were destroying the crops, he threw a spear at the direction of the movement and fatally injured his neighbor's wife. He was tried by a major court and convicted of negligent homicide. After he had been sentenced to imprisonment, the Abyei Chiefs' court tried the tortuous aspect and assessed the compensation on the basis of negligent homicide. The plea of accidental death was dismissed on the grounds that he should have known that the woman might also be guarding her field, especially when he had seen her hut closed.

Another case showed a clearer instance of negligence. A man saw the stalks of durra and corn waving in a field immediately behind the homestead. Believing it to be jackals spoiling the crops, he threw a spear at the area and killed a small child. The Ngok usually plant fast-ripening durra and corn in such nearby fields to supply food before the main crops ripen. Although the crops were not entirely ripe, they were sufficiently ripe for children to gather corn or sugarcane. The man was held guilty of negligent homicide by both the major court and the Chiefs' court. Being a kinsman of the child, he was made to pay *awec*, conciliation fee, and not *puk*, blood wealth. Since *awec* is often greater than compensation, and the child's father in this case was the paramount chief, the amount paid was much greater than usual.

contamination leading to death. This taboo must continue until full settlement and possibly longer. One of the leading chiefs, who is aware of the case, then intervenes in person or through a representative of his lineage.

The chief calls upon the relatives of the deceased, sacrifices a bull known as *mior de kueng*, "the bull of peace settlement," and asks the aggrieved group to take an oath to keep peace and avoid vengeance. The chief then asks the relatives of the killer to collect the blood wealth cattle and hand them over to him. On an appointed day, the two groups are convened and a bull known as *mior de yuom*, "the bull of the bone," is sacrificed. The chief, or one of his relatives acting on his behalf, takes the bones of the right hind leg of the animal, breaks them in two, and throws one half to the killer's kin group and the other to the relatives of the deceased, who must at first show resistance and wage a mock attack of vengeance on the killer's relatives, until they are persuaded by the chief to accept the settlement. Being interested in the well-being of all his people, the chief receives one cow from the blood wealth and hands over the rest to the relatives of the deceased.

Thus, the divine aspect of well-being, the pivotal role of the chiefly lineages, the need for forceful retaliation prompted by their traditional ineffectiveness, and the realization of the higher value of unity and harmony they stand for, all combine in the ceremonies of feud settlement.

An area in which the dichotomy between crime and civil wrong is blurred in customary law is that of homicide and compensation rather than capital punishment. But the law has, of course, been evolving and changing, with Western ideas incrementally becoming reflected, especially on the issue of crime and punishment. In the words of Michael Makuei, the Attorney General, capital punishment is an innovation that runs against deeply held values: "There is a strong cultural bias against capital punishment … In our customs, capital punishment never existed … To avoid vengeance, it was decided that people should be compensated … With the introduction of statutory laws came the idea of sentencing the offender to death."

The increase in the reckless use of arms in homicide and the military justice through court martial has fed into the new trend toward capital punishment. In a 1987 case reported by Monyluak Alor Kuol, "a local SPLA officer in charge of Akot area, in Rumbek County, murdered Chief Majok Derder in relation to a court case concerning the officer's brother that was before the chief. I later participated in the proceedings of the court, which was convened to try that officer. He was convicted of murder and sentenced to death by firing squad."[8]

In another case, also reported by Kuol, a pregnant girl escaped from her home and went to the family of the man who had impregnated her. A group from the girl's relatives decided to attack the man and his relatives when the matter was discovered. Some of the attackers were carrying firearms. Their Chief pursued them to dissuade them from the attack. When he reached them the two groups had already started to exchange fire. Whether intentionally or accidentally, the chief himself was shot and fell dead. On realizing what had happened to their chief, some of the attackers hurriedly left the scene of the fighting and ran to the nearby village where the chief of the other section lived. They found him, attacked him, and killed him, in revenge for the death of their own chief. An even greater catastrophe was only avoided by the quick intervention of some SPLA forces in the area. The High Court Judge of Bahr el Ghazal Region tried the case in 1998 and sentenced four of the ringleaders to suffer death by firing squad.[9]

The proliferation of arms and the general atmosphere of violence resulting from the war also encouraged armed confrontation in intertribal conflicts, although the SPLM/A also took stringent measures against those responsible. However, when tribal wars erupt and large numbers of people are killed, neither capital punishment nor full blood wealth is possible. In most cases, reconciliation and some appeasement payment is the preferred option. This was the case in a conflict between the Dinka and the Nuer that erupted in the mid-1980s before the SPLM/A went into the area. A peace conference was later organized by the SPLM/A and a Chiefs' court presided by an SPLM judge later settled the matter by imposing a blood wealth of only eleven cows "for reasons of expediency, as the number of people killed was too large, and the ultimate objective was the reconciliation rather than the redress of every single damage."[10]

According to Monyluak Alor Kuol, "The introduction of the idea of hanging the murderer by the State authorities has had some bearing on those relatives who may refuse compensation when they are given the option. The generated feelings that might he caused by killings with impunity, exacerbated by the use of guns, have affected the local inclination for blood compensation. However, many members of the traditional Dinka communities still see *apuk* as the best compensation for murder."[11] Kuol cites a case that took place in Yirol County and in which the relatives of a man killed by an SPLA soldier opted for cattle compensation over the possibility of referring the soldier to a court martial that could sentence him to death. The relatives of the deceased were primarily guided by their cultural conceptions.[12]

The law, however, now balances between customary preference for compensation and the option of capital punishment. If the accused is found guilty, then before the court passes the death sentence, it will ask the relatives of the deceased if they want the death sentence to be passed against the accused or will opt for compensation. And their preference will prevail.

It is fair to say that the cases of families opting for capital punishment must be rare. And the reason is probably not so much because of the lure of material compensation, although that too is significant, but a deep disapproval of capital punishment that is rooted in their value system. Putting a person to death is seen as a cold-blooded murder by the State. As the Attorney General underscored: "In most cases people prefer compensation because this capital punishment is … not part of our culture." Referring to the position international human rights advocates take against capital punishment, he said, "Opposition to capital punishment was already there in our customs."

5.2 Bodily injuries

Depending on their gravity, personal injuries not resulting in death are matters of less concern to the respective groups of the conflicting parties than cases of homicide. If the injuries are severe, they may provoke group violence; otherwise, the matter is usually settled by the court's imposing liability for reasonable compensation on the assailant, with or without penal sanctions. There are traditional rates of compensation for certain injuries that guide the court in reaching a settlement which will restore the equilibrium.[13] If an injury is inflicted by a kinsman, payment takes the form of a conciliation fee rather than compensation.

The Dinka often fear the reoccurrence of injuries caused by means other than spears, and a considerable number of deaths are attributed to early injuries. In such a case, it will be material that *athiol* and *riem* cattle had been paid as a demonstration of good will toward the injured. Under such circumstances, compensation in the event of death is reduced. This anticipation of full loss of life is significant, for while injury deserves compensation for its own sake, focus is on elimination or weakening of life as a self-generating force. For this reason, cattle paid in compensation of injury are ideally used for marriage.

Such proceeds as are recoverable in personal injuries usually benefit the family as a whole, for if the injured party is a dependent member (a child or a wife), he or she will be expected to hand the compensation over to the guardian, and if he is a family head, then it naturally forms part of the family property. Indeed, if there is no material dispute as to the facts, the Dinka practice is that the case may be brought by one member of the family for the benefit of all or of any one member agreed upon by the family.

5.3 Liability for animals

The distinction between domesticated animals (*domitae naturae*) and naturally tamed animals (*mansuetae naturae*) on the one hand, and those naturally wild (*ferae naturae*) on the other, seems to be recognized by the Dinka. Liability attaches to the former and not to the latter.[14] Apart from the obvious case of intentional injuries, the owner of a domesticated or naturally tame animal is liable if he knows of a dangerous propensity in his animal and unreasonably neglects to keep it under control or to give adequate warning to those within its zone of danger. Such duty of care as is imposed seems to focus on imminent danger. Thus, an aggressive cow is stopped when attacking a stranger or the stranger is warned against the cow on the spot. Similarly, a vicious dog has to be held when a stranger approaches or else he is told to avoid the danger. But a cow that is aggressive against people is not necessarily kept from grazing with the herds in fear of its harming passersby. Nor is an occasionally vicious dog necessarily kept in bondage. But if a cow becomes ferocious, which is extremely rare, or a dog becomes rabid, which is more common, it must be destroyed.

In cases of negligence, reasonable damages are assessed by the court depending on the harm done, the degree of negligence, and the relations of the parties. In the absence of negligence, strict but nominal liability is imposed and the injuring animal itself must be surrendered to the injured party or, if he has been killed, to his heirs as nominal damages.[15] The beast is then used for marriage, either immediately or after it has increased naturally or through trade.

The Dinka do not impose liability for naturally wild animals, perhaps because they are normally not owned. However, a form of ownership and possession attaches to a number of wild creatures that symbolize divinities, *yieth*: these are snakes, lions, crocodiles, and the like. An animal representing a divinity of a lineage must not be killed by that lineage. The animal may be aware of the friendliness of that particular group and be gentle toward them. Thus, cases are cited in which lions have come into the homes of their "relatives" and received offerings of cows, sheep, or goats.

Snakes, some of which are deadly, are frequently encountered in Dinka homes. If they are "related" to the clan, they are given butter to lick, anointed and patted on the back, carefully persuaded to enter a basket, and moved by the elder members of the family, who declare that it is for the snakes' own protection from accidental injury that they are returned to the forest. While the snakes are often gentle under such treatment, they are unpredictable and may bite when a person stumbles over them or frightens them in any manner. When a snake or any other totemic animal injures a person related to it, the matter is easily explained in terms of a wrong committed by that person or any other member of his kin group. Propitiation of the creature and ritual atonement must be done.

Thus, while the Dinka consider domestic animals as causing nominal liability to their owners unless the owners are negligent, their religious thought makes them accommodate dangerous creatures, a practice which leaves these creatures secure and generally in harmony with people. But should this harmony fail and they injure people, the Dinka attach no liability to injuries caused by them. Instead, liability is imposed on their "hosts" if they are injured, for not only must they be ceremonially buried, if killed, but sacrifices and dedications must be made to them in compensation and appeasement.

5.4 Employment of curers

Although they are now exposed to modern medicine, the Dinka are still largely dependent on magical cures, and while divine rulers like the chiefs and prophets do not demand remuneration (though they may welcome gifts), other curers are generally professionals who are paid for their services. They undertake divination, blessing, herbal treatment, and other aspects of doctoring people, crops, and livestock. Their skills are mostly hereditary, but there is training within the group.

When summoned, a diviner or a curer often demands an honorarium *in limine*, in the form of a coin, a spear, or an animal.[16] The actual fee for services performed differs according to the nature of the work done and the seriousness of the illness. It varies from money to cattle of ranging value. Generally speaking, the fee is paid after the services have been effectively performed, but the amount is agreed upon before services are rendered; where the employer is a man of wealth and the practitioner has no reason to fear default in payment, he may render services on the tacit understanding that a reasonable amount will be paid.[17] Some well-reputed functionaries refuse payment prior to their success. Others, even when successful, insist on only a nominal fee without which the divinities and ancestors are believed to be unhelpful. They see their functions as humanitarian and not materially motivated.

The less interested in material gain a curer is, the more divine he is believed to be and the more popular his services are. But since the success of their cure is generally a condition precedent to their remuneration and recognition, all diviners and curers are very concerned about their patients' recovery. If successful, a curer may sue for his fee, and the court will enforce it. If the fee has not been agreed upon before the practitioner's performance, the court will assess a reasonable amount. Usually, disputes do not arise over the value or the payment of the fee, because the practitioner's dissatisfaction is believed to invoke his divinities and ancestors to undo the cure or inflict a new evil on the cured person or another relative. Moreover, there is always the expectation that his services will be needed again. Since the success of divination and cure is largely dependent on the diviner's understanding of the social environment of the patient and the possible psychological cause of discord, a local diviner, who will be more interested in such a social environment for this very purpose, could be more effective than a stranger.

The fact that traditionally the Dinka pay for medical services has recently been extended to modern medicine and has been taken advantage of by local medical assistants and dressers. The Dinka sometimes pay for services due to them from the state. The projection of traditional practices and the abuse of these by the modern medical men have so interacted that many Dinka genuinely believe that a government medical officer cannot treat a person adequately unless paid. Some keep out of hospitals on account of this belief. Others receive services they have no faith in because they have offered no money to their doctors. The writer is informed by medical practitioners that they are not infrequently forced to treat Dinka patients in their private clinics instead of in state clinics on the request of the patients. A doctor is then obliged either to receive much less than his services are worth because of the poverty of the people, or to render cheaper and less useful services than the patient could have received in a state clinic without payment.

5.5 Social health insurance

The Dinka practice of paying for medical services should not imply lack of public "health insurance" in traditional society. But it does show the importance of individualism within communalism. Health protection for the individual took various forms, from ancestral protection to mutual dependence among the living. A popular saying among the Dinka is for a person to sometimes call upon illness to visit him so that he may distinguish between those who are "really his people" and those who are not. A sick, aged, or otherwise needy person must be taken care of by his relatives or friends. The circle of such people usually extends to neighbors and even strangers, with reciprocity as one of the incentives.[18]

During illness, a man in need of an animal to sacrifice may seize anyone's beast, if necessary without the owner's consent, though on the understanding that it will be compensated for. A similar practice is authorized where there is danger of starvation, or any case of imminent peril. Collective herding and protection against external animal or human aggression are other aspects of mutual dependence.

Legitimate obligations to fellow men, relatives, friends, neighbors, or even strangers may be enforced by the chief. A sick or poor man without an able relative may trust in the chief's care. In numerous ways, the chief receives material benefits from his people so that they indirectly support such public services.

Part Three

Voices for Customary Law

1. Introduction to Part Three

As part of my preparation for this study, I conducted extensive interviews – or, as I will prefer to consider them, conversations – with leading policy makers, thinkers, and actors in the justice system in Sudan and in particular Southern Sudan. A leadership training workshop organized by the Sudan People's Liberation Movement and Army (SPLM/A) in collaboration with the university of South Africa, at New Site, Kapeota County, in Equatoria in February 2005, at which I served as a facilitator, provided a unique opportunity to discuss the issues raised in this study. I then proceeded to Rumbek in Bahr el Ghazal, the interim capital of the Government of Southern Sudan, where I held conversations with more judges and lawyers. I later took advantage of being in Khartoum in August 2005 to interview more judges and lawyers from both the North and the South, including the minister of justice of the Government of National Unity.

I was struck by the fact that the Southerners I spoke with all seemed to reflect a remarkable degree of agreement on the main issues raised. While these issues ranged considerably, the conversations were structured around a number of principal themes. The starting point was a discussion of the sources of customary law, with a focus on the fundamental cultural values or norms on which the legal system was based and which it intended to promote. Within that broad normative framework, we discussed the substantive content of customary law, its rules of procedure, and the role of traditional leaders. Since most of customary law relates to personal affairs, in particular family matters, gender, and age issues, specifically the status of women and children figured prominently.

Much of the emphasis was placed on the prejudices of the Arab Islamic-dominated national legal system against African customary law and how promoting customary law in the South was an essential part of the liberation struggle. With less tension, comparisons with Western legal thought and practice were made to underscore the positive aspects of customary law that have tended to be viewed negatively by applying Western criteria. In particular, much emphasis was placed on the contrast between the Western adversarial system, in which the judge or the court plays the role of an umpire, and the customary law approach of mediation and conciliation, with the judge or court playing an active role in searching for a point of consensus and reconciliation. While even in this comparative context, customary law is valued as an integral aspect of a highly prized identity, which the South had fought to protect and preserve, the comparative debate with the West is approached more creatively and constructively than the virtually zero-sum confrontation with the Arab-Islamic North and its agenda for the application of Sharia Islamic Law.

It is clear from all accounts that customary law now enjoys a great deal of emotional and intellectual association with the struggle the people of the South have waged for half a century. And the aspiration of the leadership is that it should figure in all aspects of nation-building: constitutionalism, governance and, of course, the administration of justice. In its optimal vision, this will elevate customary law to a normative framework whose postulates and stipulations are all-embracing, as guides to the political, social, economic, and cultural processes of nation-building. This is an enormous challenge whose dimensions and long-term implications will still have to be thought through and worked out.

The vision is clearly ambitious, if not yet well defined. Judging from the experiences of Sudan and other African countries, customary law is still faced with the prospects of being relegated to a subordinate role in the context of legal pluralism that still favors the received English common law for the secularists and Sharia for the Islamists. And yet, in their approach to the challenges before them, the leaders of the legal profession interviewed clearly see the preservation, promotion, and development of customary law as central to the development of Southern Sudan.

One of the issues on which those interviewed came across as sensitive and somewhat cross-culturally defensive is the potential conflict between customary law and international human rights and humanitarian law. While some acknowledged that there were areas in which customary law will need to be reformed, such as those relating to gender inequality, the general tendency was to see customary law and tradition in general and the value system they represented as conforming to human rights and humanitarian standards. In their view, even accepting international standards as universal norms, the best way to promote them among the people in Southern Sudan is to present them as an embodiment of their own traditional values and not as an imposition from the outside.

Meanwhile, issues pertaining to the preservation and promotion of customary laws ranged from recording them, analyzing them, harmonizing them to address the problems of diversity, restating them with a view to reform, and eventually codifying them to guide the courts in their administration of justice. While there was some difference of opinion on whether customary law should be codified or not, there was virtual unanimity on the need to ascertain and record Southern customary laws comprehensively, so that no group will feel left out. Coming out with a common code that will either be unified or will still accommodate a degree of diversity is a challenge still to be addressed.

Clearly, there is still a gap between this positive outlook and the enthusiasm with which the future of customary law is viewed, on the one hand, and the need for a clear articulation and practical plans for achieving what at present should be seen as broad aspirations. Many questions still remain to be answered. How much can the laws of such diverse groups be fully harmonized to form a unified system of law capable of general application among increasingly interactive and pluralistic communities? To what extent is customary law capable of addressing the needs of the complex modern society beyond the cohesiveness of any homogeneous ethnic group? Is customary law capable of being adapted and modernized to deal with the emerging challenges of a modern state? To what extent is reform with a view to addressing issues of gender inequality and human rights protection in general possible without challenging and undermining the integrity of customary law? What is meant by making customary law a source of legislation generally? Does this imply legislation in areas in which customary law has competence or is it envisaged to be reinterpreted and applied to areas outside the traditional scope of application? What does making use of customary law and traditional cultures in general in the areas of constitutionalism and governance mean and how in practical terms can that be accomplished? And how can customary law be synthesized with elements of other laws, such as received Western law and relevant Islamic principles, to produce a legal system enriched rather than threatened and undermined by these outside sources?

These are only some of the questions that need to be raised and addressed in a practical way. And while the responsibility for addressing them lies mostly with the national leadership, those interviewed see a major, if complementary, role for international partners by providing both funding and expertise.

Whatever their ultimate implications in practical terms, these conversations give a remarkable insight into the thinking of individuals who will be among the leaders whom history has placed at the frontiers of revolutionary leadership, challenged to steer the process of reconstruction and nation-building in the South. That there is such a degree of consensus among them is an indication of how unified Southern leadership is on these challenges. If, on the other hand, they are a self-selected sample who might be at variance with others, then other perspectives not reflected here will have to be ascertained and comparatively reflected too. Then the search for an even wider common ground will be necessary. In my view, what is critically important is to generate debate on the issues involved – and as the South moves toward establishing a Government of their own, for the first time since their country became exposed to outside rule, the timing could not be more opportune. The conversations with prominent legal professionals included in this volume are almost certain to add to the debate on the role of customary law and contribute constructively to addressing the legal and broader issues facing the Government of Southern Sudan.

The interviews with the Minister of Justice and Northern lawyers differ significantly from those with Southerners, mostly because they focus on the legal situation at the national level, where Sharia has been dominant. But even here, as one might expect, the views of the Minister differed from those of the lawyers in that he represents the official view, and as he has contributed significantly to the development of the system he naturally defends it, characterizing it as more reflective of common law principles than of Sharia, despite perceptions to the contrary. The lawyers, on the other hand, see the legal situation and the interplay of religious and secular laws as "confused," "uncertain," and "chaotic," and see the post-conflict challenges of the CPA as the urgent need to address the crisis. In the discussion with the Northerners, customary law hardly figured, partly because they did not seem to know much about it. Indeed, with the abolition of the Native Administration in the North by Nimeiri and the repeal of the Chiefs' Courts Ordinance of 1931 and the Native Courts Ordinance of 1932, and their replacement by the People's Local Courts Act of 1977, they thought customary law had been abandoned, at least in the North. The truth, of course, is that it is being administered by the People's Local Courts, which function in much the same way as their predecessors.

2. Dr. Peter Nyot Kok

New Site, February 8, 2005

Francis Deng (FD): This is an interview with Dr. Peter Nyot Kok in New Site, Kapoeta County, Southern Sudan, February 8, 2005. Peter, as I mentioned to you the other day, I am interested in revisiting this whole area of customary law in Sudan. It has been quite a long time since I worked on customary law. On the other hand, Sudan seems to have been in a situation of flux, where one doesn't really know what the changes in the legal system are, and what the place of customary law is. I'd like us to sort of range and talk about various aspects of the legal system, with special reference to customary law. Let me first ask a rather philosophical question about the kinds of values that customary law is supposed to promote.

You and I have been to Yale Law School, and we know that according to the theory of law propounded by the late professors Harold Lasswell and Myres McDougall, law is supposed to regulate processes in which people seek values, using resources, through institutions, with certain outcomes and effects. We also know that different legal systems have their own normative frameworks, determined by their fundamental values. I think I am right in saying that in the evolution of Western law, property was the basis on which the allocation of rights and responsibilities were based. Accordingly, the process of reform was premised on property relations. We know that in other countries, Sudan today being an example, religion is supposed to be the point of entry, and everything else should then relate to that.

In the history of jurisprudence, we have seen how different schools of thought emphasized different sources for law. Natural law advocates emphasized the divine origin of law. Others adopted the historical approach that saw law as a reflection of the spirit of the people of a given society. And yet others emphasized the importance of the courts. More recently, the critical school emphasized social justice as the premise of law. What would you say are the fundamental values that the customary laws of the peoples of the Southern Sudan, as you know them, are based upon?

Peter Nyot (PN): Thank you very much Francis. I became interested in the customary law of the Dinka effective from 1999, after I became actively involved in the Sudan Peoples Liberation Movement (SPLM). It was an interest reinforced by the choice which I made to come and practice law in

Southern Sudan. I found very quickly that you can't practice law in a meaningful way without an awareness of what the customary law is. So, I sort of got into it from the angle of legal practice. I deferred defining what law was until the time I felt I had sufficiently immersed myself into customary law practice. In short, I will say that I can identify three main sources of customary law. Property is in place all right. I will still put it as a number one source of the customary law of the Dinka. I haven't really determined what I should put second between religion and what I will call the way of life. The two are not the same. On reflection, I will put the way of life as second to property.

FD: What do you mean by the way of life?

PN: Way of life is that part of the culture that is not predetermined by religion. It is the way people do things, such as the way people get married, that is not prescribed by religion; the way people bring up their children, that is not prescribed by religion; the way people bury their dead, that is not prescribed by religion. Those kinds of things. I distinguish these from those prescriptions laid down by religion. For instance, Dinka religion says that you should mourn your mother for four days, and that you should slaughter a cow on the death of your mother. This is the sort of thing I regard as having a religious dimension. Way of life is determined basically by what people have observed to be the way according to which their forefathers and foremothers had conducted their approaches to life; how life has been lived. Take cultivation, for example, there is no religious prescription for cultivating and for storing crops. It is what has been seen to work. I distinguish between those two categories. But I find it difficult to determine which one should get the priority over the other, between religion and the way of life.

Then there is the other category, which is the massive and pervasive influence of received law. As you know, English common law has the greatest influence; to a limited extent, Islamic law has also exerted some influences. These sources of law have had an influence over our customary jurisprudence. With the increasing coming into the practice of law by different lawyers, law itself has had to be interpreted according to the principles of interpretation in English common law. This too is not an insignificant source of influence. These are what I will summarize as the basic guiding principles of customary law.

FD: Although we'll come back to the influence of received law, it is interesting that you say that through interpretation you can transform the customary legal system. Will you give an example of the kinds of principles of interpretation that are transforming customary law?

PN: The area of commercial relations is an example. We didn't have a rule of customary law which required contracts over US$20 to be in writing. Due to the influence of received law, that is common law, contracts above fifty Sudanese pounds now have to be in writing. Sometimes they are written in Dinka. Contracts touching on land laws also have to be conveyed in writing. Traditionally, it used to suffice to have witnesses determine how much money was spent. On that basis, you could have the contract enforced by the court. But now, it has to be written to confirm the contract. If people don't know how to write, they have to look for somebody who knows how to write.

FD: It is interesting you identified those areas, because as you will recall, when I did my doctoral dissertation at Yale Law School, which I published as my first book, *Tradition and Modernization: A Challenge for Law Among the Dinka of the Sudan* in 1971, I attributed the logic of Dinka customary law, whether you are talking about substantive or procedural law, to certain basic values. I identified as number one, the importance of procreation, which Professor Harold Lasswell called the myth of permanent identity and influence. That overriding goal, or modality, as Lasswell preferred to call it, determines the way resources are distributed or shared, and the hierarchy of authority, starting with God, other deities, the ancestors, and coming down to the parents. The next overriding goal I identified was the notion of unity and harmony, subsumed in the Dinka concept called *cieng*, which advocates the ideals of human relations as a means of collectively pursuing lineage or ancestral values. Solidarity of the lineage required that members be united behind the clan, even though they do so as individuals. These values are then projected onto the community in its varying formation. A third and related value was the dignity of the human being, both as an individual and as a member of the community. This value is embodied in the concept of *dheeng*. Respect, *atheek*, is an aspect of *dheeng*. I always give the example of how in Western jurisprudence the dead person has no reputation and therefore cannot be defamed, whereas, among the Dinka, the reputation of a dead person is more important than that of the living. Will these be representative ways of looking at the system of values behind the law or are we being selective of what I consider important?

PN: I think we are being broader than what I consider to be the Dinka way of life and religion.

FD: For example, could *cieng* be considered a way of life?

PN: Yes, *cieng* will be a way of life. In fact, *cieng* came to mind immediately when I was attributing the sources of the legal system to religious beliefs and the way of life. I failed to mention *cieng* because the imposition of Sharia has affected our thinking. I was partly trying to make a distinction between those aspects of law that had sources in prescribed religions, such as the Islamic Sharia, and those, again drawing from the Islamic sources, that are known as *sunna*, or the practices of the people.

FD: So, in a sense, we are really interacting with the impact of Sharia and Islam in general?

PN: That sort of thing. I was reacting to that.

FD: That makes sense. I wanted us to begin with the logic of any one given legal system, and then move to the pluralistic situation of the modern world, specifically in Sudan, where different systems are brought together and interacting. This includes the traditional system, with its logic, the received English common law system, with its logic, and now Sharia, or Islamic law,

FD: Now, if we follow the argument that different systems have their own logics, their own value systems, and that in the modern context they have come together, how is the resulting pluralism being managed? We used to know the system under which customary law was part of a bilateral or trilateral system. Bilaterally, the system was divided into the civil branch, which included received common law and customary law, and the Sharia branch. The trilateral system included the received common law, Sharia, and customary law. We know that there has been the Islamization of the legal system. What is the situation today in the country as a whole? Let us begin with the North, and then we will turn to the South.

PN: The situation in the North is based on Sharia and the official position is that non-Muslims have special courts to go to in Northern Sudan, especially in personal matters. And I also noticed that most of the judges are scrupulous about that; once they detect that the case involves non-Muslims the tendency is to refer it to the non-Muslim court.

FD: These will be civil courts or customary courts?

PN: They will be civil; and they are part of the hierarchy of the judiciary.

FD: And they will be required to apply the parties' customary law?

PN: Yes, they will really go out of their way to look for that, unless, of course, it proves difficult, time-consuming or too expensive. I have known of cases where judges will say, "You people, there is an alternative; there is Sharia."

FD: I guess their reasoning will be, why worry about this difficult search for applicable custom when you have Sharia to apply.

PN: I have seen such cases. And in the cases where I had to offer such a choice to the parties, to consider Sharia as an option, they said, "There is no problem; that is OK."

FD: I suppose they will see the substance of the law that was applicable, in terms of the justice and good conscience and all that, to be in conformity with their sense of justice.

PN: Exactly; it was acceptable to them.

FD: Is this mostly on distributional issues, such as property suits?

PN: Yes, it was distributional issues like property. For instance, on the issue of inheritance, Sharia was acceptable, but not as often as the question of distribution of property. Inheritance tends to invoke strict adherence to the customary law of the Dinka, rather than the accepting of Sharia. Although in two Greek cases, the parties accepted Sharia, because it was almost the same as their own Greek Orthodox law.

FD: In these cases, was there a tendency at all in the minds of some litigants to see Sharia as a reflection of the cultural values of the Arabs, and therefore, that there was a conflict of identities in having Sharia applied to them?

PN: It was acceptable to them purely on the basis of justice. They felt that it was just; it was fair.

FD: So they didn't worry about the fact that it was Islamic? On the broader issue, how is the legal system, as we knew it, functioning today? You and I were trained in the old system. Many of our colleagues, who are judges or practicing lawyers today, were trained in the old system. What has the impact of Sharia been in the legal profession, and the overall administration of justice?

PN: Where Sharia has been enforced, as in Northern Sudan, it has definitely affected practicing lawyers, who must make intellectual adjustments to get informed about what Sharia says or does not say. And some of them in the process have become really good legal practitioners in Sharia. In the legal profession, it became clear that practicing lawyers had to get closer to Sharia. People will say, "You should go to so and so because he is knowledgeable on the law." We have not had that challenge in Southern Sudan for two main reasons. First, there is no competition in receiving the common law on matters of procedure. Most of the time, the procedure is derived from civil or common law. And we didn't make any fuss at all on why it should be so. Second, the question of Sharia did not arise because the Islamic clientele in the South was not that significant. And then our judges have always used the British-based legal provision of justice, equity, and good conscience, which is still useful, because in the absence of any provision, you apply the English common law. And it has come in handy to know.

FD: Because it allows the judge to borrow from any legal sources?

PN: Yes. As a result, we have introduced a lot of things in the administration of justice. So, those are basically the elements of the legal system. First, the legal system itself knows that it is inadequate in a number of ways. It knows very well that in the customary law area, you can be guided by the realization that it is eclectic. That is very liberating. And second, the hierarchy of courts has been flexible enough so that in customary law you can always go to any customary law court which has a reputation of competence and wisdom. People will say that the court in this or that area is well known for its fair administration of justice.

FD: And this will be irrespective of which tribal division is involved, or will it be within the same jurisdiction? For instance, if you have a tribe that has its own chief and its own court, will it be acceptable for that chief to allow his people to go to the jurisdiction of another chief?

PN: At the appeal level you have that choice.

FD: You make it sound as though the system at the national level, specifically in Khartoum, has found its equilibrium, and that there is now a functioning, well-defined system. My impression, admittedly from afar, was that despite the imposition of Sharia, various things are happening that, sometimes, judges, because of their legal education and disposition, might apply Western jurisprudence and sometimes Sharia, and that the system is being tolerant of these diverse ways of practicing law. Is that true, or has the system become fully Sharia oriented?

PN: No, you are right. And it was true even during the days when the system was very Sharia oriented. There has always been tolerance, by the way. Even during the heydays of Sharia.

FD: And this is in the North?

PN: Yes, in the North.

FD: So, people were doing different things despite Sharia being the normative framework?

PN: Yes, we lived through that, which was amazing. At the height of the celebration of Sharia, we had cases in the non-Muslim courts in which the judge openly came and said, "You go and look for your witnesses who can come and testify on this item of law."

FD: On the basis of the non-Muslim old procedures?

PN: Yes, on the basis of the old procedure. And this was at the height of Islamic enforcement.

FD: Would it be a case of the system turning a blind eye or would it be that they actually knew and consciously tolerated it and even accepted it? Did they pretend that it was not going on, or did they know it was going on and accepted it?

PN: They knew; they knew. They knew that it was also the right of the non-Muslims to avoid Sharia where their own law existed.

FD: So this was a concession for the non-Muslims?

PN: Yes, it was a concession for the non-Muslims.

FD: What about the Muslims, could they opt out of Sharia?

PN: At that time, no. Those were the hard cases.

FD: There was no flexibility there?

PN: I did not come across any; not at the time.

FD: Is the law well known to the practitioners today, or is it a situation where a few are well versed in Sharia, while most who were trained in a totally different legal system are ignorant of Sharia? I know you said that a few became experts in Sharia. But what does this say about the legal profession as a whole?

PN: If you take the bench, for example, I had the impression that judges, especially of the senior courts, that's from the province courts upwards, were well versed in Sharia. But the same was not true of the lower courts, where you had Sharia judges who were ignorant, who could cut corners, and were generally not well versed in the provisions of Sharia. That was clear. But at the higher levels, judges of the bench were reasonably good in how they understood and applied Sharia. And you had debates even within the judgments of those judges of how Sharia should be understood or should be applied. So, there was a reasonably learned debate going on among the judges. The same thing applied to the legal practice. As I said, over time, people became well versed. They, in fact, got some confidence that Sharia, in the last analysis, was not something that should be left to the Muslim Brothers. It was for everybody who could understand it, could interpret it, and could take cases to court on it, irrespective of the political monopoly, or political implications of Sharia, according to the political parties.

FD: What about customary law; is there any documentation of the law that lawyers and judges can refer to, or is it still very much a question of finding the law as you go along, in a practical sense, without any code or any documentation of the law?

PN: I have a feeling that what will have seemed to have been a shortcoming in research was not necessarily a shortcoming in the practice of the legal profession. I mean, documentation in terms of books, your book and John Wuol Makec's book, were immensely helpful, but there was a lot of room for going out and finding what the people were feeling and were living. There was a challenge of constantly being forced to go and see if what Francis Deng had said, and what Wuol Makec said, were still valid. But most of us were assured that what you people wrote was still valid.

FD: I think it is very interesting that you talk about the source of law being the way of life, which translates in Dinka terminology into *cieng*. Now, if that is the case, then it is pragmatic and dynamic, because *cieng*, or our way of life, is not static. It is constantly transforming itself, changing according to the needs and the dynamics of the situation.

PN: Exactly.

FD: So, you will say then that reform is built into the sources and the processes of the administration of justice?

PN: It is inherent in the way of life and the very nature of change. And that gives a lot of room for flexibility, both to the chiefs, who are the lawmakers, and to the administrators, who sometimes improvise laws, and without any embarrassment, particularly in the situation of war that we have gone through. For instance, the whole question of blood wealth payment became so flexible as to be unrecognizable. And the whole question that people have nothing, specifically cattle, in their hands, had to be addressed.

FD: So people used money and called it cattle?

PN: Yes, that sort of thing.

FD: By giving a money value to a cow?

PN: That's right.

FD: And then leave it for times when things will stabilize. Whether these cows will actually be collected or not is left to the unknown future.

PN: That's right.

FD: Last year, I attended a meeting of lawyers in Uganda. It was organized by the New Sudan Law Society. One of the themes which emerged that really surprised me was women complaining about being punished for adultery. It used to be that men were the ones who paid compensation for adultery. Later, some punishment was introduced for both the man and the woman. Now, they say that there is a strong women's movement against the idea of punishment for adultery. What principles are being advocated for reform, or in what areas is customary law being reformed in a visible way?

PN: Customary law is being reformed in a visible way in the area of personal law; I will say specifically in the area of property law, largely because of the pressure from women. There is pressure for equality of treatment, in the area of inheritance, for example. The women's movement is taking the whole system to task for the unfairness in which men and women are treated on issues of inheritance. The question of adultery was mentioned in apprais-ing customary law. Two issues were raised in Rumbek-Yirol area discussions of the issue. Traditionally, the female adulterer was obligated to confess whether the accused male adulterer was the only man that had slept with her. A lot of pressure was put on her to confess other men who had slept with her. When that happened, as it sometimes does, that she would confess the other men that had slept with her, the conclusion will be that she was an adulteress. That will actually mark her, that more than one man had slept with her.

FD: She will therefore be considered promiscuous.

PN: Yes, she will be considered promiscuous. And this actually protected the adulterer. The idea is that the alleged adulterer should not be the one to bear the punishment alone. The punishment is usually in the form of cattle, ten cows collected from the adulterer. If there are three other men whom she confessed, then the four men will have to share the payment of the ten cows.

FD: So, it would in effect be a protection for the first adulterer?

PN: Yes. In terms of reputation, it doesn't really matter, because adultery destroys reputation whether or not it involves one man or several men.

FD: The reputation of the woman?

PN: Of the woman and of the first adulterer, as well as any other men involved. The situation would be that today X and Y have been cited, in a case of adultery by woman Z, and it is done. Those who have been accused would be called and questioned whether or not they have committed adultery. In most cases people admit to having done it. Our people can be very honest, Francis; a man will come and say, "Yes, I have done it." Then he is made to pay compensation. The women then took the case further, and asked, "Why should we be the ones who are forced to confess, when men are not asked to do the same?"

FD: To confess other women with whom they might have slept?

PN: That's right; the man is not asked to confess. And women put the case on the basis of equality. They want that rule of evidence also applied on men. "Let the men be asked to confess, 'Have you slept with other women?' And we will see whether the same thing will wash by the men." They took that as a case of discrimination: "Look what is required of us, while the same thing is not required of men. That is inequality, based on sex. And that's because men have the power." In Rumbek, that rule of procedure was actually abolished. So people no longer require women to confess.

FD: So, emancipation is becoming a major factor of law reform?

PN: It is; it really is.

FD: Especially with women?

PN: And that is a logical place to begin from, really, because it was so blatantly unfair. All the women needed to do was to go public and very soon men listened to them.

FD: In these cases of people innovating, introducing new rules, is the general tendency to try to find the law, reinterpret it, and reform it, or is it because of the war and the disruption of society that the whole process is becoming haphazard and sporadic with respect to what law applies or does not apply or even what the law should be? Are people making a deliberate effort to find the law and reform it, to interpret it in a progressive way or even to invent it?

PN: Unfortunately, it is neither of those, given our educational background. When you talk of law reform, you are thinking of scholars, intellectuals, jurists, or even specialists who see the situation on a regular basis, following the law, and being provided with papers by scholars and so on. But that is not how it is in our culture. I have a feeling that soon people will demand that it be done in a more effective, more organized, and more predictable way.

FD: In the 1960s, what you are talking about is exactly what was done in both west and east Africa on law reform. There was the recording of customary laws. Then people looked at received common law. And then they looked into how to restate the law with a view to reform. Now, obviously the war situation does not permit this. And the national situation will not allow the development of customary law within the context of Sharia. But now that there is going to be a Southern government, do you see this happening? As you say, this is an area where there might be some deliberate effort to record the customary laws, to analyze them, to appraise them, and to then restate them with the view to reform.

PN: That's an area with a lot of possibilities, I must say.

FD: But so far nothing has been done?

PN: No. I have a feeling that the situation cannot go for long without something being done. It is an area that calls for action.

FD: If we speak of law in a holistic way, one will have to think not only of customary law, which deals mostly with personal matters, but also the issue of governance in general, which goes into constitutionalism. How do you see the challenge in the South, where most people are still ethnic groups that have not been that much transformed by modernity? To what extent do you think the system of governance that is going to develop in the South, given the fact that SPLM talks about decentralization, is going to be influenced by traditional principles of governance? Are customary law institutions, including such areas as the choice of leaders, going to become part of the modern system, or is it going to be relegated to a subsidiary or marginalized system?

PN: At the beginning of this interview, I thought that I should have mentioned that the challenge to law came, as we can identify now, from two main sources. One is what you have said, the challenge posed by notions of human rights, the rule of law, and good governance, including democracy. That is a big challenge. And then there is customary law as the way of life of our people, which also has its own dynamics. Those two challenges are coming almost at the same time, and it is difficult to prioritize them, that our priority should be this one or that one. People realize that the rule of law is something that you cannot put off for tomorrow; it is for now. Then there is the question, also, of the way of life of the people having to be accommodated, having to be monitored very closely, having to influence governance; that too cannot be put off, especially as people come back from war, try to resettle, and pick up their lives. It is something you have to do something about. Again this applies to the areas of customary law. Maybe criminal law and the rule of law areas are different because they involve constituencies with defined agendas. As far as the Movement (SPLM/A) is concerned, it has already talked itself into a frame of mind from which it is difficult to go back on the proper observance of human rights law; the language we have used, and the endorsement we have given, bind us. I mean, we will have to do a lot of explanation if we are not forthcoming, if we don't deliver.

FD: It's tough.

PN: Yes, it's tough. And especially, if you add other issues that may crop up. For instance, the question of truth and reconciliation which people will have to grapple with at a certain point in time; it is bound to come up anyway. So, on that basis, I don't see any embarrassment on the part of the executive, because it could be said that on these issues we have always thought that violations of human rights, where they occurred, have been individual responsibilities, not collective. And secondly, they could have been explained in terms of the war situation. Again, it cannot be collective guilt. In fact, as a member of the SPLM/A, I have come to believe that. In truth, the record shows individual cases of violations of human rights. It was not a collective responsibility of the SPLM/SPLA. So, I don't see any embarrassment in that field, honestly.

What we may decide to do will be an exercise in nation-building, in reconstituting the Southern Sudanese soul; that there is need to be truthful about what has happened and forgive what has happened. This is important for catharcism, for our own people themselves. In any case, it is not a cause of embarrassment; it is a case of being courageous, of admitting that, for the future itself, we need to be very clear about how these things happened and why, and how they should not happen in the future. We need to do that. So, human rights, the rule of law, and so on, are areas that should be confronted with absolute openness and with no embarrassment.

FD: But if we go back to seeing law as a way of life, then whether you are talking about democracy or human rights, or even nation-building in a broader sense, is it not possible to derive some of the principles from the traditional norms as guidelines? For instance, if you talk about the *shura* in Islam, this is a principle which you could say is an Islamic tradition; couldn't we talk of *cieng* as a traditional principle among the Dinka that is relevant to respect for human rights, that is relevant to being heard in a democratic way, that is relevant to the rule of law, knowing where you stand in the legal system, the values that the system is all about? Is that doable? We might say, yes, for instance, pertaining to Dinka society, but could we find equivalents from which we could draw comparative conclusions that will guide us? Yes, there are constituencies that are well known, advocates of human rights who are trained in the Western system and the global order, but can you reinforce them, as Abdullah An-Na'im might say, by normative interpretations that relate to the culture of the people?

PN: That one is an option that is very challenging and I am sure that the challenge can be met. It is not difficult, by referring to our own system of governance that we have been used to, to find that issues like forgiveness, tolerance, the absence of capital punishment, can be positive factors to build on. With respect to capital punishment, for instance, in the last analysis, the life of a human being is something that is very precious. That life should be spared is of prime value in our traditional system.

FD: Otherwise two families and the society lose.

PN: Yes. And there was logic for that in the culture itself. For a number of reasons, we tended to project our governance as, in most cases, self-governance, when in fact we have been continually under foreign domination. Every time we spoke of governance, it was under the District Commissioner who was a foreigner, or a *jallaba*, a Northern Sudanese. That did not allow us to focus on our governance very sincerely and consistently. There has always been somebody else who has always been above us. Policies were initiated by those above us, and our own norms and practices were tolerated by those above us. And that gave us a superficial view of our own system of governance. Certainly, it made us not emphasize our own principles consistently. Otherwise, the way we ran our traditional societies, given the sphere or the space we had, is full of examples of good governance.

Now, in the area of human rights, we have the opportunity to look into what these human rights are about, look at them point by point: freedom of speech, freedom of movement, whatever the basic human rights. And then we come and see the practice in our society and what we have done during our struggle. We will find that if there were issues of human rights that were of great concern, we will definitely have developed a human rights movement. It will have spawned to a reality. That reality was not all that glaring; it was not a daily issue which we had to confront. We didn't have institutions that were set up for that, for you could see that human rights were respected. There was always a Dinka equivalent of the human rights values that were being protected. It was probably the case that the meaning was not so clearly spelled out; it was not clearly articulated. The notions that these were things that should not be done, that this was not a good thing to do, that this was disdainful, were all there. Those are the core of human rights that will become issues to be confronted. And that was why your book with An-Na'im on cross-cultural perspectives on human rights in Africa was an important contribution. It was a very useful reading, and I thought that it was something that should have been taught in our universities, to force people to think about the equivalents in our culture.

FD: It is a case of different logics leading to the same conclusion, the universal dignity of the human being.

PN: Yes.

FD: If you discuss with the members of different traditional societies, explain to them what *cieng* is all about, and then ask them whether they have similar concepts in their society, I feel confident that they will have them. If you talk about the concept of *dheeng* among the Dinka, the essence of which is dignity and respect, I'm equally confident that other societies, such as the Nuer, the Shilluk, indeed all Southern communities, will have the same. That's why I think it is important that, rather than criticize me for having written on the Dinka, to encourage others to write on their own societies.

PN: Others should do that as well.

FD: Exactly, then we can all sit together and make a comparative analysis of what we have gathered, where we may differ, and what we have in common to build upon.

PN: By the way, I haven't come across people criticizing Francis for writing on the Dinka.

FD: Well, sometimes it is said jokingly, but sometimes seriously. Take that Northerner, Khalid al-Mubarak, for example. He specializes in attacking me, and sometimes John Garang, accusing us for advocating a vision of a New Sudan that he believes is anti-Arab. He criticizes me for writing about Dinka law, Dinka songs, Dinka folktales, Dinka oral history, and Dinka cosmology, and asks rhetorically, "What is Sudanism about that?" Of course, he omitted that I had written books about national issues as well. For him, what is national is what is Arab and Islamic. Anything else is parochial. He even criticized me for writing a biography of my father instead of writing about national figures like Ismail-el-Azhari or Mohammed Ahmed Mahjoub, his national heroes, of course all Northerners. He omitted that I also wrote a biography of an Arab chief, Babo Nimir. He considers me a Dinka chauvinist. To him, at least Garang talks about the whole Sudan, which makes me the blatant tribalist. Mansour Khalid once told me that John Garang had asked him, I assume somewhat jokingly, "Is your friend [meaning me] still writing on the Dinka." Anyway, I take all that with a sense of humor. I know Garang appreciates my writings on the Dinka as much as he does my works on Sudan. And I know that Mansour Khalid is very fair minded on the value of cultural diversity and the need to document all our cultures. As for Khalid el-Mubarak, I find his attitude a good example of the Northern chauvinism that we need to correct.

Thank you Peter for this stimulating conversation. Now, are there any other aspects of the whole system that you would like us to talk about?

PN: In fact, I wanted to pose questions to you, arising from my own experiences in the field, and on matters of law. First is the question of the absence of procedure in Dinka customary law. As lawyers, teachers, and practitioners, what do we do about the absence of a body of customary law on procedures? And then there are issues of property law that have come up, that will have to be given attention.

FD: I think we need to clarify what we mean by procedure. If somebody commits a wrong, let's say, in the case of homicide, what happens? Both sides, of course, get ready for the confrontation of almost certain vengeance. The wronged family gets ready for an attack in vengeance. The chief takes the initiative to intercede, to have certain rituals carried out in order to prevent people from attacking one another, the initial carrying out of the rituals, and the sacrifice of an animal to at least ensure truce, relative security or protection, before people go for peace talks or litigation. In the process itself, there are certain rules of evidence, some of which I tried to cover in my book, *Tradition and Modernization*, and which John Wuol Makec covers in his book on Dinka customary law: who qualify as witnesses, what evidence is permissible, what is not, and why? The argument is usually that the goal of the procedure, indeed of the whole lawsuit, is to find an amicable solution that will not only do justice, but bring people back together and reconcile them. Therefore, your evidence should not divert from that objective. This is why, sometimes, if a person says something outrageously divergent, he or she might be hushed, silenced, or the *agamlong*, who repeats what is said, will recast what is said in order to polish it up. And then there is the question of how to execute the ruling. If there is an award of compensation, how is that to be executed or enforced? So, it is a question really of what you are thinking of when you speak of procedure. You may be thinking in a quite different legal framework. Could you give examples of the kinds of procedural issues that you think are lacking in customary law?

PN: The area of corroboration is one. People seem averse to being called as witnesses, in court. The general tendency seems to be that this is not the way to conduct oneself. This is something in the culture that will have to be tackled. It is particularly true of criminal cases, when evidence is needed. The police will come and try to take the statement to prepare what they want to conclude. Somebody comes away with the impression that what was an innocent statement is misinterpreted to the extent that he is viewed as having become a witness against X or Y, which is considered antisocial and a betrayal of the accused.

FD: I think this is a case of conflict of cultural values. There is a strong bias among the Dinka against what is known as *lom*, to gossip [the perpetrator of whom is known as *lum*]; back-biting or repeating hearsay is considered despicable. So, on the one hand, when, for instance, somebody says, "That man insulted me; he said that my family are known to be witches," or he said, "There is leprosy in my family," and he goes to court to plead defamation, the court will ask, "Did you hear him say that yourself?" If he says, "No, I was told," his case will most likely be dismissed. The bias of the Dinka chiefs, or court members, will be to discourage your going about repeating something that you did not actually hear. In a sense, it is as though you are promoting your own defamation, by wanting the issue to be raised when you yourself did not hear it said. They do not want to encourage gossiping. By discouraging hearsay, they are in effect saying, number one, that you are spreading the defamatory material against yourself, and number two, that you are accusing another person of having gossiped. That person might have said it in a situation of confidentiality. People say things, for instance, about women's infidelity, where there are suspicious circumstances. And in any case, there are built-in social processes for unraveling secret acts that are considered wrongful. This is a well-connected community. So, if somebody has some inkling that someone has done something wrong, should misfortune befall that person, for instance, a woman suspected of adultery, word will go around confidentially and people will come and press upon her to confess her wrongdoing. The same is true of a man suspected of secret killing or who may know some wrong within the family that could be a dangerous source of spiritual contamination and should then be made to atone for the wrong. These things will surface on their own without public gossip. And at the right time, when the wrongdoer becomes discretely exposed, appropriate compensation will then be paid and the wrongdoer cleansed of the curse that was his wrongdoing. I think another factor, especially in criminal cases, is that punishment in the form of imprisonment and, in murder cases, capital punishment, is alien to Dinka culture. There is, therefore, a natural distaste about giving evidence that would support that form of punishment. It is as though you are betraying your culture values to serve a system that is alien and repugnant.

So, I think that one has to balance carefully these contradictory principles. One is knowing the truth, which the Dinka value very highly. Truth must be told even against your own relative, for it is dangerous to conceal the truth. When you swear, you must tell the truth. That is why our people, the Ngok Dinka, were infamous for exposing their people in their conflicts with the Missiriya Arabs, whose tendency is to harbor and conceal their wrongdoers. My father would call different people who, in one way or another, might have been involved, and would know what was happening, and press upon them to tell the truth. In contrast, the Arabs will cover up their culprits; they never reveal the truth. The other principle is the Dinka attitude against spreading rumors, gossiping, or hearsay, accusing people of wrongful deeds, unjustly. This is considered particularly abhorant if it means providing evidence to punish a person. This may have the effect of discouraging corroboration. But then there is another side, which is telling the truth. One has to balance those things. It may be a question of sharpening our understanding of the norms involved, and then seeing how you begin to change the value system. In a way, one can be sympathetic to that normative principle, because bad things get said which, if we retell them all, society will fall apart. Given the fact that the culture is against punishement by imprisonment and particularly, capital punishment, providing incriminating evidence, in such criminal cases is viewed as unconscionable and deeply disturbing.

PN: Then we come to the issue of land ownership, on which an agreement could not be reached in the peace negotiations. It was left open. We speak generally of collective ownership, but when we come to look at it carefully, there are a lot of loopholes. The government will have to deal with the question of collective ownership in a more understandable way than is being done at present. Government's hands cannot be tied indefinitely. On the one hand, important investors will be interested, definitely. They will want security of tenure from the government to hold the land long enough to make economic sense. On the other hand, there are culturally prescribed principles of land tenure which are very sensitive and to which people adhere religiously. How are these conflicting considerations going to be managed?

FD: You know, Peter, I was confronted with a similar issue in London when I was working on customary law. Professor Anthony Allott, who was teaching African law in the London School of African and Asian Studies, asked me to assist him on a property law project. Actually, he wanted me to go straight for a PhD in customary law. Having benefited from earlier research in the field, I guess I appeared to be more knowledgeable in the class than most students. In fact, even students who were doing their PhDs would consult me on their research projects. Allott's plans for me were interrupted by my crisis with the Sudan government when I was accused of masterminding the Southern movement in Europe. I had just written to the university that Professor Allott had recommended that I proceed with the PhD instead of an LLM program. Although not directly related to my course work, Allott and Professor Richard Gray asked me to join them in thinking out principles of property law, or what they called land tenure. I think the gist that we came out with, which I included in *Tradition and Modernization*, is that the whole notion of ownership and possession of property is misconstrued in absolute terms, when in reality it involves degrees of sharing of ownership and possession. Nobody has absolute right of ownership to do whatever he or she wants with property. There are always certain restrictions.

The Dinka combine the notion of communal land with very strong emphasis on individual possession, but with flexibility over the use of the land over a period of time, with the exception of *panom*, which is ancestral land. This is what you would call the clan land, where the ancestors are buried. It is a sacred place which you pass on to the eldest son. The youngest son has certain inheritance through the mother, but the clan property, the collective land, is passed on through the eldest son.

When it comes to land use, if a woman has been allotted her agricultural land, all the husband can do is help her in farming that land, but the produce is entirely under her control. It may be that the husband expects that she will use that produce to serve certain communal purposes, food for the family and things like that, but the Dinka emphasize that the man must not interfere with her land or with the produce from her land. If you have the land that you cultivate, that is also considered yours or that of your family. On the other hand, if you should move somewhere else, abandoning your property, that land should not remain fallow for long. If somebody else comes and finds it fallow, having now regained its fertility, and wants to cultivate it, he has the right to do so. It may be that if you are still interested and want to use it, you may have prior right. Otherwise, the principle is that you must use the land, or it will be used by somebody else.

So, I think one has to break up these concepts of property into different categories with different principles. It is a question of categorizing on the basis of different principles. I think *panom* is the collective land of the family, although it is under the care of the elders. Cultivating plots of land is under individuals, including women, as the producers. Land must be used, and if it is not used over a long period, others can come and use it.

PN: Another issue that is going to confront us very soon is the question of the property of the *jallaba*, the Northerners who used to be here in the South.

FD: Actually I should add something, in response to what you were saying before. Now, we are confronted with a new situation, where there are investors who want some security over possession of land, at least over a certain period of time. You also have these dilemmas of the country becoming one, and the freedom of movement, to settle wherever one wants. We have this particular problem in the Ngok Dinka area of Abyei, because the Arabs want to move in. In fact, there are parts of Ngokland that they have already settled and cultivated. For a while, we have been struggling with the central government authorities who argue that people have the right to go wherever they want to go. What do you do? If you allow that, then you are really breaking down the territorial elements of the identities of the ethnic or tribal groups. I don't think we are at a point where we can ignore these notions of tribal identities and the land associated with those identities. The question then is how to reconcile, on the one hand, the need for development, including encouraging investment, which will require some fundamental prerequisites of property control, with, on the other hand, respect for group identity, of which land or territory is an essential element. I think this needs a lot of thinking and work as to how it should be managed.

PN: The question of the *jallaba*, the Northerners, abandoning their plots of land has now gone on for 15–20 years, about the same time the war continued in the South. I can imagine them coming to claim the lands, the plots, they used to have in the South. In the process, of course, those lands and plots and so on have changed hands and so on. At the same time, some are still identifiable and some houses or buildings are still intact. There is need for a policy on this issue. In some cases, this will constitute injustice for some people who thought, in good faith, that they had acquired the land and established themselves on their own land. There are real issues to be addressed. I thought this is an issue on which we should reflect.

FD: You know, Peter, this is an issue that comes up very often with respect to problems associated with internal displacement. It's a big issue. We have commissioned some studies to deal with the property implications of movement. People are forced to flee their properties, sometimes for a long time.

Their properties get occupied. Then they return and want to reclaim their properties. I think, rather than give any vague recollection of the themes from the studies, what I should do is get those studies, and then see how problems like that were settled in other situations. One of the experiences that could be looked at very quickly is that of the former Yugoslavia, because these problems occurred in a massive way. The period of absence from one's property was not so long in the case of Yugoslavia, but the duration of time is a problem in the case of Cyprus, where the occupation of the land has gone on for a long, long time. Any resolution of the conflict, including reunification, will have to address the question of land. I'm sure the issue is already being discussed. I think it will help us to look at some of these precedents. So I'll see what I can find when I go back to Washington.

PN: Those were my concerns.

FD: Now what about the Arabs who are living in the South, do they tend to hold to their Sharia, or are they flexible enough in how some of the customary laws may apply to them, in practical areas like property and personal family problems? Is there a sense in which people see their law as part of their identity, or does the situation begin to impact on the people, just, as you said, the Southerners in the North, pragmatically say, "This particular principle of Sharia seems fair and acceptable?"

PN: What has happened in the South, in most of the SPLA-controlled areas, is that we now do not have Northerners. Not at all.

FD: Really!!

PN: Yes.

FD: So separation has already taken place.

PN: Absolutely. In terms of Northern presence here in Rumbek, it is my view that it has. If I were in Wau, then the situation may be different, because in Wau you can find a Northerner owning a house or as a government representative here and there. But in Rumbek, Yirol, and so on, there is none. So we have an experience of a different Sudan, which is free of *jallaba*, or Northerners.

FD: Very interesting.

PN: People find it difficult to believe.

FD: That's why Garang says that self-determination should be precisely what it says, to be self-determining. So Southerners seem to be already exercising the right of self-determination.

PN: You know, Francis, it has become a different experience altogether. You live in a place for a year without seeing a *jallaba*. The whole question of *jallaba*/Southerner relationship is no longer there.

FD: Do our people feel themselves freed, or do they find new problems with their own people administering them?

PN: I see a sense of freedom. They are more relaxed in dealing with their own people. I also discovered that there is a high degree of intolerance toward the authorities, especially seeing something which is oppressive from your own kind.

each in the Nuba Mountains and Southern Blue Nile, making five circuits. However, these judicial circuits have been made to fall under one senior judge, for want of judges. So, I preside over circuit 3 and 4, which comprise Western and Eastern Equatoria. By virtue of that position, I am Chief Judge for the Equatoria Region at present. Having said that, for the last three years, I have been involved in the process of restructuring the system.

FD: Thank you.

John Luk (JL): My name is John Luk. I am also a graduate of law from the University of Khartoum, 1977. Prior to that, I worked briefly as a local government officer in Bahr el Ghazal, specifically in Yirol. I then went to the university after a year out. On graduation, I went and worked for the Southern Regional Ministry of Legal Affairs, as a legal counsel, until I went for postgraduate studies in the United Kingdom to do a Masters degree in law at London University. I finished in 1983, coinciding with the outbreak of the war in the South, so that I couldn't go back to Sudan. Of course, the Southern Regional Government by then was dissolved. The South was broken into three regions and we were all transferred back to the Attorney General's Chambers. I couldn't go to Khartoum, as I joined the struggle. For some time, I was in London as the spokesperson for the SPLM/SPLA until 1988–89. I then came to the field, to the front, trained, and was deployed in Central Upper Nile. After working in some other areas, I was deployed as a civil military officer in charge of judicial affairs also. I was a Judicial Officer for Central Upper Nile, until 1991, when there was a split in the SPLM. I then went back to London, and later came back again to the field, and became Secretary of Information and the Official Spokesman of the SPLM/SPLA.

Currently, I am participating in different capacities. I have a center called the Center for Documentation, which I run there in the United Kingdom. I try to follow events in the South and document, or get documents, and keep them as archives. I am involved with the Civil Society Organization, training in advocacy issues of human rights, women empowerment, paralegal training, for the NGOs, helping them with their constituent documents, and so on. That is where I am. I have also been a member of the negotiating team of the SPLM until peace was signed. We don't know what is next.

FD: Thank you very much. I want to begin with an approach which may reflect my own bias, but please feel free to come in with your own perspectives. As a point of entry, it's my belief that every society has its own fundamental principles and values that determine the logic of its legal system: what the rules are, who gets what out of the system, what procedures they follow. In some societies, there is the moral code, attributed to natural law, descending from divine sources. In other societies, the logic of the system is based upon property as the most important thing. For instance, in the Western system, it is known that property was the basis for determining status and much of the distributional principles. Some schools of thought take the historical approach to law. The so-called realists emphasize the role of the courts, while the sociological school considers a whole lot of things in the social context.

In my first work, I looked at our Nilotic legal system as premised on the fundamental principle of continuity through the lineage, a principle of biological and social immortality, to continue life hereafter, through the family one leaves behind as one joins the chain of ancestors after death. Every individual is vitally important, but as part of a chain in communal solidarity. The solidarity of the clan, which emphasizes the values of unity and harmony, is subsumed under the Dinka concept of *cieng*. The notion of individual and collective dignity and respect becomes very central to being remembered. In the Western legal system, it is said that there is no reputation for a dead person. So, you cannot defame a dead person. With us, defaming the dead is even worse than defaming a living person. I say all this in order to ask you, in your knowledge of the legal system of traditional law, what you consider to be the fundamental principles or values that determine the substance of the law and procedure in customary law.

PM: I will start from the premise that where I come from, being a Dinka Agar, the people start to point a finger when talking about something that is criminal or a civil wrong. They start to say, *kerac*, it's bad, whether a civil wrong or a criminal act; something that is not desired to happen; something that does not promote the harmony or the coexistence of the people, either as a family or as members of a clan or as a community that is living together; something that is evil; something that should not happen to interrupt good relations, the pleasurable enjoyment of human existence or the sharing of whatever is good in the life of the people. This to me is what I regard as the basis of law where I come from. *Kerac* is something bad, something wrong.

But the distinction did not develop between what constitutes *kerac* as an aspect of something criminal, and *kerac* as an aspect of civil wrong, something that has not offended the public interest but has offended an individual. And this goes on to the present day. In the communities that are living still intact, there is no clear distinction between what should be described as a crime and what should be considered a civil wrong. You will find that when the court arrives at a decision, what was initially a civil, or for that matter a criminal offence, starts from the premise that *acaa luoi kerac*, "he has done me wrong." This, to me, is the way I conceive the entry into what constitutes a crime or what constitutes a civil wrong in our particular community. The essence of it is, should such a thing have happened and what should be done about it? If there is no *kerac*, then people live in harmony, and the society is free of evil. If it is free of evil, then that is a good society in which, what you mentioned earlier, *cieng baai*, the good *cieng* of the land, is maintained and thrives. Life goes on and history is recorded in the oral form in which it is passed down. This is one.

Number two, for purposes of communal protection, in order for the localized community to protect itself from any adverse action by another clan or subsection, *kerac* must be prevented. *Kerac* coming from outside must be faced by all. It starts in the family, where a child should be prevented from committing *kerac*, something bad. And whatever comes from outside should be collectively faced by the members of the family, or the clan, or the community, in protection of their good state of affairs that is free of *kerac*. And *kerac*, with us, should come from outside; it should not start from within. It is a very conservative way of thinking. Of course, *kerac* must always come from somewhere, but it is prescribed that it should not start within the group. With the socialists they will want you first to scrutinize yourself on what happened, are you free? Are you free from any wrong? Are you not part of what happened? And once you are clear that you are not part of what happened, then you can point a finger in the other direction. In our case, *kerac* does not come from inside, and that is why evil, *kerac*, must be prevented within the group.

JL: That is very interesting. Taking the Nuer perspective, I believe the Nuer will have an answer to the question you asked as to what the fundamental values, or principles, of customary law are. The Nuer have certain words they use. They have the word *dhuer*; *dhuer* is wrong. When they judge, they look at an act, and measure it against what they think are their benchmarks, or their standards of norms. They will look at an act committed against an individual, which could be, say, a tort or a criminal offense. They will come and bring the whole range of community perceptions of what is right and what is wrong. So, the Nuer will talk in terms of, "This act is *dhuer*," which is a wrong. The opposite of *dhuer* is *cuong*. *Cuong* means what is right. This is how every case is judged. It is giving *cuong* or it is giving *dhuer* to the persons concerned.

And there is a sense of collective protection, because, given the village system, the segmentary lineage system in which Nuer society is structured, an act of an individual does not end there. If it is judged as *dhuer* in the eyes of the society, it has implications that threaten the security of everybody. An individual is not held responsible for his acts alone. The consequences of *dhuer* flow over, so that if he doesn't make a redress quickly, so that people feel that he has recognized his wrong and has really repented, the consequences are self-help on the part of the wronged party. And in Nuer society, enforcement of customary norms, of violations of customary rules, immediately triggered self-help, because there were no courts then.

Even today, that is still the case. If you don't acknowledge your wrong, and you are seen as arrogant, the person who has been violated is encouraged to defend his rights, and challenge the wrongdoer to a duel, for instance. And should it happen that the wrongdoer is physically stronger than the wronged person, and believes that he can commit an offence with impunity, because he is strong, the rest will join in support of the wronged person, to show the culprit that he is wrong. Sometimes, this may bring communities into conflict. For that reason, those who are close in blood relations to the offender will immediately intervene to correct him, because they know the matter will not end there. So, one is not taken as an individual.

But if things get out of hand, and people come and find that the situation is out of hand, then it becomes a different matter, because there is a kind of mutual defense among relatives, whether you are wrong or right. A Nuer man, if he finds a fight raging, and he sees, for example, Paul Mayom, whom he knows, being beaten, and is on the losing side, will immediately jump in to defend him, without questioning whether he is wrong or right. Later on, they will make him sit down and ask what the problem was. "How did you get into this?" And if they find out that he was in the wrong, then they will get on him, and put all the blame on him. In terms of resolving the conflict, they will then go to the other side, to make apologies for what had happened, and be ready to pay compensation, because they recognize that the wrong is on their side. The feeling of common survival is always a motivating factor. It is an urging feeling that you don't let your kinsman suffer a beating or a misfortune without you coming to his defense.

These concepts are also underpinned by a feeling of spiritualism. People will tell a wrongdoer, "God will not accept this." They try to link up these values to divine will. "What you have done is wrong," they will tell him. And that is a source of fear. So, you abide by certain principles within the community because you are afraid that going against them will have consequences for all, apart from the communal self-help that can also affect all. Nevertheless, there are strong people who believe that they can act with impunity. And there are people in the community whom people fear because of their prowess in fighting. Despite that, there are still spiritual powers, of whom all people are afraid. There is a strong spirituality among the Nuer.

So, those principles, the principles of wrong and right, which provide their yardstick in judging, are also underlain by fears of doing wrong to somebody, which is not right. There is a punishment for it by an invisible power. Even if you are very strong you may find your children get sick, and you will begin to feel that it is because of a wrong that you have done. Relatives come and plead to God to find out if a wrong has been committed. A diviner may be asked to help find out the source of sickness or misfortune in the family. He will come and say, "It is because of some injustice you did in the past. God is angry. That is why your children are dying." The man will have to confess, repent, and get an animal to be sacrificed. He will pray, "God, I did this and it was wrong." This helps also in keeping the community in harmony. It reduces conflict. One source is that a person fears the kind of reaction he will get from the people he offends. But if you think you could get away with that from the people you offend, then, still, the wrong will hunt you in a different way. You do not want that risk. You want your family and your relatives to live in peace and security; you don't want to earn divine wrath, the wrath of God, which can punish you severely. So, I think these are some of the underpinnings and guiding principles in customary practices.

It is important to bear in mind that the individual is not alone. Whatever you do has got some impact on the nuclear family, and on the extended family at large. Therefore, if you commit some offence, which could be a tort or whatever, or do harm to somebody, you know that you will also offend your own relatives, and they are going to come to you. They have a name, and they have an interest in you as a relative. What you do goes back to them, even to the far distant relatives. You may not feel that you have a responsibility, or a duty of care to a third party who is not a relative, but you have a duty of care to your own relatives. In your moral conduct you always think of them.

So, I think that is what helps maintain public order. Nuer society has no centralized authority. We never had chiefs before the British came. So, how did people maintain order? I believe it is through these principles that order was maintained. And, of course, we have the traditional institutions that also have to enforce, or reinforce, customary norms, like the traditional spiritual leaders, such as the *kuar kuac*, the leopard-skin chiefs. So, you cannot commit a wrong and keep quiet about it; you must go and report. Even if you kill a person by accident, it is important that you go and report yourself, so that you are cleansed before anything else. You can't keep quiet about it. Whether you killed a person in a tribal fight or in a separate duel between the two of you, for instance, it is your duty to go to the *kuar kuac*, the leopard-skin chief, and tell him what you have done. He will tell you, "Go and get a bull," maybe of two-stripe color pattern. "Bring it." He will slaughter the bull, make a small cut on you, mix your blood with the bile of the bull, and have you drink it. Now you are cleansed. Your next problem will be confronting the relatives of the deceased and preparing to defend yourself before the settlement is made, and the compensation is negotiated and paid.

FD: You know, there was something in Paul Howell's book, *Manual of Nuer Law*, and I believe it is also in Evans-Pritchard's book, *The Nuer*. They argue that it is only if both parties desire the involvement of the leopard-skin chief that he will intercede or intervene successfully. The point was made in Allott's class on African law in London. I raised my hand to say that the word "successfully" means that the leopard-skin chief could intervene any way, even if not successfully. On the other hand, I argued, whether he will succeed or not is a question that cannot be predetermined, because, once he intervened, other factors could enter to affect the outcome. Professor Allott was very impressed by that argument, building on the use of the word "successfully." If there is a conflict, even before the conflicting parties give their consent, people will approach the leopard-skin chief and ask him to intervene. He will get involved. Evans-Pritchard and Howell made it sound as though the leader is passive until called upon by the parties. Doesn't he actually intercede immediately, once a wrong has been committed?

JL: In fact, he does. First of all, even if the conflict is still on, he intercedes. He is in the community and is recognized for playing that role. He also knows that whatever the level or intensity of the fighting, he is always a protected person. No side will harm him. He will even penetrate into the middle of the fighting. He will make certain spiritual sounds or noises, which, if heard, will make people become frightened. If you continue fighting, then you are going to face the consequences of God's punishment. So, he is always very active. He will just get into the middle of the fighting. Of course, in the heat of fighting, people get locked in fighting, and might not notice the chief. But the moment people say that *kuer mon* [spiritual leader] is here, even if only for his own safety, people will begin to be careful, because killing a spiritual leader inflicts a terrible curse that nobody will want to risk. So, he has a kind of restraining effect, once he is there.

Of course, usually, the elders come in and intervene and try to stop the fighting. Fights break out only when the elders on both sides have not discussed, or have not agreed, but there will always be elders who do not want conflicts to start or continue. And so they will normally join in the effort to end the conflict. They bring in the leopard-skin chief and use him, because he is a law enforcement officer to them, until the fighting is stopped. Once the fighting is stopped and there are casualties, then people sit down to negotiate a settlement. People run to look for the chief to mediate.

These days, with the use of guns, a man accused of having committed homicide will say, "I fired in front of me and I saw somebody fall. I don't know whether I killed somebody or not." But such cleverness will not pass; that won't be enough. Your people will pressure you to tell the truth, for, otherwise, you will get contaminated. You will not be able to rest or sleep, until you admit, repent, and carry out the appropriate rituals. Physically, your people will protect you against the other side; but spiritually, you get protection after you go and report yourself, "I have done this wrong." However, nowadays, because of the spread of firearms, it is easy for a person to say, "I fired, but I don't know whether I shot somebody." So, it will take a lot of investigation to be able to identify the culprit. But even if there is doubt, they will not explain it in your favor and assume that you are not the culprit. They will compel the suspect to go to a spiritual leader, who might take a decision on the issue.

Nowadays, someone accused of having killed in a fight may argue, "I was fighting on this front of the battle; I could not have shot and killed someone on the other front." Previously, with spears and sticks, you knew your victim immediately; you were immediately identified. These days, things are changing, because of the introduction of the firearm: How do you get the evidence? Who did this? It is a problem. Recently, I was in Akobo, and I got a case of a relative of mine who was being accused of having killed somebody. He said, "No, I am his brother." His younger brother had killed somebody. Then that younger brother died; he was killed in a fight. Now, the relatives of the deceased, the first one who was killed, were seeking compensation, the *dia*, blood wealth. The brother argued that it was a disputed case, because even before his brother died, he said that it was not he who had killed the person because he was on a different side of the fight. When they went to court, they argued their case. The court held that nothing could be decided, because there was no way of ascertaining the evidence. So, again they resorted to the spiritual remedy, and told the parties to go to a man in Ayot area, who was supposed to have the spiritual power of divining any wrongdoing. They went. I found that they had already gone to Ayot. When they came back, they found me in Akobo. I asked what had happened, and how it was decided. They said the spiritual leader said that it was the deceased who had killed the person.

PM: And his death was interpreted to constitute guilt.

JL: Yes.

FD: But will that be enough punishment?

JL: No, that imposed on the relatives of the accused, who was also killed under different circumstances, the obligation to pay compensation. The killed killer was held responsible for the first killing.

FD: But the point is whether his being killed in the subsequent fighting could be construed as punishment for the wrong he had done, a form of spiritual capital punishment, which should not require his family to pay compensation.

JL: That's possible. In fact, one of our other relatives came and confided to me that the deceased had confessed to him that where he fired, he saw somebody fall in the grass, and that he might indeed have killed a person. That meant that unless the wrong was redressed, there could be spiritual contamination. So, now, they are going to pay the compensation, even though the culprit is already dead.

FD: There seem to be similarities in what both of you have said.

PM: Yes, you are correct; there are similarities, taking specifically the key word that you emphasized, that is "successful" intervention by *benydit* [big chief]. The process explained by my colleague, John Luk, is an accurate reflection of the situation, even among the Dinka. The first stage is one of engagement to stop the parties from fighting. I am convinced that this is what happens. The other complication comes with the intervention of *benydit* or the spiritual master, to initiate the reconciliation or the settlement of the case. Whether he will be successful if he is called upon to reconcile between the relatives of the deceased and the relatives of the offender or the accused is a challenge. The status and the reputation of a particular *benydit* comes in. How much is he valued in the community? If he is a man of his word, is believed to have close relations with the spirits, and is well connected to godly powers, he will be respected. He will perform his function, and his word will be taken as final. The most complicated situation I see is, if this *benydit*, who, for particular purposes, wants to bless a given section in order for that section to get an upper hand in the fight against another section.

FD: As a means of empowerment?

PM: Yes, as a means of empowerment, a means of imparting luck to them, so that they do not suffer harm or that they inflict harm on the other party. If they go and the fight takes place, and he is later asked to mediate in the reconciliation process, it becomes problematic, since he had blessed one side against the other.

It becomes particularly complicated if he were sitting as *benydit* that has been awarded judicial powers by the local administration. As *benydit*, he will then be the Chief Administrator with judicial powers. If he does what I have just explained, that he blesses one side into battle, people move, the fight takes place, and people get killed from the section that he did not bless, how could he then be an impartial judge in the court proceedings? He had approved of the war and, as *benydit*, had asked the spirits, and probably, with the aid of whatever other powers he could invoke, and the wrong has been committed with his approval, how does he now stand qualified to try the case? And if his reconciliation process results in reconciliation, what the Dinka call *cuil*, how valued will that be?

This is where the question of whether he will be successful as a good judge or not is really pertinent. You cannot authorize a fight and sit as a judge, and mediate the reconciliation. The whole process of customary law is, in fact, reconciliation. It boils down to the norms of peaceful coexistence, reconciliation, and living together harmoniously. This is an intricate part of the challenge before us, and which I see will need to be carefully considered.

FD: Building on the two points both of you made about rights and wrongs, the spiritual dimension, and the power of the divine leaders, if the leopard-skin chief blesses people to go to war, in principle, can he bless his people successfully if he doesn't believe that they are in the right? Could he bless his people when they are actually the aggressors? In contrast, if he knows that there is aggression coming, and believes that his people are justified in their fight, and he then blesses the warriors on the basis that justice is on their side, will that make a difference?

PM: Well, precisely, and in brief, I am aware of the spiritual masters who are *banydit* [plural of *benydit*], who have specializations in the areas of say, blood, *malual*, "red." This is a group which is specialized in occasioning death or life based on what group of people comes to them and requests to be blessed as they go to battle, calling on the spirits, for them to be fortunate and to inflict losses on the other side. He is paid for this. And you go all the way to engage him. That becomes a sort of commercialized transaction which is supposed to benefit the group.

I know of people who do this. They call themselves the "people of blood." These people do not necessarily have judgment on the events. People come to them and say, "They have killed our brother." Sometimes, compensation will even have been paid. And yet, they want to revenge. This is not justified, but for a man of *riem* [blood], or *malual* [red], or a spiritual master, who commands these particular spirits, and this line will give you all that he knows and ask that you go and do whatever needs to be done. He has nothing to do with things like blessing you to increase your wealth; this is the specialty of another person. Blessing you to be endowed with children is the specialty of yet another *benydit*. There are people who are specialized in settling disputes who do not necessarily engage in matters for which people request their blessing.

take procreation as the fundamental principle, then it means that the ancestors come above the fathers and the elders next, and that kind of thing. And it also influences defamation; for instance, who gets insulted and how grave is the offense, if directed against somebody in a particular category. Those of you who deal with issues of rights and wrongs, how do these rights and wrongs begin to influence the substance of the law, and the procedures of the legal system? Which of you wants to start?

PM: I will just want to make a brief comment on the aspect of the blood cattle, of the compensation for homicide, and the main logic why, for example, the Dinka, will want a specified number of cattle paid to the relatives of the deceased. I believe the principal reason is what you stated. The main logic behind it is what you said. These cattle are received and should expectedly be used to perpetuate the lineage of the person who has been killed. A woman has to be married to live with a relative to bear children in the dead man's name.

The reason for why the blood wealth cattle should be divided gives another reason. They say that there is no way in which you can eat a human being, a relative. The only way for you to eat a relative is if he is dead, and blood compensation becomes due. Now, you will be entitled to take what portion of the bones with the attached meat is due to you in the established distribution of a sacrificial animal. And this is very clear in the way they divide the parts of the meat, when the animal is killed, and especially when it is killed for ritual purposes. Each son, the elder son, the next, other sons, the sisters, and the aunts all have their predetermined shares. Using the same logic, they consider that this is the only way to taste the blood of your deceased relative, in the form of animals that have been given the family in compensation.

Now that marriages have gone high, and the compensation is still low (thirty-one in Bahr el Ghazal, unlike Upper Nile which varies from twenty-five up to one hundred), there is a discussion now among ourselves to revisit the Wanh-Alel statement of Dinka customary law, so that a clear balance is made. Of course, there is no price for human life, but you will have to balance whether the war has sufficiently affected all, and that some number, equivalent to twenty-six cows, has continued to be confirmed as the legitimate bride wealth or not.

JL: With respect to compensation, of course, there is a co-relationship between the blood wealth and the bride wealth. In marriage, you do not pay the bride wealth alone. All your relatives collect to assist you, to be able to pay for the marriage, to perpetuate the lineage by bringing forth children. In that same way, if you are dead, you have been killed, the very same people who actually contribute cattle to your marriage to found a family have a right to share in the cattle of compensation for your death. When the compensation is paid, it is distributed just like bride wealth.

So, in terms of the substance, on this question of rights and wrongs, there seems to be a commonality, or collectivity, of interests and rights. For the family, of course, there are other things a person does for them and which will be missed when he is dead. There are so many services which he is supposed to perform. I think keeping his name alive is most important. And it is the duty of the family to ensure that one's name continues. Even if he were to die, he will have power over them. They call it *colwic*. This sometimes manifests itself in lightning. To honor him, the family will be under duty to see that a woman is married for him, so that his name is maintained. It will be as if he hasn't died, as if he is still there, with all his rights among the living.

In terms of the rights we were talking about concerning the violation of rights, certain rights are conferred, based on the recognition of right and wrong. Whether it is cattle, marriage, your house, or any other property, it is recognized by the community that you have certain rights that should not be violated. People keep an eye on the recognition that a person, though an individual, which they also value, has rights that should not be violated. I think it is a kind of collective protection, because the community comes up in defense of individual rights. Why is this? Nobody will say it is up to the individual to defend his own rights, except on such small causes that you pursue in the Chiefs' courts. But in areas of social rights, your interests are protected. In the case of adultery, for instance, it becomes not your problem alone. The fact that your rights on your wife are violated becomes a clan issue. In fact, people used to fight on that issue. Even now, they still do, although the ferocity of these fights has been reduced.

PM: The way I look at how our people grade what constitutes a wrong and what constitutes a right is directly related to the community establishment. It becomes right when we are peaceful, settled, conversing, and sharing things equally as a community. That is right; a state of stability. A state of something wrong causes tension and destabilization comes to the community. This is the bottom line; it is wrong, something needs be done to right the wrong in order for people to be stable.

JL: To achieve an equilibrium.

PM: Yes, to bring people to stay in harmony. This is the bottom line for what is wrong and right. As for the other aspects of what constitutes a right, that is another matter that concerns either an individual or a family. These are rights that are due by way of continuity and so on. This is, of course, different. You were investigating the normative framework of customary law, the values behind the law, what constitutes right and wrong. This is what I wanted to say about that. As we are here now, we know what is right, and what is wrong. If one of us here throws a stone at a person outside there, a tension will arise; a wrong will have been committed. Anything that destabilizes is wrong; anything that stabilizes is right. It becomes much more of a wrong when you relate it to something higher than purely human considerations, for instance, when you relate it to heavenly or spiritual values. For example, theft, the way people regard it and want to discourage it is a matter of human prestige, that the son of X has shamed his family by stealing. But compare that with the crime of adultery. Compare a person who has committed theft with someone who has committed adultery. Of course, God doesn't like theft, but if it is adultery, the spirits that guide you as a human being won't be happy. You will not have protection from them. This is where they grade you. And actually later on, it becomes the basis for the determination of the penalties to award: which one has God's prohibition, and which man also says is wrong? There are certain things that are wrong, but minor in nature, which, to them, have no immediate relation to God's prohibition. And I think what we said earlier about stability and maintenance of harmony really forms the logic and the basis for determining what is wrong and what is right. What keeps you settled, and happy, with no problem, is what is right; what keeps you in trouble and unstable is what is wrong.

JL: Just to add to that, I think in terms of the substance of the law, the generalized reactions to a particular act, and describing it as right or wrong, set the standard, and this standard has evolved into common values. I think in terms of the substance of the law, that depends on the society, the community viewpoint on a particular act, and the way it judges certain acts that they consider repulsive to standards they have set within themselves. And I think in that way, depending on the events in the community, societies, over years, begin to develop concepts of norms and values which they adhere to, which they view with respect and follow. I think this is how our customary law systems have developed and are developing.

Now, with assistance from the customary courts, even though most of the customary courts' decisions have not been recorded, still, the old chiefs remember the cases. These are open courts and people come and sit. As in parliament, you come and sit and listen. A case of really serious implications will normally be followed by almost everybody in the community, how it has been decided, how the community has reacted to it, and how other customary courts have reacted to it. They keep it; they remember it. So, I think the sense of right and wrong evolves and becomes consolidated, to define the value system within the society.

Even when they had no such law enforcement agencies, like the modern ones, still the community took certain things as essential values for harmony within the community. They maintain this social equilibrium in the community. Individuals begin to feel that if they engage in certain kinds of activities, they will be unacceptable to the community, their own community. And the price of being notorious is, of course, isolation. What an individual does, if it is negative, has a bad implication for the immediate family, and maybe for the distant relatives too, and perhaps his society at large. And the way people carry themselves, the pride with which they carry themselves in their community, is such that you will not want to be seen to be going against what have been established as important values in the society.

Take cattle theft, for example. You have people living in a very large area, with different clans and without cattle theft. It is only because of the war that you now see the Nuer going to steal cattle from other Nuers. Traditionally, you seize cattle from your relatives as a matter of right. If your relative is greedy and you are in need, especially during famine, you say, "I have a right to get from him what I need to survive because he is my relative. I must get it." Even if he wants it back, he will get it back in good times, when things are alright. So, you do it and the community would accept that. In fact, at times, the community will say, "If this family is so poor and there is famine in the land, they have the right to bring the relatives to court." Their relatives will be told, "You have to give this family some cows, so that they survive the famine."

This is the kind of mutual assistance needed during times of difficulties. In terms of values, this feeds into what becomes custom or the cherished norms of the society. I think these evolve as reactions in the society. People develop the feeling that you must be a decent person within your society. It is only now that people go to Khartoum and get lost there. Previously, it was difficult and extremely rare for people to get to a very far distance. You may move to a territory of a neighboring tribe, and go with only some of the reputation about the terrible things you have done. You go to hide there and not come back. But if you want to live in the community, then there is a compelling demand on you, that you live according to the community's sense of wrong and right.

FD: That is all very interesting. Let's now come to the context of today, in particular, the pluralistic context of modern Sudan and the place of customary law in this context. But before getting to that, what you are both saying reflects a society that is cohesive, that accepts fundamental values and cultural norms, and in which, in a sense, there is consensus behind a normative framework of rights and wrongs, including entitlements. What about the situation today, given the degree to which there has been some impact of modernity and people are no longer confined to the traditional context, and a large portion of whom are no longer preliterate, and in fact have varying levels of education in the community? What you both say is premised on a society that is coherent, cohesive, where people share fundamental values and cultural norms, and accept these norms as sacrosanct. They see it as the way God wants them to live. But given the fact that we now have a pluralistic society in terms of levels of education, that we live in different, far apart areas, and in the context of the modern nation-state, with the impact of other cultural and legal systems, as we converge into one national system, are these norms beginning to be challenged, being reformed, or being revisited, with the view to addressing new concepts of justice?

JL: I think there is a real problem right now. Our society, the old traditional society, is no longer what it used to be. There have been very strong external influences, and there has been a great deal of mobility. People now have new values. People have been exposed to education. People have got exposed to other societies. Local societies are no longer local societies in their localities, as they used to be. The means of travel has now increased a lot of things. People live in other communities and see different ways of doing things, especially in the cities, for instance. Also the modern system, the state administration, has come to intervene. This plurality of systems, of norms, has had its own impact in the way traditional systems, traditional institutions, their resilience, are being greatly challenged. And there is also a degree of lawlessness that has taken place. Our areas have been devastated by war for many years.

So, the tendency has been to get away from what used to be our normal way of life, our traditional values, that we cherish so much, that we wanted to preserve. That life has become so difficult, no longer what it used to be. For instance, now, almost every young man in the area has got a gun. Violence has become rampant. The means of prosecuting the conflicts are different. The tools of the conflict are different. So, I think, there is a great challenge to be met. The elders are bewildered. If you go to our villages, you will find the elders are so bewildered that if you talk to them, and even to the chiefs, they will say, "Nobody listens to us anymore." The young generation is a different generation; it is a generation that is no longer attached, or afraid. The fear that people used to have, the fear of divine powers or the curse or contaminations of wrongdoing, these are not effective anymore. These are eating into the traditional values that we used to have and the harmonies that our traditional societies used to enjoy. This is a very big problem and a big challenge. I think the war has played a very big part in this.

PM: Yes, I totally agree with you, John, especially in highlighting that aspect of the war. I would like to take it from its initial stage that this regime was predominantly governing, and specifically prescribed by our people for a stable community, that was not being influenced by any external sources. With the sudden or gradual change to this pluralistic life, and the modernity that is coming in gradually, the first category that got affected really in our communities are the values, not necessarily the laws. The values that people live by have been profoundly affected.

Earlier on, there were certain values that were being respected, not necessarily because acts in violation constituted a wrong when they were being done, but because they cost the violator and degraded him before the people. But they were not necessarily wrong. These values have really been affected greatly. To give an example from my community, Agar, where I come from near Rumbek, when I was young, I never saw a gentleman who was not married, getting into a restaurant, to go and eat. There is, of course, nothing wrong with going to a restaurant to eat. But at that time, it was something, which, if you did, a song would be composed insulting your name, that things have deteriorated to the extent that the son of so-and-so was seen to be entering a restaurant to redeem his stomach from hunger. This is an element of some of the values that were regarded highly. You shouldn't eat in the house of your in-laws, leave alone a young man who is engaged, but not yet married. Even if you have completed the marriage, or have followed all the requirements of a valid marriage, you still have to perform certain social rituals before you can partake of food among your in-laws. This ritual is called "washing" or "cleaning" the mouth. Of course, you did not come with a rotten or dirty mouth, but you should not appear to be eager to eat your in-laws' food without performing the ritual. This ritual usually entailed your being given a cow or cows after which a feast was prepared and you were persuaded to eat.

Now, the effect of what you mentioned, such as the haste which has been introduced by modernity, the need to move, the need to get employed to pursue a means of living, and the imperatives of war, that life is no longer lived at ease, have all affected our society a lot. And, consequently, the stringent thinking of our people on these matters has either been reduced or has been abandoned. They are not being seen the way they used to be seen in the past.

This has its own implications in terms of people coming to reside with communities that were stable, the impact of their stay, and the attitude towards life. To cite one example, an American, whom the Dinka named Makuen Anyiel, was once penalized for having passed very fast, on the road, with a motorbike that had a bad exhaust and was causing too much noise. Normally, the Dinka did not have a crime, or a tort, that will penalize someone for having caused noise. Nor were there means for making such noise. People used to pass by quietly. You can see we are importing things and losing some essential aspects of certain values that were intended for that stable past. With time, some of these values are getting relinquished slowly, and without much concern.

The fundamentals are still the ones that constitute the stability of the people. These are the ones with which they are concerned, and they will want to resist changes in these areas. But even these are getting affected. To give another example, in the past, when someone died in a nearby house, children were not allowed to go to that house until after three or four days. Children were not supposed to know about death. It was feared to inflict a curse that might cause some evil, such as bringing disease. But these days you find people burying a person, and you just pass by, greet them, and express sympathy, "Sorry this tragedy has hit, but nothing can be done; it's God's will. Strengthen your hearts."

A very strange thing happened in northern Bahr el Ghazal. This is a true story. It happened last year. People had a misfortune. One of the young men of a family died. He was living with his mother. Some relatives and friends came to assist in digging the grave. In the course of the burial, relatives brought some alcoholic beverages, and people drank while digging the grave. Maybe it was meant to make them work faster in digging the grave. The body was still inside the hut. One of the volunteers seemed to have had too much alcohol and fell asleep nearby. It was getting dark. When the grave reached the required depth, by mistake, people went and picked up the man who was now lying drunk and placed him in the grave. Unfortunately, this is a true story.

FD: Where was the body?

PM: The body was inside the hut, and the mother was there, inside the hut.

FD: And where was the man who was drunk?

PM: He was lying nearby, in the vicinity.

FD: But not in the same hut?

PM: Not in the hut. They buried the man. When they realized what had happened, they said, "Nothing can be done, God has taken him." And that's all. The mother could only say, "What can you tell me now that you have not put your brother into the grave?" All were astonished; this was a serious matter.

Now, you can see the element of alcohol being introduced in the burial as a new thing. This is coming with this *karama* business, a burial feast which is alien to our community. The impact is gradual and there is no way of preventing it. The economic aspect of life among the people is dictating these changes. Now, people can work, and earn money. The value of the cow as wealth that was left to you by your ancestors is being reduced. And if you can get money when you are working, and if you can get treatment in the hospital when you were supposed to go to *tiet*, the traditional healer, then some of the old ways gradually begin to change. And you find now that people do things in disregard of what *bany bith* [chiefs of the sacred spear], the spiritual leaders, say. And these have their own implications on the authority of the spiritual leaders who sanctioned the customary practices that constitute our customary law.

JL: Let me add to what you are saying. Now, there is another aspect, Christianity. If you go to Upper Nile, especially in the Nuer areas, Christianity has spread to the extent that even an elderly man will say, "I want to be baptized." Elders will come and ask to be baptized. And the young people, you find them in groups, traveling, traversing the whole area. They will travel from Akobo up to Nasir, maybe up to Gaijak area, very far out to Ayot. You see them together, boys and girls, mature young people, eating together and sleeping together. In the past, that wouldn't happen; you wouldn't be eating with any girl just like that.

So, Christianity also has come with some impact. The result is that people feel that our traditions have become something of a lower category. As a Christian, a man will say, "Oh, those traditions, we do not follow them because we are Christians." When we try to remind them of our real values, they look at those values and say, "We are Christians; we are people who have been baptized." Baptism is now seen as a way of getting out of tradition, mainly by the youth who are now getting baptized.

PM: There is no *jok* [plural, *jak*, traditional spirits].

JL: No, nothing, no *jok*, no *wal* [traditional medicine]. They don't take *bany bith* [spiritual leaders] seriously anymore.

The war is another source of negative change. Among the Nuer, they say that a soldier has no shame; a soldier can do anything without feeling shame. So, the young men, the SPLA soldiers, will come to the village, ask for some *dura*, sorghum, and pound the grain themselves. Traditionally, a young man could never do that at home. As a soldier, you are armed, you are given some sorghum, then you go pound it and do what only women are supposed to do.

They will also grind the grain on the *pil*, the stone grinder. In the beginning, it was something very surprising. These young men who are gentlemen, how can they be doing these kinds of things!? And with brewing the local beer, the *merissa*, when it has not yet been filtered, soldiers just take their socks off, wash them, and help themselves by filtering the brew with their socks. So, a lot of things are changing.

PM: On this issue of Christianity, John, the way our people take Christianity, and from your example, this is also true with the Nuer; they accept that they are Christians and that salvation comes through Jesus. But I have been told a story, in which the legacy of our hierarchy of beliefs, the hierarchy from *Jok*, to *Aciek*, to *Nhialic*, seems to be maintained in line with Christianity. They take Jesus as the Son of God. And God is there. An incident occurred in one of the places where people sat and were praying. One of the people, who was a very famous man, is reported to have said, "Look here, you Jesus, son of Mary, we have been praying for the last several years and you have not come to our help. Now that you seem not to be passing our message to your father, please get out of our way and let us talk directly to God, your father." That was not from the Bible; it was from their preconception that you can perform *wal* [medicine], go to the spirits, but if all that does not help, you sacrifice a bull and plead directly to God. This sacrificial animal is *muor Nhialic*, "the bull of God." This is another aspect of African religion. And I will want to believe in that, because, if later on, things fail in the middle here, you will want to take another way out.

JL: Our traditional way.

PM: That's right.

FD: This whole issue of change is very intriguing. We should get back to the impact of the war, even on litigation, on the judicial system, and the impact of Sharia in the Northern Sudanese context. But on the specific point you just raised, as you were talking about the impact of change, I was wondering whether there are different categories of values, some fundamentals that our people will consider to be part of their identity, of their human dignity, things that are so deep that they cannot be discarded easily, things that are likely to continue, even as they change. For instance, we talk about the concept of *cieng* among the Dinka. I don't know the equivalent among the Nuer. *Cieng baai* is how people relate to one another.

JL: Yes, it is *ciang* among the Nuer.

FD: So, it is the same. It is *cieng* with an 'a' for 'e'.

JL: Yes, 'ia'.

FD: That's very interesting. In the United States, in virtually all the Diaspora conferences I go to, our people are calling on their people not to abandon *cieng*, to remember our *cieng*; that kind of thing. Obviously, it does not mean that you should conform literally to the way people used to live, but it means that there are some fundamental values or principles that you should not discard. Are we able to distinguish between those categories that are deeply rooted and those patterns of behavior that are more prone to change, such as people eating standing or going to a restaurant, or pounding grain? I want us to come to a concluding question, as to what all this means to the future of customary law for our people. But we will come to that later.

PM: In the process of change, there are fundamentals, the fundamental premise from which our great-great ancestors based their lives, and which need to be preserved. Those bases have successfully helped them continue to support their lives from time immemorial to the present. One example will be respect of a young person for an elderly person. That is *cieng*. That is the way people live together in the land. *Cieng baai* is based on learning from the experience of the elders, not the young teaching the elders, a thing which is now getting affected, as the young acquire modern education and become more knowledgeable than their elders. *Cieng* meant something equivalent to biblical teachings: respect your mother, respect your father, respect the elders, don't destroy the property of the family, take care of the members of your community, defend the community. These examples, and much more put together, constitute *cieng*. Our society was based on the premise of respect of the young for the elders, and the duties each generation, or each group, was required to perform for the community. This particular aspect, which we should hold to, is the strong need for our young people to maintain respect for the elders. No society can function happily without respect for certain norms or mores. I do not know about other societies, and the way they organize their social life. The possible way all of us can contribute to preserving some of these fundamentals requires that we sit and investigate, identify, and find out precisely what constitutes the essential principles of *cieng*. And we should see if they can be purified. Purification means improving upon them, establishing them, and entrenching them into our systems as a basis for our laws or principles of customary law.

FD: This means respect for our ancestors, our forefathers, and their legacy as embodied in the culture and inherited wealth of knowledge, and that kind of thing.

PM: Exactly. As in your case, for example, the Sacred Spears of your Pajok lineage. These spears did not stay there for nothing. They did not continue all this time, and generate all the stories about them, without a value that is implicit in them. That really needs to be discovered, and clearly made to be a strong base for the continuity of the people and the society.

FD: Could what we are saying include the tradition of age grading, even if we stop cutting their heads? Other ritual forms of age grading could be developed. Among the Jews, there is the ritual of *bar mitzvah*, when a young person reaches a certain age, and is ritually made to assume certain responsibilities. This could be a tradition that helps organize people according to the needs at the various stages of life.

PM: Exactly, giving them duties, assignments and qualifying them to do or not to do certain things. For instance, a child shouldn't drink alcohol. That will not constitute *cieng*. He shouldn't insult an elder; that is not *cieng*.

JL: That is a very interesting point. When I was in Central Upper Nile, I saw these young men being initiated and given scarification on their foreheads. When this ritual is done, they are considered as having now gone into manhood. And they take a different way of life. They become gentlemen, warriors, fighters. You can no longer send them on errands to go and get this or that. They can no longer milk the cows. They can no longer look after the goats and sheep. And yet, they were really minors by our modern legal standards. They were children. I called a meeting with the chiefs and explained that these boys were very young and marking their heads was not good because it put them into a stage which they are not mature enough to handle.

FD: What age, roughly, will they have been?

JL: I believe about 13 or 14.

FD: Among the Dinka, isn't it about 16 to 18?

PM: Yes.

JL: If you had gone to Upper Nile, you would have seen that they were just 13 or 14. I don't think they will even be able to carry a gun. But they carry guns now. So, we tried to stop that. I thought we should stop it because they were too young. I didn't think that was the age for them to take such a major decision. But, of course, this was the custom, the tradition, after a young man reached a certain age. Earlier, that was 18 or more. But then each family began to feel that if their young men were not initiated with the marks, it was as if they did not have a man in the house. Given all these deaths resulting from the war, people needed men to fight. You could see the attachment they had to the custom. Some chiefs argued that it was permissible, even though they were still very young. They admitted that when they themselves were given these initiation marks, they were already quite grown up, perhaps between the ages of 18 and 20, as you said was the case among the Dinka. So, they sympathized with my concern. But when I gave an order that nobody should initiate his son, and that whoever did so would be made to pay a fine in cattle, they tried to respect my order for the first month. But after a few months, they will take the children to some far away place, and they will come back with the scars, still very fresh. I imposed fines on some people. It became a big problem, as some of them resisted. The oldest of the men argued, "This is our tradition. What are we going to be if we leave this tradition?"

FD: Their young men would remain perpetual children.

JL: That's right; they will remain children, what they call *dhol*, uninitiated boys.

FD: Exactly. In fact, it is the same word among the Ngok Dinka – *dhol*.

JL: But then I said to them, "Look at me, I don't have initiation marks and yet I have children." They believe that if you are not initiated, there are certain things you cannot do.

FD: You cannot date girls, for instance.

JL: Exactly; because you are a boy.

FD: And you can only flirt with girls after you are initiated.

JL: That's right; not until you are initiated. In fact, if you went with somebody's wife, and you are a "boy," not initiated, you cannot be found guilty of adultery and be made to pay compensation. Even in fighting, if the enemy finds out that you are a "boy," not initiated, they cannot kill you. So, it has some privileges, you might say, as well as problems. If you are not marked, if you have not been initiated, then you cannot legally commit certain offences. Even if you commit certain offences, that will not be illegal. You are not culpable, because you are still a minor; you are considered a minor because you have not been initiated into adulthood.

FD: That's a very sophisticated view.

JL: Yes; you are considered not capable of committing certain offences; so you will be left alone.

PM: There are some legal implications for initiation.

JL: Yes, exactly. You cannot be held guilty of adultery, for instance.

FD: But if a woman commits adultery with a boy, that will be a big disgrace for her.

JL: Exactly; it will be a major disgrace. But we also have found a similar situation with the leopard-skin chief, the *kuer kuac* or *kuer mon*. He does not commit adultery; he is not held responsible for adultery.

FD: Really? Why?

JL: Nowadays, that applies to his wife too. There was a case where one soldier, who was from the family of *kuer mon*, went around and had an affair with a married woman. But by tradition he cannot pay *aruok*, compensation for adultery. Also, if you commit adultery with the wife of a *kuer mon*, you don't pay, because he can't claim cattle. So there was a young man who was involved with the wife of the *kuer mon*. People claimed that he should pay compensation. The decision was that he could not because the husband was a *kuer mon*, a leopard-skin chief who was not spiritually allowed to receive the cows usually given to a husband whose wife has been violated. That is a problem. So, we decided there must be some punishment, a fine to be imposed, but to be paid to the government, not to him. They accepted that.

PM: Let's go back to the concept of *cieng*, which we were talking about earlier.

JL: Yes, we were talking about *cieng*. I digressed from that. But *cieng*, which in Nuer we call *ciang*, we actually speak of a good *ciang* and a bad *ciang*.

PM: Ideals.

JL: Yes, the pursuit of ideals. We will say this person has got a bad *ciang*, because he does not observe the norms of the society; he doesn't respect them. He will become notorious. People around him will say, "Isolate him, ostracize him." He is ostracized because of his bad conduct. He does not respect children; he does not respect women; and he does not respect his colleagues. He doesn't have the integrity or the dignity the community wants to see in its members. You will get some people like that and people will shun them for not observing the values of *ciang*.

Now, with our young people who go abroad to other places, when they come to leave, people give a party for them, and advise them, "Please don't abandon our *ciang*. The *ciang* you are leaving behind, don't abandon it. You must hold to it until you come back." That means keeping our values with you. "Don't abandon them, because you will be nobody if you go and take up other people's values. So, remember how you used to live back at home." You already named a number of these values: the question of mutual assistance within the community; the question of respect for the elders; the need to protect your community. And when they go, say to America, the advice given to them is to hold together and not forget our *ciang*.

With women, in particular, one of the things we hear that is against *ciang*, is that they go and get involved in extramarital affairs and leave their husbands, whom they left here at home. People come to hear what is going on. Cattle had been paid for their marriage. The relationship had been established between the two families. It should be considered a sacred bond. But now, the word that comes back from there reports that she has gone. Stories begin to circulate that so-and-so has been left by his wife. The parents at home lament that their children have forgotten their *ciang*; they have forgotten our values, by which the wife should respect the husband and keep the family intact. So, different factors are coming in to affect *ciang*.

PM: Whether *cieng* has deep roots in our history, or is the result of a dynamic process that has developed a set of values in changing circumstances is something I am still speculating on. I think *cieng* is an accumulation of values, over time, again and again. And my concern now is the way *cieng*, which entails the values of our communities, is becoming disadvantaged somewhere. If we take the example of Christianity and baptism, the spiritual values of our culture that constitute our history as an embodiment of *cieng* have been destroyed with the shrines. The priests move all over the villages and begin to destroy them as symbols of Satan. They have forgotten that apart from the spiritual beliefs associated with these shrines, they represent the manifestation and values of *cieng*. They carry with them values that are institutionalized in spiritual terms.

FD: And they provide a link to the ancestors.

PM: They are a connection with the ancestors.

FD: Which is itself an embodiment of a code of moral conduct; a legacy.

PM: Exactly. So, essentially, we are losing. And this is, of course, as Dr. Francis was saying, the impact of modernity on our culture and our customs. I will not want people to destroy these symbols, because they should remain as concrete references from which we should be deriving, and investigating in depth, our legacy and our cultural heritage. If you go to our villages, there are men of small gods. We call them *kulaang*. They tell you things. These are people possessed by small spirits. Now, you come and find the young people in the family becoming Christians. They will begin to try to discredit all these people by saying that these things are of Satan. They must not be tolerated, because they contradict Christianity. The young people come into conflict with the older people on these matters. But I think these beliefs and practices have their own power for spiritual survival. People are attached to them. In fact, these spiritual functionaries try to find out what is happening within the community, including people who are sick. People come and gather around them to perform rituals, trying to connect with the ancestors and the gods.

FD: I think we need to have some principles for remedying this problem. In fact, I would like to raise some questions about that. But before we get to that, there is an aspect of change, of modernity, of the destruction that I would like to raise. What has been the impact of the central government policies, particularly the introduction of Sharia, in our societies? When we were in law school, when I was doing fieldwork that gave me the material for my book, *Tradition and Modernization*, I was the only one in the Faculty of Law who was able to conduct a study of customary law, because of the strong resistance from the system. The Northern Sudanese establishment did not want it. So, my British and American professors were the ones who encouraged me to conduct fieldwork, including preparing substantive areas of law to investigate. My colleagues, Gordon Abyei and Natale Olwak, when they went back to their communities to study customary law, were suspected, even by the chiefs, and certainly by the government authorities. They were considered subversive.

In my case, because my father was the chief, rumors were going about that I was being prepared to become the appellate authority who would see my father's cases. And so, when these rumors became rampant, I talked to my father, at one point. I told him that I was hearing things that I was not happy about, and that instead of sitting in court, recording cases, I would like to interview people at home. I asked him to tell the chiefs, so that when I called on them to come to talk to me at home, they would be responsive. My father smiled in a way that indicated that he knew what I was talking about. Earlier, at one point, he asked me, "Mading, this study of Dinka law, is it only in our tribe here, or is it throughout the country?" I assured him that it was an academic exercise that applied to customary law throughout the country.

At that time, there was prejudice on the part of the Muslims, especially the Arab-Islamic-oriented central government, which I believe, with the introduction of Sharia today, should be even more. I know that later on, when I graduated, or just before I graduated, the Faculty of Law began to send students into the field to look into customary law. At our time, it was discouraged. What is the situation of customary law today in the modern Sudanese context?

JL: If you go back and look at the constitution of 1973–74, the Nimeri Constitution, custom got recognized in the constitution as one of the sources of legislation. Before that, of course, it was in the laws, the civil justice ordinance. The laws that replaced it in 1973–74 also carried customary law; it was recognized as a source of legislation. And, in fact, in the courts, there are decisions that upheld customary law, at certain levels of the court system. But that was in the North. In the South, in 1977, the People's Local Courts Act, that replaced the Chiefs Courts Ordinance, was enacted. It also recognized that the chiefs were to apply customary law within their own communities. And the bulk of litigation, especially in the South, was, and still is to this day, under customary law.

I do not know whether this is still the case after the introduction of Sharia and the coming to power of this NIF regime, but it seems that there are customary courts in Khartoum. And they always talk about them. Even during the peace talks, they said, "Your chiefs are there and they are applying their customary law. Nobody is interfering with them." And indeed, when we were holding the Wunlit conference we had a lot of Nuer chiefs from Khartoum. They were based there. There were chiefs from Akobo, chiefs from Wau, chiefs from Ayot. They were based in Khartoum. They had their courts there. They had their *alamat* [robes] on them. They were there applying customary law. They would collect heads from different clans, and put them together to act as an appellate authority on customary law matters.

But I think, customary law as it is, whether in the constitution or in the laws, is still subordinate. The stipulated condition is that it must not contradict justice, morality, and good conscience. Even in our own laws, we have put those preconditions for customary law to be recognized. And customary law used to be taken as a matter of fact, not law. When an issue of customary law arose in court, you would call witnesses to come and testify on the custom as a matter of fact, before you would take it into account. But I think we now have the opportunity to really consider the application of our customary laws. Now that we are going to have a government for the South, I think this is the time to reenact the statutes on customary laws that were originally derived from the colonial legislation. No serious work has been done in this area, except perhaps the Bahr el Ghazal conference of the chiefs, in Wanh-Alel.

FD: Is that document available, by the way?

JL: I think it should be available, including in John Wuol's book on Dinka law.

PM: I have a copy.

FD: I will really appreciate having it.

JL: So, that is where the customary laws have been restated, codified, and enacted into law by the Bahr el Ghazal parliament, after the South was divided into three. So, I wouldn't think the introduction of Sharia in 1983 has any impact on our customary laws. The attitude of the Northern judges, of course, would be that these definitely are inferior laws or customs.

FD: So, the meeting of the chiefs, in which they adopted the reform of the law, was when my father was still alive, because Peter Nyot said that my father was invited and expected to attend, but could not make it the last minute because of other commitments in Khartoum. There, the chiefs got together and reassessed customary law with a view to reform. I think you mentioned it earlier.

PM: Wanh-Alel.

FD: Perhaps they were talking about my brother not my father.

JL: It must be your brother.

PM: As for the impact of the subsequent Sharia laws on customary law, the way I saw it, in 1983, when Nimeiri declared these laws, they were meant to be of universal application. There was no exception as to the South. He abrogated the Addis Ababa Agreement and declared September Laws, which were the Sharia law, to be applied countrywide. This actually became one of the major reasons that fueled the resumption of the war, the liberation struggle. That was also what made the youth and the officials to join the liberation movement. It was also the very reason why intellectuals defected and the Southern Sudanese judges chose to resist the application of Sharia law in their respective courts. I think Sharia continues, and to some extent I was able to get some sections in the criminal code, which we translated, Dr. Mansour Khalid and myself, that were excepting, exempting really, the three Southern provinces from the application of Sharia laws.

FD: Isn't there a provision under the new constitution to that effect?

PM: Yes, there is. We had to translate it to support the argument that the exemption should also be accorded to Southern Sudanese who are resident in the capital city. To me, not much of effect really, has been occasioned by the imposition of the Sharia legislation, because people have protested against it in the same way customary law resisted the application of Sharia laws in areas where customary law would be preferably the pattern or the law of the day. As to its merit in the legislation, of course, the North prefers to have Sharia as the number one source of legislation, albeit with the recognition of customary law as also a source of legislation. But now, we seem to have very clearly parted ways. The source of legislation in the North will be Sharia, with all its components, while the sources of legislation in the South will be the customary law and all other sources of values. So, essentially, I have not noticed any great change in the position of customary law. The application of customary law has persisted against Sharia law in the same way people decided to rebel against the imposition of Sharia.

FD: Let's consider the diversities of our communities. It is clear that there are different customary laws in the South. However, when I studied customary law in London University, it used to be said that there was as much that united African customary laws as there was that divided them. The first question will be, is it now time to collect these customary laws, at least the major ones, to conduct a comparative analysis to identify the common themes in order to then restate the law with a view to reform? An aspect of that will be, as we reform, is it possible to have some fundamental principles stated, along the lines of *cieng* [*ciang*], which will guide us in terms of a moral code that can then be translated into legal principles, and that could provide a basis for a reform agenda that is philosophically grounded in the culture, but also specific in its principles, covering various aspects of the law, whether we are talking about criminal law, or torts, or family law, or evidence?

JL: I think where we should start is what you said; you have to ascertain the different customs, the customary laws of the various communities. Even when we speak of custom as a source of legislation, in our new setting, we will be expected to build on our traditional values, and identify what are common within our communities, which we can use as principal sources of legislation. Otherwise, we will just be continuing with the old colonial statutes, borrowing and borrowing. Of course, there are areas in which customary law will completely fall short of meeting the needs. Those areas we will leave to modern legislation.

So, I think, even for us to draw up an agenda for reform, we must be able first to ascertain, codify, and restate customary law principles that are being applied within our various communities, and have a comparative look at them, with a view to regularizing them, and trying to deduct the rationale behind the principles. From our findings, we will then look deeper behind the customary law provisions and their rationale, so that we are able later to generalize and compare among the communities, and how those values and rules developed. So, it will be important that research be conducted with a view to codifying customary law, reforming it in the light of the new developments, and modernizing it to meet contemporary needs. For instance, our women today cry very loudly against some of our traditions and customary law provisions that tend to discriminate against them. They see these as very negative and that they retard the progress of women. I think we will have to sit and scrutinize the customary law provisions in each community.

Reform should take into consideration some other standards in certain areas. Some of the customs, although they are ours, may not qualify to be graded up to the level of where we can use them in our future legislation. But I think the key is really to know exactly what exists in the various areas of the law, whether it is in family law, or in the area of torts, or in the area of property. For instance, with land tenure, we need to know what different customary laws are out there. Land will be a very important issue for us. We have been saying that land is owned on the basis of customary law, but we have to establish what exactly the law is in our different societies. Say, for instance, in the Dinka society, how is land owned? How is land owned in the Nuer society? What is the situation among the Bari and the Azande? What about the resources that are part of the land? We now have oil and other resources; what will be the role of the state in the ownership and management of those resources?

So far, we seem to be promoting custom, and rightly so, because this is our base. But you cannot promote it when you have not made a thorough research to know exactly what it is, so that you are able to reform it. Reform should come after the laws have been recorded, then restated and codified. That is when we can crystallize the principles that we can generalize in terms of legislation in the South. We could then produce what we can call our own law. The source of that law will be from us, and it could be powerful.

PM: I wouldn't, I'm sure, differ with you. My reaction will be to the question of whether it is really about time to act on this matter. My answer is in the affirmative. Action is very urgently needed, in fact. We urgently need to undertake the task of recording our customary laws. First, we need to identify the ethnic groupings that are closer to each other, record and analyze their laws, try to distinguish, compare, and contrast various views on the laws, and put together those that do not have serious contradictions. After such analysis, you come to the process of harmonizing the various laws. And once you have harmonized them and ensured that all the stakeholders accept the process of harmonization, you can then take those that qualify, and use them as the basis for codifying what you could then call your customary law, which you now take and legislate upon.

Most certainly, our thinking has been, yes, we must have our source of legislation in our custom. But we are falling short of providing the basic fundamentals from which we should be deriving our laws as of now. And I really commend your initiative. We should undertake this, even during the pre-interim period. It wouldn't take too long to discover some of these regimes. And as John was saying, we should cover all aspects, going to personal matters of succession, issues of interpersonal relationships, and so on. That basic material can be collected in a very short time. What may take time is the process of harmonization. Even analyzing the material is not a big issue to me. Once you have recorded it, you simply analyze it. Harmonizing the different laws is what will need a larger group of people.

I think this is a very critical time in which we really need to undertake this work. It is very important, and we are focused. I know many of my colleagues, with the presence of somebody like you, will be able to produce in about four to five months, the material that will really be a good reference, as a base for our future laws. And as John was correctly saying we will borrow where we are deficient, and we really use our customary base. I think it is very important that we undertake this very quickly. That will be good. It is probably resources and time that we should be thinking about.

JL: There was a workshop in October on customary law. It was based on a research project sponsored by the World Vision, and funded by the Germans.

FD: I believe they have sent me the reports of that project.

JL: So, that was a beginning.

PM: They are very valuable.

FD: As a matter of fact, I was thinking that instead of rushing back to Washington tomorrow, I might stop in Rumbek for a day or two and talk to more lawyers. But even more than lawyers, one should talk to other people who are involved in the administration. Now, I have two more questions, specifically on what we are talking about. First, is it possible to talk about cultural values, like *cieng*, for example, as a source of normative principles that can then be legislated upon? In other words, it is agreed that customary law should be the source of law. But is there a cultural framework, a cultural normative framework, which in itself can be a guide that can be a basis for innovating to determine what laws will be in harmony with our ideals and also serve modern needs? This would be a little different from the way lawyers go about things. What is suggested is that law would then be guided by the philosophy of the society and its moral code, as a guide for legislation.

JL: And it is what makes *ciang*. What are the values that constitute this thing you call *ciang*? It must be an embodiment of certain principles that add up to make the concept.

FD: In fact, in Dinka, *cieng* is also law. It is custom, law and way of life.

JL: Yes, so you can extract from it the values that really comprise *cieng*. *Cieng* comprises a number of values and we should try to identify them. And so it becomes the frame from which you try to pull out some principles and say, "This principle constitutes good *cieng*."

FD: Or this is bad *cieng*.

JL: This is bad *cieng*.

PM: Mine is almost the other way around. I was thinking, John, that we use *cieng* as a major reference, what constitutes *cieng*, as a major reference from which we first select the basis for what we should introduce into our accepted customary practices that constitute our law, and make them the fundamental principles of our approach to our legislation.

FD: Interesting.

PM: It is the other way around almost; this is my personal view.

FD: This is circular. I think what could happen is that *cieng* could be your guiding principle, even in selecting or appraising your laws.

PM: A reference point.

FD: Yes, a reference point. Then you begin to see what is in them.

PM: What is in *cieng*.

FD: What promotes *cieng* and what contradicts *cieng*. So, in a sense both become relevant, I think.

PM: Take defamation, for example. It is not part of our ancestors' *cieng* for a boy to insult an older person. If he is strong enough, he can beat an older person, but must never insult him. If you take this in the case of defamation, and you will want now to frame what constitutes defamation, the original *cieng* is that a younger person can beat a person older than him in age, but should not insult him.

JL I want to give you an example from our situation in the Akobo area. It was in 1965, during the time of Anyanya. Anybody who was found collaborating with the enemy at that time was executed, in extreme cases. So, we had our head chief, the Paramount Chief, called Colwic. He was one of our leading chiefs. Now, a certain group of Anyanya came and arrested him and began to beat him. Then one of them insulted him, saying "*aci laac*" [he has soiled himself]. This was serious. The chief said, "You, stop that. I am above insult. If you want to kill me, kill me, but don't insult me. I am above it."

PM: That's it.

JL: And this is why I put *cieng* as a guide. He said, "Nobody should insult me among you. If you want to kill me, kill me, but I am above insults."

PM: *Cieng* requires that as an elder and even because of the authority he has, he should not be insulted.

JL: With the respect he commands within the society, he cannot come down and be seen to be insulted, whatever the situation might be, even if he is assaulted. The level of dignity he had was that high.

FD: It's interesting what you say about dignity. One word we haven't talked about in the Dinka context is *dheeng*. *Dheeng* is dignity, and it has to do with mannerism, with appearance, with the way you conduct yourself, the way you talk, the way you eat, the way you walk, the aesthetics of dancing and singing, and all that. *Dheeng* is a very central value among the Dinka. This is why they say respect is of paramount value in our society. Anthropologists have highlighted the importance of respect among the Dinka and the Nuer. And respect to me is directly related to the dignity associated with *dheeng*. I see *cieng* and *dheeng* as closely related, and linked to the ancestral heritage through the lineage.

PM: When they say, "He is a son of *adheng*," it is not because his father was a good dancer, but because of the respect, the status, and the gentle behavior of his father in society. This gives him a good name.

JL: He inherits that good name. He derives advantage from it.

PM: That is a part of good *cieng*, a component of which is being an *adheng*, because of his good *cieng*, you cannot be anybody.

FD: Without good *cieng*.

PM: No, you cannot.

FD: And good cieng confers on you the status of *dheeng*.

PM: That's right.

FD: Let me now come to my other question. I am close to the end, unless you people want to raise other questions. We are talking about tradition in the context of customary law, but I think tradition can also be relevant in the broader issue of governance and the related areas of constitutionalism. That will mean we administer ourselves by building on our social structures and organizations, including the various institutions that we have been talking about, such as the age-set system, modernized and reformed, the role of women, the elders, the chiefs. It seems to me that if we use tradition as a basis for building our society, it has to go beyond law. It will have to extend to the area of administration and constitutionalism. I think our context of Southern Sudan is a fertile ground for that kind of innovation or experimentation. In your view, is that a valid proposition, and what will be the position of the Movement on that proposition?

JL: I think that the implication of this will be that we have to talk about institutions. What kinds of institutions do we want to create that will engage these categories of our society, the women, the traditional authorities, and the youth. And, indeed, in our culture and terms of reference, there is a point which relates to what the role of the traditional authorities will be in the governance of South Sudan in the coming period. This is a question we are asked to answer.

PM: We will have to provide some answers.

JL: This is particularly important for the traditional authorities, the chiefs. The Movement, in fact, recognizes the very important role they have played since the inception of this war. They have preserved the integrity of the society. They have fed our army. They have contributed selflessly to the struggle. During this hour of peace, are we going to discard these leaders, and forget them? And are your structures, which start with the Boma, going up to the Payam and the county, going to establish a system of local administration that will tend to push the traditional authorities away? Will they be replaced by other bodies or will these others coexist with them in exercising the authority of governance at that level? These traditional authorities, who have persevered our institutions of indigenous governance during all these years, what are we going to do with them, to make them part and parcel of our governance structures, and part and parcel of the peace that we have achieved, their share in the victory of peace?

Now, the existing structures at the different levels seem to be in conflict. Some people were suggesting that at the Payam level there is a conflict with some of the traditional structures that are there on the ground. The SPLM authorities are seen to be replacing the chiefs in those areas. They are transforming the institution of chieftaincy into elected counsels at that level. That means you will be discarding this traditional structure and, of course, cutting the links with their communities. Instead, you will now have elected counsels. Anybody can come, contest, and perhaps win. In some communities, leaders are illiterate. Take the Shilluk, for instance, a kingdom, you go and impose a Payam on them. What will happen? What is the role of the Anyuak king? They are there. They came to New Site for the conference of the kings and chiefs. They were recognized and told that we recognize them, that they will be part and parcel of the administration. But then, these are not small leaders in their communities. Some are kings who have absolute authority over their whole population.

The challenge now is how to harmonize their role with modern structures of local government. A way must be found to involve them. For instance, take this state of Eastern Equatoria. There are chiefs here. Are you going to have a governor with his cabinet, or at the county level, a commissioner and his team, people whom the population considers to be like the colonial authorities, and who see the usefulness of traditional leaders as indirect rule? Will that still be the case? As citizens themselves, can they come through the other structures, the modern structures, that we have organized, for instance, parliament at the state or the Southern Sudan level? They are not abandoning their people and their people want them, and actually people have found them to be very useful. They have found these structures to be good and have served them, even at the most difficult times. Now, do we adopt a negative attitude to them and say, "*Khalas*, finished, your usefulness is over?"

In the resolutions of the New Site conference of chiefs, which are wonderful resolutions, there is much about what the role of the chiefs will be, but it is mostly at the level of generalities. So far, nothing, no policy has come up to institutionalize what will be the status and role of the chiefs. There is now uncertainty about the system of local government that is being introduced. It is still under discussion. Nothing is said about retaining their present status, leave alone uplifting them to a higher level of participation. Of course, there are ideas that have been floated outside the structures of the SPLM. You have heard of the House of Nationalities, or the House of Chiefs. Some will want to see and learn from the experience of other countries. In Ghana, for instance, the chiefs have a recognized role and status. And even matters relating to customary laws, before you upgrade these laws to the level of a common source of legislation at the national level, can we upgrade the courts that we have now? Should we have higher courts of customary law, which can hear appeals from the traditional Chiefs' courts? Judges of higher courts are hearing these appeals.

But as customary law is not codified or restated, judges find it difficult to ascertain the law. This young man, the son of John Akot, who is here in Toposaland as a judge, what does he know about the Toposa customs? It is very difficult. He can't just sit there waiting for appeals from the Toposa Chiefs' courts. It is quite a problem. Judges are finding it very difficult. At best they are obliged to learn on the spot. And definitely, they are bound to make mistakes. They will be making a lot of mistakes. They cannot be the final authority. Do we need to establish customary appellate courts? That is one question. On the administrative side, do we need to create structures within which the voice of our traditional leaders can be heard and can have inputs into policy matters, at the county level, the state level, or even the Southern Sudan level itself? So these are questions which are under discussion and nothing has crystallized on them.

PM: I will start with the question of what will be the position of the Movement with respect to these traditional authorities. I think the Movement is open-minded on this issue. There are several reasons one can give for that. As John correctly said, the resolutions that were passed here by chiefs' conference were much more of a general nature, recognizing the importance of, and the role played by, the traditional authority. So, as I was saying, my personal view is that the Movement is open-minded about this matter. All that is required from the concerned group is to come up with a clear proposal on what should be the status and role of the traditional authority. Many reasons can be given for advocating an important role for them, such as their support of the Movement to come to where we are now. It is one of the areas for which we should find time and resources, and sit down to develop a well-considered opinion on what constitutes traditional authority and what role it should play in our system of governance. And traditional authority really has behind it our very history. We cannot easily begin to abandon it.

What is competing with what I am saying is the service delivery machinery that we intend to establish through the local councils and the local administration, a thing which is not difficult to harmonize. Instead of bringing the local authority to absorb traditional authority, let the traditional authority absorb the elements of the local administration, which should strengthen, and create systems that can be efficient in service delivery as well as keeping the component of the traditional historical needs that we will want to preserve. This will be my personal opinion, because, if you take the local authority preposition at present, with the intention to maybe absorb the traditional authority into local administration, you will be slaughtering it.

This is the difficult aspect. The challenge is only service delivery. It is very easy to establish bases for service delivery to flow. This is doable; I don't think it is very difficult. This is a pressure area, by the way. Our people have not seriously thought of the value of the traditional authority, that it is the very custodian of our history. The spiritual leaders, the kings, and the chiefs, the great ones, they are the might of our people. This is where you get the history, and this is where you get the values as they are being developed.

FD: That's what impressed me, when I interviewed Dinka chiefs way back in the early 1970s, and they were talking about the way they used to organize themselves. The way people like Giir Thiik, Makuei Bilkuei, Arol Kachuol, Ayenh Aleu, and all the big chiefs of the land, the way they used to function, sounds like a confederal arrangement. I mean, they would all get together to discuss the big issues that affected their whole community.

PM: The whole of Bahr el Ghazal. They would send for your father, on the serious issues, and say, "let us get together and make history."

FD: Not only that, Giirdit was going back even to the time of Arob Biong, my great-grandfather, and Kwol Arob, my grandfather. And how the leaders would all gather, and in terms of connecting to the center, channel their resources, like cattle contributions to the government through Arobdit, Arob Biong, or Kwol Arob, who would then come back with the message of what was happening up there in the North, at the center. They will call the chiefs and they will gather and discuss the affairs of the land.

Now, if one assumes that resources could be made available, and this is a project that the US Institute of Peace, for example, will expect me to come out with some recommendations that they will consider supporting, and given the need to prioritize, should one think of a meeting that will bring all those that are directly involved to brainstorm about some of these issues? That could be one step in the order of priority. Other steps could be, first to collect the material, to commission studies of major groups, and then use that as a basis for workshops. That probably will take time. But perhaps those who are already reasonably knowledgeable could put something together as a working paper for discussion, and make the other function, of collecting the necessary materials from all the various communities, a mid- to long-term project. What will be your sense of how best to go about it?

JL: I think we should be emphasizing the necessity to start something in this area, and, of course, the starting point as you said, a brainstorming without waiting to go to the field to collect data. There is already some experience, and some rough ideas, such as the ones we have been discussing. And then these could be crystallized into a kind of program or project. Our objective will be clear by then, once we discern the needs in this area. This is particularly urgent now that we have peace, and are trying to establish a government for South Sudan that plans to use custom as its principal source of law-making. And if it will be used, then what difficulties can we expect to be encountered? There will be difficulties, of course. Customary law is scattered; it has not been put together. It has not been recorded and harmonized. And there are so many ethnic communities in Southern Sudan. That makes it difficult. Where do you start? With whom do you start? The government in the South, whether at the Southern Sudan level, or at the state level, will have those difficulties. Some states have a number of ethnic communities that have different traditions or customs.

So, I think the brainstorming as a start, with which you come and try to define what the problem is and what is required, is a good idea. What is required eventually will be got from the field, and that will be useful. So, I think that the priorities really should be creating a forum that defines the needs, the problems, and the difficulties that are out there. To overcome them, you have to do more research and do things that can enrich our understanding of the situation, so that the longer-term objective can be set.

FD: Even the report that I will prepare out of these discussions could be a background paper.

PM: I entirely agree. Such a meeting would facilitate planning for certain activities, and would help narrow the areas of focus. And it would help us prepare the ground for a specific focus on what we intend to achieve. And there are various ways of stimulating discussion. You can send people to meetings. And you can do it by e-mails or by telephones. But you may not find what you need. Following, as you correctly stated, a clear discourse and target specific areas that we are interested in at present would enable us to come up with a material that we need for the start. It would be the basis for probably dividing the ethnic communities into some rough categories that form a basis from where we can take off. I really agree with that approach.

JL: There is pressure now coming out of the agreement on the issue of land ownership, which has come up as a very urgent matter. The agreement says, very simply, that laws have to be revised to conform with certain customary concepts of land ownership. These customary concepts of land ownership have not been studied. Nobody has done much work on them. But NPA [Norwegian People's Aid], with those of William Kon Bior, seem to have done something. I met William Bior and he said they were doing some study on land law. There are a lot of activities underway.

PM: That is under the Secretariat of Agriculture …

JL: And this is in terms of potential investments. We are being swarmed by a lot of people who want to invest. And they are curious about what they read in the agreement, which says that land belongs to the communities. Now, as a government of South Sudan, how do we respond?

PM: There is a contention now …

JL: How do we come in, as the Government of Southern Sudan? There is no mechanism yet established. I don't know what the constitution of South Sudan will say. Even the issue of giving out concessions on the oil, for instance, when we have already said in the agreement that land ownership is communal, will be a problem. The revision that we are going to make in the laws makes it imperative that we develop a land policy. Such a policy should clearly identify the categories of land tenure and all that. What kinds of interests in land should be taken into account? Similarly, we will have to consider the activism among the women for their property rights. Women's movement for emancipation is emerging as a powerful force for change.

FD: For instance, on issues of inheritance.

JL: Yes, on inheritance, and land ownership, property ownership, succession, all those issues. So there's pressure. People are debating, which some groups in the community, especially the women, feel very concerned about. But there is nothing they can do because the practices in the various communities are presently outside their control. No one will be able to stop these practices until the power structures and the normative principles are changed. You will then be able to bring certain practices in line with certain standards, on human rights, for instance. All this makes the whole exercise a very critical one, especially in Southern Sudan.

FD: Thank you so much. This has been very helpful. I wonder if any of you has any concluding comments, or whether there is an area we haven't touched upon that you would like to bring up.

PM: I personally would want to repeat what I said before by way of emphasis, that your initiative is wonderful. And all that I would want to add is my real sense of urgency on the matter. I really feel very happy about the decision you have taken not to leave tomorrow and to go to Rumbek and discover and identify for yourself some few instances of contributions that will form part of your report back to the US Institute of Peace. But the matter really requires a sense of urgency. The last remark made by John clearly makes the point that is an urgent issue for all of us, as the elites of our society and as people who have fought for this cause and who bear the responsibility to really avail ourselves of certain basic takeoff requirements for the Government of South Sudan. We will not spare time to assist you in helping us come out with something that forms the premise from which we should base the administration of our people, to provide them with proper support in pursuit of their freedom and human dignity.

JL: I would like to add that, in the years since independence, the development of law in our country has been Sharia and the law we inherited from the British, the colonial masters, the common law. Our own values and social systems have been down. And any development has been at the expense of our own values, our social systems. But at present, having reached the peace agreement, the challenge for us is to show what is ours, really; we must highlight what is ours. I think this is an opportunity we cannot afford to miss. We have no excuse to continue to build our legal system on the bases of what has been imposed on us in total neglect of what, tangibly, we could call ours. Or maybe we will need to supplement ours with something from somewhere. African law need not be neglected. I think people need to build on it, and crystallize its principles so that it is not dismissed as nothing, as not a worthy legal system. I think, as you said, Paul, the elites of the South have a challenge on them. This is what they can leave for posterity; that we have developed our own legal system, that Sharia cannot be imposed on us. Sharia has been fought, of course, by our own customary and traditional systems. Our people really kept true to their culture, to their values, in spite of lack of assistance from anyone. But experience has proven over the years that our customs have been resilient. If you compare us with other societies, I believe the penetration of other cultures into our own has not succeeded much. So, I think with peace, the challenge is urgent; the call is truly urgent. It is good that you are taking up the challenge.

FD: Thank you very much; I really appreciate your contribution and your very kind words.

4. Attorney General, Michael Makuei

Rumbek, February 11, 2005

Francis Deng (FD): It is my great pleasure to be talking to the Commissioner for Legal and Constitutional Development, popularly known as the Attorney General, and to pursue some of the questions related to the future of customary law in Sudan, particularly the southern part of the country. So, Mr. Attorney General, could you just kindly introduce yourself very quickly, in terms of your background in the field of law, and then I have a few questions that I will want to ask you.

Michael Makuei (MM): Thank you very much Dr. Francis. I am Michael Makuei, the Commissioner for Legal and Constitutional Development. I am a lawyer by profession, graduate of 1975, Faculty of Law, University of Khartoum.

FD: Thank you. Some of the questions I would like to ask you are almost philosophical, but I think they are also very pertinent. It is my belief that every society, in terms of its legal system, is governed by some fundamental values that are related to the culture of the people, and it is those values that then determine how the system regulates power or resources, who gets what, the distributional aspects of things. I wonder whether you could tell us, from your experience, whether with reference to the Dinka specifically or any other groups that you know, what the main values that condition the legal system are, including procedure, in the culture of our people.

MM: In terms of our cultural values, of course, customary law is one of the main sources of law in Southern Sudan. These sources are used by the legislators for enactment of some of the laws of the New Sudan. For that matter, the values of the society are actually embodied in the customary law, and these values are what are transformed into laws. However, customary law at present in the South, or in the New Sudan, is not yet codified. It is not written. But, at present, we have set up a Customary Law Steering Committee that will conduct research on the customary law. Of course, there are a lot of regimes of customary law in Southern Sudan. And for that matter, we decided that instead of leaving these customary laws unrecorded, they should be recorded, harmonized, and, if possible, enacted. And in so doing, we have set up this Customary Law Steering Committee. Of course, this is a process. We do not expect to finish it in a day or overnight. It is a process that will take a long time. It may go on for ten years or more. But we have started the process. We are optimistic that within the coming few years, we will be in a position to come up with something on customary law.

FD: We will get back to the issue of the future of customary law specifically. For now, I would like to build on my study of customary law in my doctoral work at Yale Law School, which resulted in my first book, *Tradition and Modernization: A Challenge for Law Among the Dinka of the Sudan*. In my dissertation, I used the jurisprudential approach of Professors Harold Lasswell and Myres McDougal, in which law is seen as a regulator of a process by which people pursue certain goals or values, using resources, through institutions, with specific outcomes and effects. For them, the goal of human dignity was seen as the overriding objective in a democratic society. I thought that among the Dinka, and indeed in most African societies, three main principles were at work. One had to do with ancestral continuity through procreation and the continuity of the male line, which is a form of immortality. Law is very much structured to promote those values that are associated with ancestral legacy. The second is the notion of *cieng*, a concept of unity and harmony that envisages a community with a common cause towards the fundamental goals of the family, the lineage or the community at large. And the third is a concept of personal and collective dignity, *dheeng*, which is also connected with the normative principles of *cieng*. Interestingly enough, in my discussions with the colleagues with whom I have already talked, mostly Nuer and Dinka, there were variations of shared principles, and particularly the concept of *cieng*. I want to see whether it is possible to discern certain values that are pertinent to law, in terms of both substance and procedure. Would you have some observation on that?

MM: Well, of course, customary law is actually the basis of everything in the society. And for that matter, if you take Dinka customary law as such, you will find that nothing is outside customary law. Customary law is associated with the ancestral lineage and legacy. That is, you must know your origin, to which section you belong, and the code of conduct of your society, or your community. You must all the time represent that community at your best, in the sense of proper conduct. And this is where *dheeng* comes in, because you must be presentable. Wherever you are, you represent your people. You must always be seen to be doing the right thing. You must be proud of your section, be proud of your people, and be proud of yourself. All this goes back to custom.

The other part is *cieng*. In Dinka custom, *cieng* is associated with so many things. In cases of marriage, for example, if I am marrying, *cieng* requires that my uncles and other members of my clan must contribute cattle towards my marriage. Here, it becomes a right. *Cieng*, in the Dinka community, is a right. If I am marrying, it is the duty of others to pay for my marriage. This constitutes one element of *cieng*. Another element of *cieng* is that if my daughter is being married, my relatives will also be entitled to share in the bride wealth. This is *cieng*. If I do not distribute the bride wealth of my daughter to my people, then they have every right to take me to court. Even if they had not paid for my marriage for that matter, they still have the right to take me to court. This constitutes *cieng*.

Anybody who does not abide by the principles of *cieng* is ultimately considered an outcast. He has abandoned *cieng*. It is because of our customary way of life that you find some houses full with relatives. This is part of our *cieng*. People must be together, and it is your duty to take care of whoever comes to you. You must address their problems. This is how I see *cieng*. It is actually the source of everything. If you go to the courts, at times, because of *cieng*, you will find cases of hunger brought to the court. When there is famine, relatives have the right to take you to court and demand that you provide them with something to live on. And the court will decide accordingly, on the understanding that you will be paid when things get back to normal. If you have cattle, you will be forced to give some to your needy relatives to live on. This constitutes *cieng*.

That is the substantive part of it. Another aspect relates to procedure. In customary law, it is difficult to differentiate between a criminal offense and a civil suit. These are almost the same. What happens is that, if I am aggrieved, I go to the court. The chief sits under his tree or in his *luak*, cattle byre. I go and complain. I go and sit and at the appropriate moment, state my claim against a particular individual. The police of the chief would be sent to go and summon that man. He comes. You both sit. And the case is seen on the spot. There is no delay. The procedure is that you come and sit and everybody narrates his part of the case.

You find that when it comes to the decision of the court, it is not the chief who actually decides. It is in fact an open court. Anybody who is not a party to the suit is a chief, or a member of the court, and has a right to give an opinion. When the time for decision comes, even the least person who is sitting or standing somewhere, will say, "I want to talk." He will be allowed to talk and talk, and at the end, pass his judgment. And the process continues, with people talking and passing judgments until in the end it reaches the chief. The chief is usually the last person to decide. And he will have learned a lot from all those judgments or opinions which were given by these gathered. At the end of the day the chief decides on the final judgment. In so doing, he reaches the correct decision, which usually reflects a consensus, because he will have benefited from all the opinions expressed.

So, here we have a procedure different from our statutory procedure, by which you come to the court and have to present a petition. The judge will interrogate you and find exactly what your cause is. Thereafter, if it is a civil suit, it is allowed on the payment of fees. You must pay the fees. Someone is sent to summon the defendant. Thereafter, the issues are framed, if the case is disputed. If it is not disputed, then it is decided on the spot. But if it is disputed, the issues are framed and another date is fixed for the hearing, and all those processes. With customary law, all these procedures are covered at the same time. And in fact, in accordance with the principles of *cieng*, we believe that the customary procedure is more powerful and fast. It is faster than the statutory procedure, in the sense that the statutory procedure causes a lot of delays in the process. This is why in Sudan at present you can get civil suits waiting for ten years. And every time you come to the court, the defendant will be reported sick. That is an excuse. Then next time you engage an advocate, the advocate may decide to send away his client. Then he comes to court and says, "Yes, we are waiting for my client."

In the customary courts, everybody sits there. There is no question of a witness being kept outside. You sit there. Everybody comes and sits and the process starts. The hearing will continue. If you are there as a witness you will talk. And in the course of your talk, you will be interrogated by everybody around: examination, cross-examination, and re-examination. In the course of the process, the court eventually reaches the correct decision. That is how I see it. We are just waiting for this customary law project to start, and then we will begin to consider all these issues and determine how best we can incorporate these procedures into our future statutory laws.

FD: Excellent. Let me ask you about the reported correlation between blood wealth and bride wealth. In my own work, I observed that the amount of payment for compensation in homicide and the amount of cattle needed for marriage were related. The question was raised whether this was related to the idea of the continuation of life. If a man is killed, you need enough cattle in order to marry, to have children born to his name. This is something that has struck many people. There appears to be a correlation between compensation for the life lost and the value of children, that is begetting children to the name of the deceased. I understand that in some cases now there is a change, particularly among the Agar. They say that the chiefs decided to lower the value of the bride wealth, but that has not affected the value of the blood wealth in homicide. How do you see the correlation between blood wealth and bride wealth?

MM: By blood wealth I assume you mean the *dia*.

FD: Yes.

MM: In fact, there is no correlation, even though they appear to be almost the same. In marriage and the payment of bride wealth, the intention is to guarantee the continuity of the family. When a person dies he is a loss to the family. If he is not married, then the blood wealth, the *dia*, which is paid, is actually used for marrying a wife for the deceased relative. In so doing, you have now guaranteed the continuity of the deceased, despite his absence. Children will be born and they will be named after him. Even though they do not know the father, when they grow up, they will know him and become proud of their father, whom they have never seen. This, in a way, is what adds to the population. It is said that a Dinka man never dies. If he dies when he is not married, then a wife will be married for him and he will continue to live through the children to be born. If he dies after marriage, then people will take care of his family, his children, and his wife, and more children will be borne by his widow to his name. They will be recognized as his children begotten by a relative, so that his continuity is guaranteed.

However, in cases of marriage, you cannot set the maximum price, because this is a social transaction. What is usually done is that whenever there is any dispute in the marriage, you set the minimum. So, in case the parties disagree, and they come to the court, the court will set the minimum for dowry. But if the parties agree and understand themselves, they can go as far as their wealth can take them. And here, nobody will interfere with their agreement. It is a question of understanding. But once there is no agreement and people go to court, the court will impose the minimum payment. This is the procedure.

Now, in terms of the bride wealth and the *dia* (the blood wealth), the correlation to me is not clear. The value of the *dia* is something that was agreed upon by the chiefs. An example is in Wanh-Alel, where the *dia* was set at thirty cows plus one. That one cow goes to the court, but the thirty goes to the relatives of the deceased. This is in Wanh-Alel and this is what is applicable in the whole of Bahr el Ghazal. But if you cross to Upper Nile, say to the Bor area, the *dia* is fifty cows, but the bride wealth is not fifty. The minimum is thirty cows for marriage. And it has no maximum. So, if you disagree, and you go to court, the groom's family will be forced to pay thirty. But in cases of *dia*, irrespective of whether or not the family marries a wife for the deceased, the *dia* is fifty cows. Out of the fifty, the court takes about ten as court fees. Now, you are left with forty. An additional two are taken, one is killed for the ritual ceremony of atonement, and one is given to the specific court that made the settlement. So, actually the relatives of the deceased receive only thirty-eight head of cattle.

Of course, human life has no value in the first place, but this is something symbolic, to make people feel that their loved one is compensated, and as such, they will not decide to take law into their hands and revenge, as it was in the past. There have been some complications here and there because there is also a conflict of customs. Now, the people of Wanh-Alel, if any of them is killed, say among the Nuer or the Dinka of Upper Nile, the family of that person pays in accordance with the Wanh-Alel custom. Of course, you apply the custom of the deceased. If someone from here, in Bahr el Ghazal, kills a person from Upper Nile, he will pay fifty. If someone from Equatoria kills a Dinka from Bahr el Ghazal, he pays according to Wanh-Alel, fifty head of cattle. And if he kills somebody from Upper Nile, he pays according to the custom of the deceased; that is, he pays fifty. The question arises, if one kills someone from Equatoria, where people do not possess that level of cattle wealth, how much *dia* should be paid? Of course, human life should be the same everywhere, so, in principle, should the compensation for life. And yet, conditions differ. These are some of the issues on which we need to harmonize the law.

I remember a case, a traffic case, in which a car overturned and killed a lot of people, including some Equatorians, some from Bahr el Ghazal, and others from Upper Nile. They all died. Now, when the case came before the judge, they decided that compensation should be based on the customs of the deceased person. So, the same people who died in that same car accident were compensated differently. That created a very big problem. This is where we need to harmonize the customs, so that we can come up with something fair to all. Keeping the situation as it is now will drag us into problems one day.

FD: That is a fascinating challenge. We will come back to the modern challenges for the application of customary law. On this question of compensation for homicide, is the thinking in the South now against capital punishment, which is currently in place in the country? Judging by customary law, it is obvious that people would prefer compensation to capital punishment. What is the thinking behind that; is it simply to compensate, or is there more to it than that, such as, in human rights terms, a principled stance against the idea of capital punishment?

MM: Yes, in fact, even though undeclared, there is a strong cultural bias against capital punishment. This issue with reference to human rights principles has just come up recently. Customarily, it seems as though the intention originally was to fight against capital punishment. In our customs, we do not have capital punishment; it never existed originally. Capital punishment was introduced by statutory law. At the beginning, if you killed someone, his family will just revenge. To avoid vengeance, it was decided that people should be compensated. You are paid *dia*, instead of taking the law into your hands and killing an innocent person who never participated or had a hand in that offense. Compensation was always there until statutory laws were introduced. With the introduction of statutory laws, it was thought that the best way of addressing this capital offense was to sentence people to death.

Nevertheless, if the accused is found guilty, and before the court passes the death sentence, the court has the right to ask the relatives of the deceased if they want the sentence to be passed against the accused or if they want the alternative punishment through compensation. If the family of the deceased says, "We don't want compensation; let him be sentenced to death," then that goes. Otherwise, if the family of the deceased says, "We accept that he pay compensation," the court will rule accordingly.

FD: Am I right in assuming that in most cases, people prefer compensation?

MM: Yes, in most cases people prefer compensation because this capital punishment is not part of our customs. It is not part of our culture. So, it is just a mere coincidence that human rights advocates came up with new principles against capital punishment. Opposition to capital punishment was already there in our customs, except that it was not officially recorded. People did not go down to analyze why people objected to it. In addition to opposing capital punishment as such, the intention, of course, as I said earlier, is to guarantee continuity. If you are close to someone that is killed, that is a loss to the family and to the society. People did not want to lose more lives.

Instead, they wanted to guarantee the continuity of life and secure the life of the accused.

So, our people actually agree with the idea of discouraging capital punishment. But, for the time being, there is the case of the habitual offender, who has killed so many people. He can kill a person today, and if he is not sentenced to death and is eventually released, he will commit another murder. He becomes a habitual offender. These are the types of criminals on whom we cannot avoid passing the death sentence, as long as he causes death, plans it, and executes it intentionally. Our policy is to adopt our customary law, and, in most cases, a person is only sentenced to death when there are certain severe circumstances, so that we deter others from following the same line. But, generally speaking, courts look into the customary legal practices to mitigate the sentence.

FD: That's a good analysis of the balances that need to be made. Let us now look into the place of customary law in our legal education and practice. When I was in the Law Faculty, in Khartoum University, there was such a strong prejudice against customary law. In fact, I think I was the only one who took advantage of my vacations, with the encouragement of my professors, to study customary law. I used the material from that research later on when I did my postgraduate studies in London and at Yale. My colleagues, Gordon Abyei and Natale Olwak Akolawin, wanted to do fieldwork, but could not. The Northern administrators and even the chiefs were suspicious about that kind of research. In my own tribe, when I went to do fieldwork, rumors were going around that I was being prepared to be the appellate authority, over the paramount chief, my father. At one point, my father asked me, "Mading, this recording of customary law, is it carried out all over the Sudan or only in this tribe?" And I knew what was on his mind. Considering the situation, I told him that I did not want to sit in court anymore, and that I would only interview people at home, which was what I did. More importantly, we had the central government prejudiced against customary law, which they associated with the South, and which they considered primitive and subversive. They wanted to encourage Sharia and modern Western law, even though in the North too, over 90 percent of the population were still governed by customary law. What is the place of customary law today, both at the national level, how the central authorities see the role of customary law, and certainly in the South?

MM: Well, for the central government, of course they are somewhat hostile towards customary law, even though, personally, I consider Sharia as custom. So, if Sharia is a custom, then it is a customary law based on the society in the North. All the laws that have been enacted and even the behavior of the society are based on custom, whether it is Islamic or other sources. For us in the South, our sources of legislation are led by customary law. This is why we are trying to develop customary law and codify it, if possible. In the course of doing that, we will be conducting a great deal of research. We will involve many researchers who are interested in our customary law, so that they go down to dig and find out these customs. We must back up our policy decisions with empirical knowledge. In the course of doing that, we will need to go and find out from the people exactly why they do what they do. Even though they will not be giving you the same explanation in terms of human rights, in terms of women's rights, in terms of child rights, and so forth, you will be in a position to reach your own conclusions on the basis of your interaction with those communities.

So, with us in the South, our source of legislation is custom. And because custom is not developed, we need to do some work, to conduct research, and then come out with what may constitute a substitute to the current statutory law. Yes, it is true; in fact, the Northern government did not have any interest in developing our customary law, because they feared that it would replace the other laws, including the Islamic Sharia laws. So, it was a policy of the national government to see to it that customary law did not find any home, and should not be developed. They inculcated it into our minds that these were primitive customs, and that we did not need to talk about them. And we believed them. Some people, like you, did not believe them and you continue to record and project our customary laws, because you did not believe that they are primitive. Our laws have been there. They have existed from time immemorial and have been inherited by generations after generations. Our customary law is rich, and is valuable. It is only that we were made to believe that customary law is primitive and that we do not need to entertain it. This is how the government was fighting customary law, especially in Southern Sudan. Time has come now for us to develop it, and show the international community that all these human rights they have been talking about, like child rights, we have them; we have our own child rights. And we have women's rights. You have everybody's rights in the community. All these things are there, except that we have not gone down to record them, study them, develop them, and promote them so that they are known by the international community.

I remember a time when we had a workshop here on juveniles. It was attended by a lady, a judge from Norway. She was talking to us about children's rights. When we told her about child rights in our Southern communities, she was very surprised. We said to her, "After all, have you seen street boys here in Rumbek? Do you see street children here in the town?" She said, "No, I was indeed surprised that I did not see any street children. Despite the effect of the war on your people, I have not seen any street children." I said to her, "This is one of the issues that is actually addressed by custom. It is our duty to take care of any child, any homeless child, any child who has lost parents. It is the duty of the next of kin to take care of such a child. These things do not exist everywhere. Even in Europe, where the modern ideas about human rights are now coming from, you find children in the streets. In our society, it is also the duty of every person to discipline a child, when he sees him going astray. Meanwhile, in the modern world now, if you begin to discipline somebody's child, it amounts to child abuse, an offence." So, we talked to the Norwegian lady judge and she was very surprised by what we said. She said, "You have very good customs." We said, "Yes, we have good customs, except that they are not known." The Arab-Islamic government has been depicting these customs as primitive. And the international community also believes that our customs are primitive, backward, and that we do not need to build on them. They believe that we are against women's rights, against children's rights, and so forth.

Even our women now have come to believe that customary law is hostile to women, and are fighting it. This is not correct, because in our customs, women's rights are entrenched. Contrary to Western belief, in our customary law, women have the right to inherit. Once her husband dies, she is fully responsible for her wealth. If the children are young, she takes care of them until they grow up and they take over from their mother. It is the right of the mother to take anybody to court if he misappropriates her properties, and the court will grant her right. You hear some women now crying for women's rights, land rights. After all, land with us is not owned by the individual; it is owned by communities. And it is the right of the community to ensure that the family stays in their homestead. There is nowhere where women are evicted simply because they left their husbands.

FD: That is interesting. On this question of land, my view is that actually there is no society where individuals have absolute ownership of property. There are certain rights and entitlements over property. Among our people, if a woman has been given a plot of land, even though her husband can help in cultivating the land, he has no right over the land or the produce. It is her property; it is her land and the produce is hers. The same can be said, as you said, about cattle, which are allocated during the husband's lifetime. If the man dies and the women have already been allocated their share of cattle, men are not going to come and say, "These are ours." What is known as '*panom*' is what stays as the collective family ownership, the ancestral land, because that is where the ancestors are buried. But you have to use the land productively. If you leave your land to be fallow for so many years, then others can come, occupy it, and use it productively. Even in terms of humanitarian law, traditional society has valuable principles. Dinka values relating to warfare, for example, are arguably in conformity with international norms. You kill face to face; you do not ambush. If a man is fallen, and a woman covers him for protection, you should not touch him.

MM: You do not hit a woman; you do not hit a child.

FD: These are fundamentals that people do not realize. They are principles of a strong moral code, which are now being destroyed in the process of modernization. Now, what is the best way of proceeding forward? You have already indicated an approach which I tend to agree with. First of all, we should recognize that we have diversity of legal regimes. We need, as a first phase, to record as much as possible. Then we need to sit and analyze what we have recorded, to identify the differences and the commonalities. We should also see the weaknesses and what kind of reform is needed, so that we restate customary law with a sense of reform, and in a comparative way. Then we can put the reform legislation into place. And there are international partners who will like to assist us in this endeavor. Should we aim at organizing a meeting first that will then plan all of this, or should we go ahead and commission studies of different communities, and then organize meetings afterwards? Or should we do both concurrently? What is your sense of the strategy for doing that?

MM: In fact, there are some customary laws which are already recorded, like Wanh-Alel, the Panjab, and Nuer law. All these are recorded, and they have been operational all this time. These are recorded laws. We do not need to start from the grassroots again. But we need to revisit them, in the form of meetings, conferences, and so forth. We need to look at them critically and see how far they have changed, because some of these customs, of these recorded customs, have already changed. So we need to go down and find out exactly what is going on through workshops, conferences, and seminars involving the communities themselves. Then we will see how far the laws have changed. We can review them and adjust them accordingly. There are other customs which still need to be recorded. These ones, which are not yet recorded, need to be recorded. After recording, we should organize workshops or seminars to discuss and ascertain whether the supposedly recorded custom is exactly what it is. You want to ensure that nothing comes up later, where people will say that, after all, this is not their customary law.

So, it is after recording that we should begin to hold workshops with the communities concerned. After ascertaining or ensuring that these are the customs of the people, you can then sit down to study them. You study and harmonize; you identify the areas of commonality and put it aside, and you identify the areas where there is complete disagreement. Then you pick up all these pieces and organize more workshops, conferences, and seminars with the elders of the communities concerned. So, you identify in the course of the recording how many customary law regimes are there. Then you start with each regime, and harmonize it within itself. And then you harmonize it with all those other regimes. After finishing with those regimes, you come up again with another process of harmonizing the regimes that should constitute a national framework of legal regime management.

At the end, it will not be necessary that we come up with only one customary law, but we can come up with regimes that will be applicable in these areas, and then we will provide a basis for resolving the conflict of customs. There will be a law also to regulate these customs. In case of any conflict, what should be done? That way, we will be in a position to at least come out with a formula for response. So, we have the two approaches. One approach is to start with workshops on the present recorded customary laws. The other relates to unrecorded laws, where you have to start with recording first, and then you organize workshops and conferences. This is how we look at it.

FD: I take it that the committee you have formed will be given responsibility for managing this process. Or is there a need for other institutional structures to help carry out the process you have just described?

MM: This body is just the beginning. We call it the Customary Law Steering Committee. In fact, this Committee will be transformed into an institution. In our plans, we had the idea of setting up an institute for legal studies. We actually wanted to set up a paralegal training center as a springboard to help us meet our legal needs in the institutions. And, thereafter, we would like to transform this center into an institute for legal studies. It is this institute for legal studies that should take up this process, including the required research.

For the time being, we have not been able to set up the training center, and we are running out of time. So we decided to set up this steering committee to start the process. Meanwhile, we will be thinking of how best it could be transformed into an institution, a research institute or something of that kind. This body, given the problems of funding and so forth, is unable to take off now. But it is an ambitious process that will involve many researchers. And if we can, as soon as we start, we will begin with the training of the researchers themselves. They will recruit people, train them, and then send them to the field for the recording of these customs. After the recording, we will have their recordings, and we will have those who conducted the research. They will come and sit down to analyze the data. We expect them to come up with some observations, conclusions, and recommendations. That is the process we intend to follow.

FD: This is very interesting, and, as you say, very ambitious. It is difficult, of course, to cover all the different communities and subgroups, but is it possible to have major clusters of what we call customary laws? It is just like the recordings that have been done: Wanh-Alel, Wunlit, and Panjab. I don't know whether these documents are actually available for one to consult. But could you break down the South into major customary law groupings, and what will those be? Obviously, they will have to be somewhat flexible.

MM: Yes, of course; in fact, this is why we set up the Customary Law Steering Committee. They are supposed to sit and subdivide the South into areas, because the South is so vast and the customs are so varied and conflicting that they are difficult to harmonize. But, nevertheless, it is they who will come up with their plan. They will come up with their plan of how best to approach this challenge. They cannot start with the whole South; otherwise they will end up in disarray. We have given them the prerogative to sit down and work out their plan. We will be there to help them whenever they need our support. I am sure what they will do is to divide the South into zones. And in the course of that division, they will, say in Bahr el Ghazal, start with a certain area, in Equatoria they will start with a certain area, and in upper Nile they will start with a certain area. Or else they may take a state or a region, study it, finish it, record it, put it aside, and then move on to other areas. In the course of their work, those who are recording will be doing the recording and moving ahead with more recording. Meanwhile, whatever is recorded will be brought to the researchers, who will sit, study it, and organize workshops, conferences, and seminars.

The process will continue like that, because these recorders will not necessarily be the people who will be conducting the seminars and workshops. In doing their recording, they will be moving systematically until they cover the whole of Southern Sudan. This is what I think they will do; but they have not yet come up with their program.

FD: Thank you very much.

5. Deputy Chief Justice, Bullen Pancol Awal

Rumbek, February 12, 2005

Francis Deng (FD): It is a great pleasure to be meeting with you, Deputy Chief Justice Bullen. I would like you to say a word of self-introduction, including your legal background and what you are doing now. I will then have a few questions to ask you.

Bullen Pancol Awal (BP): Thank you very much Dr. Francis. I am glad to be with you personally, as a very distinguished Sudanese. It is a pleasure to have this interview with you. My name is Bullen Pancol Awal. I am the Deputy Chief Justice of the New Sudan. My educational background is simple. I graduated from Khartoum University in 1975. During the struggle, I had a chance of going to Germany. I became a Fellow of Max Plank Institute for International Law. I pursued postgraduate work in constitutional law and international law at Heidelberg University. So far, that is the background to my education. If you have anything to ask me, please; you are welcome.

FD: Thank you very much. That is very kind of you. Now, as I mentioned to you earlier, my focus is on the future of customary law in Sudan, or the place of customary law and its future in the country, with particular focus on Southern Sudan. My first question is of a somewhat philosophical nature. In studying law at Yale Law School in the United States, with the New Haven school of jurisprudence, called Law, Science and Policy, the approach was that law regulates to a process in which people are seeking values using resources, through institutions, with certain results, outcomes, and effects. In that context, human dignity, defined as the broadest shaping and sharing of values, was postulated as the overriding goal. I personally saw that in our own society, the overriding values were continuing one's identity and influence, even after death, a kind of immortality through the lineage, ideal human relations reflected in the concept of *cieng*, people living together in unity and harmony, and the dignity of every individual and group, reflected in the principles of *dheeng*. I will be interested to hear your own views of what are the main values our people consider important in shaping their legal framework, whether we are talking about substance or procedures. And you can agree or disagree with the things I have just said.

BP: I personally agree with your views as expressed in some of your various writings. I cannot claim to have understood most of your writings, but I have attempted to read through some of your writings. Customary law, in my view, is a foundation of any society. At certain points in time, the Northern Sudanese have sometimes referred to us as people without culture, without traditions, and so on. Every society has its own norms by which it lives. But we, the people of South Sudan, have never organized our life at the national level, as people with their own way of behaving, their own way of doing things, their own ways of approaching life. Therefore, at this particular point, the time has come to elevate the values of our society, codify them, and start a proper work. I believe customary law will be the founding law for our society, just as it was in the history of English law. When we talk of precedent in English law, it actually emanates from customs. Therefore, the time has come to develop our customary law.

FD: In the past, we found that in Sudan, at the level of the government, even in the Faculty of Law, there was a discouragement of customary law. In fact, when I did my fieldwork, I was the only student who was able to do research in the tribe. My colleagues, Gordon Abyei and Natale Olwak Akolawin, had difficulty with the chiefs. Even in my own case, rumors were saying that I was coming to study customary law in order to prepare me to become the appellate authority, over my father, the paramount chief. And at one point, my father himself asked me, "Is this recording of customary law only in this tribe or is it all over the Sudan?" I decided that I will not sit in court anymore, that I will just conduct my research at home, and interview the chiefs at home. What is the general climate at the national level today? How is customary law being seen by the authorities? Then we will focus on the South.

BP: In the past, anything about customary law used to be second-graded; it used to be something hateful to the government. It was, in fact, discouraged. The other aspect was that the history of Sudan was not taught in most Southern schools. If anything, it was taught in terms of how we, the Sudanese, were related to the Arab world, Islam, and related associations. As we speak now, there is an overriding consensus to start developing our own laws, in respect to our customs. The question really is, how do we do that, because we are many nationalities in the Southern Sudan, fifty to sixty in the region. How you harmonize all these is actually the problem.

FD: In the process of developing customary law, we now have a national legal framework, based very much on Anglo-American, or should we say, English common law, whether it is through precedents or through statutes. How do we see the way this received law will be harmonized with customary law, considering that many people see customary law as reflecting a tradition that is fast dying, and especially given the way our society has been shattered, with people spread all over the world, where other systems are prevailing?

BP: In the past, most laws in Sudan used to provide for Sharia; that will be one of the main sources for law in Sudan. Another source which was referred to is custom, but in a very faint way. At present, since the start of the rebellion in Southern Sudan, customary law has been emphasized by the SPLM, that any statute passed by the SPLM must have a reflection of customary law before that statute is applied. This is a big revolution. From that departure point, they moved forward and took strides. I think it is now a national strategy to develop customary law as the main source of legislation in Southern Sudan.

FD: That being the case, what will you suggest should be the process by which we can develop customary law? As you said, we have so many nationalities; some of the laws of these groups have been recorded to some degree, although not in a comprehensive way. The process of recording, analyzing, making comparative analysis then synthesizing, and coming out with commonalities or some fundamentals that can provide a basis for a restatement and reform of the law, will seem to be a logical one, but one that is often time consuming. Do you have a strategy, or does the legal profession have ideas, that will be useful in strategizing on how to move to make customary law more useful?

BP: In fact, if I am not wrong, one of the strategies is that already developed by you. I heard from some people that you were interested in committees to embark on the harmonization of customary law. That is one aspect. An example of what can be done is found in Uganda, where the tribes of southern Uganda, the Buganda, the Musoga, the Bunyoro, all these tribes, started a process between 1969 and 1970, and organized the customs of these major tribes in southern Uganda. When I last visited Uganda in 1998, I found that a language had developed in some areas; some aspects of the law had been developed. So, I think this process of organization will depend on the proximity of tribes. There are tribes with similar ways of doing things, similar behavior patterns, similar approaches on matters of custom. You could group these tribes together, and then find other tribes with other ways of doing things, and come up with a final commonality, and try to harmonize these tribes into one legal regime.

FD: You said that the tribes of Bahr el Ghazal, through a conference at Wanh-Alel, collected laws and suggested certain directions for reform. Is this document available? And is it being used, or was this an event of one time that needs to be revived and developed?

BP: That document is very much alive. We even, I suspect, have copies in the judiciary offices. That document is being used in Bahr el Ghazal as a source of reference. It has been improved by Justice John Wuol Makec, who made commentaries on the document. And this document, I believe, is a major contribution as far as the law of the Dinka of Bahr el Ghazal is concerned, and of course, there is your own work. These three, the work of John Wuol, your own work, and the work of Wanh-Alel, put together, can bring something tangible to Bahr el Ghazal.

FD: Are there concrete areas in which [international partners] can be of help in what's going on? Will this be in the collection of materials or recordings? Will it be better to organize meetings on specific areas of customary law? What ideas will you suggest for their assistance?

BP: First of all, we already have a committee consisting of the judiciary, legal affairs, local government, and others. This committee, to the best of my knowledge, will have some ideas about what could be done. This is an area of start. The other area of start is to make similar committees gather work on what I referred to before as proximity tribes. Tribes with certain commonalities could be grouped into one, other tribes with similar ways of doing things could be grouped together, and we move to yet another group of tribes. Then these committees should be engaged in Bahr el Ghazal, in Upper Nile, and in Equatoria. At a certain stage they will come out with something roughly representative, for instance, of the Dinka. They will come out with something about the tribes of Western Bahr el Ghazal. They will come out with something rough about tribes in Eastern Equatoria, something on the Nuer in Upper Nile and other tribes there. This will require a lot of help from various institutions. Once that is done, that will be one major area of achievement.

The other area is the NGOs which have done some work with the chiefs and other people in Southern Sudan; World Vision is one, Norwegian People's Aid (NPA) is another. These two have commissioned studies on customary law. You should ask them about these studies. These materials should be put together and a study made to encourage legislation and the documentation of customary law in Southern Sudan. The other area where action is needed is the role of traditional institutions. Time has come to deploy some of the chiefs, even as senior members of the judiciary, so that when they are trying cases they record what they know about tradition, about history, about customs or the law. This could be another source of training materials. In the final analysis, we will come to a situation where we have some sources, some substantive materials, and can then try to put it into volumes, organize them into something useful for legal education. Another thing, the SPLA has suggested the establishment of an institute of legal studies, which I think will take customary law as one of the main components of developing law in Southern Sudan. It will also be useful to give some help to scholars to do research on their own. At the end of the day, we will find a direction in this area of customary law.

FD: That's all very helpful. I appreciate it. Now there is much complaint against customary law, particularly on the part of women, and questions about land tenure and the pressure for investment from outside. How do you credit these questions about the status of women in customary law; is there a just case to be made and are there plans for reform?

BP: I think so. That has been the pattern all over the world. Women are known to have suffered in the past, even in Europe and in America. Now, women are claiming their rights. So it is only a matter of time. We Sudanese must recognize that women must be brought up to equality with men. This should be the position of the law in my view. We should abrogate, modernize, or otherwise reform those areas of the law that seem to discriminate against women. For instance, in property law among the Dinka, no woman owns property. Land is property and women in Dinka tradition are not supposed to own land. So, I think it is one of the main areas where customary law will have to reform itself. Those are areas of injustice to a human being as a human being. Of course, the situation must be viewed in the context of change. Those areas which support the protection of human rights and non-discrimination generally must be seen in the context of development and encouraged.

FD: An aspect of land law that is presumably controversial is the argument that land is communally owned. Of course, I personally think that there is no society where an individual has complete ownership over the land, because there are all kinds of restrictions. Ultimately, it is a function of degrees of ownership, or certain entitlements to land, and land must be used. You cannot leave the land empty and exclude others from using it. It will be allocated to others who will use it. But once you have land to your name, it is yours until you move on to another area and leave it fallow for an unreasonably long period of time. When we now talk about land tenure, outsiders coming in to invest, and wanting to be allocated land, what plans do we have for regulating the fact that land is communal, owned by the community, while those who are coming to invest want to be assured of a certain degree of secure holdings over the land for a period that will make investment worthwhile?

BP: First of all, to assert the fact that land is communally owned is a philosophy that I accept, but not absolutely. Land principally must be for use; it must be to the benefit of mankind. If you say that you are making a railway line from Wau to Juba, it will take you ten years or twenty years to persuade the community along the railway line to allow you to pass the railway line over their land. For me, to say that land is communally owned is a philosophy to safeguard the land of Southern Sudan against unauthorized encroachment by the administration in Khartoum. But, to me, it is not a correct policy. Land must be used. If the government wants land at any point in time, it must acquire it for development in the interest of mankind. And, therefore, we must find some other formula than saying land is communally owned. The government must find a way of acquiring land when it wants it for development, in the interest of the whole country.

FD: Our people have been very much shattered by the war. They have gone everywhere inside the country and abroad. They have gone from the rural areas to the towns, where they are exposed to many other influences. In your view, how much continuity is there in people's belief in customary laws and traditional values, or are people abandoning their traditions? And is it important to try to revive them? And how do we do that?

BP: During the years of the fighting, the main problem has been displacement. Communities have been displaced and they have migrated to other areas and countries around the world. The host communities have always been hostile, thinking that these people had moved in permanently. What you said about the philosophy of communal land is correct. The displaced have been rejected and they continue to be rejected. The present government seems committed to wanting people to return. They want people to return to their communal land. To me, that should be encouraged as a means of reducing tensions among our people. It is necessary to do it.

I think that land must be developed. It must be developed for the benefit of Southern Sudan. We need land for mining in Kapoeta. The locals might get some benefit from it, but land must be developed for the benefit of the people of Southern Sudan. You will need land in Maridi for cultivation. That must be done with some compensation here and there. If we need land for development purposes, then it is necessary to relocate people in order to develop the land. To me, government policy should be that land must be for the benefit of all.

FD: What about the relevance of the overall cultural values to the development of the law?

BP: Well, our society has been broken. During the war, there has been a lot of displacement. So such an institution like marriage, for instance, has become unstable. You could find your wife being married to another man in another part of the world. During the liberation struggle, there have been massive movements and social disintegration. It is essential that our values are restored. One priority area will be to find jobs, to bring people back home, to find suitable areas of settlement for them, and to make their situation more stable.

FD: Deputy Chief Justice Bullen, thank you very much.

6. Tilar Deng

Rumbek, February 12, 2005

Francis Deng (FD): Tilar, it is a great pleasure to talk to you about some of these issues of current importance to our people in Southern Sudan. As I said to you earlier, I am interested in looking at the status of customary law in Sudan today, particularly in Southern Sudan. As you may know, I have been interested in the study of customary law from the beginning of my legal studies, but it has been quite a while since I last looked at the situation in our country. I would like to ask you a number of questions. We can then go to some philosophical issues, and move on to the status of customary law today, and the prospects for the future. It is my belief that every society has a system of values and cultural norms that shape its approach to law. It is a question of law being a promoter of fundamental values in a society, regulating relations on the basis of those values. Before we get on to some of the specifics about the legal system and customary law, could you first introduce yourself in terms of your background, your studies, and your involvement with the legal profession? Then I would like to ask you what the fundamental values or cultural norms are that condition law in our traditional society, what values law is supposed to promote, and how they determine the law, whether we are talking about the substance of the law or the procedures.

Tilar Deng (TD): Well, Dr. Francis, it is also a pleasure to be talking with you. We have a very long relationship, since I was a student in the US in 1978. And we have continued that relationship in various ways. I appreciate having you here since our last meeting in Addis Ababa. Focusing now on the area of the customary law, I will start by asking, why it is called customary law. It is a law that is based on culture, and there are values that condition the people to respect it. But before I get into that, let me say that people are trying to codify customary law, and my view has always been consistent, that once you codify customary law, it ceases to be customary law; it becomes statutory. It cannot expand as the people go along. Our people, for generations and generations, had their own values, and these values are what form their way of behavior. There are constraints on what you can do and what you cannot do. They have lived this way for a long time. Whether it is marriages, divorce cases, or tort cases, they are based on their own customs and values. Those customs and values have shaped their outlook, the way they perceive life, the way they perceive their relationships, whether as a family, as a clan, or as a tribe. It is a very strong component of our social systems. And our systems are based on our norms and values. That is what made us to exist, even our name, as a distinct people. If we did not have those laws and values, we would have been assimilated for a long time.

FD: Thank you. By way of some jurisprudential background, let me say that I went to Yale Law School, where law according to the theory of Law, Science and Policy was seen as based on certain overriding goals that shape the way society functions, from a legal point of view. What they considered the main value, the overriding value, was human dignity, defined as the broadest shaping and sharing of values. In my dissertation, I emphasized a number of factors, including *koc e nhom*, a notion of continuity through the family line, what you might call immortalization of every individual through a lineage, as a major goal that shapes the distribution of values, such as power, wealth, respect, and others. The other is the normative principle of *cieng*, how people relate to one another, and the norms implicit in the concept of *cieng*. Then there is the notion of *dheeng*, which is a concept of human dignity, whether that of the individual, or of the group. These principles shape the rules relating to marriage, power and authority, respect, and wealth. Will you agree or will you add something else?

TD: I read what you wrote. It was very similar to what I developed. I read parts of your thesis on the issue of *cieng* and *dheeng*. I didn't have any disagreement with them. But let me make a few remarks. *Cieng*, as you put it, is related to how an individual relates to other people. As we sit here, we are relating to one another. This is *cieng*. *Cieng* is the way we live together as individuals, the way we respect one another. What makes good *cieng* is that people are staying together, are respecting one another and deferring to one another in expressing their views. You know, of course, that there are a variety of meanings to *cieng*. *Dheeng* too has a variety of meanings. It can refer to the physical appearance of a person, that he is handsome or beautiful. You can say, "He is *adheng*," in the physical sense God created him. But *adheng* also goes further, and relates to a person's conduct; that he is generous; respects other people's views; advises people; and is a person on whom you can rely. That is *adheng*, one on whom people can rely. In times of difficulty, people can depend on him for support. I forgot the third concept you said …

FD: *Koc e nhom*, standing the head of a dead person upright.

TD: That relates to having your name continue after your death.

FD: It's a form of immortality.

TD: Yes, which a lot of Western people do not understand. Why should a dead person have *dheeng* privileges like a living person? The point here is that in our own culture, you are physically dead, but you still exist in the society. Although you are gone, people say, "His soul is still with us. We must marry a wife for him." Relatives have to marry a wife for him, and the children will be named after him. So, it has that element that there is a blur relationship between the living and the dead. And there is also the element that his name can never be lost, because we believe in the fact that your name can only be lost if you don't have children alive.

FD: There used to be a strong bias against customary law in the system. When I was at Khartoum University, customary law was not taught. I did fieldwork on customary law on my own, supported by my professors, who guided my research at home. My Southern colleagues were discouraged even by their chiefs and by the attitude of the officials in the South. In your view, how is customary law being perceived today by the authorities?

TD: The point is that when this movement, the SPLM/A, started, it started as a military movement, and there were very scanty provisions in the SPLM penal code of 1983. So, customary law was not considered as a vital part of the control systems. The law was purely military. Until I'm speaking today, the customary part of our law is still being neglected. That's why you see now a lot of breakdown of law and order. The traditional leaders are no longer in control. And since people are armed, when you kill with a foreign weapon, it is considered that the ghost of the deceased will not haunt you, because there was no proximity between you and the individual you killed. You did not kill with a traditional weapon, which requires a face-to-face confrontation. That means that the intervention of firearms, and of Western culture in general, is now beginning to erode our cultural and moral values. So, if I kill someone now with an AK-47, I will not go through any of the traditional rituals any longer. Traditionally, when you killed a person, you would go and stand outside, whether in the homestead or in the cattle camp, and you would shout out loud, calling on the people to hear you. People would come to you and you would make a public confession and say, "This is what I have done." Immediately a bull would be brought out to be slaughtered. You would be cleansed ritually before you were allowed to associate with the people.

This doesn't exist any longer. These are the difficulties we need to correct. If we don't correct them, then the element of law and order, based on our cultural norms, values, and customs, will disappear. And if we don't apply our customary law, which is very rich, even in our contest over the land issues with the North, we will be weakened. In our traditional law, land is owned communally. It is the community that leases the land to the state, rather than the state leasing or giving land to the individual. People have not looked into this matter carefully. The implications of undermining the customary law are serious.

FD: That's very interesting. I have two more questions. One, if we assume that we should place emphasis on customary law, and we know that there are foreign interests that are looking at investing in our land today, but for whom predictable entitlement to land is a prerequisite, how are we going to reconcile community ownership with attracting investment? I can understand that following the traditional land tenure principles is a way of also protecting our people, our land, from the encroachment of outsiders who would overwhelm them, but how do we balance these two?

TD: Well, even in our customary law, we have never refused land to any foreigner. I come from Yirol, and if I go to Abyei today, and I'm attached to a family in Abyei, I will be given land. There will be no question at the end of the day, I will be given land. We will, of course, need to adapt customary law to new phenomena that are coming in. We never had traffic laws because we didn't have cars. We never had company laws because we never had companies. There will be new areas in which a variety of laws that we never had will have to be adapted. And yet, even in those areas, there will be need to consider also elements, or the values, of the customary law. For instance, look at humanitarian law. I worked with the ICRC for a long time, and I made a comparative analysis, as a consultant. I found that there was not much difference between our traditional law and the law of war applied by the ICRC. On such issues as taking prisoners, child protection, women, and all these things, the only difference I find is that we did not commit our values into writing. I compared the two and I used to give lectures at Heidelberg University on international humanitarian law, using as a basis African, particularly Dinka, customary law. There was not much difference.

FD: By the way, do you still have those materials, your comparative analysis of international humanitarian law and the Dinka or Nilotic value system? And could I have access to them?

TD: Yes. They are not here, but I have them in Nairobi and you have unrestricted access to them. If I can have your address, I will send them to you. By the way, I forgot to introduce myself at the start. I am Tilar Deng. My academic background in the university is that I had a double major in political science and anthropology. Then I went on to the UK, where I did my LLB with honors. Then I joined the Movement, and worked as one of the judicial officers, as they used to be called in the Movement. So, I worked with my two colleagues, Deng Arob and Monyluak Alor. In 1992, I went back to Britain, where I did international commercial law. Then I came back to the Movement and worked with the NSCC [New Sudan Council of Churches]. I was the one who invented the term "people-to-people peace process," using our methods of reconciliation. That's why it is "people-to-people." You know in Dinka there is no authority. Authority is in the people themselves, who are thrashing out their differences.

FD: I'm sure that initiative has been very influential in promoting peace on the ground, and will continue to be used in promoting comprehensive peace in the country. What you said about land, I agree with entirely, including the fact that we had ample land and anyone who came into the community would be provided with land. I suppose the problem comes if you want the land to be now used as a resource for massive development. That could easily make those with the means invest in a capitalist economy that could marginalize the true land owners. They would take over the land and turn the people into a subservient status, as opposed to engaging in family-oriented agricultural production and ownership of the land. Is there a way we can conceptually, legally, reconcile the two?

TD: I'm one of the people who would strongly resist turning our people into a role that is alien to them and that they cannot conceptualize. I remember, when I was working with John Burton, and there were no teachers in Yirol Junior Secondary. So I went there to teach English. I used the same books that I was taught from, which had such things as the train leaving from Euston station to Liverpool. I could not conceptualize it until I went to the UK. I saw Euston station. I even went to Liverpool. So I said, instead of saying the train is leaving from Euston station to Liverpool, why don't we say, the cattle were moving from one cattle camp to another, because the child will conceptualize it immediately.

Although I believe in modernization, I do not believe in the type of modernization that will displace our people from their land, and impoverish them. We must keep the land. You get everything you need out of the land. So, any changes in land tenure should be gradually done. I am biased. I don't think I will accept foreign investments that will take over the land for the purpose of building skyscrapers and that sort of thing. I'll go for supporting the people, for improving their agricultural ability to benefit from their land. There is no contradiction between education and culture. I always say that I have nothing against the Arab language; it is what is inside the Arab language that I'm against. So, I am not against development, but I am against any form of development that will make our people dependent on others. And they have never been. If we make our people dependent on others, we will have defeated the purpose of this war. Our people have been resisting domination by others, not because they didn't like them, but simply because those people wanted to come and take over their land, erode their culture, and turn them into nothing.

FD: That is very well said. Now the point is, we have so many communities, as we say, so many nationalities. There are certain groups that have similar customs, but they are quite diverse. What will you say is the best way to move forward with customary law? For instance, should we have massive recording of customary law, then do an analysis to see how they harmonize with one another, so that we then use them as a basis for developing the law, if not codification, at least a restatement with a reform agenda in mind? Such a restatement of the law would aim at remedying some of the weaknesses in the law and borrow from outside in a more positive way.

TD: Well, you are absolutely correct. We have various customary laws, practices, values, and ethics. I will not object to research; I am for it. I've been working closely with Deng Biong. He is the one leading the steering committee on various regimes of customary law. They collect all the necessary data, and see how they can be harmonized. I will not predict how they will come out. There are a lot of bases of similarity within our customary laws, but at the same time there are variations. Take the Nilotics, whether they are Nilo-Hamites or Nilotes proper. They have many similarities. If you go to the Bantus, then you will get differences. Even within the area we are now in, we have the Jurbel and the Agar; they will agree on the *dia*. If you kill a person, you have to pay compensation. They will have the same thing with *aruok*, compensation for adultery. But the amount paid varies. The Dinka will demand thirty-one for a murder case. Some tribes cannot afford that, because it will wipe out the wealth of the whole clan.

With the Nuer we don't have a problem. In fact, their *dia* is higher than ours. In the conferences where we met with Deng Arob, we had to make a compromise on the *dia* and adultery cases. We had cases where a Dinka is killed by a Nuer, and a Nuer is killed by a Dinka. You have to harmonize the compensation in such situations. And then we have divorce cases, where, according to custom, you have to trace your bride wealth cows. But if a Nuer man is married to a Dinka, and the Nuer is far away, you will not be able to trace the offspring of the cattle paid initially. So, we say that if you paid thiry-one or twenty initially, that's what you get back, because there is no way of tracing the increase through offspring. You have been too far away. It relates also to the Dinka. So, I agree with the need for the harmonization of the laws and the preparation of reference documents.

FD: Connected with the idea of customary law is the broader issue of administration and constitutionalism. I've always thought that the challenge for African constitutionalism is, first, to deal with the issue of diversity, to manage ethnic diversity to prevent conflicts, and second, to orientate constitutionalism to the cultures of the people. And this goes beyond just customary law; it has to do with the political authority; it has to do with constitutional principles that relate to democracy, human rights, and those issues. Do you see a role here for tradition in the building of society in the broader sense of constitutionalism that manages diversity and is responsive to the culture?

TD: Absolutely. There is a very big role. Let me say something and then I will come to your position more specifically. You know that the African Charter on People's and Human Rights recognizes very strongly, more than any other human rights document, the responsibility of an individual towards his family and society. The other human rights documents don't have that. This is based on African culture. So, I would think that our customs should form a very important basis for our constitutional framework. As I said already, in our culture, we didn't have cars, we didn't have many of the things we have today. So, there will be some borrowing from the outside world, from other people's experiences with all these things. But if our constitution is not based on our own experience and culture, the respect for it will be very much less. Law has to appeal to the sense of the ordinary person. That is what law is all about. Let's give an example. We make a law to fence the airstrip, in order to prevent cattle from crossing. This is modern. But our culture will say that cattle must have access to every place. That will have to change. We tell our people, "Look here, we didn't have planes before. We now have them and they have to fly in and out. Cattle will cause an accident if we do not control them."

FD: But is there within the Movement, which is about to become a government, a consolidated ideological or policy perspective on these issues?

TD: Absolutely none. Michael Makuei, who is now the Attorney General, has been drafting the interim national constitution, with the help of others. He has not had the time even to think of asking the ordinary people on these matters. This law has to originate from the ordinary people. We have to solicit their views. We have all the time assumed that this is what the people think. We say, let's go, because that is what the people think. So, in a nutshell, I don't think there is a valuable opinion, within the Movement, about the perspective and the importance of consulting the ordinary person.

FD: How should we remedy that; what do you think has to be done to bridge that gap?

TD: I think we have to talk directly to the leadership. The way the system has been working is that the leader of the Movement is the sole authority. In fact, he has to be influenced to understand other perspectives and the importance of involving our people. Without his approval a lot of things will go wrong. Even writing this interim national constitution, there will be a lot of things that we will be surprised by at the end of the day. And coming to the constitution of South Sudan, there are things that our people will be very surprised by. We have not even sensitized them at all.

FD: That is interesting because, when I hear of these interim constitutions being drafted by a committee that works with some foreign organizations, it seems to be contradictory to the practice of constitution-making that, for instance, the Eritreans, the Ugandans, the South Africans, to mention a few, went through, and that is to consult a broad-based constituency. That hasn't quite happened here. Is that likely to raise problems later on and can it then be remedied, or will it have been too late?

TD: Well, it has already raised questions about the process. There is a concern that things are being done without involving the people. My own hope is that when institutions in the South are established, and they are strong enough, they can challenge the constitution of the South. But, of course, there will be difficulties later, because if the constitution is being written for the interim period, then the provisions of the interim national constitution cannot be contradicted by the interim constitution of the South. And that is where the big difficulty will be. Once you commit yourself strongly to the interim national constitutions, then you weaken yourself in your government of South Sudan, and the constitution of the South. And that is the danger. People should be instructed more on the interim national constitution, because it will give us a broader base, for even writing our own constitution. So, we will be restricted later on. The constitutional government of South Sudan and the constitutions of the states will very much depend on what those people do at the national level.

FD: We were talking earlier about so many interest groups coming into the South, supposedly offering help, but there always is that fear that the help might be externalized in its perspective. For instance, with this constitutionalism, I understand that many outside experts are involved. What specific role they play should be a matter of interest.

TD: I think the research on customary law, to me, will be a priority, because it covers a lot of areas. So, I think it will be very important to engage in the recording, analysis, synthesis, and the development of customary law.

FD: Thank you very much. This has been a very interesting and constructive conversation.

7. A Group of Southern Sudanese Judges and Lawyers

Rumbek, February 13, 2005

Francis Deng (FD): First of all, let me express my deep appreciation for your receiving me and particularly for taking time off on Sunday when you would be either in church or with your families. I just want you to know that I appreciate it very much. I wanted us to have a conversation around the future of customary law in our country, and in a number of interrelated areas. One is with respect to the administration of justice, the other relates to the role of culture in governance, in the broader sense, and the third is the relevancy of our cultural values to constitutional democracy.

Let me begin by a brief anthropological overview. I believe every society has a system in which justice, administration, and the principles of constitutionalism are governed by fundamental principles, major goals, that society aims at promoting, and which determine the system. In my own work on the Dinka, I premised the system on three main principles. One was the continuity of the ancestral line, which really aims at immortalizing every individual, so much so that even when a person dies without marrying, a woman is married to beget children in his name. Another is unity and harmony. We know that in African law, as contrasted with European law, the notion of restoring the unity and harmony of the community is the principal element of dispute settlement. The aim is not simply to apply the law so that you win or lose, but to bring people together, to have consensus behind decisions, so that people can go back and live together. That was a major principle which I think influenced much of the judicial or legal process. A third principle was respect for every individual. I always give the example of how in English law it is said that a dead person has no reputation and cannot be defamed. With us, the opposite is the case; it is a more severe offense to insult a dead person than it is to insult a living person.

Today, it seems to me that we are confronting a situation in which the relevancy of custom or tradition can no longer be seen as just contributing to the status quo, or looking back in a reactionary way. To the extent that every society is not only organized around fundamental values and institutions, but evolves on those bases; you don't just leap from nowhere to somewhere, into the so-called modernity. In *Tradition and Modernization*, I go into details to see how one can build on tradition to promote development or progress.

I remember that my brother Bol, when I published my first book, *Tradition and Modernization*, wrote to say, "This is the immortality I believe in." He was trying to contrast scholarly achievement with the Dinka concept of immortality of having children to continue the male line. Later on, when I got married and had a son, he sent me a message to say, "Now you can die in peace, because you have a son." So, this in a sense is a mix of tradition, looking back or continuing in the old-fashioned sense, or modernity, building immortality on accomplishments, so that the memory of the dead is based not simply on begetting children, but on accomplishing. If we want our leaders, for instance, to be motivated to do something progressive, maybe by honoring achievements we motivate people to do things that will perpetuate their memory instead of simply having children.

I think that we today, in Southern Sudan, in a way, are fortunate, even though it is a fortune that is also a curse, in that we are the least influenced by Western culture in terms of development. Our societies are really at a basic level, which allows room for creatively modeling development, building on what we have. I have always been impressed by how the leaders of Botswana have managed to build their progress on their existing social structures and institutions. Botswana is now a country which is reputed to be very stable. Some people think it has to do with their small size and their diamonds and things like that. It probably helps to have diamonds and to be small in size, but I think much has to do with the extent to which their leaders from the beginning built their system on the existing institutions and cultural values.

I want us to just think out loud, to discuss how customary law is going to be relevant as we build our societies. In what way can we inspire our judges and our lawyers to see customary law, not as something that is holding us back, but as something that can be dynamic and even be reinterpreted in a modern context to promote development from within? Whether we are talking about legal or other aspects of development, and governance in general, principles that guide the rule of law or the way people administer themselves, the question is whether we can apply some of these values.

I am thinking of the Dinka concept of *cieng*, and in the conversations John Juk and I had. They also have something very similar among the Nuer, with the word spelled and pronounced a little differently, *ciang*. This is a principle of how people should relate to one another with a sense of cooperation, mutual respect, and harmony. We can also take another Dinka concept called *dheeng*, which is a normative principle of dignity, concerned not only with how you carry yourself, including physical appearance, but also with the propriety of conduct, in terms of personal behavior or of how you relate to others. If we were really to understand these principles, interpret them, promote them, and project them as guides in whatever we do, I think we can motivate our people to look on themselves with respect.

I always feel that we have fought the Arabs and promoted our cause as a kind of culture of resistance, which we defined almost negatively, that we are not Arabs, and not Muslims. I think the time has come for us to be assertive, to be positive about what we are. And what we are is not simply calling ourselves this or that, Southerners, Africans, Dinka, Nuer, but the content of what that means, what we are, whether it is in a spiritual sense, in a political sense, in a cultural sense or in a broader sense. So, this really is a free interaction in which I would like to benefit from your thoughts, including ideas on the kind of support we will need from the outside world. There is a keen interest today around the world from people who would want to help. Because Africa is finding that all the models we have received from outside don't seem to be working, people are interested to see if we have something authentic to build on

African leaders have always endeavored to develop indigenous ways of promoting their government, although very often they have tended to exploit African culture for purposes of domination. For instance, in the attempt to legitimize the one-party system, African leaders argued that traditionally we didn't have parties. This argument could be well intentioned, but could also be a perversion aimed at trying to inculcate domination. When Kenneth Kaunda of Zambia talked of humanism, he was motivated by the desire to have an African normative guiding principle. But very often, this quest for indigenous values is not fully utilized. In Tanzania, Julius Nyerere's *Ujamaa* was close enough to be founded on indigenous values. In Ghana, Kwame Nkrumah talked about consciencism, also a search for African normative frameworks. Now, we hear in southern Africa of *Ubuntu*, a concept which is being explored as a guide to nation-building. Constitutionalism in South Africa is said to have been guided by that concept. The way that they are interpreting the constitution and applying it is said to be guided by the principles of *Ubuntu*. It is something they are even projecting as part of the African renaissance.

I think we in the South, and in Sudan, are frankly the least "contaminated" by foreign ideas. We have to begin to think consciously about who we are, what we have, and how we can make our people become more aware of themselves, let others become aware of who we are, and how we perceive ourselves, and then build our society from within; I think we will have done ourselves a great deal of favor. So, what I would like us to do is, we go around, whoever wants to speak, and please hold the microphone, the tape recorder, close to you, because, sometimes it doesn't pick up from too far. I'll pass it around. I have no rigid agenda. This is a free conversation. Any ideas are welcome about what we may propose, whether to the authorities, or to our partners abroad, including ways in which they can help us in developing our own concepts.

I have already discussed with Justice Michael Makuei. I told him that the way our constitution is being developed strikes me as a top-down process. We get experts from outside to help us with constitution-making, people who may not have any sense of the values that are important to our cultural system or concepts of governance. Everyone knows that in our traditional society, whenever there was a conflict or a public issue to be debated, we sat under the tree and debated and debated until we would come to an agreement. This was used by some against a multiparty system, but it could also be an important principle to build upon. Some societies have developed their constitutions from the grass roots step by step, up. This is really becoming the trend in Africa. Democracy has to affect not only the outcome of constitutions but the process by which they are developed. Maybe certain circumstances in developing the constitution from the top down have compelled us to move the way we have moved, but I think it is also important that as we begin to make our constitution work, to make it a living document, we have to involve the people with their cultural values. I think awareness of the broader issues, of the cultural values, of institutions of our society, and how they could be made relevant to our system of governance, or constitutionalism, could help in making what was a top-down process be reinforced by a bottom-up implementation. So, who would like to speak first; you don't need to make this a protocol process. Anybody who wants to say something can speak.

Michael Makuei (MM): Deng Biong, you are the right person who can start, since you are the chairman of the Customary Law Steering Committee.

Deng Biong (DB): Thank you; yes, maybe I will start. The point is that I may be repeating myself because this morning I had an interview with Dr. Francis. By way of self-introduction, I am Deng Biong Mijak, and am a high court judge now at the Judiciary Headquarters here in Rumbek. I did my law at Khartoum University, graduated in 1985, and joined the Movement in 1986. I served in the Movement in various units and in various liberated areas, sometimes as a judge and sometimes given other responsibilities. At times, we combined what was called legal affairs office with acting as judges to settle cases, and also giving advice to the commanders, on legal matters. It is true that I gained an interest in customary law in my work as a judge in different places, especially when I was in Equatoria. In 1994, I thought I should do something about recording some customary laws, especially in Equatoria. I realized that my colleagues who worked there, even in the old Sudan, before the war, did not do anything to record the customs in Equatoria, unlike the case of Bahr el Ghazal, where judges took the initiative of recording customary laws. This is why we have the Wanh-Alel statement of customary laws in Bahr el Ghazal.

So, I initiated a process of bringing chiefs together. Two seminars were held: one was in Umbasi, that is in the Yei area. By then, Yei was under the control of Khartoum, and we were operating about eighteen miles from Yei, in Umbasi. So, we held a seminar for one week. We invited chiefs from the clans' headmen, to subchiefs and senior chiefs, and some elders. Some records of those meetings are available. We touched on various customs. That was in February of 1994. And in March, 1994, I went to Kajokeji and did a similar thing there. The recommendations that came out of those two meetings were improved upon, and culminated in the customary court that is operating now in that area of central Equatoria. It was the result of that work. When I got transferred here to Rumbek, I did some papers for the Sudan Law Society, through UNICEF. That one was on adultery in Dinka and Nuer customary laws. It was to touch on issues of women's rights and all that. And, again, I did another issue paper on child legitimization and custody. That was also tackling issues of child rights. Both were done for UNICEF. I have also compiled some ten cases involving customary issues for the South Sudan Law Society, through the same project. Later on, I did a study for UNDP. I am currently doing some work also on the interface between traditional authority and local government, in terms of structures and the administrative and judicial roles of the traditional authorities. This is what we are doing now.

In October, during JAM cluster II, that is the rule of law cluster, when we did a workshop here in Rumbek, it was felt that customary law is important to our legal system. There were several panels, one for the legal affairs secretariat, another for the local government, and a third for the judiciary. All these panels, when they realized that issues of customary law were coming up, and customary law certainly is going to play a role in shaping our legal system, decided that a body be formed, composed of five representatives from five units or institutions that were thought to be stakeholders on the issue of customary law. And these are the judiciary, the legal affairs and constitutional development secretariat, the South Sudan Law Society, representing civil society, the local government secretariat, and the secretariat for the women's agenda and child welfare. These units sent in their representatives. I was seconded by the judiciary to this body. The body is supervised by the Legal Affairs Commissioner. When this body was later on formally constituted, I was appointed as its chairperson. So, we put out proposals for a work-plan workshop in Nairobi, which was funded by PACT. The workshop was held in Nairobi last December [2004], from the 14th to the 16th. We had put out proposals for a comprehensive recording and ascertainment of various customary regimes in Southern Sudan. This one now is pending funding. So far, we have got hints from some organizations that they are ready to support us. It is only a matter of time, but I believe they will go ahead with the funding.

So, this is what we are doing now. Customary law definitely is going to play a significant role, because, as is clear in the agreement, this time the legal system in South Sudan will stand on a different philosophy altogether from that of the North. The question will be what are the main sources of legislation in the South? The answer is that custom is the main source. Our laws should be reflective of our customs and our values. This is where the importance of customary law comes in. Essentially, before the advent of the modern state, we had our own social structures, our own laws. And today you cannot come and say, "Let us forget about them."[1] The war we have just ended was a cultural war. The reason for the war was that the North thought the South was suffering from a cultural vacuum. They were calling it in Arabic, *el faragh el thagafy*, "Cultural Vacuum," which was not true. The idea was that the system in Sudan was trying, of course, to build itself on Islamic principles, Arab and Islamic culture, and all that, but now our argument in the South is definitely that we are a people with cultures.

Before the introduction of the modern state, our societies were stable, with an established social order. People did have rules to govern their affairs. The colonialists found them living as communities in an organized society. We have now realized through our studies that these customs, these rules that were governing our traditional societies, did have a lot that was admirable in them, such as a code of ethics that could be relevant even to modernity. As I was telling you this morning, our societies used to observe certain ethics and values, such as the rule against abusing a vulnerable group, like women and children, in the course of a fight, or taking sexual advantage of a woman who is captured by the enemy. These norms were there in our societies. Today, people talk about the Geneva Conventions and they are not aware that these values have been there all along in our societies They are ignorant of this fact. They say, these are international humanitarian and human rights standards, but we have them. It will be very much convincing to tell our people that we want to enshrine these principles in our constitution, simply because they were there. Our ancestors had observed these principles. It will convince them more than telling them that the Geneva Conventions require it.

So, customary law, even in terms of governance, is important. Recently, in 2002, in this area, the authority went, dismissed all the traditional chiefs, and installed military officers. Some were made executive chiefs, others were made to preside over local courts, and some were made subchiefs. What happened was that it did not succeed. People avoided these imposed structures. People suspended cases waiting for this emergency to be lifted so that they could go back to their normal way of doing things. So, in terms of governance, there should be a rule whereby traditional authority is given room. If we accept that they were playing an important role in social organization, in establishing order in their communities, then now, with the modern notions of governance, there is a need to try to harmonize the traditional notions of governance with the modern ones. A line should be drawn in between, whereby the state structures should stop, and the local traditional structures continue from there, downward. That also goes even to the courts. There are certain levels where the modern state courts should stop and the local traditional system take over. So there is much to be gained from the customary law; it is relevant to the administration of justice and it is relevant to the constitution-making.

FD: Thank you very much, Deng. There is nothing wrong with repeating what one has said before. But you have added much that is valuable. As Deng has done, I would appreciate it if you will introduce yourselves as you speak.

John Luk (JL): Yes, my name is John Luk. I too had an interview with Dr. Francis, but let me try again. There is no doubt that every community's existence is based on certain principles, fundamental principles. Even in the animal kingdom, you see that animals have their own ways, their patterns of conduct. As human beings, our societies have rules of conduct that guide them. That is how they have kept together and maintained their social order. There are rules that guide them in maintaining peace. There are rules that govern their relationships with one another. There are rules that regulate family matters, public matters, and even private rights. Those are there. One thing, though, is that talking about South Sudan, we are too diverse. The communities are so diverse that there are a lot of variations in customary practices, although maybe you can categorize them into larger groups with much in common. In terms of trying to promote customary principles, and bring them into modernity, and in terms of governance, this requires that a lot of work has to be done first to ascertain those values that we talk about in our various communities. We can then later on crystallize them into general principles that can guide us.

We talk about the word *cieng* among the Dinka, and in Nuer it is *ciang*. These concepts embody the way we live, the way of living. There are certain principles, and as I said the other time, we make distinctions between *ciang migua* and *ciang mijek*. *Ciang migua* carries with it certain norms, social values, that people would like to identify with so that you gain status within the community, as somebody who is conducting himself in accordance with the principles of *ciang migua*. In the Nuer context, there are certain principles which you look for in somebody. To say that a man is *wut pany* is as saying in Dinka that he is *adheng*. For instance, the values of valor, the values of generosity, the values of respect, and above all the element of spirituality, that you are a God-fearing person, were all there and highly regarded. These are the things that guide us. Also we talk of *nguot* as laws. In Nuer, we talk of *nguot*. These are the rules, the laws, that have been laid down; what we should not do. This amounts to what we would call customary law. *Nguot* applies in every respect; every way of life has certain *nguot*, certain principles that are laid out. They also govern other aspects of life. For instance, in the area of marriages, there are certain laws you must follow, certain *nguot* you follow. And in war, there are also rules to follow: how you treat women and children, or those who are not initiated into manhood, if you encounter them in battle. So, the *nguot* of war are there. How you treat your victims, under what circumstances you are permitted to finish off your enemy, and what you do with a wounded enemy.

There are also laws that relate to leadership, which we call *ric*. *Ric* means leadership. To become a leader in the community, what kind of criteria should you meet? What will people look for in a person to qualify as a leader? And what are the ways by which we choose our leaders? I am now talking in terms of governance. Nobody simply appoints himself as a leader. There are certain qualities which the community looks for in a leader, and which a potential leader must satisfy.

In the Nuer community, leaders are people who solve problems, people who deny themselves and serve the people. These are the people who will be watched, and at a certain point of time an old man will come and just say to him, "I give this man my daughter because he has convinced me of his qualities of leadership, the way he conducts himself in the community." Somebody will come and say, "This is my daughter, I want to be related to you because I like the way you conduct yourself, the way you are so gentle, and what you do." Some of those people will really be so outstanding in the community that the community is able to build a consensus when they look for the person to be their leader.

There are also many stages in leadership growth among age-mates. Young people, among themselves, know who has what qualities and potentials for leadership, whether in war, in peace times, or even in managing their own youth affairs. The elders also know each other, and they always look for certain leadership qualities. When you reach a certain age, you are expected to acquire a certain level of decency and dignified behavior. These are among the things considered very important in the society. You must show decency and dignity within the community by being of service to others, even denying yourself in the service of others. So, for the leadership, there are things which qualify people to be leaders. It is not anybody that can become a team leader or a group leader. There are things to look for in a potential leader.

Our societies have struggled to maintain our culture and our customs. Modern education has had its own impact on our culture and our traditions. In Kenya now, when we sit in the evening and watch the TV, around 4:00, you will see school shows, in which children perform their own traditional dances, dressed in their own traditional attire. High school children come and present their traditional dances, and sing the songs their people sing in the village. That reflects a conscious effort through education to keep people attached to their cultures and traditions.

In Southern Sudan, the war has affected us a lot. There have been no long periods of peace during which modern education could have been adjusted to our own way of life, our own social values. People come to towns and leave their relatives in the villages. People are disjointed, disconnected. I think the challenge now is to find a way of getting back together. Many of our people have gone to far distant lands and are picking up different cultures. When they come back, some, particularly the children, will find themselves uprooted, unless conscious efforts are made to orientate them. When they come back from the cultural values in which they now live, which are totally different from our own, it will be necessary for us to make it a really urgent issue to orientate them to our own customs, values, and way of life. We should not just talk about our cultural values; they should be practiced and made available, especially to the people who are now in the Diaspora. Our culture cannot remain only in the minds of the elders. The elders are perishing. This war has made a lot of people to perish. So you need to document these cultural values. That raises the issue of the recording, codification, and restatement of customary law, which we talked about when we had that earlier interview. This is important; otherwise our custom will be threatened, as we move further into modernity.

As we start again to build a system of governance, and build our towns, there will be a tendency to ignore our traditional structures, and to make them disappear, in fact. So, our traditions are seriously threatened with disappearance. People are coming together from different communities. And that is a good development. Some common positive values will emerge through living together, interacting, and getting to know each other's language. But back home, if we just ignore the situation, the result could be very negative. Our local government structures are now being built that will bring with them, in the name of modernity, new approaches to democracy at the grass roots. Democracy now is taking a different form from what we had traditionally. Without looking very seriously at what we are bringing in, in the name of democracy or good governance, we could have serious problems. Now, we are told about the so-called good governance and we immediately jump to the World Bank criterion of good governance with accountability, transparency, and all these sorts of things. But how different are they qualitatively from our values, the basic way we have been running our communities long before we heard of the World Bank or the Western world? And now they are preaching to Africa, saying, "This is how you should govern yourselves! This is the good governance that enabled the Western world to advance."

This is apart from the issue of technology, of course. But the basics at the grass roots, at the start, are important for us. This is where our soul is, really. This is where we should start before we add other things, such as technology and other concepts of modernity. So, I think the challenge is great. The coming period is a struggle of cultures, of civilizations. And we must respond to that challenge. As Justice Deng said, we have been viewed as a cultural void, a cultural vacuum that is being filled by the Western world, by Arabs, or by Islam. This is what has been encouraging the people in the North to encroach upon us. They always ask us, "What do you have? Show us what you have." And we say to them, "We are fighting for something precious to us." Of course, their own excesses made us angry, the naked operation that has been meted on us. But now that we are a little bit peaceful, especially with this peace agreement, you definitely must show what you are and what you possess.

Now, we claim Sudan to be ours. You hear some of our leaders trying to trace back the glory that was ours, about what happened to us in the middle, and how we have been made to lose everything, so that we are almost starting from zero. I might not go that far, but I think at present, before we lose totally what we have, it is important to make efforts, very conscious efforts, to promote what we have, and to deepen our understanding of what we are, and the values that have kept us to this day, as a people. This is very important. So, I think it is right for people to feel that we have something that we should not leave to die in the name of modernity. What does modernity mean? Does it mean that you attach yourself to values that are not originally yours? Of course, cultures do interact. And definitely, we will be able to take from other cultures, based on the resilience we will create within our cultures to interact with other cultures without losing the core or integrity of our own. It is a matter of a balance; you take in from whatever is positive around you and add it to what you have. You must not abandon yours, thinking that the best is what others have. If we do that, we will be rootless. And, of course, a tree that doesn't have roots dies.

FD: Thank you very much. Just for the new arrivals, as you can gather from what you have heard, we are focusing on the challenges of customary law and culture in the administration of justice, governance, and constitutionalism in the broader sense. Who is next?

MM: To continue from where my colleagues stopped, in fact, it is true, it is through our customs and traditions that there is a threat. This is simply because we have been made to believe that after all we don't have cultures, that we don't have anything, that there is a vacuum to be filled. Others came to fill that vacuum and convince us that we don't have anything, and that the best way is to pick whatever they bring and adopt it to be ours. As a result, most of our intellectuals have actually lost their culture. It is unfortunate that even our languages are threatened. Language is one of the outstanding means of actually maintaining a culture. You will find today that because of the war, and massive displacement, there are many families which have completely abandoned their mother tongue. And their children have never learned their language. Now that we have signed a peace agreement, children will be coming back who don't know their mother tongue. These children have become the victims of a situation which, to me, is the making of their own parents.

We strongly believe that we have our culture and our customs. These need to be maintained and promoted. If you look at the conventions and protocols on human rights, for example, you will find that in our customs, every citizen or member of the community has rights and duties. This is what the modern constitutions and conventions talk about. You have the right to live in the community; you have the right and the duty to do whatever serves the interest of the community; and one of your duties is to defend your community. Whenever anything happens that threatens the community, such as fighting between two sections, you are under duty to defend your community. You have the duty to defend your property as well as the property of other members of the community. And so on and so forth. So, if we get down to really scrutinize all the protocols and the conventions that are now said to be modern, we will find that we have them all in our customs. They are there in our culture and they are all over. But because we have been made to believe that ours are so archaic, so primitive, we tend to pick those of others, forgetting that it was perhaps ours that were picked up and developed by other people.

That is in terms of human rights generally. In terms of women's rights, and children's rights specifically, they too are there. For example, in our rules of war, you don't kill a vulnerable person; you don't kill a person who is disarmed; you don't kill a woman; you don't kill a child. This is something that is in our custom. But the conventions come and tell us, "Don't do this, it is against the convention and should be done like this." And yet we already have them in our own customary law, except that we were made to believe that we don't have them because we have not recorded them. When we talk to people, and tell them that we have these in our own customs, they will say, "Where is it?" That's because they want it in writing. They want it documented. But if you send them to that old man who is sitting there in the village, to go and interview him, they will find out that these things had always been there with us, in our customs, which are not written. As our cultures are not written, those who read believe that we do not have anything. That is not the case. We have our own code of conduct; we have our own humanitarian law.

Coming to the system of governance, it is the modern system of governance that we have now been made to accept. But in the past, we had our own system of governance. Whenever you go to any village now, you find elders sitting there, either in the *luak* [cattle byre], or under a tree, discussing issues that concern the community. Among them, you find that there is a leader who is not actually elected, but is accepted by the people. And you find that there are certain conditionalities which must be met for a man to become a leader. Although he is not elected, he emerges within the community, with the acceptance of his age-mates, and the elders. Ultimately, he will be known as the one capable of leadership among his age-mates. The elders will be observing what the young people are doing. At the end of the day, when they come to the selection of a leader, they will not ask you, the young people; they will just say that so-and-so is the chief. And that's that. Nobody will question their wisdom, because if I am selected from amongst my age-mates, they already have known the role I play among them. The system of democracy that has come up now, whereby people go to the balloting box, is new to our people. It was never there with our people. But we had our own system of democracy and leadership.

In terms of legislation, we have our customary laws. These laws are not written; they are not statutory laws. But they are there and they operate effectively. And they are actually dynamic, not static. It is the same community that keeps developing their customs in accordance with their needs. So, in our system of legislation, it is the elders together with the chiefs who sit and decide on a course of action. Even this terminology of the chief may be misleading. But we have an elder, who, whenever there is any problem, will sit with elders and discuss the problem. And they will agree on how best it will be handled. This is how we have been living all this time. Whatever decision is taken, on a particular issue, that is the legislation. It then gets adopted as the customary law of that particular community. This is how we have been going on all this time. So, here now comes the difference between our customs or traditions and modernity

It is time now for the intellectuals to go down and record these customs which are tragically almost vanishing, because the elders who really know them are perishing, as was correctly noted by my colleague, John Luk. And the young generations coming up are not fully versed with the customs. At the end of the day, we end up with the modern way of doing things and will have discarded all our valuable customs. So, there is need for us to go down and record our customs, our customary law, our cultures and so forth. Of course, it is not all the customs that we should preserve. We have been made to believe that all of our cultures and customs are bad. It is true that there are some customs that need to be corrected. Some are inhumane in a way. There was a time when I had a talk with some of our people. I told them that one of their customs must be changed. According to that custom, if I kill a person, my daughter or sister is paid to the relatives of the deceased. In compensation, she is paid to the relatives of the deceased. This is a bad custom. But there are good customs. There are bad customs which we must discourage, and there are good customs which we must promote and develop

In terms of the judicial system, there are situations whereby you find that a law completely contradicts a custom, that there is a conflict between the custom and the statutory law. This situation needs to be remedied. In fact, we are now waiting for the result of the work being done by the steering committee under the chairmanship of Justice Deng Biong. My personal opinion is that it will be good if we could set up courts of customary law at higher levels. We now have them only at the grass-roots levels. But as soon as a case goes beyond the grass-roots level, it goes to the statutory courts. At times, you find that the judge is completely ignorant of the customary laws of these people. As such, he will decide in accordance with the statutes before him. Those decisions often cause a lot of problems. There is a need to set up courts that will be receiving appeals based on traditions and customs, so that the traditional authority continues to review its decisions from the grass roots up to the top. That should be a separate system altogether. It will be a structure that follows the customary laws of the people. In that way, we will be in a position to maintain our customs, develop them, and promote them.

I remember there was a case in Wau, when the late Gordon Abyei was the Province Judge. A case was decided here in Rumbek. It was a case of adultery. In that case, the trial judge sitting here was a Northerner who did not know the customs of the Dinka or anything about the local cultures. He saw an appeal case of adultery that had been decided by the Chiefs' court. The adulterer was made to pay compensation. When the case was brought before him on appeal, this Northern District Judge, who was the Resident Magistrate, asked where the husband of the woman was. They told him that the husband was dead. He asked who was then raising the case of adultery. When he was told that it was the relatives of the dead husband, he dismissed the case on the ground that the woman had no husband since her husband had died. That was the end of the whole case. The plaintiffs appealed again. They went to the Province Court and found Gordon Abyei, who was himself a Dinka and knew Dinka customary law. He reinstated the decision of the Chiefs' court. Then he wrote to the Northern judge, saying, "For your information, the husband of a Dinka woman never dies."

This is how customary law is being affected. It is being applied by judges who do not know the law. As a result, it is being distorted in one way or another. These are some of the issues that we should look into in the near future, when the customary law research has taken shape. That way, we will be in a position to develop our customary law and update it. In fact, if you go to our own documents, we talk about customary law being the source of legislation. But we have not even gone down to know it. What is that customary law which we are making our source of legislation? We need to study it thoroughly. Then we can develop it so that we make it a source of legislation based on a particular understanding. We have a great deal to learn. The field of customary law in the South is vast. And there is a lot to learn. In some areas, there is even a conflict of customary laws. These need to be recorded. We need to identify their origins, record them, and then harmonize between them. After harmonization, we need to go down to enacting them. This is a process that will take time. Nevertheless, there is need for us to adopt these customs, so that they become our source of legislation.

If we go down to conduct research and look at these modern principles of rights, we will find that we have them. The problem is that we have not gone down to document them, and show them to the international community: "This is what we have. What you are telling us, we already have." This is where your own contribution comes in. There are some among us who pick those modern principles and beliefs and come and say our customs are archaic; they are oppressive. They just discard them like that, even though they have not gone down to study these customs, when they would discover that they are, in fact, fair. Where they are unfair, and it is true that some of these customs are bad, we need to change them.

One of the main issues that is of concern to us is the question of language. Language is the source of culture. With us now, our young people feel proud when they talk a foreign language. Here in Kenya, our young people talk to us in Kiswahili. They think they look modern by speaking that language. And when you try to talk to someone in his mother tongue, you find out that he doesn't know the language. Once you have lost your language, you have lost your culture, because culture is closely connected to language. This is why you will find today that the Northerners want everybody to speak Arabic. With Arabic comes Islam, and with Islam comes the Arab culture, and with all these come an Arab-Islamic worldview. They are all interconnected. So, it is important that we maintain our cultures, or customs, promote them and develop them, and tell the world that this is what we have. Above all, we must ensure that indigenous languages are maintained and promoted. I think this is one of the policies we have to adopt.

In the agreement, we made all the indigenous languages to be national languages. This is a very big achievement, because this is now a recognition, after so many years of struggle. In the past, Arabic was the only language. Now, all the other languages have become recognized as languages, not just dialects, as we were made to believe. These are now all recognized as national languages. It is now our duty to develop them. By developing them, we will be able to promote our cultures and customs. So, this is what I wanted to say about all these issues.

DB: This is Deng Biong again. I would like to add my comments on this issue of statutory and customary laws. I have observed particularly recently on my tour of Western Equatoria that our statutory laws put adultery as a criminal offence, and therefore triable by a second-grade judge. That could be the correct interpretation. But then, I have observed in other areas that it is relaxed, and you could still see chiefs handling cases of adultery. In Western Equatoria now, they have taken all of these cases to the criminal courts. That is a real problem, because adultery by its nature has civil and criminal aspects. I believe the intention in taking these cases to be tried by a second-grade judge is to tackle the criminal aspect. But the criminal aspect will not address the civil aspect, which is supposed to be handled by customary law as administered by the chiefs. These are some of the issues that we need to address quickly. This is a case which an executive chief, or even a subchief, should handle in these communities.

Again on the issue of our traditional notion of democracy, you know the Western style of democracy by election. But our people do not believe in that form of democracy. This notion of bringing people and asking them to stand behind the candidates, which is what they do nowadays, is alien to them. Three candidates are asked to stand and people then line up behind the candidates. Our people don't like it because it creates a lot of tension within the same community. The chief who is elected will not be at peace with some of the people who did not support him. The traditional notion of democracy is that people sit, they nominate the candidates, people debate and dialogue, until they come to a consensus and select one of them. People first dialogue over the candidates and decide by consensus. That is the traditional way, the traditional concept of democracy, which I believe we should preserve, especially in selecting traditional leaders. Now, in areas of Yei and Yambio, they are electing chiefs. They have introduced Bomas and they say, "Now you have to elect the chiefs." People are not even asked whether election is the best way, or whether they would prefer to nominate people and then select through the traditional way by which they used to select their leaders. From our own observation, people don't like it when they see it as something being imposed on them from above. This is what I wanted to address.

Harriet Kuyang (HK): Thank you. I am Harriet Kuyang, and I work with the Law Society. I just wanted to raise a question in our customary laws and cultures with regard to the administration of justice, governance, and constitutionalism. My question is basically on the documentation of our cultures that has been done by people other than us, Southern Sudanese. This has led to generalizations about our cultures. I myself wrote an article in which I said that we should treat our customs and cultures as reflecting the human rights that are being incorporated for us. I said that our customs and cultures cannot be modernized. How can they be? Which aspects are we going to modernize? These have been our norms, our way of life. Our customs have identified and guided us for all these years. It is unfortunate that with the prevalence of this long, protracted war, there have been infusions from other areas, with practices and customs that vary. Traditional cultures should not be generalized because they have differences that should be developed, and they have a commonality that should also be developed.

When it comes to our justice system, our customs and cultures are a bit unfair. They contain practices that disregard certain groups, for instance, women and children. I think these are the parts that we should look at to determine how relevant they will be in the future, and how they could be codified with the view to reforming them. We have to consider the fact that they are not fair in certain aspects, especially when it comes to the justice system.

I had a meeting with one of the chiefs in Yei. We were discussing our customs and cultures, looking at a lot of things. We looked, for instance, at widow inheritance. Of course, there are a lot of arguments in favor of the custom. It provides for continuity in the family and for the maintenance of the widow. These are valid arguments for it. But, of course, with the development of our society, and certain emergency issues, for instance, the issue of HIV/AIDS, I think this is something we should look into because a widow could be a victim of HIV. And once she has inherited that, it could cause a lot of complications for her and the family.

I also raised the issue of inheritance in the event of the death of a male spouse in the family. Normally, what happens with death is that inheritance goes to the male heir. What happens in female-dominated families, where it is just the wife and the daughters? That means that the property that was accumulated during the marriage will have to go to the hands of another person outside the immediate family. That leaves the widow and the daughters probably begging for their own property. What I wanted to look at was the issue of property rights and how a woman, in the event of the death of the man, and the property passes on to other hands, women in the family become beggars.

Another aspect to look at is that there is a lot of biased superstition against women embedded in our cultures. I take the issue of the adultery. When we discussed with those chiefs in Yei, they were looking at adultery in a superstitious way. They were saying that in the custom of one tribe, a bowl is put under the bed and then if it is eaten at night, it means the woman has committed adultery. I told them that it could be coincidental that maybe a rat could have eaten the bowl, and then the custom victimizes the woman. So, when it comes to the justice system, these two offenders, the man and the woman, are viewed differently. Both have committed the same offense, which is adultery, but the female counterpart is viewed much more harshly than her male counterpart.

On my first visit to Yei prison, I found women who were alleged to have committed adultery. I am not saying women should go ahead and commit adultery. I am looking at the way they are viewed. Since it is the same offense, there should be some commonly applicable rules; there should be some justice. And if we continue this way, women can never realize justice, when they are viewed like that. The judge who took us around revealed his obvious prejudice against women. This was quite apparent from the way he was saying, "This is a woman who has committed adultery." The way he was viewing them was enough to show his verdict. With a man, they just say, "He slept with a mother and a daughter."

So, when it comes to our justice system, our cultures raise a lot of concerns. This is an issue that should be addressed, with a view to remedying the gender prejudices. Some say that women are just making a lot of noise, that they want to advance their position at all costs. That's, of course, not true. We are looking at a culture that looks at the men as a superior group of persons. Probably what can do for the man can do for the woman. Even in our African customs and cultures, women have their own needs. It is unfortunate that some of our cultures go to the extent of defining what a woman should eat. This is defining from the social, the cultural, even economic aspects what you should eat. Some of the women are deprived of some of the smallest delicacies in life. This is something that is minute, but I think these are issues that should be looked into.

When it comes to the issue of governance, it also raises other dimensions. What is happening is that our customs and cultures recognize the fact that women cannot be incorporated into governance. What happens is that their role in governance is kept at the informal level. It is clear when we look at our legislature, a quick count will show that it is male dominated. The women who were there were probably either professional, or they were included because of the demand from the international community. What I'm really saying is that our cultures should look at the contributions of a woman, not in terms of solving disputes among family members, children and the men, and the other people who are living in the house, but to advance just a little bit. In Yei, when it comes to the Payam court, and there are women there, but the role of the women is to cajole the woman to confess to an offense she hasn't committed. The women are purportedly for representation. But what they really do is go down and tell her, "Please, if you did it, then just say you did it." And she hasn't done it. Because of pressure, many women have confessed to offenses they haven't committed. So, if we could look at the women's role in governance in a more formal way, I think it will make a difference. In this process from the signing of the peace agreement, to brokeraging governance structures, to establishing a proper system, we need both sexes. And if we look at our cultures and customs, they try to hamper the role of women. So, these small, discriminatory practices should be looked at.

When it comes to the issue of constitutionalism, of course, we are faced with a situation where we don't even have an interim constitution; we are making one and it will be ratified. So, the recommendation I would like to make at this point would be that our customs and cultures are part of us. Personally, I have gone to the Diaspora, and I can say that I was fortunate enough to have my customs and cultures instilled in me. I cannot speak for everybody else, but I know that for most of us, it is probably a way of identifying oneself in a foreign land. I wrote an article on my own experiences, being uprooted from South Sudan to another country. There are challenges. Sometimes you will have to call yourself other than what you are, not because you want to, but because no one will know what you really are. Probably, it will be a source of insult. Then there are some of our children who grow up in the Diaspora, that can be pinpointed. The main victims in my experience have been the Dinka and the Nuer. How are they supposed to meet, mingle, and socialize? They had to adhere to English, or Luganda, or whatever. But, of course, when you start looking at the reality, all of us want to come back to our own culture and be proud of what it is. It is fortunate that we are now going to be identified as a country. I think that's all and maybe I will add more later.

FD: Thank you very much. I think that is very helpful. I particularly appreciate getting a different view from a gender perspective. On the issue of inheritance, among the Dinka that I am familiar with, during the lifetime of a man, he distributes cattle to his wives or children. When a man dies, according to my knowledge, what has been distributed to the wife cannot be taken away from her. That is her inheritance. If she has a plot of land, which has been given her, even if the husband were to help her cultivate that land, he cannot interfere with the produce; it is absolutely her domain. Are there differences among our various groups on this issue? I have heard this from a number of sources, and it is true in my own travels around the world that on questions of inheritance and land-holdings, women are very disadvantaged. But am I wrong about the Dinka practice, or is it that the Dinka practice is different from other communities in the South? And then I didn't quite get the thing that is put under the bed.

HK: They will put a bowl under the bed. I repeat that in itself is a bias, because in the existence of the marriage, you already have the bowl under the bed. That bowl is put there to check how loose the woman probably is. But this is not done for the man. If the bowl is eaten, probably by a rat, it automatically means that the woman has committed adultery. So, what I was trying to raise with the chiefs is that this is superstition. The rats could have eaten the bowl. Maybe it's too hot and they are all too hungry. But they will say, under no circumstances could such a thing happen.

MM: Concerning the issue of inheritance, this is where I said that there is diversity even within Southern Sudan. To give the example of the Dinka, you put it correctly. A husband distributes his cattle in his lifetime. Whatever cows come, that is additional to his herd; it is his duty to see to it that it goes to a certain wife. If he has only one wife, then there is no problem, but if he has two or more wives, then he must ensure that whatever new cattle arrive should be assigned to someone among his wives. This has been the situation. Once you die, it is the duty of the eldest wife to take care of the younger wives. In the case of a young wife, whose children may still be small, it is the duty of the family to take care of her wealth up to the time when her children are fully grown. That woman has the right to go to court at any time and sue anybody who misappropriates her property. It is her right to claim her entitlements and she will be given her cattle. These are rights which are there. I think this is where we differ in terms of customs. In terms of land, the land women talk about is the land in the urban areas. Otherwise, in the rural areas, land is not owned by individuals; it is owned by the community. And once you stay there, once you get married, then you settle somewhere within the land of the community. That land continues to be owned by the community. Even though you have settled on that piece of land, it is not yours; it belongs to the community. For the urban areas, what I know is that whoever applies to Rumbek County for land, a man or a woman, is given a land. That land is registered in your name. If I am a husband and I have two, three, four, or five wives, and I have acquired pieces of land, then before I die, it is my duty to see to it that this plot of land belongs to this wife, this one to this wife, and this one to that wife. If I have only one wife, then I distribute it to her children, this one belongs to this boy, and this one belongs to this boy. What is missing in our custom is that girls do not inherit.

FD: They are assumed to get married and move out of the ancestral line.

MM: They will be married to others and as such, they don't have the right to inherit. It is different from Islam. In Islam, when you die, your daughter gets her share, half of what the son gets. But with us, girls do not inherit because they are not considered to be members of the family.

FD: And that could be injustice …

MM: Yes, that could be an injustice. At least for the one who is married, she is with her family, there is no problem. But there are girls who stay in the house. Sometimes they are married, but the marriage fails and they come back to the family. These ones are entitled because they are considered to be part of the family. Actually, they are given the status of sons in the house. In terms of the evidence that is usually given by women, I agree that there are certain situations in which you will find that men are unfair to women. These are the areas on which I say we need to work to correct. In terms of fines for adultery, the same applies. In fact, the courts are harsher on the adulterer than on the adulteress. He is more severely punished. He pays the fine and *aruok*, which is compensation, and it is high.

What happens is that the man pays the compensation and is also fined; in default of payment, he goes to prison. The woman is only fined. Now, it is the duty of the husband to pay the fine of his wife, since he has received the compensation for her adultery. The adulterer is actually under duty to pay the compensation. But because the husband is angry, he may decide to punish the wife by making her spend her term in prison. And nobody else, other than him, can come and pay for her to be released on bail. If you come and pay, then you are part and parcel of that offense. These are the problems. And this is where you get so many women in detention. If you go to the prisons now, you will find that the numbers of women who are charged with adultery are many. Their husbands have decided not to pay for their bail, because they see it as another way of punishing them. This is the situation in which we are. These are the real issues we need to visit and work on. This goes back to the issue of sensitizing the man himself to understand that, after all, the property you own is not yours alone, but is a common wealth within the family. So, whoever commits an offense and is fined, the payment should be from that common wealth, and not the other way around.

FD: Thank you very much. Who is next? Judge James Bol, the floor is yours.

James Bol (JB): James Bol is my name. I will try to illustrate a few items by case law. I think that cases always give us hindsight into the culture of the people, and exactly what was the prevailing opinion by then. The first thing I want to comment on is *cieng*. How far do we relate to one another according to our traditions and customs and so on and so forth. I believe that this concept of *cieng* is under threat, in view of the height of the war and conflict always. In 1965, here in Rumbek, I was with a friend of mine, who was in the same dormitory with me. It was during Anyanya One. His older brother, who had just been married, was killed by the Arabs some four miles from here. His mother cried out and told him not to join the movement, because nobody would be left if he were killed. The new bridegroom was in the house. His brother was buried. There would be nobody in the house to take care of the family. The other one had gone to war. The remaining one was dead. It meant that that family was nearly going to be extinguished. So what Archangello, my friend, did was that he gave his gun to some of his friends in Anyanya One and stayed for a while. Then he convinced his mother that they should all move outside the town, so that he could continue looking after the family as well as being part of the struggle. It took time for the family to agree with that arrangement of continuing to be with the women and also be in the movement. On reflection, I asked Archangello later, when we met here in 1973, how he came to such a hard decision. He said he was forced between adhering to custom of being a responsible person in case of the death of your brother and joining a movement which he felt was very dear to him. It was a difficult decision. But again, there were many other difficult decisions for Archangello.

The same period, another girl's brother from Tonj Intermediate School was captured here and imprisoned at Laido, the new *dakhaliya* [dormitory] after 1963. People knew that the *shawish* [Sergeant Major] who was there would butcher them, always at night. So, the younger sister came and stayed in that *dakhaliya*. When she was asked to leave around four or five in the afternoon (most of the civilians were sent out of the area by then), she said she was not leaving. Someone asked why. She said, "I have no other place to go to." He asked why she had no other place to go to. "Don't you have parents?" She said, "That one in prison is the only brother I have." So the matter was reported to the Sergeant Major. And he said, "What, therefore, do you want?" She said, "I only want one thing, and that is my brother. I am willing to be your wife if I can have my brother. That's all."

I later read the book of Dr. Francis in 1986, *Cry of the Owl*. The characters really came visible so much to me. The sister volunteering to be the wife of that person she didn't know in order to spare the life of her brother. That is *cieng*. There is cohesiveness for the family to exist, which is the main reason why we marry, why we stay together as brothers and sisters, why we stay together with distant cousins and so on, and why we go to war if our cousins are attacked by others.

This concept of *cieng* was tested again in 1965, when our people were killed in Wau. Among those who were killed, I knew about five or six very well, including the women they had married, and so on, when I was still here in Rumbek or in Bussere. A Catholic priest asked me to check on them five years later, in 1970, to see how their families had fared. I found out that three families stayed well. The women were inherited by their respective brothers-in-law. They continued to rear their children well in the church, and continued to take them to school. The other two did not do well. They were married into families which were not their original marital families. And with the conflict with the other women in the house, they were being seen in a negative light, as wandering women, going from family to family. They ended up in very bad shape. They didn't take good care of their children in schools. And that affected their children. That's what I found when I came to the court in 1973.

But there are other cases also, like the case of Kelueljang here in Rumbek, in 1976. Kelueljang left here in 1963 to go to Khartoum as a young man, to work in a factory in Khartoum North. He conceived a girl in 1965 who bore a son. And later, when he came back, that boy was already in primary one or two around here. Kelueljang didn't have enough money, so he didn't buy cows. His older brother's marriage broke down and the cows were sent back. Now, when he married in the section of Makuer Gol, his brother put that marriage to a stop. He said those cattle had to be distributed, "You need to pay the *aruok* for my son." So, they went to *mahkama shabiya*, the people's court. The court ruled that most of the cows from the marriage should continue to go to the elder brother. And since the younger brother did not bring money to buy cows when he came from Khartoum, he was not a very good member of the community. He appealed and came to me. On reflection, I came to the conclusion that the cattle that were in the family belonged to all of them. That is in principle. But according to the Dinka, marriage is by birth order; it is not *sampala*, or haphazard. If it were haphazard, it would cause confusion, which is why our elders made that device. The order of marriage had to be the eldest first, followed by the next, and so on. I came to the decision that since he married earlier, the first cows that came back from his broken marriage belonged to him. But with the other cows that were in the family already, they had an obligation to support their brother to pay the *aruok* for his child. The older brother disagreed and went to the late Martin Majier. Justice Majier said that I was mistaken, that the cows all belonged to the older brother to use for his marriage.

Now, on reflection, you might ask, what the disagreement was basically about. If this child was a daughter, I assure you, they would have paid *aruok*. Why? Because she was going to bring in more cows later. But this child was a male who had two problems coming up with him; he needed to be redeemed, and then he himself would later ask for cows to be married. Since this man, who had returned from Khartoum North, did not buy enough cows, he was considered a useless person; he was not a good person. So, I asked, if those of us who were able to buy cows were seen to be good people in our families, why should we punish the others who did not fare well economically? Will the Dinka always go with those from whom they will get benefit? Is that *cieng* proper?

The next thing is the question of our widows, or abandoned women. In many war situations they are there as victims. In most cases, they are taken care of well. But in many cases also, some do not fare all that well. And that brought us to the suggestion I made last September, and on which I happened to be in the minority. I made a proposal for an emergency legislation for family law. And Justice Michael Makuei said no, you cannot make an emergency legislation when you don't know what the situation is in customary law.

This is the time now to sit down, study our customary law, record it, and then present it to the leadership. I believe by the time we are going to present it to the leadership, you will find that a large sector of our community is very angry with us, because we are not trying to adjust to the changes. The question is, "What are these changes?" We know that in most of our customs, women are supposed to be inherited by the next of kin, and the first choice is the older brother, then the next brother. In cases where many male relatives have died, they go as far as the third ring. Now, under the conditions prevailing today, why our elders made that decision is being challenged. A woman will say, "I see nobody here with whom I want to live to take care of my children." And they always argue, "If this man comes into my family, he is going to get rid of my cattle, or sell my goats, because he is not known to be an economically responsible person." The question is, are they asking for too much when they say, "Give us a chance to choose whether to stay in this family or opt out?" In the other cases, we are reminded that if she is not able to bring back the cattle paid for her marriage, since she has opted out now, this means that she will stay in that no-man's-land, until her father or uncle pays back the cattle to the family. That's what we are facing in Rumbek and Yirol and in other areas. So, we have a lot of hard work to do during this phase. Thank you.

Bol Pot (BP): My name is Bol Pot. I would like to contribute a very little thing to your question about the ownership of the land and property. Actually, Nuer culture and other cultures are quite similar. But on the issue of ownership of the land and property, I see that there are very small differences. In relation to women and children, it seems that they don't have full rights of ownership. When a man gives cattle or distributes land to his wives, they have only the right of use, which means that they cannot dispose of the property

forget that our way of living is reflected in our laws. The way our community controls itself is also the law.

When it comes to the administration of justice, Nuer people, as a tribe, have their own culture, their own customary practices. For instance, when we come to war, as some of our colleagues have already mentioned, and John Luk mentioned some of the points in relation to the Nuer, they have strict rules for controlling themselves in war. These rules govern what a warrior is permitted to do or prohibited to do in war. They fear the consequences of violating these rules. If there is fighting, and it happens that one group is defeated and is chased, if you run and enter a cattle byre, you will not any longer be victimized. They leave you. The notion is that it can also happen to us. It may happen that we too may be defeated and chased. So, if the enemy runs and enters a certain place, he must no longer be harmed. Then also children were not to be killed. Any boy who is not yet initiated as an adult must not be killed. This is still the practice. If you kill a boy, then his people will retaliate by killing a boy from your side. They will not kill a woman or a girl or an adult. They will look for a boy of the same age as that boy that was killed. The same thing applied to women. If you kill a woman, the other side also will look for a woman and kill her. And the same applied to killing a girl. So, because of the consequences, these rules were seriously observed. Any violation would immediately trigger a response, a retaliation. The side of the person who has committed the offense may even offer to pay compensation far above the normal, because of fear that the revenge will be swift and severe.

Coming to the issue of adultery, the situation among the Nuer is the same as the practice among the Dinka. But they differ in certain aspects. Among the Nuer, if a man dies, the widow will not be liable for adultery. If her husband is dead, then she should not be held liable. Anyone who has an affair with her will also not pay compensation. But that would be a ground for that woman to be divorced by her dead husband's family, and would deny her access to her share in the family's wealth. She would be dismissed.

When it comes to inheritance, the situation is the same as among the Dinka. But they differ in certain details. If a woman has no children, if her husband dies before she begets children, she cannot inherit. But she will be given the right to choose another man within the family to live with her. If she refuses, then she will be divorced and she will not have anything from the family. Even if she gave birth to two or three children and they are still small, she can go her own way, and the family of the deceased will pay the cows, of *aruok*, compensation for those children, and keep the children. That is an area where Dinka law may have a difference with that of the Nuer.

I now end with the point about governance and also constitutionalism. I see that there is now a conflict between our culture or customary law and foreign methods of law-making. We now receive many suggestions or offers of contributions from our foreign partners. They want us to depend on them to make our laws in the way they want. This may completely contradict our laws. I think it is important to build our laws on our culture and customary practices. As lawyers, we know that custom is one of the sources in international law. But the way it is defined by some of the lawyers, in the context of international law, may differ from one society to another. In international law, they see it as a law of morality, because there are no sanctions against violations. But in our case, customary law has sanctions beyond the force of morality. These sanctions are imposed not only for civil wrongs, but also for criminal punishment. So, we need to look into customary law very seriously and see how we can incorporate them into our statutory laws, instead of just importing everything into our legal system, because it may conflict with our own way of life. This is what I wanted to contribute.

FD: Thank you very much. Will somebody else like to speak?

DB: Yes, maybe as a contribution, to what should be done, by way of recommendation. To me, as a recommendation, I will suggest that a study be done to ascertain our public policy. It is true that we are now acting on some sort of public policy, that we need to encourage our customary law; we need to encourage our values; and we need to incorporate our values into our legal system. How that can be done needs to be ascertained from the people themselves and the views of the government authorities. This will give a clear picture that could be drawn upon in developing public policy on the issue of customary law. That is one. And again, this is what we are doing now as a steering committee on customary law. Our immediate target now is to ascertain the customary laws we talk of, to record the values we talk of, and to be comprehensive in our approach, such that no people should feel that their laws are undermined, or their custom is overlooked simply because maybe they did not even have educated people, or people in government. This is why we are doing it as a comprehensive undertaking that should cover the whole of South Sudan. This is for the purposes of availing the custom, in a written form, as a source of legislation to facilitate the work for the legislators in using custom as a source.

And again, the issue of knowledge of custom itself, by the sitting judges, is important. If you don't have it recorded, and somebody invokes a customary rule in a case that is pending before you, and you don't have the custom in front of you in a written form, you will have difficulty knowing what the law is. I remember a case here that came to me by way of appeal, where a certain lady invoked a Kuku customary rule, and the judge who was not aware of Kuku customary law, found it difficult. But he just went ahead and settled the case. He did not know whether or not that was the real Kuku customary rule. When it came to appeal, my background and my experience in those areas helped me. I could know if the lady was really invoking a true Kuku customary law or not. So, recording customary law will help the judges to have knowledge of the customary laws and regimes that are available in South Sudan. It will also help the human rights agencies and NGOs that are concerned with child protection, human rights, things that are related to customary law. Their ascertainment will help also give an insight or will allow them to have knowledge of the real custom before they can come up with criticism or make statements about that particular custom without having prior knowledge of that very custom, and others.

We should also bear in mind our people who are in the Diaspora. Because of the war, they took refuge there. Some of us were talking about those who have lost contact with their original communities and the customs of their communities. Definitely, with the peace now achieved, people will come back, and they will return to their centers, to their villages, and conflicts will arise. The newly applied cultures will come into conflict with the cultures that might be exercised by the people who remained at home. For certainty purposes, you need to have these customs ascertained, in their original form if possible, such that we could also monitor the variations and we could say, "This is a newly acquired thing you are bringing into our culture; it does not represent our culture," and all that. There are so many reasons why we should embark on the ascertainment process as of now. These are some of the recommendations I wanted to add.

FD: Thank you. Well, I have kept you quite long on Sunday. But I have a couple of questions, quick ones, that I hoped to get your reaction to. The first has to do with the collection or documentation of customary law. I was wondering whether it was possible to identify major groupings that could be the categories for recording. You were saying that there is a need for a comprehensive approach. What does being comprehensive mean in a society where you have some fifty or sixty ethnic groups or tribes? Can we begin with major categories? It might be difficult for you people to respond now, because this could also have some serious policy implications, as to which ones will be recorded and who will be left out. The other is, I was wondering what areas of the law we will consider most pertinent to customary law. I know that criminal law and civil law, such as torts, are interconnected in our societies. Sometimes punishment takes the form of increased compensation, rather than imprisonment. In fact, in some of the materials I collected, not just customary law materials, but also songs, our people felt strong bitterness about certain police treatment. As our societies didn't use to have prisons, didn't use to have police, the idea that a gentleman who has been initiated is caught by the police and whipped, or driven into prison was seen as absolute indignity. There are a lot of songs about imprisonment, in which people are lamenting, and the lamentation shows a violation of major values that were associated with the dignity of a human being that it is being violated. In any case, what areas, is it marriage, is it torts, is it property, that should be covered in recording customary law? Can we just list areas that will be worth looking into? And then specifically, as a question, given the fact that there may be cases to be tried by people who may not know the law, as Justice Deng was saying, can we begin some training of lawyers using available resources, so that although it is not perfect, it at least sensitizes judges to the issues of customary law? Is this one of the things we could do? Any response?

DB: On the issue of comprehensiveness, you know we have a project proposal in which we have categorized all the groups, the cultural groups, the ethnic groups in South Sudan. There are, I think, about fifteen groups, and these fifteen groups, we have proposed that they will be covered by fifteen or so teams of researchers. Each research team will have one international expert and one national expert, plus some four or five, depending on the area occupied by that cultural group. So, they will be supported by the data collectors, about four or five, depending on the size of the area. That is what we mean by comprehensiveness. We want to target every group in Southern Sudan, and then we will ascertain and record all the customs related to many aspects of life, issues to do with marriage, or with family law in general, torts, and all that.

You are right on the training of judges. The available material that we have today could be used to train judges. And, actually, we are doing some sort of training here. Another study could be done, where the material is available. There is no problem. And apart from training of substantive customary law, even the concept of how, as a sitting judge, you allow a custom to govern a case needs training. In case of conflict of customs, what custom should apply to a suit, that is, a suit of personal matter? These are issues that you have to train judges about. There is no problem about that. It could be added as one of the recommendations that could be given priority for study, if there are funds for that.

MM: To add to what Justice Deng Biong has said, I think, as he has said, the customary law steering committee has already gone ahead and I think they have selected or proposed fifteen groups. This is what I presume to be the customary law regimes that are actually operational. Within these fifteen groups, there are some variations. This is their first task. They will go down to do the research. They have a long way to go. Nevertheless, this is a good beginning. We are sure that we will be in a position to at least record customary law, and try to harmonize it so that we can address these issues of conflict of customary laws, and so forth.

The area where customary law is pertinent is in cases of family law mostly. And, of course, with the family law there are so many things involved. In family law, you may find many other aspects of the law. After all, in customary law, we hardly differentiate between a criminal offense and a civil suit; they are the same. Take the issue of adultery which was quoted earlier. In customary law, adultery is both. But you go to the penal code; it only addresses the criminal aspect of adultery. It is silent on the civil aspect. Sometimes, this is where the misapplication of the law comes in. When the judge sitting there says, yes, adultery is a crime, the criminal procedure will consider only the criminal aspect and is silent about the civil aspect. But if it is a customary law court, a Chiefs' court, it will address both aspects. This is where the accused is made to pay compensation. And he is also fined as a punishment for the criminal offense committed. This is an area which has a lot of cases. In fact, what is usually applied by the court is the statutory law. It is actually meant to apply to the urban centers. These courts are seeing cases of adultery as a crime. They are not County courts; they are Payam courts.

The Chiefs' courts out there are also seeing cases of adultery. When we go down to the level of a second-class magistrate, the powers of a second-class county judge are almost the same powers as the Payam court. They are the same powers as the Chiefs' court. There is not much difference.

On the issue of training, it is true that there is need for us to train the judges. In the past, I remember during the colonial period, there were records. You would find that the District Commissioner, who was by then the judge sitting in his court, would record all the customs of that area. When he was transferred, and a new person came, the first thing that person did was to read the file on customs. He would acquaint himself with all the customs of the area and then he would follow from there. After independence, when the Arabs came in, all these documents disappeared. Nobody bothered to continue the recording. We lost them all. That was a very good attempt. There had been a lot of records on customary law. All these things have gone. So, at present, there is need for us to keep on training not only the judges, but all the lawyers actually, on customary law, especially with these changes, with a lot of judges who will be coming from the Diaspora, who have acquired new cultures, who will think that these cultures are archaic and old, we don't need them, they are primitive. These people, we will need to change their outlook, to remold them into becoming Southern Sudanese again, so that they live according to the realities of our situation here. I agree with you, this is something that we need to work on. And we will try to develop it so that we give training to the will-be lawyers in Southern Sudan so that they can also participate in the development of our customs.

FD: Lastly, but importantly, I would like to ascertain your views about areas in which you think potential international partners could make some contribution to assist you in your endeavors. I am aware that there a lot of people who want to come and be of help. Sometimes, they might get to be a little too crowded. So, we have to be careful about seeking support where we really think it will be useful, not where people will become crowded. The question is whether you still need international partners and in which areas do you think you will make good use of their contributions.

DB: What we have done so far with the committee is that we invited stakeholders, I mean the agencies that are interested in customary law development, or who are interested in addressing issues of customary law. We invited all these to a workshop, which we called a work plan workshop, in Nairobi, last December [2004]. Actually, we wanted to know from them what they had been doing, and what they intended to do, even how we could coordinate with them. We separated the issues. There were agencies that were interested in specific issues. UNICEF was interested in women's rights and child rights; and FAO was interested in issues to do with land, simply because of food security. But then we threw in the general proposal on ascertainment of customary law. Among those who were very interested was PACT. They were the ones who funded the workshop in Nairobi. Max Plank also expressed their readiness. By then, they were connecting it with the final signing of the peace agreement, which is now done. If there are other potential partners, what we will do is to engage them and discuss issues and areas of mutual interest and possible cooperation.

MM: Yes, of course, we welcome those efforts that have been exerted from anybody who is willing to offer us services. On the issue of constitution-making, and the work of NCRC [The National Constitutional Review Commission], we have already gone a long way. We have finished the draft constitution. The draft is now ready. This draft will be presented to the NCRC when it is constituted. In the meantime, we cannot say that the process is over and that we don't need additional technical support from the others. It is true, there are some institutions that are working with us, but it is not enough to be fixed to one institution. It is good to vary, so that you can get more information and expertise from various sources. The same is true of the Southern Sudan constitution. The drafting committee is not yet set up. This is where we will need their contribution. There are some institutions that have promised to provide the necessary technical expertise as well as funding for the process. But, of course, that is not enough. We cannot say that we don't need anything more, because we need their contribution also in the development of the Southern Sudan interim constitution.

As for the composition, the NCRC is supposed to be sixty, and the representation is supposed to be according to the ratios agreed in the power sharing, in terms of representation in the executive and national assembly. As for the timetable, we are actually behind schedule because the NCRC should have been set up on the 23rd of this month [February, 2005], because the agreement was supposed to be adopted by the parties on or before the 23rd of January. It was adopted later. None of us made the schedule and the NCRC will start the process after its composition and it will work for a maximum of six weeks. The Southern Sudan constitution is supposed to be out four weeks after the adoption of the interim national constitution. Because we are behind the schedule, we were of the opinion that we should start the drafting of the Southern Sudan constitution. As long as the interim text is out, we can use it as a basis, along with the agreement, for the development or drafting of the Southern Sudan constitution. By the time the Southern Sudan constitution is adopted, we will just be making a comparative study to make sure it conforms with the provisions of the national constitution. The Southern Sudan constitution drafting committee will be forty representatives.

The other areas where we will need technical expertise, or technical assistance, are the review of the Southern Sudan laws. The laws we have now are the New Sudan laws. In fact, we need to establish a Law Review Commission in which we will review all the laws of the New Sudan, so that they incorporate the new structures and the agreement, in addition to the development and the drafting of new laws in the areas where we have none. Up until now we have set up forty laws only. You cannot govern a state with only forty laws. So, that law review commission has a task of preparing laws in all the fields of governance. Here too, we will require technical assistance that will enable us to prepare these laws.

In terms of identification of priority needs, we have already worked on the JAM, and all our priorities are identified and are with JAM. This is what will go to the donor conference. We will also not object to whatever technical assistance we may receive in that area. What we have given is the overall plan up to the end of the interim period. We have not provided for the period thereafter, whether the people of the South vote for unity or secession. Nevertheless, you need to plan for that, and we have not done it. So, this is an area where we need to revisit even the plans we have laid down, so that we can ascertain as to whether we have actually met our needs, or need more, and in which areas.

For customary law, we will also ultimately need support. This area has already been covered by Justice Deng Biong. This issue of customary law has been a problem for us. You find that most of the NGOs will rush in with their money and they come and say, we are conducting research in this field. After conducting the research, they just end up there, because all these activities were not coordinated. After finishing the research, they don't know where to present it, and it ends up there. Now that we have set up the Customary Law Steering Committee, it is our policy that whatever organization has interest in the study of customary law should liaise with the committee. There is no way we will allow people to conduct research here and there, which is not controlled. People come up with very wild conclusions. This has been putting us into crisis with some of our constituencies. So, this customary law research should be organized, systematized and, in fact, the representation now in the Customary Law Steering Committee is the judiciary, legal affairs, women and child welfare, local government, and law society. These are the institutions that constitute the steering committee. This body will continue to operate and, sooner or later, instead of being a committee, it may develop into another body. This is how we are starting now, but we may have more plans for this body to transform itself into another body that will be more established than continue to be a committee as it is now.

On the issue of legal dialogue between the Sharia and non-Sharia systems or whatever other systems, this is where the lawyers or professionals could come together and brainstorm. In that process, we may be in a position to address some of the outstanding legal issues that we have not seen for the time being. This is where we will be sitting as lawyers, as professionals, and address some issues to do with the violation of human rights in some legal systems. This is another area in which we will be willing to explore for possible collaboration with international partners.

FD: Well thank you very much. I really appreciate the time you have given me and I believe our conversation has been very constructive. A lot of good ideas have been articulated and it is for me now to put them to good use. Thank you very much.

8. Ambrose Riiny Thiik and Chan Reec Madut

Khartoum, August 2005

Francis Deng (FD): Well, Molanas, the two Honorable Judges, I am delighted I have this chance to talk to you both on certain issues. Could you first please briefly introduce yourselves in terms of your name and what you are doing now?

Ambrose Riiny Thiik (AR): My name is Ambrose Riiny Thiik. Currently, I am the Chief Justice of what we, until now, still call the New Sudan, comprising, of course, of Southern Sudan, Nuba Mountains and Southern Blue Nile. I am also President of the Court of Appeals, the highest court in the New Sudan.

Chan Reec Madut (CR): My name is Chan Reec Madut. I am a judge. I work for the Sudan Judiciary as a Court of Appeals Judge here in Khartoum. A couple of years ago, I was a human rights officer at UNICEF. Now, I am back in the Judiciary, in Khartoum.

FD: Molana Chan, can we begin with you because, before we go to the South, we want to have a broad overview of the Sudan legal system. At our time, in the olden days, we had the common law system, the Sharia system and the customary law system. You could say it was a three-tier system. The system was also divided into civil law, which comprised the common law and the customary law, and the Sharia branch. Could you give us an overview of the situation today?

CR: I think what we have right now is a mishmash of Sharia and the common law system. Of course, the main thrust is on Islamic law, because of the political developments in this country in the past few years. But the whole legal heritage is still there. Common law is still applicable in the form of precedents. Otherwise, the leadership is gearing the law towards the Islamic system. And so, officially, the thrust is the Islamic system, but there is plenty of the common law within the same system.

FD: Could you give us the court hierarchy, the process by which decisions of the courts are made, and where appeals go?

CR: At the top, you have the Supreme Court, then the Courts of Appeal, and then the General Courts, which previously used to be called Province Courts. Then below the Province Court are the District Courts. Below the District Courts are what they call Town and Rural Courts. The Supreme

Court has branches in Khartoum, Port Sudan, and Madeni. For each of the twenty-six states of Sudan, you have a Court of Appeal. And the Province Courts are the General Courts within the states. District Courts are divided into three: District Courts of first grade, second grade, and third grade.

FD: Is the first higher than the second?

CR: Yes, the first is higher. Below this you have the Town and Rural Courts. These are established by the decree of the Chief Justice and I think they are a kind of replacement for what used to be called Native Courts, or Town Bench Courts. The Chief Justice has the power to set up town and rural courts. He has the power under the Judiciary Act to set up these courts in terms of numbers, substantive jurisdiction, and geographical jurisdiction as well. These are the ones that take care of legal disputes in the villages and in the towns. This applies mostly to Northern Sudan. As far as the South is concerned, it is restricted to what used to be called garrison towns. Beyond that, the system is under the SPLM administration.

FD: And what law do these lower courts apply?

CR: The lower courts apply mostly custom, subject to the requirement that a custom should not contradict Sharia. This is the basic situation. Most of the natives in Northern Sudan are Muslims, and most of their customs are Islamic. They are not so distinctive or so distinct like the customs in the South. And if those customs are contradictory to Islamic law they will be scrapped because they are contrary to Sharia. Even in the South, by the way, the regulations for Rural and Town Courts stipulate the same condition, that custom should not contradict Sharia law. It also should not be contrary to justice, equity, and good conscience. This is in addition to the requirement that customs should not contradict Islamic law.

FD: Could you describe the institutions of the legal system, the role of the Minister of Justice, the Chief Justice, the Bar Association, and other organs?

CR: The Minister of Justice is part of the Executive organ of the Government and it is manned by legal advisors to the Government. Their main task is to prosecute cases before the courts. The Ministry of Justice has nothing to do with the judiciary. The judiciary is mainly for the adjudication of cases and is under the Chief Justice. It is an independent institution. The advocates form an independent institution for private practice. They are lawyers who defend individuals or corporations in cases against the Government or against others. Of course, the qualification for lawyers in both the Ministry of Justice and the Judiciary is the same. You have to have a law degree, a Bachelors degree, and you must pass what they call a professional or bar examination. The bar examination qualifies you to be recruited into the judiciary as a magistrate or to the Ministry of Justice as a legal advisor, or to the bar to practice as an advocate, provided you practice under a licensed advocate for some time.

FD: What is the substance of legal education these days? Is it common law, Islamic law, or a mix?

CR: It is a mix. They have Islamic law, but they also have all sorts of other common law subjects, such as evidence, criminal law, and all the sort of subjects that we used to study under the common law system.

FD: In English or in Arabic?

CR: Most of them in Arabic, but some, such as public international law, are taught in English, especially in the University of Khartoum. In other universities I think they are being taught in Arabic.

FD: Molana Ambrose, could you pick up and tell us about the situation in the South?

AR: Our judicial system in Southern Sudan, or in the New Sudan, started in earnest in about 1999–2000. The court structure still exists. The apex begins with the Court of Appeal. Most judges now in Southern Sudan are members of the SPLM/SPLA. They were previously in the judicial service or legal practice in the old Sudan before the war. There are those who were on the bench as judges or magistrates, and those who were in the private practice or in the Attorney General's chambers in the Ministry of Justice. Anyway, we now have a six-tier court system. We begin with the Court of Appeal which has a limited number of people, four Justices of Appeal. Three sit as a panel for decisions of the Court of Appeal. The court is chaired by the Chief Justice, but the panel can be chaired by any of the four judges. Then you have High Courts, there were about six of them, although we were not able to effectively run some of them because of lack of personnel. What we did was to group a number of counties. It is important to know that our administrative structures are also slightly different from those of the old Sudan. Until now, we have regions, five of them: Bahr el Ghazal, Equatoria, Upper Nile, Nuba Mountains, and Southern Blue Nile. These regions are divided into counties, and the counties are divided into payams. These are the administrative units.

Our courts follow that structure, not exactly, but to a great extent. The Court of Appeal is on top of all the five regions. The High Courts do not necessarily fall into one geographical entity. In Bahr el Ghazal, for instance, we've grouped a number of counties to fall under one High Court circuit; we call it Circuit One. Because you have a higher volume of litigation in those areas, we have had to make part of Bahr el Ghazal counties a High Court Circuit Two. Equatoria is also split into two High Court circuits. In Upper Nile, a group of counties under us form the other High Court. The Nuba Mountains has one High Court, and the Southern Blue Nile has another High Court.

Then you have the county courts. The Justices of the High Courts actually take care of the administration of the courts in the counties that fall under them. They are also the ones responsible for trying murder cases, or the more serious cases that used to be tried in the old Sudan system by what was called a major court. The major courts now are headed by a High Court Judge and sometimes even by a member of the Court of Appeal where you do not have a High Court Judge. We have a number of young graduates who came into the movement in the last ten years or so, and who had graduated from Egyptian universities in Sudan. These are the ones that have been running the county courts. Because of the shortages still, we find ourselves having to group a number of counties, two or three, under one County Court Judge. Then, later on, we began to select lay people as county court judges of second grade to help in the counties. In some counties, you will find that it takes a hell of a time for the county judge of first grade to be able to go from one county to another. He may be stuck in one county, unable to move to the next county.

Then below the County Courts you have Payam Courts. It is envisaged that the Payam Courts, in the medium term, will be run by people we will train to be qualified paralegals. At the moment, we have a panel of three lay magistrates that are selected, one a chairman and then two other members, to make a Payam Court. These are the ones that now run Payam Courts throughout Southern Sudan and in the other regions of the New Sudan. These are what we call State Courts.

Below them come the traditional, customary, or Chiefs' courts and they are two: you have a regional court, what in the past was called a regional court, but is now sometimes called a Boma Court. This court is formed out of areas of two chieftaincies or more, from which you select five people as members of the Regional Court. This court has regional jurisdiction, but it also has an appellate jurisdiction over the Executive Chiefs' Courts. That is the next level. A chief in his area is the president of his court, assisted by four others to make five. We try very hard, but we don't always succeed, to get women to be members of the Chiefs' Court and even the Regional Courts. We even try to recruit women into the Payam Courts, if we can.

That is the general court structure. This is going to change. With the coming into force of the Sudan New Constitution, the structure will change. We are going to have a Supreme Court of Southern Sudan, this time without the Nuba and the Ingassana, not even Abyei area. It probably will be manned by about seven justices of the Supreme Court. Then we will have three Courts of Appeal, each responsible for the States of previous greater regions. In other words, we are going to have a Court of Appeal for Bahr el Ghazal states, a Court of Appeal for Equatoria states, and a Court of Appeal for Upper Nile states. And each state will have a High Court. Now there will be about four Justices of Appeal in each of the three Courts of Appeal. At the state level, High Court will also have three members. Then at the county level, we will have County Judges. Any number of first- or second-grade magistrates or judges will run the County Courts. Below them, the traditional courts will continue the way they have always been. They are patterned on the basis of the old Chiefs' Court Ordinance of 1931, even though it is now defunct.

FD: What is governing these traditional courts now?

AR: We were thinking of putting into place a Local Courts Act. We haven't yet done that. But we have always maintained those structures even during war. Later on, in 2000, we had a judicial committee under the chairmanship of the Chief Justice that went around and then issued a report and that gave what, in effect, you may call a circular that provided for the formation of those courts, which I think are also mentioned in other acts. The Civil Procedure Act, the Criminal Procedure Act, and the Judiciary Act may have mentioned them, but have not quite provided them with jurisdiction the same way the Payam Courts, the County Courts, and the other courts have been provided under those laws.

FD: Could you tell us something about the institutions of the justice system: the Attorney General, the Chief Justice, and others?

AR: We have what we call the Secretariat of Legal Affairs and Constitutional Development, which is being headed by a Commissioner. He is himself a lawyer, a man who was a judge previously. He has a very limited number of personnel. They are responsible for drafting laws and giving advice to CANS, the Civil Authority of the New Sudan. The Commissioner and one of our senior judges in the High Court have also been involved in the peace negotiations to provide technical legal advice there.

FD: Are they prosecutors?

AR: No, unfortunately they aren't for a variety of reasons, not least because of the number. There is an acute shortage of personnel. So, it is the police who are responsible for the prosecution of cases. The police force also has its own challenges. It is not well organized, not well trained, and it has a shortage of personnel as well. And so are the prison services. They too have serious problems. These are some of the challenges that face the justice system in the SPLA-held areas, the New Sudan or Southern Sudan. We are now optimistic that as we set up a formal government in Southern Sudan, these issues will be addressed. But there are difficulties, and their implications for the delivery of justice service are considerable. You have now judges that find themselves trying cases that are never well investigated. Sometimes, it is not easy to apprehend the criminals, or people accused of crimes. Even if they are arrested, sometimes keeping them in custody has its own problems. When they come before the courts, the courts tend to impose fines rather than to impose custodial sentences because of the problems pertaining to the prison system. There are serious inadequacies in the establishment of the prison authorities. These are some of the challenges facing us. They gravely affect the kind of justice system that we are delivering.

FD: You did talk about capacity, which is probably very obvious in the South, lacking qualified lawyers as it is. Could you give us an estimate, even if one does not have precise figures, of the numbers of the human resources in the justice system, beginning with the national level, in all its different forms and institutions? Do we have adequate lawyers? Do we have an oversupply of lawyers? Are the lawyers well qualified? And then we will go to the South.

CR: I think there is no problem of capacity as far as Northern Sudan is concerned. They have enough lawyers to man the judiciary at all levels. I think we have the largest Supreme Court in the world. It has about eighty judges, although some of them have gone to the Gulf. There are supposed to be around seventy to eighty Justices of the Supreme Court. The Court of

international standards. And yet, when outside observers speak about the status of women or children in our societies, there is always a concern that there are shortcomings in the customary law system. Will you comment?

CR: I think it will be unreasonable to say that all our customary laws are good or consistent with human rights or humanitarian standards. This is not true. There are some aspects of customary law that are clearly inconsistent with human rights standards and some of them need to be scrapped. I can cite a few examples, say in relation to children. When sending children to school, our people used to prefer to take boys and leave the girls behind so that they can be married with bride wealth. That means that, already, we are interfering with the child's right to education. You have the issue of early marriages. This again has problems for female children. It becomes a health issue, apart from the matter of her consent, which is often missing in such situations. You have some harmful traditional practices for children. Although we don't have this FGM [female genital mutilation] in the South, we do have, for example, scarification on foreheads. Now, once this is done, you are considered to have become a man and you cannot remain behind in case there is fighting. And so, although you are still a child, you are considered already a man through this customary practice, and then you get exposed to hostilities. This, I think, is an issue affecting the rights of the child.

FD: Usually, at what age do children get scarification? Is it between sixteen and eighteen?

CR: It used to be about that. It could be even lower than that because they believe it is a way of improving the social status of young men and making them responsible. The children too are eager to have their social standing enhanced that way. But it also imposes on them serious liabilities. Then come to women. The husband's power to chastise his wife is already problematic because it is really being abused. There are certain attitudes associated with the way we treat women. Unless we dissociate from this kind of behavior and treat women as equal partners in a marriage, we have a problem. We have been made to think that as the head of the house, you have the right to chastise your wife and that sort of thing. Now, if a father decides to give away his daughter in marriage, traditionally, she won't say no. Although courtship is encouraged at a certain level, once you have missed that chance and it comes to the level of deciding whether you are to be married, you could be married without necessarily giving your consent. This is a serious issue as far as women are concerned.

Then, if a woman loses her husband, if her husband dies, the custom says that someone within the family will have to step into the shoes of the husband and beget children with her to the name of the deceased husband. Traditionally, there were good reasons for doing this. But it now presents very serious complications in terms of human rights. There are many cases coming before us of widows refusing to be inherited, and for good reasons. The custom is automatically opposed to the human rights of these women not to be married or to get into that kind of relationship based on custom. In fact, I have a small paper which I prepared for UNDP, titled "Customary Law from the Human Rights Perspectives," in which I have highlighted some of these issues. So, in brief, I would say that there are certain customary law aspects which need to be revised and brought in line with human rights standards.

AR: I couldn't agree with him more. Human rights, or even customs that are inconsistent with equity, justice, and good conscience, are problems that we face in the courts. The SPLM, as a political movement, has also faced issues of gender equality and has come up with policy positions, especially with regard to the right of women to public positions. When we were setting up our court system in 2000, and we were touring our areas with a view to inspecting and establishing the courts, our job was to try to highlight the issues of women's rights and their membership in the courts. We were also concerned with child rights on that trip. Our experience is that within certain conservative communities, especially among the Dinka, in Bahr el Ghazal in particular, the question of getting women to be members of the court was such an uphill battle. I know of a case where a woman was willing to be a member of a court, but felt unable to apply until her husband returned from wherever he had traveled, and gave his consent. And in fact, we asked the committee to await the return of her husband. When the husband came, he refused to allow his wife to be a member of the court. And so the woman could not become a member of the court.

That is one thing. The other thing is that, as Justice Chan has just pointed out, even our own laws tend to run counter to the principle of gender equality. Take the provision in the Penal Act concerning rape. It is a rape offense for a man to have intercourse with a girl less than eighteen years old. But girls get married at the age of fifteen to sixteen. When we tried on our campaign to tell the people that they should not give their daughters away in marriage before the age of eighteen, it just fell on deaf ears. It is something they have done for centuries. It is a problem. The issue of consent in these cases is a problem. Can a girl consent to marriage when she is under age? She has no capacity, for one thing. Even if the girl being married is of age, and does not want to marry the particular man, she again will be compelled by her family to get into the marriage forcefully. That is the custom. So, there is a lot that we need to do.

Fortunately the courts have some power in some cases. There is the power that subjects a given customary law rule to the test of whether it is just, equitable, and in good conscience. There is also the requirement that when there is a conflict between a customary law rule and state legislation, the state legislation has precedence over the customary law rule. These are some of the small things that can probably help. What is true is that there is a lot to be done in this area.

We should begin with research into the customary systems, holding customary law conferences with chiefs, with a view to influencing change in the customary law rules and practices. In the end, the legislative authority of parliament may be used where things are difficult by any other way. The courts will also have a role to play. Here, you need our judges to be instructed sufficiently. This has not been the case in the past. Our legal education in the University of Khartoum did not address the question of how much customary law we were supposed to know. This time around, research into customary law as part of the curriculum in the legal education will be an imperative. These matters should be addressed so that courts become active agents again in influencing change in the customary law. In the last five to six years of our role as members of the Court of Appeal in Southern Sudan or in the New Sudan, we have found occasions where we have had to make certain pronouncements that we thought were laying down precedents, even in the area of the customary legal system.

FD: My last question has to do with the prevailing legal system in the country. Talking to some of our Northern colleagues yesterday [the last interview in this volume], the picture that came across about the legal system, particularly at the national level, is that it is really chaotic and confused. Lawyers have an eclectic knowledge about this kind of legal system and that kind of system. When you are short of any principle or rule to apply, you use your *ijtihad* [creativity] or effort in interpreting Sharia. What will it take to have a system get better established, almost to the point where we used to be, so that there are clear, predictable rules, which is the essence of the justice system or of the rule of law? Where is the problem, what are the obstacles, and how can they be overcome?

CR: It is good to be open-minded about what went wrong. It needs people to face the issue head-on and I think the best way to proceed from here will be to revise the whole system, so that recruitment to the judiciary is based on qualifications. As far as the new recruitment is concerned, it should be based on qualifications. For those who are already in the judiciary, I think they need to be exposed to some kind of training, preferably in other sister countries that have better judicial systems, so that they know what others are doing instead of looking inwardly. And I think that Southern Sudan now has a chance that it is beginning from scratch. It has the chance to benefit from the experience of other countries.

AR: The description in terms of chaos is correct, even though we are not familiar with what goes on in the judiciary here in the North. The political environment, what the Islamic thing has done, and I will expect reform not just in the judiciary, but also in the legal education itself. I think there should be a return, and I'm glad to say there are a few voices that are now being heard these days calling for a return to the old ways at the University of Khartoum. I hope this will spread to the other universities and we make the decision that we are going to have either a common law-based or a Sharia law-based system. For us in the South, up to now, we don't have this problem. Our problem now is the need for competent, qualified, judicial personnel, properly trained. We also have the problems of budgetary provisions for the institution. We also need all the other things that make for running an effective judicial system and judicial services. Even the infrastructure, development of courts, and judges' houses, transport, libraries, sufficient legal reference material are among the things we urgently need. As has been pointed out, we are now in a better position, as we have, in the last few years, tried to look at systems closer to us, such as in the Ugandan legal system and the court system, which we think are as good as what we used to have in Sudan. That's why we are finding the legal training institute in Uganda as being very useful to us. We are quite conscious of the fact that we should start to set up our legal system, court system, on a correct path. I'm glad to say that we do not have these clusters of Sharia constraints and things like that.

FD: By the way, do Southerners have the option to have Sharia applied to them?

AR: We anticipate that because, obviously, there will be Muslims in the South and we anticipate that Sharia application will come in. But we would like to see it happen the way it used to happen in Sudan, where personal law applied to personal matters. We wouldn't have a problem with that. But the kind of Sharia that goes into other areas, such as criminal law, is what we would have problems with.

FD: Thank you very much for this very illuminating information on the legal system which will help me a lot. I would like to switch, if I may, to another item for discussion and that is what I call the challenges of war, peace, and the future of Sudan. Basically, it is a question of seeing where we came from, where we are now, and where we are headed. In particular, looking at it from a Southern Sudanese point of view, what really was the war about? Have we achieved those objectives through the Comprehensive Peace Agreement [CPA]? How do they relate to the objectives of the other rebel groups in the North? And how do all these add up in terms of our vision for where we are going?

CR: This may look like a very complicated question for me. But I think we have come a long way. During the first movement, Southerners fought for the separation of Southern Sudan, and this was problematic in a way. The thrust of the SPLM, right from the beginning, has been the vision of the New Sudan. Some of us didn't appreciate the full dimension of this thrust at the beginning, but as years went by, people who had been fighting us came to join the ranks of the SPLM so that, in the end, it looks like the haves and the have-nots, or the dispossessed against the rest, and this is a positive development. I consider it to be one of the biggest achievements of the movement. People who have been sleeping have been awakened so that they know their rights and understand that we are not their enemies, but indeed have something in common with them to fight for. This is important. At the same time, we have the peculiar interest of the South, in the form of self-determination. We have achieved that too. So, you could say that we have a chance for this New Sudan, if people are willing to make it attractive. No problem, we will go for that. This is good. Otherwise, if it cannot work out, we fall back on this self-determination of ours. So, I think that a great deal has been achieved already. But, with the big loss of the leader, John Garang, we need to close our ranks. We need to be mindful of the fact that we have a common destiny. I believe we are still in midstream and there is a need for people to close their ranks so that we reach across, and this is something that calls for our collective effort as Southerners and any other disgruntled people.

AR: Yes, put another way, what we suffered is political, socioeconomic, and cultural marginalization. That is what we were fighting against. And that includes even law itself, the treatment that was given to our traditional customary law systems in many parts of Sudan. And, as has been correctly pointed out by Justice Chan, the vision put forward has made it clearer to even people beyond Southern Sudan who have suffered similar marginalization but who, before then, were cloaked, their eyes were cloaked by religion. As time has unfolded, I think the picture got clearer to them. So, the chance for a united Sudan on a new basis is there. But that will depend on the extent to which the identity of interests in the country will be shared by those who have suffered similar marginalization and treatment in the West, in the East, and even in the far North. Otherwise, in any event, if people feel again that they have greater identity with the groups that have marginalized us together by reason of their shared religion, then we have a fall-back position. But that fall-back position can only be realized if we work well as Southerners during the transitional period. Otherwise, I agree entirely with what has been stated by Justice Chan in this respect.

FD: You know, the paradox, it seems to me, is that while we are making headway, and I agree with both of you, our success, in a sense, generates a threat to the old establishment. They then entrench themselves to counter what is happening. We therefore have this paradox of two extremes coming together to form a partnership. How sustainable is that partnership?

AR: Well, how sustainable remains to be seen. What I see clearly is that the chance for transformation and reform in the country is greater now than at any time before. The question is to what extent the other political forces coming in will see that and identify with this new vision for the country, rather than take the traditional Northern Sudanese, Arab, or Islamic view of the country. If they don't prove progressive enough to be able to see this new vision, and instead ally themselves with the traditional position, the chances could be unpredictable, and would leave little optimism for change in the country. But we are not alone in the expectation that the CPA, depending on the way we will play it out, is a great opportunity for change in the country and the realization of the unity of the country. This view is shared by many African countries. They would like to see Sudan wake up and play its role in Africa, not as Arab or Islamic, but rather as an African country, democratic, open, and following the values of good government.

CR: Partnership presupposes that the partners have certain objectives to achieve through the partnership. In this context, I assume that the purpose of the partnership is to implement the CPA. It shouldn't go beyond that. The movement has the right to deal with the government of the day. There is no question about that. So, I don't agree with those who think that the whole thing is a bipartisan arrangement. This is a government that has been around since 1989, and the SPLM as a movement has the right to deal with it. Now, the question will arise, as to the interest of the other political forces. The CPA has the built-in mechanism for bringing about a democratic process at a certain point. So there is a chance, for those who think they have enough political weight, to come in. Also there is this built-in thing called inclusiveness. It may be little, but the underlying principle that power has to be shared is good by itself. People who want a share only need to be persuaded to be patient.

This is how I look at this partnership. If the other party doesn't respect the agreement, then there will naturally be a problem. This is the reason why the partnership was formed in the first place. I think I take this chance to complain about certain things we have heard in the past few days. For example, the CPA says the opinion of the experts on the Abyei Boundary Commission [ABC] will be final and binding. But when the experts came up with their report, a lot of fervor was made against it. So I'm beginning to be worried. The CPA says that sharing oil revenues will start as from the 9th of January, 2005. Now, from what we hear, things are not as clear as they should have been. And there are so many other things. This, in the end, will determine whether the partnership should continue or not. Otherwise, I would call it just a marriage of convenience. We should part ways at any time, if people fail to honor the CPA.

FD: I think the things you have pointed out are quite valid, including what I've been told, that the violence that followed the death of Dr. John Garang, and the reaction of the authorities, completely highlighted the division between Northerners and Southerners, when we thought we were coming together. Even such small things, as how at home Southerners feel when they are in their national capital, can be significant. How free do they feel culturally to behave the way they feel like behaving? Although people don't want to overstate the fact that being free to have your drink or so is the crux of the matter, it is an important aspect of how you feel as an individual, whether you are comfortable or uncomfortable. Why shouldn't I have my wine or beer with my meal? The mere fact that I am in a hotel room instead of in a private home deprives me of that freedom. So, this is part of what we are talking about. When we say that we have agreed and will endeavor to make unity attractive, are we going to solve these small little things, or will they linger on? And, I guess, part of that is what ideally would you want to see as making unity attractive? How should unity be made attractive to the South? What is needed?

CR: I have heard people asking this question before, during certain workshops. I personally think that attitudes matter a lot. Apart from respecting the terms of the agreement, apart from addressing the issues of infrastructure in the South, attitudes have to change. This is crucial. If the other side doesn't recognize me as an equal, it is meaningless, even if he builds an *amara* [a development complex] for me. So, attitudes have to change so that the Southerner feels that he is just like a Northerner, the Northerner feels the same, and the same with the people of the West and the East. This would make unity attractive. Today, if you look out of the window, what kind of equality is there? I tell people that when I go to East Africa I come back with a heavy heart. When I go to central Nairobi, I ask, whose development complex is this? They say this is that of Mungu, this is that of Alexander. Then where are we here now? These are some of the aspects that would make unity attractive. But if you walk about and you see that your kinsmen are the garbage collectors, you see the cadets running in the morning, and you don't see your people there, how attractive is that? And this is the future? You go to the Bank of Sudan and you see none of your people on the staff. What type of unity are we talking about? To make unity attractive, we should be frank. It is only one side that can make unity attractive because, as a Southerner, what do I have that I can offer to make unity attractive? It is enough that our people have given unity a chance during a specified period. It is the other side which has the means and the power to make unity attractive by doing certain things. There is no rule of thumb to say once this is done, *khalas*, finished. It is like if you are attracted to a girl, it is your duty to convince her that you are serious and if, at the end of the day, the girl is not convinced, she can be expected to turn her back to you. So, this side of Sudan has a lot to do to make unity attractive.

FD: But, you know, the point though is, ideally, frankly, the kind of New Sudan I would like, and I believe John Garang wanted, would so transform this country that the people here, who are enjoying their present status, would feel threatened by the change. The kind of New Sudan we want, which means making unity attractive, would certainly threaten the interests of these people. So, why do we think that they will cooperate with us in making unity attractive, if it threatens to turn the tables and disadvantage them in the long run?

AR: I don't think anybody in his right mind wants the tables turned against anybody. Rather, the other side who has a monopoly of everything should be able to see clearly that the other side needs exactly the things I have, in terms of power, in terms of wealth, in terms of development, in terms of services. Take the little example that I am now engrossed in: I am supposed to be responsible, up to this point, for the judiciary in Southern Sudan. I've been trying to look at court buildings, the buildings of the judges in the North and in the South. There is nothing near anything in the South. And we then made a proposal about three to four weeks ago. We went to the Chief Justice and tried to see to what extent the mother unit, the national judiciary, will help address the gap that has existed. It is a gap. There should be a better English word than the word "gap" that would really describe the situation between us, because, if the three of the nine provinces of Sudan have about two courts that have been built in the last fifty years, whereas almost every city, every town, in Northern Sudan, has courts, court complexes that have been built, how can that be described as simply a gap? And when we address this issue people say: "But you are now going to have your budget in the South, so you are going to have to start the process of building the courts." And they are talking about courts that were not built in the last fifty years. What kind of attraction is that? What kind of closing the gap is that? What kind of the new bases do we have? How are we supposed to appreciate that? Although my colleague put it earlier in terms of development buildings, and feeling good as a proper owner, the issue is more fundamental than that. It is a question of really balancing the whole equation. There must be visible effort made by what is the national government, which is predominantly Northern, and is going to remain predominantly Northern. No amount of sharing we are going to have will make much of a difference. It is going to be a problem. If we do not see some effort being made to balance the equation, unity will not be made attractive in my view. While it is fine to give them the benefit of the doubt, and it remains to be seen what the outcome will be, the process so far is not inspiring, as some of the examples that were cited earlier on make clear.

FD: One last question, do you think it is possible to have a Sudan that is enriched by our complex view of our identity as Africans, Arabs, Christians, Muslims, all of that, or is it more practical to reduce it to something more simple? Should we take ourselves as Sudanese, no matter whether we are traditional African believers, Christians, or Muslims? Is it being Sudanese that should count? And as Sudanese, is multiple identity something that we should build on or does it complicate life?

AR: It is something that we should all recognize and decide that we should build on it. There are countries, there are nation-states in the world that have done this. People with even greater, bigger, larger diversities than we have. The United States is an example. But, in our case, much as it is a desirable thing to wish to be, is the other side willing to do this? Do they see any value in the identity of the other people as opposed to theirs? Maybe this is my prejudice, but it does appear to me as if they are prepared to benefit from that. They are not prepared to decide to have these diversities developed in a way that will make the country good for all, and be richer because of that culture and diversity. But that is the most desirable thing to do if only there was the political will on the other side to want to do that.

CR: I think it is a good idea to have emphasis on Sudan, Sudanese identity as such, because any other identifications have been problematic since independence. But the question is, for how long are we going to plead for this status of Sudan? Is it possible that these other guys are going to abandon their attitude? Otherwise, why do we insist on this? The Dinka say about the dog, that a dog will never leave the household. Each time you beat the dog, it will cry out, "Ooo," but then it runs around and comes back. It says, "These are affairs of the family; nothing can be done about it." It has nowhere to go to. It has to linger around the same house where it is being treated like that. I think this is not our priority now. Our priority, I think, is that each group should work to consolidate itself. And should Sudan become truly united later, it will be on the basis of full equality. Our emphasis now should be to unite to have a solid identity as Southerners, as Westerners, as Easterners, and as Northerners. And then when sanity prevails at some point, let us make

Sudan come together as a country of equals. Now, the SPLM has already done its best by the level of consciousness now happening all around. This could be the basis of Sudan for all the people. But given our disadvantages, whatever effort we make should be to organize ourselves before we talk about the affairs of Sudan. That is the way I see it.

FD: But, you know, although I said that was the last question, I think I would be remiss if we did not reflect on the situation now in light of the loss we just had. As you know, the late John Garang brought the South from a point of great skepticism about what he was saying about the New Sudan. Then he extended the war to the East and called it the New Sudan Brigade. All these were suspect. And Southerners interpreted things in their own way in order to justify relating it to their own objective. Southern soldiers were popularly reported to say, "*Ke tharku angicku*," "We know what we are fighting for." The idea was to let John Garang talk about his New Sudan while, in fact, the South was fighting for separation. But over the years, Garang's approach brought in results to the point where the South now has the right of self-determination, even though it is still pursuing the vision of the New Sudan. This has the effect of minimizing reactions against the right of self-determination which many people in the world see as synonymous with separation, and which they don't like. The agreement has now given us these two options: we are pursuing New Sudan if they can make it attractive, but in the end we will vote. Meanwhile, we don't have to commit ourselves to anything until the voting day. Did Garang do enough for this approach to continue, or is his strategy at risk because he is no longer here?

AR: This is one area where I really feel an acute sense of loss from his departure. My belief is that as he was articulating this vision, he was now going to be more amenable to being understood, to being accepted, and he probably was going to bring the marginalized Sudan in line with Southern Sudan. He was also going to be more effective, other things being equal, even in addressing himself to the Arab North to come to the belief that our diversity, based on Sudan rather than looking anywhere else, could be beneficial to all. This is the area where his loss is much more a problem than any other. We wished that he had lived a little longer. It is God that sets these things, but, as the legendary Chol Mong once put it, "If God had asked, we would have said 'Just give it another two more years,' so that this message is driven home." He would have promoted peace to be realized on the same basis in the West and in the East. He would have continued to explain the message, and expand it throughout the country because he knew how best to do that and he had already captured the imagination of people. He was charismatic enough for his message to be well understood. Had he lived longer, we would have gone somewhere towards his vision of Sudan united on a new basis and the South could, if they felt no disadvantage, accept to remain united with the North on the new basis. But now, I don't know anymore.

CR: I think he has done a great deal. This idea of New Sudan, I think, first came up with William Deng. And that led to his death. William was talking of New Forces Congress and he was trying to endear himself to the dispossessed people of Western Sudan and Eastern Sudan. It was as though he had stretched the umbilical cord and that led to his death. And when John picked up this idea, he elaborated on it more. He did more than that in terms of armed insurgency in the West and in the East. He inspired Northerners and Westerners to join the ranks of the SPLM. And there is all the literature he produced and the talks he gave in promoting this vision. I think the situation will never be the same. These people are sufficiently awoken to continue on their own from here onwards. When he recently came to Khartoum, I was in Nairobi, and what got my attention were the slogans from Darfur. The Darfurians were saying, "Darfur! Darfur! O Garang!" And another slogan was, "Welcome to the SPLM, the symbol of freedom and justice." As a child, I remember that the people of Darfur were the ones who were prosecuting the war in the South. Now, with these developments, their hopes somehow became nailed to the Southerners. So, I think these are very significant developments which show that Sudan will never be the same. Garang has done a great deal in this respect. As for the South, I don't agree with those who believe that John had neglected the issue of the South. I have heard him many times saying that he could not see how a person can vote himself into a second-class citizenship when he has a chance to be a citizen of his own country. It means that he was trying to tell these people, the Northerners, "Please Brothers, you change your ways. You overhaul the whole system." If that were done, all of us would not regret being in one Sudan, but if it cannot be done, then we have to have a country of our own. So that's all I can say on this issue.

FD: I am somewhat hesitant to pose this next question, but I am one of those who believes that even in a crisis, one must look for an opportunity. As we look to the man we have lost and the man who is taking over, what are the comparative advantages and disadvantages? Let me be more specific: Garang was a leader who did so much, but had also a lot of critics and enemies, some of them very extreme. Garang was a man who was now getting to be torn between focusing on what's happening on the national level and taking care of the South, which probably would have taken him to another level of complexity. Is it possible that some of these problems that were associated with Garang's leadership could be addressed by Salva Kiir, building on what Garang has achieved but adding whatever attributes he has in order to broaden the unity of the South? Might he, while pursuing Garang's line, bring in a new style of leadership that can become, in the end, a source of strength?

AR: Apart from the worries that I previously expressed, the change as a result of the exiting of our late leader, in terms of unity, greater unity among the people of Southern Sudan, the style is different. Dr. John Garang had a different style. Kiir's style, which has yet to be seen, seems to be one that will probably encourage more open, a more broad-based consensual approach to our problems, our governance. I don't know, but I just want to believe that people will feel probably more united now than when Dr. John Garang was at the helm of the leadership. The loss of his death will hurt our other greater objectives in the country, which were aimed at trying to achieve unity on a correct basis that would ensure equality. That is probably where the problem is greatest. But the question of the South pulling together and trying to do something for itself, I think the new leader will probably provide an environment that will facilitate that. I don't know, it is too early, but that seems to be the trend and the feeling many people now entertain. He is unassuming, a simple personality who wants to know what the people think. That is in sharp contrast with our previous leader who always felt that he knew better and knew where things were going. It is true he was a visionary, no doubt, but people always want to be associated with things that have to do with their aspirations. As you can see, it took a lot of time for people to understand his vision, as was made clear earlier on. Yes, he was definitely a perceptive, visionary leader, who looked well ahead of most people. In short, I think that people in the South will probably pull more together now. The previous criticisms I hope will go down and people will want to contribute and work for a greater united Southern Sudan.

CR: I think God gives different talents to different people. The late Dr. John Garang was talented in different ways, compared with some of his colleagues in the leadership. In that sense, it is not going to be easy to do some of the things he had been doing. But even so, there is no reason for our people to lose hope because Salva Kiir, nobody doubts is a nationalist, who has been very consistent during all these years of turbulence in the Movement. In fact, we think that without him, the Movement may not have stuck together. The people of Bahr el Ghazal, I mean some people from Bahr el Ghazal, were causing a lot of confusion. And I have known Salva Kiir from the time we were schoolboys. He was my schoolmate and he is a very likeable personality. He was very intelligent. There was Salva himself, there was somebody called Barnaba Guui, I don't know where he is now, and there was another John Akot; they were geniuses really. I am not surprised that Salva Kiir, given those talents, has been able to rise to the level he has come to. If only he could listen to people, and I believe he does this, there is no question of an all-knowing leader. You should all be around him. That you are there, and he is there, this by itself means that he has his people around and if he could benefit from your views I believe that the country will continue to be held in what the Dinka call *cieng*. Even if a great man falls, people like you will remain around. What we should do is to continue efforts toward where we want to go and we can easily cross to the other side.

FD: Well, thank you very much. On that positive note we now end the interview.

9. Ali Osman Yassin

Khartoum, August 2005

Francis Deng (FD): This is a conversation with Ali Osman Yassin, the Minister of Justice, regarding the Sudan legal system, in light of the changes that have taken place since 1983 and particularly since 1989 and in the 1990s. We are talking about the Sudan legal system as a whole, and the role of customary law, which used to be administered in accordance with the Native Courts Ordinance, 1932 in the North, the Chiefs' Courts Ordinance, 1931 in the South. Mr. Minister, could you give us an overview of the Sudan legal system today, and then we can get into some of the specifics.

Ali Osman Yassin (AO): Thank you very much Dr. Francis. It's really an opportunity to see you again now, after the peace agreement. I am so happy. And I am sorry for the demise of our brother, Dr. John [Garang]. Hopefully, people will still implement the peace agreement strictly to the letter of every word in that agreement.

Concerning the legal system in the Sudan, in the 1970s, Sudan, after so many changes, in fact, established a legal system resulting in the respect for the rule of law and tried to codify, as much as possible, the covenants of human rights in certain matters. Sudan acceded to many human rights conventions, all of them or at least the majority of them. They became part and parcel of Sudanese law, the law of the land, and in our national legislation.

You know, during Nimeiri's regime [1969–1985], Nimeiri tried his best to Islamize criminal law, through the penal code. The earlier penal code was changed as a result. All the Islamic *hudud* penalties were incorporated in the new code. In 1991, we, Government of National Salvation, decided to make some reforms in our laws, especially the Islamic provisions in certain laws prevailing at that time. We have done our best to delimit the scope of the crimes which were introduced by Nimeiri. The penal code of Nimeiri consists of 400 provisions. We thought it was a bit too much. So, we decided to shorten the code into about 185 provisions. By doing so, and I participated on that reform committee, we had in our minds that whenever you make the incriminating provisions short, more room for freedoms is made available to the people. That was the main idea behind our reform.

For the *hudud,* we inserted only four or five provisions, and we made an explanatory note, especially for the application of *hudud*, and exempted non-Muslims, especially in the South, from those penalties. In civil law, we removed matters that were in contravention with Islam and Sharia. That was studied thoroughly by us and we found no conflict between that and the Civil Code and Commercial Law at large, except in very few cases, such as interest in the banking system, and things like that, debentures in the companies, bonds, very few things which in any case would never have entered the application of the law in the country at large. So, I would say that we could unify the laws for the practitioners without being affected by their beliefs, or freedoms of belief or other freedoms or fundamental rights.

Having done that, every year, more changes took place in the Salvation Government program. The Salvation Revolution Command Council was dissolved. The President first appointed members for the parliament and then Parliament was elected. Time passed and more freedoms were given and are still being given. These changes definitely influenced our legislation very much indeed. In time, we decided that we needed to sense the views of the people. Since then, the wishes and the will of the people have been largely considered. The President was always talking about the rule of law. But the rule of law means that the machinery should work, the law-enforcing agency should do their job well, no extrajudicial decisions, everything should be within the machinery of the law. And we, here in this Ministry, did our best to pull back the Government, whenever they tried to inflate here or there, or to do something outrageous. Of course, basically, in areas like security laws we grumbled about them, and we did our best to change them through the parliament. Now, detention without warrant, detention without lawful excuse, has been lessened to a large degree. At least theoretically, we have introduced provisions to curtail security agents from doing such things. And as a follow-up under the supervision of the judiciary, arbitrary arrest has been prohibited and here we are monitoring that.

So, the core point here is that this country should be fair and just and that requires that for everything we have to have a law. And we did our best to remove the mischievous things in the law, and to help the courts to apply certain provisions by the spirit of the law in order to create for us some precedents to follow and to fill the gaps which we could not do by legislation and codification. And we have done well with Hafiz al Shaikh when he came to be Chief Justice and Obeid before him. Now with Jallal, we are also trying to help him by giving him some ideas that the judges should follow. They should come to us, and request us to go to the legislature and tell them that these are court decisions; we have to adopt them. Of course, we have to do so in a very subtle manner, so that we do not draw the attention of the executive to what we have done as lawyers.

For the codification, we have a law reform, conducted by a standing committee here. From time to time, we suggest a few amendments to the law, whether private or public law. Lawyers' law has been given room for the reform. They welcome the idea of introducing a few things.

As for Native Courts and customary law, unfortunately this part has not been given much time and attention. You know, in the North, a few customary laws have been adopted by the courts and have become part and parcel of our laws. For instance, in the Northern part of Sudan, land law has been largely admitted that is acceptable to the people, such as *toria* and *gussad*. In certain areas, research has started, and we have not yet, up to this moment, come out with results, neither in the North nor in the Southern part of the country. We need a committee to assist in this area. The peace agreement calls for the establishment of a Law Commission. This commission is expected to do a big job. We are waiting for it to initiate the codification of customary law. Here in Khartoum, we have introduced native courts, because the regular courts cannot meet the needs of the people. Justice cannot be done, or be seen to be done, unless demonstrably you give the people a chance to share in solving the problems of their people in their localities. In Kordofan and Darfur the native courts have been reinstated. I don't know to what extent there is literature on that, but I am sure we have issued a lot of circulars encouraging the native courts to do the maximum to reduce the backlogs we usually receive from the representatives of the Judiciary and the Ministry of Justice in these areas.

The rule of law in Sudan has been affected by some political problems, of course. Sometimes, certain incidents interrupted our programs. For instance, sometimes there are coup attempts, led by Shaiqi people, or as in the Darfur case. These always interrupt our program here. The people in the Government then go back to follow certain measures which we believe constitute a violation of the provisions, and the principles which we declare to be prevailing in Sudan.

The situation now, definitely after the peace agreement, can be straightened and put right. Now that the peace agreement has been incorporated in the constitution, it will establish the guidelines for us in our future program of legislation and enactment of the laws. At this moment, we are preparing more than sixty-one laws for amendment to comply with the peace agreement. And more will come, definitely. There are a few people now here in this Ministry who are studying all parts of the law, private and public, with that purpose in mind. We are doing our best to comply with the provisions of the agreement. We cannot afford any conflict between the constitution and the enabling law or the current law in the country. This is the general situation, but if you have specific questions about anything, I don't mind.

FD: Thank you very much Sayed Ali. This is a good overview. I just want to know, first, whether the old system, as we knew it, which comprised the civil, mostly common law system, the Sharia system, and the native or customary law, has now all been merged into one system, in which Sharia is the main guide? And what room is there for the application of any common law principles in the South?

AO: Well, indeed, as you know, we are very much influenced by the common law system, and as you know very well, we have two schools of law here in the Sudan: the common law, that is English or Anglo-Saxon law, and the continental civil or French tradition, which was adopted by the Egyptian school of law and similarly by schools of law in other Arab countries. But mainly, common law was considered our main law. The main features of our legal system were inherited from that legal tradition. For instance, our commercial law is based on the English law. And we did not like the idea of one book, called the commercial law book. We don't have that. We have separate branches of the law scattered here and there. There is the law of contract, law of agency, law of partnership and others. Most of the law here was based on the English system, but in broad lines, as you know, and we left the substantive details to the courts. But, for some time now, the courts could not do the job well, because of the standard of the judges in these courts. So, that influenced the standard of the law in Sudan, not because the Government changed the law, but because of the standard of the people applying the law, being ignorant of the system. So, they were helped by the civil ordinance of 1983. Even this could not fill the gaps.

We are graduates of the common law system, University of Khartoum, and we have had our postgraduate studies mostly in the United Kingdom. Sudanese company law is based on the English law of 1908. This was passed here in Sudan in 1925. It's effective up until this moment. They did not change it. What changed is procedural law; the substantive matter of the company law is left for the discretion of the judges, who still turn to English law for guidance. We would like it to continue like that, although we thought about amending that law and we have done our best to bring some treatise from English law, Gower on company law for instance, and so forth. But the people like to keep it as it is. The procedure for the formation of the company, liquidation of the company, meetings, and so on and so forth have been amended, but the substantive aspects have been left untouched; that we have left for the judges to fill the gaps from the English substantive law.

Unfortunately, when the judge comes to the bench, without having knowledge of company law as a subject, that creates a problem, but definitely that depends on who is doing the job. So, common law, up to this moment, supersedes all types of systems in Sudan. Nimeiri, when he came, made a sort of amalgamation between Sharia and the system which was applicable at that time. He did not really change the system at all; he simply introduced a few principles. To some people, it was a bit odd, because it did not look coherent with these different systems, different views, different philosophies, different backgrounds, all lumped together. But Nimeiri kept them together all through.

When the Salvation Government took over, we did not touch the civil law, as I told you. But we made some changes in the criminal code. We had in mind all the conferences held abroad, in the United Kingdom, having in mind the recent theories of criminology, law of sentencing, whatever it is. We decided that all those should be included. We should not make a departure by bringing in Sharia law wholesale. We left the provisions which were not in conflict with Sharia to continue. And we found them similar. For instance, such principles as that a person should be presumed innocent until the contrary is proved, or that nobody will be adjudicated without being heard, we found them more or less identical. So, we kept the system, more or less, as it is. You can't say whether it is common law or not, and you can't say whether it is Islamic law or not. All the principles of justice are similar. But, in black and white, we put in some provisions, like *hudud*, and we made some explanatory notes to make things easier in the application.

And I must tell you, now here, since 1989 amputation of hands is minimal, you can say three or four. During Nimeiri's period, hundreds of hands were amputated. We didn't do that. Why? Because we put the defenses, all the defenses in Islam, we included them in our application. And believe me, Dr. Francis, there are more than eighty defenses in Sharia. So, you cannot imagine that a person would be sentenced to such a severe punishment when any one of the defenses applies to protect him from the application of such severe punishment. With that understanding, we kept things together.

Now, you can't say this is an Islamic system. For the Muslims, they can say that it is Islamic because there is no conflict between what they believe and what they can see applied in the courts. But for me, as a student of common law, who has also done some reading in Islamic law, I can say with confidence that the common law system is not touched. With that full understanding and thorough study of the situation, we made the amendments to the law. That is the difference between what we have done and what Nimeiri did. Nimeiri did it rashly, without careful study of the matter, and he made a marriage between two things which could not be together. But we studied that and in fact we trimmed the law and made it very strong. As a Sudanese who graduated from the common law system, you can hardly distinguish between the common law and the Sharia law.

I had the opportunity to talk at SOAS [School of Oriental and African Studies] in London some time ago about the legal system in Sudan and I reached the conclusion that we have never deformed the common law system in Sudan. It is still intact; it is touched but not destroyed. It is still as it was. Of course, politicians say that the fate of common law is the fate of independence in Sudan. That is not true, to be frank with you.

I was teaching company law for six years in the University of Khartoum. When they Arabized the system, I stopped teaching because I could not teach that subject in Arabic. I didn't know what to say in Arabic so I stopped teaching. I apologized and told them that I could not. I quit, in fact. Now, we're going back to it. I'm introducing a new amendment to the company law. What did I do? I did not do anything except introduce certain principles, for instance, the protection of minorities, shareholder's minorities. I brought those principles into our law. I did not bother myself to go and look into Sharia, because there is nothing in Sharia. If somebody puts his finger on these principles in Sharia, let him tell me. I know they don't have them. So, to be frank with you, on this issue of Islamization of the legal system, for a person who is a scholar, who can make research, he will find that things may not be completely intact, but also that nothing much has changed. Very slight changes do not affect the roots of the whole system. So, up to the moment, I will consider the precedent in the English system as guiding and sometimes binding on our courts. Yesterday, I wrote a submission to the court here concerning an appeal. I prepared the appeal. I wrote about twelve cases, citations of cases to the appeals court, to the High Court, telling them that they had to go back to the precedents, to the cases considered before and decided and that we should not depart from the system as it is. That is the common law. So, that is what I can say. Generally speaking, I am not biased to the common law, but in fact I think that it is more fair.

FD: Thank you very much. This is very helpful. Could you give us a picture of the legal system in terms of the institutions of the system, the judicial hierarchy, your role as Minister of Justice and what we used to call the Attorney General, and all the other agents of the legal system?

AO: The system of justice here in Sudan consists of a judicial hierarchy that starts with the Justice Council. This Justice Council is chaired by the President, with members representing many different specializations. The Minister of Justice is a member, the Chief Justice is a member, some of the judges of the Supreme Court (High Court we call it) are members, and also the Undersecretary of this ministry is a member, the Prosecutor General is a member, and representatives of the Bar Association and other affiliated bodies, such as the Constitutional Court, the police, and the military judiciary are all represented. The role of the council is to make policy suggestions for the legal system in Sudan.

But when you come to the application of the law, you will find that the judiciary is an independent corporation, which is a separate entity. It has its own legal entity, headed by the Chief of the High Court, called the Chief Justice. This man is also the Chairman of the Judiciary Council. It is a commission now in accordance with the peace agreement. Its job will be the same as that of the Judiciary Council, now headed by the Chief Justice, and three High Court members. I am a member, the Minister of Finance is a member, and the legal advisor of the President is a member. The role of this Council is to make policies on replacement of the provisions of the law, law reform relating to the judiciary, discipline of the judges, promotion of the judges, and transfer of the judges from one area to another. And they keep the whole set-up under their direct supervision and control. They don't have any relationship with the judiciary, except the appointment of the Chief Justice, and the judges, through recommendation to the President. The President appoints the Chief Justice and all the judges. All of them have to be appointed by Presidential decree.

The courts are fully independent from the executive and the legislature. I represent them in the council of ministers, but by their authorization. I am not there on my own. I can't talk on their behalf, unless they request me to speak on an issue before the council of ministers, or in the parliament, involving the judiciary. They come and request me to answer on their behalf, because they don't appear there. They delegate me piece by piece, each item separately.

So, I don't have any power of supervision on them and they wouldn't like it; they are very sensitive about that. Nobody can summon them; nobody will call them to come. They don't like it. They will complain to the President. If somebody is going to administer some oath, they witness that. So, any affairs of the judiciary, of the judges, including financial issues, are completely independent. They take money from the public treasury, but they have their own money. They take a percentage from the fines, from the money they get of their own, and from the investment. They are very rich. They are extremely rich people. With respect to the terms of their employment, they have very good contracts. Salaries in the judiciary are far to the top, whereas others are low. We in the Ministry are similar to them. We fought for that very much and I succeeded in putting them to the same level with the lawyers here. I succeeded in that. Our people here are now similar to the judges.

Now, we come to the Ministry of Justice. For some time, the head was the Minister of Justice, and then it was changed to be Attorney General. The Attorney General was the top man here, supervising the whole thing. The major issue for him was the prosecution. And the Prosecutor General is one of his subordinates. The Advocate General deals with the civil cases on behalf of the Government. He is a lawyer of the Government. We have about ninety-eight offices throughout the country belonging to him. He is supervising these matters concerning advices, contracts, drafting, negotiations, whatever it is, on behalf of the Advocate General. We have lawyers outside in all organs of the Government, whether departments, or maybe public companies or whatever it is. So the Advocate General is one of the subordinates of what is again called Minister of Justice that has replaced the Attorney General. In the past, it was the Attorney General.

The main job here, what we do, is legislation. We study the law, and write memos about it. Proposals come to us from the policy makers. And we put the proposal in the shape of a law and make our comments. If it is OK, we will pass it. Otherwise, if it contravenes the constitution, we tell them. If it contravenes the law already existing, we tell them. So, we make a study from that angle. This part is headed by Solicitor General for Legislation. His job is to study the law and to recommend reforms, especially lawyers' law and the general laws. Private laws, we study them and make our comments. But sometimes we don't interfere. On mining, for instance, we give them only general remarks, but no more than that. And we leave it for them to convince the Council of Ministers about that.

So, now we have Prosecutor General who is supervising all prosecutions throughout Sudan. We don't know what will happen now after the peace agreement. As I said, we will have to coordinate, because still the job is on us here to appear on behalf of the community representing criminal cases. So, we have to coordinate with the relevant minister in the South who is similar to the Minister of Justice here. In the South, now, he is called Attorney General. But we will appoint some lawyers here and maybe we will send them to the South. That's another issue; now I'm discussing this matter with Allison on what to do. He said to me that he wants me to appoint thirty lawyers to the South. They should be appointed here, get their training here, get everything from here, and then we send them to the South. Whether that will be on secondment or whatever, we will decide later. But so far, until we resolve this matter, we are appearing on behalf of the community on all criminal cases throughout Sudan.

The procedure starts with a single person who is now supervising the investigations. Neither the police nor the judiciary gets involved; it is the prosecution who does the investigation under supervision. We have to determine whether there is a prima facie evidence, whether there is a case. Or we can conclude that we don't see any point to take this matter up. And the matter ends there; no case, no claim. At the same time, the Attorney General, whom we call the Minister of Justice because the Arab League and the African Union members all call them ministers, is doing the job. I have two jobs. As a minister I am a member of the cabinet. When I put on the hat of the Attorney General, I am a semijudicial body, because I can say, "No case; no prosecution is required." Finished, it will end here. After the investigation is completed and before the court delivers the judgment, I can intervene. You know this very well; you know the law. So, there is a huge power here. And that's legal. They say it is semijudicial, but I tell them it is judicial. When I say that there is no case, nobody on earth will bring it back. From here, I can give instructions to Zalinge, far away. If they bring me the case here, I study it. We have circuits for that. Three lawyers sit together and pass the verdict by majority. They have to decide by majority. When I decide on an issue, that is it. This concerns the criminal side.

On the civil side, we have the Advocate General who is doing all civil matters. He appears on behalf of the Government in all cases. And he gives advice, *fatwa*, to them, and legal opinion as well. By our law, his opinion is binding, unless it is changed by the President. And the President has to say why he decides otherwise. He cannot pass only a decree and say, "No, I don't like the opinion of the Attorney General." Of course, he is not accountable to anybody, but usually because this is judicial and legal he has to justify his position, if he changes my advice or my opinion. So, by law, it is binding and final in this matter. All contracts of the Government, commercial contracts, before they are signed by any agent of the Government, a lawyer from here should study them, negotiate with the concerned department, and help draft them. Only when he says that this is OK will the Government proceed with the contract. If he doesn't say OK, then the responsibility is on the person who is in charge.

So, we are also controlling Government contracts, to lessen corruption, because, sometimes, they don't make tenders. They bring relatives and give them contracts worth twenty million dollars. Such a project as the Meroe

Dam, for instance, is a big thing, and unless it is approved by us, the Government cannot sign the contract. The President always supports us, and the Council of Ministers also always supports us.

We have another department, called International Law Department, which is concerned with international agreements. They follow the development of international law. We attend international conferences to represent Sudan. We tell them Sudan's point of view on, for instance, the law of the sea, or the international criminal court. We make a note on any draft agreement and take it to the Council of Ministers. We may tell them, "No, we don't want to accede, for the following reasons." And we take it to the Ministry of Foreign Affairs as well. We cooperate closely with the Ministry of Foreign Affairs in these matters.

All agreements, bilateral or multilateral, are considered by the department here, which is also headed by Solicitor General. The person who specializes in these matters got his PhD from Cambridge and he is doing very well. We train our lawyers, by the way, in Cambridge, London, and other prestigious universities abroad. These people work on international agreements.

We also have a Legal Aid Department. We provide services for paupers, those who cannot afford to pay for lawyers. We give them advice, free advice, and we appear with them in the courts. We have won a lot of cases for them. You will find it rather funny that we represent the prosecution at the same time as we represent the defense. But I don't mind. The only difference is that in prosecution, the Attorney General or the Minister can give directives, make amendments, or change the petition. In the Legal Aid Department, we don't interfere in the work of the defence counsel; we leave it for our colleagues to do whatever they want to do. And they are very successful; they have won many cases against their colleagues who are representing the prosecution. I am happy about that because we are helping people who could not afford lawyers.

FD: Could you complete the picture about the court hierarchy?

AO: The court hierarchy starts from the General Court. The General Court starts with third-class magistrates, second-class magistrates, and first-class magistrates; and then the General Court Judge. General Court Judge is what in the past was called Province Judge. Now he is called General Court Judge. And then there is the Appeal Court. Above the Appeal Court Judges are High Court Judges. On top of that are three Deputy Chief Justices and then the Chief Justice. This is the hierarchy.

FD: What about what used to be called Native Courts and Chiefs' Courts, where do they fit in?

AO: They are at the bottom of the hierarchy, but some Chiefs' Courts or Native Courts can be given powers of the first-class magistrate in criminal cases or the first-class judge in civil matters.

FD: So those courts are still intact.

AO: They are available, but it depends on the locality from one place to another. Let's say in Khartoum here, in the suburbs, we have some.

FD: Is there a law governing them?

AO: They are governed by circulars issued by the Chief Justice. They don't have a special law.

FD: Could you also address the capacity of the legal system, in terms of personnel, just rough estimates: how many judges we have, how many lawyers we have, those inside the country, and estimates of those outside who could come back.

AO: Judges in the judiciary are graduates of law schools, who begin in the bar association and then start in the judiciary after a competition. They are admitted and appointed by a decree from the President. From top to bottom now the total will be about 2000. This is for the judges. They are distributed all around Sudan, from the South to the far North, West, and East. In each state, we have somebody who is the chairman of the judicial system in the locality, in the state. He is the head of the judicial system in the state. The Appeal Court has some branches in the states. The West, the whole West, has one High Court. In each state there is an Appeal Court. In the past, the Appeal Court was at the center only. So, we have decentralized it. Now Appeal Courts are available all over the country. For the High Courts, they are decentralized regionally. There is the Darfur Region or Kordofan Region. Each has a circuit. El Gazira, for instance, has its own circuit. And so on. But the judiciary is federal; they have one list. They also have rules for the transfer of judges. They can transfer them from one region to another. Usually, the proposal is made by the Chief Justice. It is brought to the Judiciary Council which approves it.

For us in the Ministry of Justice, in terms of personnel, we have about 1200–1300 lawyers. Some of them are on the criminal side, and some of them are on the civil sector. Some of them are doing legislation, and some of them work on contracts, as I told you. The prosecution takes the major attention from us. We represent the prosecution and in each state, we have a department. The head of the department is in the rank of a High Court Judge. He is equal to the High Court Judge over there, in the same scale, or rank. And helping him are lawyers on both sides, criminal and civil. The civil division does everything noncriminal. Some of them are lawyers to the companies there, to the Wilaya (State), and to the Wali (Governor) himself, and to the Councils, Legislative Council, State Council. We give them that human resource support. Here, we have the Minister and the State Minister. The State Minister does not fit here because the law talks about the Attorney General and the Undersecretary. The Undersecretary in the past was the Attorney General himself and then the Minister was above him. So, because the entity is judicial, the word Undersecretary is not acceptable. But still, it is there. In the absence of the Minister or the Attorney General, the Undersecretary replaces him fully. There is really no room for the State Minister. But, it is politically put in between. Sometimes, it can be delegated. The Undersecretary is the top administrator here. He is also a judicial authority because the claims come through him. Subordinate to him are the Prosecutor

General, the Advocate General, the Solicitor General, and so on and so forth. They are many. We created six posts in the rank of the Undersecretary, all six people in the same rank as the Deputy Chief Justice. So on top, there is the Attorney General, and Undersecretary, with another six, each of them supervising a sector: criminal sector, legislation sector, civil sector, intellectual property sector, and so on and so forth. I created that system when I came here. I have spent here seven and a half years as Minister of Justice.

FD: What about the bar, what roughly will you say is the size of the bar?

AO: The size of the bar is huge. They accept a lot of graduates from any university, many from the Cairo University branch in Khartoum. I think they are not less than 6000 lawyers now.

FD: What about the capacity of the police? And are the police armed, by the way? What will you say is the function of the police?

AO: The function of the police now, of course, is to maintain peace and order. This is the main function; and to help in the detection and the discovery of the crimes and to combat criminal offenders, and to avert that in fact. They are doing that together with us in the investigations, because the police are the main recipients to the claim, and they report that. But the final file should be given to the attorney, who will say whether a particular case is criminal or civil, whether to accept it or not, whether to release the accused on bail or not, to arrest or not to arrest. There are few circumstances or cases in which the police by themselves can arrest. But these are limited in the court by the procedural court. We and the police are always fighting with each other. They don't like our involvement. They always want to do everything by themselves. I don't want to talk; you understand!? There is a lot of fighting on that, but we succeeded in maintaining that within the law, the Criminal Procedural Act, in which the role of the police is so clearly defined and our role is also very clear.

While the police are to maintain peace and order, they are also doing other jobs. Recently they have made a lot of investments to improve their living standards, their own standards, both public and private. They entered into private practices, such as hospitalization, commercial dealings, some corporations. I don't like that. All they are doing is to treat people in the hospital as though they were the Ministry of Health. But anyway, they have made a lot of money out of that. Now, they are well looked after. They have their own stock of machinery, combating crime equipment, vehicles, and the like.

FD: They can carry guns?

AO: Oh, yes, they carry guns, all of them. Some of them carry pistols, others machine guns. It depends upon the job itself. But they carry guns. The main condition is that they should not exceed their powers; they should not abuse the right of using the gun.

FD: Do you have adequate police?

AO: No, they are always under-resourced. They need more. And now they are trying to enlist.

FD: What about prisons and prison wardens?

AO: They are all part and parcel of the Ministry of the Interior. For some time, big prisons in the states were annexed to the states, under the control of the governors. But they neglected them. They could not give them money for food and so on. Some prisoners died in the prisons because of lack of care. The Wali [Governors] argued, "Why should I care about criminals? I should care about the innocent people outside." So, all the prisons were brought back to the federal government, under the Minister of the Interior. And he is giving them a lot of attention now. If you talk about the prison system here in Sudan, prisons need reforms. They need more attention. There is a lot of criticism against the present system. It is the same set-up made by the British colonial administration. You know they were very meager and made rare attempts at improvement.

FD: As a last question, could you say something about how you envisage the post-conflict relationship with the Southern Government, the Government of National Unity and the Government of Southern Sudan?

AO: Well, we have had some problems, but I can't envisage that they will continue for long, since things have now been written down clearly. The 1998 Constitution could not solve all the problems. We had some problems with Dr. Hassan Turabi and his people in the Assembly, the Parliament. Accordingly, the President dissolved the Parliament because of the problems between the State Walis and the President. Now, this matter is resolved completely. The transitional constitution or the interim constitution is very clear about the relationship between the federal government and the states, the state powers, regional powers, the powers of the South as a region. We don't have other regions; we have only the Southern region, the states, and the federal government. So, everything has been written down clearly, and there are only very few things that the constitution is silent about. Because the agreement was also silent about some matters, it will need the constitutional court to help on those matters, so that we solve them amicably.

Here, in this Ministry, we are now studying the things on which the constitution is silent. I have established a committee to study the constitution and to see which matters may come up and create a problem, and to envisage a solution to them. We will give these to the President to solve with the First Vice President, Dr. John Garang. The two partners should sit together and find solutions to those problems, because, if we don't do that now, these situations will explode as a time bomb. We don't want that. So, we are preparing for this issue here. We read everything and said, "This point is not sufficiently clear. It has to be elucidated more, to be clarified." So, we identified the problems and we put forward some suggestions, one, two, three, as solutions. Up to this moment, we have not exposed these for discussion outside the Ministry. But the work has been done. So, I'm just telling you that there are problems that may not yet be obvious.

We, as lawyers, can put our fingers on a few things, but politically we don't want to talk about differences at this point. We want to talk about coherence, agreement, consensus. If there is a problem which is likely to come up, then we have to sit, in a positive spirit; we have to change the spirit. We have to accommodate each other. Law by itself, or whatever is written down in the agreement, is not enough. Much depends on who is who, and who is doing the job.

FD: On that positive note, I just want to thank you again for this very illuminating and informative conversation.

10. Dr. Amin Mekki Medani and Omar El Farouk Shoumena

Khartoum, August 2005

Francis Deng (FD): This is a conversation with Dr. Amin Mekki Medani and Omar El Farouk Shoumena, both lawyers, conducted in Khartoum in August, 2005, about the state of the law in the country today. Could you give a general overview of the sources of the law in the country today?

Omar El Farouk Shoumena (OS): In the area of commercial law we have the Companies Act, the Bankruptcy Act, and the Business Exchange Act. These basic commercial laws are still based on the common law system. We have the Land Registration Act as enacted by the British. The bulk of the laws applicable today are really common law. But at the same time, we have some provisions in the Civil Code which are in conflict with these laws. The Civil Code which was introduced by Nimeiri touches on other parts of the law, for example, Law of Contract, Law of Torts, Law of Agency. The three codes which were prepared by Zaki Mustafa, the Contract Act, the Sale of Goods Act, the Agency Act, were reviewed and left to the civil courts. That's a general view with regard to the civil law. So, you can say that there is a sort of uncertainty about what system of law is applicable in the Sudan.

With regard to the Sharia law, of course, Sharia is all there as it is. Areas like family law are governed by Sharia for the North. And then there is the Social Justice Act, which makes it mandatory for the courts to apply Sharia as a last resort when investigating applicable law. This is creating confusion, because most of the judges in the judiciary are Sharia judges and they tend not to recognize legislative law. They argue that they are bound by Sharia concepts. They are creating havoc. In many instances, this was corrected by the constitutional court.

So, there is some sort of havoc with regard to the system of law which is applicable in Sudan. You have, of course, the penal code which is still the penal code of 1929. What was introduced in criminal law were the *hudud* Sharia punishments only. I personally believe what is now being practiced is a form of *tansiq*, which means that you take from various systems of law and harmonize or reconcile them into a rule of law. *Tansiq* is a concept of law which is being followed in Sudan. Take, for instance, murder, which is a crime in the penal code of 1929. That code does not care a damn about what Islamic jurisprudence says about murder. On the other hand, Sharia judges don't recognize the penal code, which is based on the Indian penal code. Instead, they are applying their own Sharia concept. That's why, oftentimes, their judgments are reversed on appeals. With regard to the native courts, I believe the Native Administration was dissolved in the North. And we have no Native or Sheikh courts.

FD: In Abyei, as in the South, initially the Native Administration was not dissolved. Nimeiri later decided to dissolve it while on a visit to the area because he got offended. But when the Dinka later demanded its restoration and I interceded on their behalf with Dr. Jaafar Mohamed Ali Bekheit, chieftainship was eventually restored. This was later extended to the Missiriya as well. But then I thought this regime has reinstated all the chiefs in the North as Amirs.

OS: That is for administrative purposes only; they have no judicial powers.

FD: So what exists in tribal areas?

OS: I don't think customary law is being developed any more. On the contrary, it is being abandoned. If you have no courts applying customary law, then you have no customary law.

FD: So, customary courts have all been abolished?

OS: You have no Native courts any more.

Amin Mekki Medani (AM): Native Administration was abolished since the time of Nimeiri.

FD: I think it was reinstated.

OS: No, it wasn't. One of the main problems of the Darfur crisis is the fact that Native Administration was abolished. Settlement of disputes at the local level just dissipated.

FD: In the North now, the administration of justice in the tribes, what is governing it?

AM: There are courts of first class, second class, and third class. Of course you have the informal system of *ajaweed* adjudication and settlement of cases out of court. The elders will do it, but you don't have any formal means of executing their judgments.

FD: Judging from what I know about the administration of justice in Abyei, there are local courts.

OS: I don't know about Abyei, but I am speaking about the North.

FD: There are three courts in Abyei. Instead of one Chiefs' court, they established three courts in the area to administer the customary laws of the people. Is this unique to Abyei?

OS: Yes.

FD: In the Missiriya area, the son of Babo Nimir was appointed *amir*.

OS: There are *amirs*, but this is for administration purposes only, not for adjudication.

FD: So, they don't see cases?

OS: No, they don't. They are there only for administration purposes, not for judicial functions as used to be the case years ago.

FD: What are the institutions or structures of the legal system?

OS: The structure of the judiciary as it is, you have the Chief Justice, the Province Judges, Appeal Court Judges, High Court Judges. The High Court is the highest in the hierarchy. It is the Supreme Court.

FD: So we now have a Supreme Court?

OS: Yes; and then the Court of Appeal, and then Trial Courts, Province Courts, and Courts of first-, second-, and third-grade judges.

AM: Constitutional Court used to be a circuit within the Supreme Court appointed when there was a constitutional case, with a number of judges, five or seven. Now you have a totally distinct judicial body called the Constitutional Court.

FD: Separate from the judicial hierarchy?

AM: Yes, totally independent of it.

FD: Is this part of the agreement?

AM: This has been the case before the agreement.

OS: This was introduced by the constitution. It is one of the innovations of Turabi. So is the Supreme Court.

FD: What about the legal profession in terms of the lawyers, the attorneys?

OS: Before we talk about the legal profession, we should talk about the legal standards, and about the legal education in Sudan.

FD: Where do the judges get their legal training?

OS: University of Khartoum, University of Nilein, and Islamic University.

FD: And they are taught common law?

AM: The important thing is that there is a crisis. When this regime came into power, in the first year about 500 judges were dismissed arbitrarily "in the public interest." In their place were recruited people with no judicial experience, and no legal qualifications. Now, you have about 70 percent of the judiciary, including the High Court, who are Sharia judges. And the Chief Justice is a Sharia judge. So, what Omar was talking about is that, although you have these common law residues, codes, or acts, most of them were abolished by Nimeiri. Those that remained indicate, I think, that the law is in a state of flux. You read judgments, some people will quote Egyptian scholars, some will quote Abu Hanifa, and others will quote Savigny and now Deng. So the law is really in a state of flux. You don't know what the applicable law is. That is my opinion. And because of the recruitment of these judges, courts will recite the Koran instead of other legal sources. It is a matter of religion rather than law. So, this is what has happened to the law; it is a total confusion.

OS: We met Dr. Garang the other day, we, a group of lawyers.

FD: You did? I could not make it.

OS: We spoke about peace; I myself spoke about law reform. I said to him, "If you want to make peace attractive, you have to sort out the legal situation in the North. Let there be no more confusion. At present there is a lot of confusion." He was very much interested in that. Later on, he told me that he took note of what I had said. There is real confusion now. You cannot speak about the judiciary when the Chief Justice is from Sharia and you want a fusion between the system in the South and in the North. You tell me that the Chief Justice is a Sharia judge and at the same time you have a Supreme Court for both North and South. How can that be?

FD: As practicing lawyers, what exactly is the legal practice in this kind of a legal system?

OS: Chaotic. One of the duties of the lawyer is to predict what the court will say about the law, and, in a system that is intact, you can be pretty sure that the court will say so and so, but now you cannot be sure at all.

AM: Francis, the basis for what Omar was referring to earlier about the sources of the law is the Judicial Judgments Act, 1983. There is a provision in that law, still operating today, which says that the judge will have to apply the principles of Sharia according to a certain hierarchy of legal principles, but, in the end, if you find no reference, you exert your own opinion.

FD: You exert your own understanding and interpretation of Sharia?

AM: Yes, your own understanding and interpretation of Sharia. This lack of certainty used to be applied to the criminal law. That was the basis of the execution of Mahmoud Mohamed Taha. Apostasy at that time was not an offense in the penal code, but the judge applied his own creativity under the principle of *ijtihad* and came out with the judgment, "This is *ridda-apostasy*." And they executed the man without there being a specific offense for that. Now, this principle of individual interpretation has been eliminated from the criminal law, but it is still part of the civil law. But this disguises what the civil law is or is not, because it is left to the discretion of the judge. And there is no direction. You don't stipulate that the discretion of the judge is to be exercised according to the legal principles of a particular school of jurisprudence, Maliki, Shafie, or Hanbali, or Hanafi, or Shia, or whatever. So whatever he finds, he will use it and give you a judgment. That is how the system works in an atmosphere of total uncertainty and unpredictability.

OS: Let us elaborate a bit about the confusion and the clash between the Constitutional Court and the judiciary. There is a big quarrel in the High Court about the murder cases. As I told you, the penal code is just following the same Section 253 of the penal code of 1929 relating to provocation, sudden fight, and so on. This derives from Indian jurisprudence, in turn based on common law jurisprudence. Now they say, "Murder is murder. In Sharia, we don't know sudden fight, and we don't know provocation." Even if you enter your private room and find a man fornicating with your wife, it is not determined to be provocation, as provided under 253 of the penal code. You have to be executed. That is the Sharia. They sentence people to death even though the law is very clear on sudden fight, provocation, or other mitigating circumstances. When it comes to the Constitutional Court, the right to life is recognized as a basic human right. When it comes to the law, they quash the decision of the judiciary which is dominated by the Sharia judges.

FD: I once talked to Turabi about the whole idea of legal defense. I told him how in traditional society people were shocked to see that a lawyer was defending only one side instead of seeing justice from both sides. It was a case in which Mohamed Ahmed Mahjoub was defending a member of the Mahdi family who was tried, accused by the Dinka of corruptive practices in parliamentary elections, in which the Umma Party had nominated him to run in our joint Dinka-Missiriya constituency. Mahjoub representing him appeared to the Dinka to be always talking in favor of one side, that of the accused. One of the Dinka elders got up and said, "The way you are talking, you must have been bribed." Turabi said, "I agree with those people. I think we should abolish this whole idea of advocacy."

OS: He is totally against it.

FD: On what grounds?

OS: On the ground that it is not recognized in Islam.

FD: What is the current situation on the question of legal defense?

AM: It is there; it is absolutely there. In fact, they are defending Turabi in court. It is there, very much so.

FD: Refresh my memory on the functions of the Chief Justice and the Attorney General. Do we still have the Attorney General alongside the Minister of Justice?

AM: This is a matter that has been settled for a long time. Personally, in a paper I wrote on the rule of law in Sudan, I say the role of the Minister of Justice should be different from that of the Attorney General because the Attorney General is the man who pleads in the interest of the prosecution or in cases against the state. And so, his position should not be political. But the Minister of Justice is political. Since the days of Nimeiri, we have almost a clash of visions in the constitution saying the Ministry of Justice in Sudan should have an Attorney General who, by virtue of his office, shall be the Minister.

FD: So now we don't have an Attorney General different from the Minister of Justice?

OS: The Attorney General has got certain judicial powers, whereas the Minister of Justice is a political figure. He represents the judiciary in the Council of Ministers, but he has got no judicial powers whatsoever.

AM: But historically, since the resignation of Mohamed Sharif, in the case of Fereijun, they have now fused the two to be in one and the same person. The Attorney General is now the Minister of Justice.

FD: So, we don't have an Attorney General, we just have the Minister of Justice who is also the Attorney General?

AM: No we don't. A senior public prosecutor does the work of prosecution and the final word is with the Minister of Justice. In all the prosecutions, the final decision is with the Minister of Justice.

FD: Sudan was one of the countries which really had an excellent legal system, including professional qualifications, whether you are talking of judges or practicing lawyers. What is the state of the legal profession in terms of qualifications of lawyers, judges, and the legal practice in general?

AM: It is very poor. You will be surprised that there are seventeen faculties of law in the Sudan. And the smallest new faculty has now 260 students in the preliminary year. Nilein has 2000 in the preliminary class. Teachers teach by microphone; students are sitting in the windows or still listening from outside the class. In the end of the year, the teachers in other universities, as far as I know, sell their handouts to the students. It has really totally deteriorated. In the libraries, forget about law reports and legal textbooks; they are not there. You go to the Faculty of Law in Khartoum; there is no library. There is no point to go to the library because there are no recent textbooks, no law reports, no periodicals; there is nothing. With mass education, of course, there are no tutorials as we used to have; there are no essays; there is no professor–student relationship. And then, after that, there is, of course, the bar examination. About 20 to 30 percent only pass that.

OS: No, less than that. Out of 2000 only eighty-two passed.

FD: What you are saying then is that the standard by which the students are tested is higher than their legal education. Where do these high standards come from?

AM: It is not really high standards because the bar examination is still geared towards practice. It is not geared towards what you know in torts, or conflict of laws, or jurisprudence, or whatever. It is more petitions and procedures and that sort of thing, very practical.

FD: But who designs the exam for the bar?

AM: The Ministry of Justice.

FD: That means they do have reasonably higher standards than the level of education.

OS: They just recruit some justices, some university professors, to set the exams and make the corrections. And I have forebodings because they do this, and decide who should pass.

FD: One of the areas they talk about, by the way, is human rights, the extent to which the legal system guarantees rights. Now, if we remember the Special Rapporteur on the Sudan, Gasper Biro, he was, of course, very down on Sudan in terms of the extent to which Sharia violated human rights. His reports were always very critical. Is he right, that the Sharia legal system is not protective of human rights?

AM: Of course, it is not. It is not because of the institutions as we described them. It is that there are a series of arbitrary laws which, in spite of the present constitution, are still enforced by the state security courts, trade union law courts, and all these. Apart from the state of emergency, which has now been lifted, there is a whole series of laws that are restrictive of public freedoms and human rights, and they are still there. The Attorney General [Minister of Justice] says he is revising sixty-one laws. We've been hearing this for more than sixty-one days. Anyway, he says there are sixty-one laws which are being revised. And you don't know whether the law revision is a function of the Ministry of Justice or is a function of technicians. So, the law is not being publicly debated either in the press or by the bar association and the like. Of course, this raises the very important issue of accountability for the past, what you call transitional justice. And now people talk about Darfur.

Why Darfur? We for fifteen years here in Khartoum, in Juba in the South, in the Nuba Mountains, and in other areas of the country, suffered atrocious violations of human rights and humanitarian law. Nobody is talking about that. Even the peace agreement and the constitution talk about reconciliation and healing of wounds. What does it mean?

OS: This is one of the compromises struck between Garang and Ali Osman Mohamed Taha. Garang was adamant that there should be some sort of accountability. Mansour and Abel Alier advised Garang, "If the main object of this peace agreement is to make a sort of partnership with you, you cannot possibly say, 'I am going to make a partnership and at the same time I am going to try you and make you accountable for the past.'"

AM: That is why the bilateral nature of the agreement has been criticized on this basis because both have an interest in not having accountability; both have committed human rights violations.

FD: I tend to err on the side of reconciliation. My reason is that while you are still negotiating peace, if you begin to target some people, then you cannot have their cooperation. I remember talking to the American Chargé d'Affaires when they were advising President al-Bashir to at least have symbolic punishment of some of the top people, who were reputed to be responsible for gross human rights violations in Darfur. I said to him, "What if some of these people are critical to the success of the peace talks in the South?" He said, "There are some people we will not touch, because we need them for the peace talks." Once you begin to be that selective, the purpose of justice is defeated.

I know time is late and you have to go, but I would like to turn to a different issue briefly. Now that peace has been achieved between the Government and the SPLM/A, what in your view was the war about and has the agreement achieved the objectives of the war? On another front, has the message of the SPLM/A about the New Sudan reached the North so that the prospects for unity are increased? Are the linkages with the marginalized regions of the North, who have the same cause with the South, reinforcing national unity?

AM: My reaction is that although, as I said, all the people took part in the agreement because it involved the warring parties primarily, and not all parties took part in the making of the constitution, still, I think the agreement should be used as a springboard and that people should take it from there. There is no point in crying over spilt milk and saying, "We should have, should have, should have!" I think we should take it from there. The agreement has many positive elements in it, such as the emphasis on the devolution of power, the decentralization of power, the emphasis on development, and on broad-based participation, not only in the South, but for people in all the provinces to run their own affairs and involve their local people. And then there is the wealth-sharing agreement, not only with respect to oil, but also the other resources of the country. So, I think, leaving aside initial reservations, the peace agreement and the constitution will both set the basis for constructively building the future. What is important is that there be good will and that people are genuine in interpreting the agreement and the constitution to set the basis for a transition to democracy and consolidating peace. I think that's it; it depends on the human flesh to make it work.

OS: This is what I said to Garang. I said that it was not a matter of criticizing the agreement, the CPA, or criticizing the constitution. Here, for example, in Nimeiri's constitution, you have the longest Bill of Rights ever. Under the original transitional constitution, the Stanley Baker constitution, you had only five or six articles about fundamental liberties but under the transitional constitution there was a very strong observance of the rule of law. There was no qualification, no restriction on people's freedoms, whereas under Nimeiri there were violations and violations of human rights. What is really important is how people implement the constitution. How do we actually see it implemented? That is the most important thing. Even let alone fundamental liberties and human rights, other provisions of the constitution with regard to sharing wealth, sharing power, if you have the will to apply it fairly and objectively, it will be all right. But if you have the will to take people's rights or to be subjective, you will go nowhere. Where is the will of the people, and how is it represented in the constitution? This is the only thing that will make unity attractive, if the two parties to the agreement are genuine about implementing it for the benefit of the people and the unity of Sudan.

FD: Thank you very much.

Notes

Part One

Chapter 2

1 Amin Mekki Medani, *Rule of Law Challenges in the Sudan* (Khartoum, unpublished paper, 2005), 20.
2 Amin Mekki Medani and Omer El Farouk Shoumena and Chief Justice Ambrose Riiny Thiik, Southern Judiciary and Chan Reec Madut, Appeal Court Justice in the National Judiciary, interviews by author, tape-recorded, July and October 2005, Khartoum.
3 Medani, *Rule of Law,* 7.
4 The National Islamic Front later split into two parties: the National Congress Party, now in power, and the opposition Popular Congress Party.
5 Medani, *Rule of Law*, 20.
6 In the taped interview by the author (referred to in supra note 2) in August 2005 Dr. Amin Mekki Medani, a prominent legal scholar and human rights expert and activist, noted: "when this regime came into power in the first year 500 judges were dismissed arbitrarily in the public interest. In their place were recruited people with no legal qualifications. Now, about 70percent of the Judiciary, including in the High Court, are Sharia Judges. And the Chief Justice is also a Sharia Judge."
7 Information provided by the Islamic leader Hassan Turabi, who had been imprisoned. A former general and ambassador who had also been imprisoned gave a similar report to the author while the author held the position of Minister of State for Foreign Affairs.
8 Ibid.
9 Ali Osman Yassin, Minister of Justice, interview by author, tape-recorded, October 2005, Khartoum.
10 Ibid.
11 Address to the Third Congress on Federalism, (Brussels, Belgium, March 5, 2005).
12 Ali Osman Yassin, Minister of Justice, interview by author, tape-recorded, October 2005, Khartoum.
13 Aleu Akechak Jok, Robert A. Leitch, and Carrie Vanderwint, *A Study of Customary Law in Contemporary Southern Sudan* (World Vision: International and South Sudan Secretariat for Legal and Constitutional Affairs, 2004), 54/7.

Chapter 3

1 For the customary law of the Dinka see Francis M. Deng, *Tradition and Modernization: A Challenge for Law Among the Dinka of the Sudan, 3rd edn* (Washington, DC: Kush Inc., 2004).

2 Godfrey Lienhardt, "The Western Dinka," in Middleton and Tait (eds), *Tribes Without Rulers: Studies in African Segmentary Systems* (London: Routledge & Kegan Paul, 1958), 106–7.
3 Arthur Nebel, *Dinka Dictionary with Abridged Grammar* (Verona: Verona Fathers, 1954), 315.
4 Deng, *Tradition and Modernization*, describes the substance of Dinka law by organizing it into eight value categories. Four of these are deference values: power, including the appointment, jurisdiction, powers, and procedures of decision-makers; affection, including marriage, legitimacy of children, sexual offenses, vicarious liability, and intrafamily liability; respect, focusing on defamation; and rectitude, focusing on freedom of religion, or lack thereof. The remaining four are welfare values: wealth, including bride wealth, inheritance, barter and sale, custody of livestock, gifts, thefts, acquisition and rights of ownership, labor and produce; well-being, including homicide, bodily injury, liability for animals, and employment of curers; skills, including payment for experts in settlement of feuds, divination, and song composition; enlightenment, including responsibility for guardianship and education of children.
5 Douglas Johnson, "Judicial Regulation and Administrative Control: Customary Law and the Nuer," *UK Journal of African History 27* (1986), 59–78.
6 Ibid.
7 Ibid.
8 Ibid.
9 As Monyluak Alor Kuol observed, "The elections have not yet transformed the system of inheritance associated with chieftanships. Local people, in most cases, still choose the sons of former chiefs and court members to fill the positions." Kuol cites a case among the Azande of Western Equatoria when, in 1992, an election was held for a successor to the late Chief James Diko. "The election committee was presented with eleven and fifteen-year-old boys among whom the crowd will elect a new chief. We had to drop the condition of maturity for candidacy and the crowd overwhelmingly selected the eleven-year-old." Monyluak Alor Kuol, *The Anthropology of Law and Issues of Justice in Southern Sudan Today* (London: Oxford University, 2000), 44, 92.
10 John Wuol Makec, *The Customary Law of the Dinka People of Sudan* (London: Afroworld Publishing, 1988), 221.
11 Ibid., 234.
12 Godfrey Lienhardt, "The Dinka of the Nile Basin," 69 *The Listener* (1963), 828.

Chapter 4

1 Regulation 53 of the Sudan Mohammedan Law Courts Ordinance of 1902, which established the present system of Islamic courts.
2 Muslim trusts.
3 Their jurisdiction is similar to that of the civil courts under Section 5 of the Civil Justice Ordinance.
4 The Chiefs' Courts Ordinance Application No. 1, Special Order of the Governor General in Council, 1944.
5 Johnson, "Judicial Regulation and Administrative Control," 67–68.
6 Farran observed about the evolution of an integrated Muslim customary law among these tribes that "Most, if not all, of the tribes involved were converted to Islam long ago. Accordingly, and by a gradual process of change, it may be argued, their pre-Islamic customs have ceased to prevail and the rules of Mohammedan law have taken their place … as the custom of the tribe in question … What these courts in fact apply is not *pure* Mohammedan law, but Mohammedan law as modified by Custom." C. d'Olivier Farran, *Matrimonial Laws of the Sudan, being*

a study of the divergent religious and civil laws in an African society (London: Butterworths, 1963), 254.

7 Makec, *Customary Law*, 19.

8 Ibid.

9 For a comprehensive discussion of the principles of "justice, equity, and good conscience," and their kindred concepts of "justice, morality, and order," and their reception in the Sudan legal system, see Zaki Mustafa, *The Common Law in the Sudan*, *op cit.*, supra.

10 Natale Olwak Akolawin, *Sudan Law Journal and Reports* (Khartoum, 1968), 232, quoted in Makec, *Customary Law*, 27. When I asked a province judge what standard he used in applying the repugnancy clauses he said, "Of course, the standard of a decent and civilized society, not that of a primitive tribe." In one case, which I also witnessed, a young judge with Khartoum legal training was shocked by the Ngok Dinka custom of compensating the husband of an adulterous wife. He argued that it was an equitable maxim that a wrongdoer could not benefit from his own wrong, and, according to him, the interests of husband and wife were so connected that for the husband to recover for his wife's wrong was to benefit wrongfully. He therefore asked me to advise the Paramount Chief, who happened to be my father, on his behalf to abolish the custom. His argument was evidently based on one side of the case, and an exaggerated one at that. He did not know the point of view of the society in which the custom prevailed. The custom is found in almost all African traditional societies and is rooted deep in their cultures. Even in Western law, in which he was trained, it is a tort in some jurisdictions. In any case, one may wonder whether it could be established that the interests of the wife and her husband in violation of sexual rights are joint. The outcome of a case of adultery may be to their common economic advantage, but in Dinka society it is most unlikely that the wife will benefit. Even the husband must abstain from the dairy products of cattle given as adultery compensation, or any food acquired through such cattle. Usually they are disposed of in settling debts or in marriage. But whether there is a common material advantage or not, the wrong cannot be common. How and why should he be hampered from a remedy simply because one of the parties injuring him incidentally benefits from the compensation due to him? The situation will, of course, be different if the husband traded on his wife or in any way consented to the commission of the wrong. As it was, I explained the importance of the custom among the Dinka and the judge was persuaded not to insist on its abolition.

11 See, for example, Farran, *Matrimonial Laws of the Sudan,* 29–31, 66–67, and Cliff F. Thompson, "Sources of Law in the New Nations of Africa: A Case Study from the Republic of the Sudan," *Wisconsin Law Review* 1146, 1162 (Fall 1966).

12 Estimates vary from over 80 to over 90 percent.

13 Deng Biong Mijak, *Save Our Customary Laws Now* (Maridi: Equatoria Region, New Sudan, 1998), 2.

Chapter 5

1 Kuol, *Anthropology of Law*, 68–69.

2 John Luk, interview by author, February 9, 2005, New Site, Southern Sudan.

3 Monyluak Alor Kuol has documented with remarkable candor some of the human rights abuses perpetrated by SPLM/A commanders and officials, although he also shows the stringent measures which the SPLM/A took against those human rights violators. The cases he documents also demonstrate how customary law was used in the adjudication of such crimes.

4 Section 251 of the New Sudan Penal Code 2003 explicitly incorporates traditional methods of resolving murder cases by providing that relatives of the victim may opt for blood compensation [*dia*] in lieu of a death sentence for the perpetrator.

5 Ambrose Riiny Thiik, Chief Justice of the South, interview by author, August 2005, Khartoum.
6 John Luk, interview by author, February 9, 2005, New Site, Southern Sudan.
7 Paul Mayom, interview by author, February 2005, New Site, Southern Sudan.

Chapter 6

1 World Vision Study, 8.
2 Ambrose Riiny Thiik, Chief Justice of the South, interview by author, August 2005, Khartoum.
3 World Vision Study, 26.
4 Deng Biong, interview by author, February 2005, Rumbek, South Sudan.
5 World Vision Study, 8.
6 Ibid.
7 "Customary Law from the Perspective of Human Rights" (unpublished paper, Khartoum, 2005), 4.
8 Ibid., 5–11.
9 Ibid., 10.
10 Ibid., 10.
11 Ibid., 12–14.
12 Ibid., 14.
13 Peter Nyot, interview by author, February 8, 2005, New Site, Southern Sudan.
14 Kuyang Anade, interview by author, February 2005, Rumbek, South Sudan.
15 Peter Nyot, interview by author, February 8, 2005, New Site, Southern Sudan.
16 Michael Makuei, interview by author, February 2005, Rumbek, Southern Sudan.
17 John Makec went on to write a comparative study of the Dinka in his book, *The Customary Law of the Dinka of Sudan*, which has been extensively quoted in this study.
18 World Vision Study, 23.
19 Kuol, *Anthropology of Law*, 10.
20 Deng Biong, interview by author, tape-recorded, February 2005, Rumbek, Southern Sudan.

Part Two

Chapter 1

1 Harold D. Lasswell and Myres S. McDougall, *Jurisprudence for a Free Society: Studies in Law, Science, and Policy* (New Haven: New Haven Press, 1992).
2 The deference value of power, as it relates to legal issues surrounding authority and decision-making, is explored in Part One of this study.

Chapter 2

1 Makec, *Customary Law*, 60.
2 Ibid., 58.
3 Abyei, Ngok Dinka Court (1954). Adol's brother died, leaving a widow who was related to Col. She was inherited by Adol in levirate. Adol refused to live with her on the grounds that she had caused his brother's death. He brought an action claiming divorce for his late brother and the return of his brother's bride wealth. The court, considering the accusation against the widow unsubstantiated, refused the divorce. Adol was ordered to live with her or forfeit the bride wealth.
4 Makec, *Customary Law*, 54. According to Makec, Section 20 of the Bahr El Ghazal Region Customary Law Act of 1984 defines marriage to include a union

"between one barren woman and another or others for whom male consorts are provided." Monyluak Alor Kuol reports a case of an old woman, Adut-dit, from Tonj district area of Chief Guar Mading. Adut-dit bore girls and no son, until the death of her husband. She was a wealthy woman with a large herd of cattle. Adut-dit decided to marry Achol, and invited a male relative, Deng, to beget children with her who will be considered Adut-dit's and her deceased husband's. When Deng joined the SPLM/A and wanted to take the young wife and her baby boy, Adut-dit objected to movement of mother and baby to the SPLM/A area. When the couple insisted, Adut-dit successfully sued for divorce. Monyluak Alor Kuol, *Administration of Justice in the SPLM/A Liberated Areas: Court Cases in War-Torn Southern Sudan* (Oxford: University of Oxford Refugee Studies Programme, 1997), 39–40.

5 Makec, *Customary Law*, 63. "For a girl, the age of maturity is marked by the first period of menstruation, while for a boy, it is marked by certain physical or biological changes … or traditional marks designed to mark the end of boyhood." One elder explained, "We allow the marriage of a girl when she is mature. When a girl attains puberty, she abstains from drinking cow milk for one complete year. During that year she could take goat milk in addition to any other food. On the expiration of the first year, the girl is given two years to consume cow milk. But starting from the fourth year, she will be observing not taking milk (cow or goat) every month for seven days from the day her menstrual period starts. She is well fed by her parents during these last two years to appear healthy and in good shape to fetch good bride wealth later after this period." This means that if a girl reaches puberty at age 13 or 14, observes a full year followed by two more years of taboos, connected with her menstruation, before she will begin to observe the rituals or taboos associated with her monthly cycle, the age when she will be considered marriageable in the sense of being given to the man as a wife will be approximately 18 years. Deng Biong Mijak, *The Traditional System of Justice and Peace* (United Nations Development Programme, Sudan, 2004), 19.

6 In his study of Ngok Dinka law, Deng Biong Mijak discussed *agorot* as a form of marriage. Quoting an elder, he writes, "There is a form of marriage whereby relatives of the girl may like to have a certain relationship with a certain family and may decide to marry their daughter to that family's young man though the girl … is still young and has not attained puberty … She is married but not handed over to her bridegroom until she is mature or at least until she attains puberty. But until that, *lung* (a metal ornament) is put on her wrist to show that she is married."

7 Kuol, *Anthropology of Law*, 64–65. The chiefs of Yirol area have modified the rule because of the war. "The harsh and risky life of a soldier has to be accorded special consideration as many of the local young men have joined the SPLA. Now the norm is that if a soldier has eloped with or impregnated a girl, then his relatives are ordered to proceed with marriage ceremonies … If he is junior in the line of marriage then his relatives are asked to hand over 11 cows to the relatives of the girl … The rest of the marriage proceedings are then suspended until the time when it is his turn in the family to marry." See also Mijak, *Traditional System of Justice*, 19, in which he reflects the changes that are taking place in response to the exigencies of the current social context.

8 An example: Maguei refused to marry the girl chosen by his father, but the father, not considering his son's wishes, obtained the girl for a bride wealth of thirty-five cows. Maguei ran away from home. His friends, members of his family and clan, and other elders went to his residence and reasoned with him. Meanwhile, the girl had been installed in his father's house as his daughter-in-law. After a long period of persuasion, Maguei gave in, returned home, and settled with the wife.

9 Section 21(1) of the Bahr el Ghazal Code of Dinka Customary Law states: "The only consent which is material for the conclusion of a valid marriage is that of the

parents, brothers and close paternal uncles in that order of importance." Makec, *Customary Law*, 62.

10 Abyei, Ngok Dinka Court (1944).

11 Abyei, Ngok Dinka Court (1959).

12 Jean Buxton, "The Significance of Bride Wealth and the Levirate Among the Nilotic and Nilo-Hamatic Tribes of the Sudan," *Anti-Slavery Reporter* (1958), 66–75.

13 Mijak, *Traditional System of Justice*, 26.

14 As Monyluak Alor Kuol notes, "Suicide is a very rare phenomenon in Dinka culture. It mostly occurs, if at all, in the context of girls upset in their relationships [in marital situations]." Kuol cites the case of a girl called Ayen Mou who, having become pregnant, went to the house of her lover Gai Muniir in the hope of persuading him to marry her. Gai Muniir was, however, not convinced that he was indeed the father of the baby and urged the girl to return to her family. When she did, she was beaten by her brother for bringing shame on the family. Shortly after that, she went to the forest and hanged herself on a tree. Her relatives brought a case against Gai Muniir for causing her death. The court absolved Gai of the responsibility for her death. But Gai was made to pay the customary compensation of a pregnant heifer for the pregnancy. He was also held liable for negligence in sending the girl back to her family before taking the matter first to his elders for consultation and resolution. He was fined by the court for not following the traditional method for managing such situations. Her brother was also fined for his role in the crisis. Kuol, *Anthropology of Law*, 64.

15 Abyei, Ngok Dinka Court (1954).

16 Ibid.

17 O'Sullivan, "Dinka Law," 180.

18 Farran, *Matrimonial Laws of the Sudan*, 72.

19 Mijak, *Traditional System of Justice*, 18.

20 Mijak, *Traditional System of Justice*, 26–27.

21 Ibid.

22 See *The Relatives of Salvatore Atem v. The Relatives of Athilueth*, Abyei, Ngok Dinka Court (1958), discussed in Deng, *Tradition and Modernization*, 178–179.

23 This is an occasion for slaughtering at least a ram and brewing beer, among other things.

24 The girl's relatives, though known by the man's relatives to be in the know, purport to be ignorant.

25 As Makec explained, "Once the final agreement is reached over the quantity of cattle to be paid and there are no other impediments to the marriage, the agreed cattle are collected and delivered to the bride's relatives. Thereafter, preparations leading to her delivery to the husband follow." Makec, *Customary Law*, 65.

26 To consummate a union in Dinka is *bi nya ruok*, literally "to dress the bride up," a further indication of how the Dinka traditionally associated being clothed with sexual exclusiveness.

27 As noted earlier, according to Deng Biong Mijak, this is no longer in practice and is remembered only by those "who had witnessed some instances of it as part of the past." Mijak, *Traditional System of Justice*, 26.

28 Kasumu, "Integration of the Law of Husband and Wife in Western Nigeria" (delivered at the Conference on Integration of Customary and Modern Legal Systems, Ibadan, Nigeria, August 1964), 6, cited in Deng, *Tradition and Modernization*, 172.

29 Ibid.

30 Abyei, Ngok Dinka Appellate Court (1960).

31 In *Akot Ral v. Lal Ayom* (supra note 82) we saw that the payment of the *amec* entitled Akot to two children who were physiologically Lal's and to compensation for elopement and impregnation of a married woman.

32 Abyei, Ngok Dinka Court (1953).

33 Makec, "Marriage as an institution, is intended to lay down a sound permanent and cordial relationship between the spouses and between their respective relatives … Because of these mutual interests … [divorce] becomes a source of lamentation to those who hold the marriage very dearly, or those whose interests are adversely affected by it." Makec, *Customary Law*, 81.
34 Abyei, Ngok Dinka Court (1954).
35 Abyei, Ngok Dinka Court (1958).
36 In accord with this, the court also ordered the payment of a few cows as *arueth*, a reverse payment made by the bride's kin to the bridegroom's kin which is equivalent to about one-third of the total bride wealth. The court, however, made the girl's relatives pay more than one-third of the new nominal bride wealth because it was to be considered *adut*, that is, cattle for soothing his grief.
37 In explaining why barrenness is a ground for divorce, John Makec noted, "The most important objective of marriage … is the procreation of children. It is the children who maintain the link between the two families who are related by marriage." He observed, however, that barrenness need not be a ground for divorce: "A man can remain with his wife despite her barrenness and still marry another woman, if he has sufficient means to do so." Makec, *Customary Law*, 88.
38 Abyei, Ngok Dinka Court (1953).
39 Some wives deliberately have illicit sexual intercourse to challenge such imputations, and, of course, only get into further trouble.
40 Makec, *Customary Law*, 87–88. As with barrenness, Makec notes that "the death of children through *akeeth* or incest and so forth may not result in grant of divorce."
41 This is probably the ground Makec describes as, "where marriage has irretrievably broken down … for example, where misconduct of the wife has become so gross that neither the husband nor his relatives have the confidence to maintain the slightest hope that she will improve her conduct, or when she is so inefficient or so lazy or troublesome that she is not able to maintain her homestead." Ibid., 88–89.
42 This is similar to the ground described by Makec as where the wife "is so inefficient and so lazy and troublesome that she is unable to maintain the homestead." Ibid.
43 Abyei, Ngok Dinka Court (1953).
44 Abyei, Ngok Dinka Court (1953).
45 Abyei, Ngok Dinka Court (1960).
46 Abyei, Ngok Dinka Court (1953).
47 Abyei, Ngok Dinka Court (1960).
48 As Makec notes, "The problem always arises if a husband refuses to accept another man to replace him for the purpose of procreation. In this case the woman will be compelled either to have sex secretly with another man or seek divorce." Ibid. Makec gives the case of *Thokmer and Others v. Malual Cindut*, in which the court granted divorce because it was "satisfied that attempts by the wife to adopt the practice of *lo-hot* [entering the hut of the husband] were resisted by her husband." Makec, *Customary Law*, 88.
49 Abyei, Ngok Dinka Court (1960).
50 Makec, *Customary Law*, 88.
51 The case of *Manyiel Cindut and Others v. Marial Manok and Others* indicates that even in serious cases of deteriorating relations between the respective relatives, divorce may still be denied for such reasons as the interest of the children. Ibid., 89. John Makec contends that there are differing views on when divorce becomes effective. One view holds that divorce becomes effective only when the bride wealth cattle have been returned. He cites the case of *Adut Puouwak v. Tierra Macar*, Maker Macol, where a divorced woman was given in marriage to another before the bride wealth cattle were returned. The Court found the second "husband" guilty of adultery, but argued that the divorce could be made effective it they

returned the bride wealth. Another view is that divorce is effective, once it has been granted, even if the bride wealth cattle are not returned. Makec cites two cases. In one, *Macuny Malok v. Sol Amiro*, divorce was granted on the grounds of desertion, even though the bride wealth had not been returned. In another case, *John Gum v. Martin Makuek Abol*, where the facts were similar, the court reached a contrary decision. Ibid., 84–85.

52 Paul P. Howell, "Ngok Dinka," *Sudan Notes and Records* 32 (1951), 288.

53 Makec cites the case of *Maguek Atony v. Marial Dorin and Others*, cited earlier, where the court found the case for divorce too compelling to reject. Makec, *Customary Law*, 87–88.

54 Ibid.

55 Kuol, *Administration of Justice in SPLM/A Areas*, 40–44.

56 Ibid., 95.

57 During the child's early years, among the Dinka, a man pays up to six cows for a boy and up to ten cows for a girl. After the age of maturity, the rates increase to ten for the boy and twenty for the girl.

58 See the case of *Mabor Adhel and Buoi Ajak v. Amon Mon*, in which the relatives of a woman who was living with a man as husband and wife, but without payment of bride wealth given to the child of the union, unless the father paid the bride wealth. Meanwhile, he was made to pay compensation for impregnation of the girl.

59 Lienhardt reported these words from an invocation by a man calling on his ancestors: "I am not a bastard coming with its mother, the bastard fathered by some stranger outside. If such a one prays, he calls upon no clan-divinity, because he is a child who comes with his mother alone and he will be unable to do anything in a case of sickness." Lienhardt, *Divinity and Experience: Religion of the Dinka* (Oxford: Clarendon Press, 1961), 222.

60 Among the Ngok Dinka, in the absence of aggravating circumstances, the adulterer is made to pay three cows, compensation and to serve six months' imprisonment. Where there are no aggravating circumstances, the three cows paid are described as *loc*, *yow*, and *nhian*. *Loc* literally means "the selected (cow)," and, as the name suggests, it is to be picked by the wronged party from among the herds of the wrongdoer. It must be a pregnant cow; where there is no pregnant cow, a cow with a calf is considered pregnant by a legal fiction. This calls to mind the procreative basis of liability. *Yow*, literally "the front (of the woman)," is a big cow. It must not be pregnant, and if it is pregnant, the calf is returned to the adulterer when it is born. *Nhian*, literally "testicles," must be a big bull, but should there be no big bull, a young cow may be substituted. *Yow* and *nhian* are symbols of the sexual relation by which the husband's procreative interests have been violated.

61 If pregnancy results from adultery, the amount of compensation automatically increases to six head of cattle. In such a case, *loc, yow,* and *nhian* become two cows each.

62 Abyei, Ngok Dinka Court (1960).

63 Unable to follow up the case, the final outcome is not known.

64 In the case of *Magot Kok v. Dorin*, the husband of a wife who was found to have committed adultery with several men was advised by the court to sue for divorce rather than for compensation. Makec, *Customary Law*, 69–70.

65 Abyei, Ngok Dinka Court (1946). Cited in Howell, "Ngok Dinka," 291.

66 Ibid.

67 Makec, *Customary Law*, 76.

68 Ibid., 77.

69 Abyei, Ngok Dinka Appeals Court (1960).

70 Abyei, Ngok Dinka Court (1960).

71 See supra note 82.

72 Abyei, Ngok Dinka Court (1946). Cited in Howell, "Ngok Dinka," 290.

73 *Col Dau v. Four Men*, Abyei, Ngok Dinka Court (1953).
74 The standard number of indemnity cattle is three, termed *roc, yow,* and *nhian* as in adultery.
75 Abyei, Ngok Dinka Court (1957).
76 Abyei, Ngok Dinka Court (1960).
77 Evidence of Attorney General, Michael Makuei. See Part Two, Chapter7, p. 242. See also Chapter 4, p. 208–209, where the Attorney General elaborates on the same point.
78 It is considered most undesirable for a person to sue in respect of his own mother's adultery. In one song, there is a line which says, "However impoverished I may be, I am not like a man who receives compensation for his mother's adultery." Indeed, the writer is not aware of such cases having ever occurred. In any case, one hardly ever hears of adultery with the mothers of adults. This is mainly because mothers are careful to avoid embarrassment to their children, and therefore do not commit adultery. But it might also be because the matter is dropped, inasmuch as the mother will have already fulfilled the purpose of her marriage (i.e. childbirth).
79 Makec, *Customary Law*, 72–73.
80 Abyei, Ngok Dinka Court (1960).

Chapter 3

1 Makec, *Customary Law*, 210.
2 This is in contrast with Anglo-American law, where incurring damages is generally a condition to entertaining an action.
3 According to Makec, defamations made in songs are more serious because the "publication spreads very fast, far and wide." Consequently, the court may, in addition to awarding damages to the plaintiff, pass "an appropriate sentence of imprisonment or fine or both" against the defendant. Makec, *Customary Law*, 211.
4 Abyei, Ngok Dinka Court (1959).
5 Abyei, Ngok Dinka Court (1958).
6 Abyei, Ngok Dinka Court (1960).
7 In May 1960, the age sets of Acueng subtribe composed songs defamatory of Abyor's warrior groups, elders, and chiefs. Before the songs were used at an open dance, word of their composition came to Abyor warrior groups. Rumors of the Abyor group's secretly planned attack were received by Acueng, and both sides started moving to strategic points. At this stage, word was brought to the chief, who immediately sent the police to pacify the situation. For three days and nights, the police struggled in the forest with several thousand intractable warriors. It was not until the paramount chief himself joined the police force that the situation was normalized. During the trial that followed, the court decided that the songs not be repeated in court, but the members of the court were informed of the essence of the songs in secrecy. The songs were banned, and the individuals responsible received varying sentences of imprisonment, up to one and a half years. The composers were among those who received the maximum. The subtribes were fined and later paid conciliation fees to the elders and chiefs insulted in the songs.
8 It is significant to note the verb "heard" because defamation has generally been slander and not libel, owing to the lack of writing in traditional society. The significance of writing has not yet been adjudicated.
9 According to Makec, "The statement published must be false. If the publication is true, it does not amount to defamation." Makec, *Customary Law*, 210.
10 In certain cases, such as defamation against an important chief, it is most unlikely that the song will be sung in court. In intergroup defamation, hostilities may develop from the singing of songs in court, and preventive measures are usually taken in anticipation.

11 This is why plaintiffs always took the oath.
12 Makec, *Customary Law*, 212–213.

Chapter 4

1 As we said earlier, for detrimental purposes, title does not pass to the bride's kin.
2 Who intervene only from time to time and over a more definitive and limited portion of the total wealth than his living subordinates do.
3 If ownership is disputed, a man may say that "it is *amani*," which expresses the uncertainty pertaining to its ownership. Makec, *Customary Law*, 118.
4 Makec identifies occupation, conquest, and gift as among the ways of acquiring land among the Dinka. Makec, *Customary Law*, 154.
5 Makec argues that where a person "voluntarily abandons his homestead and moves to settle in a new area, he loses his title to the abandoned land. However, if he intends to retain his title to the land he has abandoned, he must clearly and reasonably express his intention … No one can be allowed to exercise the right of excluding others for ever or for an indefinite period from abandoned lands when the right of ownership of an individual over his land in not absolute but restricted." Makec cites the case of *Macar Aweckoc and Others v. Riak Dak and Others* in support of this legal principle. Makec, *Customary Law*, 172–174. (For the complexities of the law on the issues involved, see the detailed discussion of the case and the decision on appeal p. 173–178.)
6 Mijok, that is, black head and shoulders with white body and either black or white hindquarters. The hierarchy of colors is not uniform among the Dinka tribes. Marial, which has a different pattern of black and white and which the Ngok allocate to the first son of the second wife, is considered the first among some tribes.
7 Farran, *Matrimonial Laws of the Sudan*, 279.
8 Makec, *Customary Law*, 63.
9 For instance, in his compendium on Dinka law, O'Sullivan speaks of "the purchase of wives by means of cattle" (O'Sullivan, 'Dinka Law,') *Journal of the Royal Anthropological Institute* (1910), 175 as one of the bases of Dinka laws. Hartland, in his introduction to O'Sullivan"s work, states that "it is usually the payment of the bride price that authorizes [the husband] to reckon the children to his stock and gives him control over them to the exclusion of any claim by the wife's kindred," although he qualifies that "all this comes very far short of vesting their absolute ownership in him. They are not slaves, however servile their status may appear to superficial observation." Ibid., 172. Under the heading "Laws of Property," O'Sullivan includes among a man's property his wives and other dependants. According to him, "No woman can possess property, she being herself property." Ibid., 178.
10 Jean Buxton, "The Significance of Bride Wealth and the Levirate Among the Nilotic and Nilo-Hamitic Tribes of the Sudan," *Anti-Slavery Reporter* (1958), 66–75.
11 "The inter-relationships are maintained by a reciprocal system of bride-wealth distribution and the obligation to assist in the collection of bride-wealth." Howell, "Ngok Dinka," 280.
12 We give the example of birth because the Dinka count a cow with a calf as two cows.
13 Farran, citing the present writer, says, "Among some of the Dinka, although bride wealth is still necessarily assessed in varying numbers of cows, a tendency is just commencing to pay over the cash value of some of them instead of the animals themselves." Farran, *Matrimonial Laws of the Sudan*, 286.
14 Abyei, Ngok Dinka Court (1960).
15 Abyei, Ngok Dinka Court (1960).
16 Reverse payment "consists of approximately one-third of the total bride wealth paid." Howell, "Ngok Dinka," 287.

17 Despite the expression, the custom does not entail physically washing the mouth. Only payment is required.

18 Although the expression "stepping into the shoes" is alien to the Dinka, the eldest heir inherits the shoes of the deceased, thus symbolizing the nature of inheritance.

19 It may be said that the wife and her children have a limited ownership owing to the hierarchical rights of ownership among the Dinka.

20 In *Mading v. Mayol* (Abyei, Ngok Dinka Court [1957]), Mayol needed a ram to sacrifice on the occasion of his son's illness. Mading gave him a ram in exchange for a bull then still nursing. Shortly afterward, Mading paid Mayol a sheep as *ajuek*. Mayol, however, disposed of the bull when it stopped nursing and promised Mading a cow calf on the occasion of the forthcoming marriage of his niece. When bethrothal wealth was paid, he designated a nursing cow calf for Mading. The cow calf grew into a cow in Mayol's possession, and eventually Mayol disposed of it. Mading then sued Mayol. During the trial, the cow, then in someone else's ownership and possession, had given birth to a cow calf and was pregnant. The court held that Mayol should pay a pregnant cow and a cow calf.

21 Relatives often do not compensate for one another.

22 In *Deng v. Dan Bol* (Abyei, Ngok Dinka Court [1960]), Mading, the son of Deng, while a child in 1944, took two sheep to the son of Dan Bol, a young boy of Mading's age. Mading and Dan Bol's family were relatives. No conditions were made concerning the nature or duration of custody. It was understood that Dan Bol would keep the sheep to multiply and be a source of wealth to Mading when he had grown up. As Mading grew up, he forgot that he had sheep with Dan Bol's family, a fact which left the latter a great measure of freedom over the sheep. The sheep multiplied. Dan Bol sacrificed a few of them on occasions of illness in his family. Then came a disease which killed most of the sheep. Dan Bol decided to exchange them for a bull which he later exchanged for a cow calf. He put the cow calf into the herds of a nephew whose father had died leaving him under Dan Bol's guardianship. The nephew, then on bad terms with his uncle, fled with his herds, including some of his uncle's, to another Dinka tribe where he disposed of the cow calf as part of his bride wealth. Later, the cow calf was traced and found to have increased to four cows. At this point, Mading's father, Deng, who until then had not known of the arrangement between Mading and Dan Bol's family, brought an action against Dan Bol for the recovery of the four cows. The court held that Deng could recover three out of the four cows. One cow was left unclaimed in accordance with the custom that when the owner ultimately reclaims his animals, he leaves at least one of them to the custodian in appreciation or in reward for his services. *Deng v. Dan Bol* also illustrates the intricacies of Dinka transactions and the underlying family relationships together with those determinants giving the heads of families family rights and obligations. Deng benefited from his son's transaction, while Dan Bol lost on account of his nephew's act. That Deng did not know of his son's transaction shows his son's desire to accumulate wealth independent of his father's control, a motive not infrequently behind custody agreements. That Dan Bol's nephew fled with the herds also shows a similar conflict implicit in the inequities of procreational stratification.

23 Makec, *Customary Law*, 188, (for cases on the institution of *amuk* or *amec*, 189–91).

24 Abyei, Ngok Dinka Court (1955). See also *Nyuong v. Wor*. Despite the abrogation of the custom by judicial authority, the Dinka are still largely unaware of the change.

25 Abyei, Ngok Dinka Court (1960).

26 Evidence provided by Mr. Natale O. Akolawin, LLB, LLM, Lecturer, Faculty of Law, University of Khartoum. This case, although decided by the Shilluk court, illustrates the respective rights of a wife and her husband over the produce of her

field in Dinka law as well. A wife had her own field separate from that of her husband. They consumed together the produce from her husband's field. She bought a cow with her own grain. In time, the progeny of the cow amounted to six head of cattle. Payment of her marriage wealth had not been completed by her husband. When the wife and her husband were enriched by her daughter's marriage, the wife's brother (the daughter's maternal uncle) came to claim the balance of his sister's marriage consideration. Her husband gave his wife's brother the cows earned from her own produce. The wife and her brother maintained that the cows belonged to her so that her husband could not use them for her own marriage consideration. The case went to the court, which held that the cows belonged to the husband and could therefore be given by him to her brother as part of the bride wealth. Deng, *Tradition and Modernization*, 277, n.55.

27 The first person to spear an elephant is entitled to the right tusk and the second person to the left tusk, even if the wounds they inflict do not lead to the death of the animal.

Chapter 5

1 Makec, *Customary Law*, 199.

2 According to Makec, among the Bahr el Ghazal Dinka, the tribe contributes to the blood wealth only if the individual killer is not identifiable. Ibid., 202.

3 Ibid., 199. It is not clear what the situation is where a man kills his wife who has given birth to children.

4 Ibid., 209. Presumably that would influence the issue of dissolution of the marriage and the compensation he would be expected to pay.

5 Usually only six head of cattle are demanded for such subsequent death, provided that at the time the injury was inflicted the guilty party had paid the sheep of *athiol* and the cow calf of *nhiem* to express his regrets and good wishes for the injured person's recovery. If this had not been done, more, usually ten, cattle are demanded.

6 Kuol, *Anthropology of Law*, 65.

7 Ibid., 66.

8 Ibid., 42.

9 Ibid., 67.

10 Ibid., 85.

11 Ibid.,77.

12 Ibid.

13 Such as injuries to the eyes, limbs, or teeth.

14 John Makec draws a distinction between those animals with a social and economic value, such as cattle, goats, and sheep, and those without such value, such as dogs and cats. Liability attaches to the first category and not the second unless the owner is negligent by not warning against dangerous propensity. Makec, *Customary Law*, 195–196.

15 Makec cites a case tried in Rumbek in the 1940s in which a boy was killed by a cow he was milking. The court decided that the cow be given to the relatives of the boy as compensation. Ibid., 197.

16 As *agut piny,* the coin, the spear, or cow of "hitting the earth" derived from the practice of darting on the ground a sacred spear to assist divination or cure. Unless this is paid, not only is the practitioner likely to withhold his services, but if his services are rendered, they are believed to be ineffective.

17 Some professionals, however, insist on advance payment. This may be the result of fear that they will not be paid or an attempt to avoid what appears to be a universal practice that no fee is paid if the treatment is unsuccessful.

18 The Dinka illustrate the importance of reciprocity with a story. A black cobra bit Ajang's cow and Ajang speared the cobra with the spear of Akol Adiangbar, a

Index